DESTINATIONS
OF
SOUTHERN CALIFORNIA

The Guide to Exciting
Restaurants, Attractions & Lodgings

Second Edition

DAVID VOKAC

D1475792

Library of Congress Cataloging-in-Publication Data

Vokac, David.
    Destinations of southern California : the guide to exciting
restaurants, attractions & lodgings / David Vokac. — 2nd ed.
      p.   cm.
    "Fully revised."
    Includes index.
    ISBN 0-930743-05-9 : $9.95
    1. California, Southern—Guidebooks. I. Title.
F867.V64   1995
917.94'90453—dc20   95-5318

                                            CIP

West Press
P.O. Box 99717
San Diego, CA 92169

Second Edition 1995
1 2 3 4 5 6 7 8 9 10
Manufactured in the United States of America

Preface

There has been bad news and good news since *Destinations of Southern California* was first released in 1990. The bad news was plentiful. Catastrophic firestores, riots, floods, mudslides, and earthquakes have each in turn beset the region in only five years. The good news is less heralded, but more profound. Every major natural and cultural attraction is open to visitors, and many have been improved. So, Southern California continues to capture the imagination of people everywhere. No wonder. For sheer diversity and number of enticements, America's flamboyant southwestern corner is still incomparable. For example, where but in San Diego (see front cover) could you share the warm sand and clear water of an idyllic cove with a colony of harbor seals? Yet most guidebooks dwell mainly on the Los Angeles area, while providing only cursory information about the other great coastal cities—San Diego and Santa Barbara. A few also touch on the high points of the desert at Palm Springs and the mountains at Big Bear. None has attempted to describe top vacation spots everywhere in the region in uniform detail. Until now.

Destinations of Southern California is intended to serve as the ultimate guide to the thirty-five foremost leisure destinations and their surroundings throughout the Southland. The book takes a comprehensive new look at Los Angeles and the coast from Santa Barbara to San Diego. It also provides the same level of detailed coverage for the thirty-two other vacation hubs. Features of most interest to locals and travelers alike—the best restaurants, attractions and lodgings—are systematically described and rated in and around every locality.

I personally visited each feature in every destination hub during more than one year of full-time, independent effort. No payments were accepted. Thus, every listing is described and rated on merit alone. As a result, I believe that this guide is honest and accurate, with consistent, detailed information about more than 1,500 appealing places in Southern California.

For everyone who intends to plan and pursue adventures in the dazzling metropolises or peaceful hideaways anywhere in the region, the completely new, second edition of *Destinations of Southern California* has the answers. All the information you need to create a visit tailored to your time, finances, and interests is in this guidebook.

To Joan

SOUTHERN

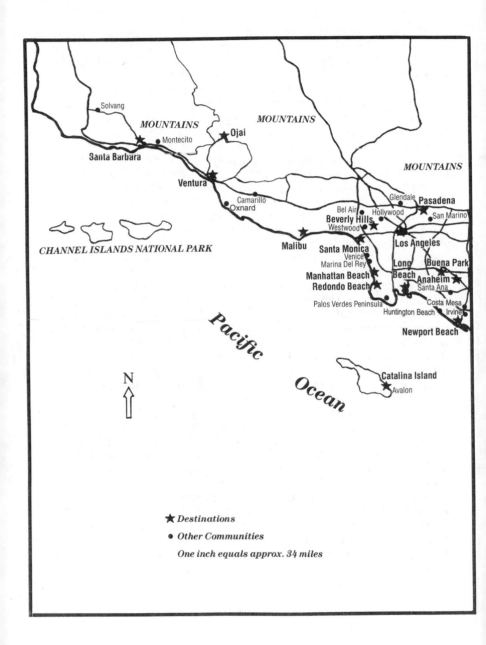

Solvang

MOUNTAINS   MOUNTAINS

Montecito   Ojai

Santa Barbara

MOUNTAINS

Ventura

Camarillo
Oxnard   Glendale Pasadena
Bel Air Hollywood San Marino
Beverly Hills
Westwood

CHANNEL ISLANDS NATIONAL PARK

Malibu Santa Monica   Los Angeles
Venice
Marina Del Rey   Long   Buena Park
Manhattan Beach   Beach Anaheim
Redondo Beach   Santa Ana

Palos Verdes Peninsula   Costa Mesa
Huntington Beach Irvine

Newport Beach

Pacific

N

Ocean

Catalina Island
Avalon

★ Destinations

● Other Communities

One inch equals approx. 34 miles

CALIFORNIA

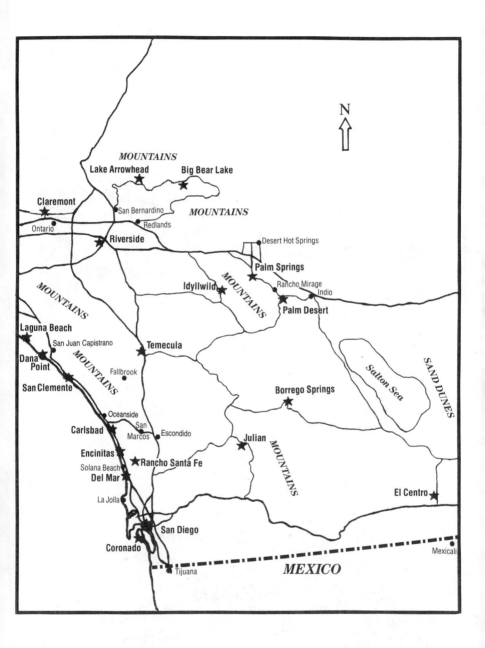

Contents

Introduction

This is the only complete guide to all of Southern California's desirable destinations. It was written to help you discover both famous and little-known places that make the region remarkable, and enjoy them to the fullest.

A wealth of new information is presented in five ways that set this guidebook apart. (1) All of the best attractions, restaurants, and lodgings (instead of random features) in every engaging locale throughout Southern California are identified, described, and rated. (2) Attention is focused on recreation and leisure pursuits primarily of interest to adventurous couples and individuals. As a result, isolated hot springs and promising young wineries receive the same careful regard as famed museums and amusement parks. (3) The likelihood of good weather is rated each month in every locale, and supporting data are provided. (4) Intimate details are presented for more than 1,100 extraordinary bedrooms in notable lodgings throughout the Southland. (5) All material is consistently arranged in a simple, uniform layout that makes it easy to scan and to use.

The contents and format are designed to quickly provide all of the information you want to get the most from these exciting destinations within your time, finances, and interest.

Destinations

A "destination" is defined in this guidebook as one of the thirty-five localities with the most scenic appeal and memorable leisure-time features—natural or cultural attractions, restaurants, and lodgings. Each destination and its environs is well worth a visit.

This general concept provided the basis for identifying the destinations of Southern California. Two measures—natural setting and leisure appeal—were used in a sequential process of elimination involving all urban places in the region. Water bodies, dramatic landforms, and/or luxuriant vegetation provide the backdrops for the most desirable natural settings. Therefore, places lacking impressive surroundings, i.e., more than a few miles from any of these characteristics, were omitted. Two exceptions, Anaheim and Buena Park, are destinations because of their world-famous attractions.

Thirty-five exceptional localities were found along the coast, in Shangri-La valleys, high in the mountains, and in desert oases. All are featured in this guidebook as the key destinations of Southern California. Communities and their environs ranging in size from Los Angeles (the West's largest city) to Julian (a historic mountain village) are included. Collectively, they are the prime sources of leisure-time excitement. Individually, each has features that make it a worthy destination for a delightful weekend or a lengthy vacation. A full chapter devoted to each locality addresses all natural, historic, and leisure-oriented attractions; restaurants; and lodgings.

Weather Profiles—the "Vokac Weather Rating"

Weather plays a crucial role in recreation and leisure, and in successful vacations. Because of this, a great deal of care was taken in obtaining and presenting detailed weather information for localities throughout Southern California. The copyrighted weather profiles for each of the thirty-five locales are the most complete in any travel guidebook.

The "Vokac Weather Rating" © (VWR) measures the probability of "pleasant weather"—i.e., warm, dry conditions suitable for outdoor recreation by anyone dressed in light sportswear. Average high and low temperatures, rainfall, and snowfall for each month (plus the frequency of precipitation), and the impact of air pollution during hot days throughout the Los Angeles area are correlated. The typical weather that can be expected each month is rated on a scale from "0" to "10." A "0" signifies the most adverse weather with almost no chance that shirt-sleeves and shorts will be comfortable. Every increment of one on the VWR scale represents a 10% greater chance of pleasant weather. For example, a "5" is used where there is a 50% chance that any given day in the month will be pleasant. A "10" pinpoints "great" weather, with warm, dry days almost 100% assured. An easy-to-follow line graph is used to display the month-to-month VWR. Generally, ratings of "7" or above indicate a high probability of desirable conditions for outdoor activity. Ratings of "6" or less suggest an increasing likelihood that the weather may restrict comfortable enjoyment of outdoor ventures and/or require special clothing.

As an added convenience, each month of the weather graph has been subdivided into four segments roughly corresponding to weeks. Readers interested in "fine-tuning" the VWR will find the smaller segments helpful. For example, if the ratings for September and October are "10" and "6," the position of the connecting line during the last week (segment) of September indicates an "8" rating. The implication is that weather during the last week in that month is normally still "very good" but no longer "great," as it was earlier in the month.

Attractions

Every distinctive attraction in and around each locality is described and rated, and free attractions are noted. Included are leisure-time destinations of special interest to adults—like wineries, golf courses, remote beaches and hot springs—as well as family-oriented places with special appeal to children. In addition, all kinds of outdoor recreation—bicycling, ballooning, horseback riding, sailing, sportfishing, etc.—are described, and key sources for equipment rentals and guides are named. As a convenience, popular categories of attractions are listed alphabetically under general headings such as "boat rentals," "warm water features," or "winter sports."

Restaurants

All noteworthy restaurants from temples of haute cuisine to mom-and-pop cafes are described in terms of food and atmosphere (including scenic views where available) for each locality. Service is not mentioned because it can vary so much even on a given evening. Prices are summarized. Meals served (B=breakfast, L=lunch, D=dinner) are identified under the restaurant's name, along with days closed, if any.

Fast-food shops and themed chain restaurants are generally excluded because of the author's preoccupation with distinctive dining. The cloning of successful restaurants is one of Southern California's least-endearing bents. Happily, many great chefs are unwilling to sacrifice their unique contributions for the lure of lucre and ubiquity. They, and a growing coterie of talented newcomers (including many bringing authentic ethnic skills) are providing an increasing selection of novel dining adventures. As a new service to readers, the author has narrowed the field down to his fifty favorite restaurants in each of the region's four culinary capitals— Santa Barbara, Los Angeles, Newport Beach, and San Diego.

Lodging

All of the best and all of the bargain accommodations in and around each destination are described and rated. Most chain motels and humdrum lodgings clustered near freeway off-ramps are excluded. These places do not convey the charm of an area, and they are seldom bargains. As an additional trip planning aid, each locality is also summarized in terms of its: overall number and quality of lodgings; busiest season (prime time); and average percentage by which rates are reduced off-season.

All leisure-oriented amenities available at each lodging are described, whether natural (like a location on a beach or in a forest) or manmade (i.e., outdoor pool, tennis courts, restaurants, etc.). Where available, toll-free phone numbers are provided.

The overall quality of an average bedroom in every lodging is rated according to the author's six level hierarchy. The following descriptions are used throughout: humble (frayed or no-frills); plain (or simply furnished); comfortable (or nicely furnished); attractive (or well-furnished); beautiful; and luxurious. Room features—phone, balcony, etc.—and the size of beds are always identified.

As a unique bonus, more than eleven hundred bedrooms with special views and/or features are highlighted. Thus, exceptional rooms or suites (starting with the best) in the foremost resorts, inns, etc., in each locality are identified by room number (or name), described, and priced. The "regular room" price which completes each listing is the lowest normal (rack rate) price charged during the busiest season for two people.

In addition, every effort was made to include and describe all of each area's safe, clean bargain lodgings. A threshold of $40 per night per couple was used, based on "high season rack rates."

Location

To help you locate any listing without a map, all addresses are referenced according to (1) mileage and (2) direction from the heart of downtown, plus (3) a street number. (There are two exceptions—mileage and direction are calculated in Anaheim from Disneyland and in Buena Park from Knott's Berry Farm.) The term "downtown" covers all features within one-quarter mile of the busiest portion of the main business district in each locality.

Ratings

Every feature listed in this book is rated. Three levels of quality are reflected in the ratings. (1) A star preceding an entry indicates an especially worthwhile example or source of a product or service. It is worth going out of the way for, if you are interested in that thing. (2) An entry is included, but not starred, if it is a notable (but not exceptional) example or source of a product or service. (3) Many features and activities were evaluated but not included in this book if they were judged to be of only average or lower quality or readily available in numerous other places.

Every feature was personally evaluated by the author. No payments were accepted. As a result, each listing is rated on merit alone, and solely reflects the author's judgment. Ratings are comparable among all features and communities. Each listing was consistently evaluated both in terms of overall quality and how well it succeeds in being what it purports to be. Thus, if a restaurant is proclaimed to be a temple of haute cuisine, its rating was based both on the quality of food and decor and on its ability or failure to live up to a lofty aspiration.

Rating information is somewhat perishable in any guidebook. After all, chefs move on, bed-and-breakfast inns change ownership, and so on. However, the single-star rating system can help to simplify your selection of attractions, restaurants, and lodgings. The author's opinion regarding each feature's relative importance is more fully expressed by the length of its description.

Prices

Information is provided about the relative cost of every restaurant and lodging. Because prices change with the economy, it is impossible to know how long specific figures quoted in the lodgings section will be in effect. However, the prices shown will continue to represent comparable values. This is because relative price levels usually remain constant. For example, a "bargain" motel (with rooms costing $40 or less in 1995) can be expected to remain a relative bargain in later years when compared to other lodgings—even though the actual price of a room increases—because the other lodgings in that area will typically increase their prices by about the same percentage as the bargain motel. Similarly, a restaurant will usually continue in its relative price category as years go by.

Lodgings: All quoted prices are prevailing rates during the "high season" (summer along the coast and in the mountains, winter in the desert). They were obtained for every lodging listed in this book through field work and follow-up telephone surveys conducted into 1995. Each price is a per-night rate for two people in a room with one bed. Rates for one person are usually a few dollars less, and rates for two beds (or more than two people) may be more. Prices are for "European plan" accommodations (no meals), except as noted in the text for the few "American plan" lodgings that include one or more meals in their daily rates. The use of on-premises facilities (like swimming pools, saunas, etc.) is included in the price of a room unless fees are noted in the description. Nowadays, travelers should feel free to negotiate the price of a room since most lodgings offer discounts from "regular (rack) rates" to members of auto clubs, business travelers, government employees, military personnel, retirees, and others.

Restaurants: A basic price code was designed to provide a summary of the cost of an average meal at each restaurant. The same code is used for all listed restaurants in all locales. Five categories are used to define the cost per person for a "normal" dinner (soup or salad, average-priced entree, and beverage) not including tip, tax, or wine. The categories and related prices are:

Low: less than $9
Moderate: $9 - $16
Expensive: $16 - $24
Very Expensive: $24 - $32
Extremely Expensive: more than $32

For Southern California, as elsewhere, field work confirmed the following general conclusions. Lodging and food cost substantially more in the metropolises than in more remote locales. Away from major cities, first class facilities are relatively less expensive, and bargains are more plentiful.

Some Final Comments

All information has been carefully checked, and is believed to be current and accurate. However, the author cannot be responsible for changes since these are beyond his control. No malice is intended or implied by the judgments expressed, or by the omission of any facility or service from this book.

Because this guidebook attempts to address all of the best localities and features in the region, it will be challenged about some places that were included and others that were left out. Regardless, the author hopes that *Destinations of Southern California* will encourage you to discover and experience the special pleasures of these delightful locales.

Mr. Vokac welcomes your comments and questions.

c/o West Press
P.O. Box 99717
San Diego, CA 92169

Anaheim

Anaheim is the home of Disneyland. A few miles inland from the ocean, the city sprawls across the broad valley of the Santa Ana River. German settlers founded a town here in 1857 and named it after the river and their word for "home." Farming prevailed. Lush orange groves still dominated the area a century later. The development of Disneyland began during the 1950s and quickly changed all that.

Today, Anaheim is the second largest city in Orange County. Oranges have been replaced by the West's premier amusement park, a gigantic convention center, a major league stadium and sports arena, and the largest concentration of lodgings in California. Thanks to Walt Disney's original "Magic Kingdom" and a burgeoning array of related facilities, Anaheim is firmly established as a renowned year-round destination for family fun, exhibitions, concerts, and sporting events.

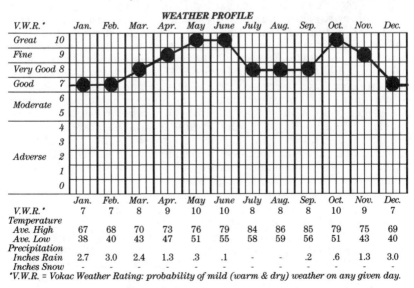

WEATHER PROFILE

V.W.R. *		Jan.	Feb.	Mar.	Apr.	May	June	July	Aug.	Sep.	Oct.	Nov.	Dec.
Great	10												
Fine	9												
Very Good	8												
Good	7												
Moderate	6												
	5												
	4												
	3												
Adverse	2												
	1												
	0												

	Jan.	Feb.	Mar.	Apr.	May	June	July	Aug.	Sep.	Oct.	Nov.	Dec.
V.W.R. *	7	7	8	9	10	10	8	8	8	10	9	7
Temperature												
Ave. High	67	68	70	73	76	79	84	86	85	79	75	69
Ave. Low	38	40	43	47	51	55	58	59	56	51	43	40
Precipitation												
Inches Rain	2.7	3.0	2.4	1.3	.3	.1	-	-	.2	.6	1.3	3.0
Inches Snow	-	-	-	-	-	-	-	-	-	-	-	-

*V.W.R. = Vokac Weather Rating: probability of mild (warm & dry) weather on any given day.

Anaheim

Population: 266,406   Area Code: 714
Elevation: 158 feet
Location: 27 miles Southeast of Los Angeles
Anaheim Area Visitor & Convention Bureau   999-8999
.4 mi. S at 800 W. Katella Av. (Box 4270) - 92803

ATTRACTIONS

★ **Crystal Cathedral**   *971-4000*
   2.5 mi. SE at 12141 Lewis St. - Garden Grove
The aptly named church is a massive all-glass sanctuary with nearly 3,000 seats. The 1980 landmark houses the world's largest church organ, with approximately 16,000 pipes. Noon organ demonstrations are usually held each weekday year-round. More than ten thousand windows provide views of the stainless steel carillon tower and extensive surrounding gardens.

★ **Disneyland**   *999-4565*
   .5 mi. S of I-5 at 1313 Harbor Blvd.
Disneyland has been the West's ultimate destination among family attractions ever since it opened in 1955. It is a modern miracle of master planning and imaginative development in which high technology has been blended with history and great stories into an enchanting collection of eight themed areas. Each has its own rides, live entertainment, dining facilities, architecture, and gardens designed to transport young and old into the past and future. You enter via **Main Street USA**, nostalgic 1890s America with a railroad station, ice cream parlor, penny arcade, collectibles shops, and street-cars. Beyond through Sleeping Beauty's Castle is **Fantasyland** high-lighted by a "Bobsled Ride" through the Matterhorn and "It's a Small World," a marvel of animation. **Frontierland** is the Old West with runaway mine trains on "Big Thunder Mountain." **New Orleans Square** features the delightful "Pirates of the Caribbean" and a "Haunted Mansion" full of restless spirits. **Critter Country** has "Splash Mountain," a whimsical log flume ride with a spectacular drop. **Adventureland** has an extraordinary "Jungle Cruise," and (new in 1995) the "Indiana Jones Adventure," a perilous thriller where (for the first time) guests experience differences on every trip. **Tomorrow-land** features "Space Mountain," the park's fastest ride. **Toontown**, Mickey and his friends' neighborhood, appeals to young visitors. A monorail connects the park with the Disneyland Hotel (see listing). Other modes of transportation in the park include an old-time passenger train, sailing ship, sternwheeler, submarines, and people movers. "The Blue Bayou" by the "Pirates" ride is the most memorable among many eateries ranging from fast-food stalls to elaborate restaurants. Live entertainment is similarly diverse. "The Happiest Place on Earth" is open daily year-round. To minimize waits for rides, go midweek from late fall through winter.

★ **Richard Nixon Library & Birthplace**   *993-3393*
   11 mi. NE at 18001 Yorba Linda Blvd. - Yorba Linda
Nine acres of beautifully landscaped grounds contain an expansive gallery and archives, theater, gardens, and Nixon's original home. The president's public and private life is presented during self-guided tours in film, interactive video displays, exhibits and memorabilia. Original furnishings distinguish both the re-creation of the White House's Lincoln Sitting Room and the little farmhouse where Nixon was born.

RESTAURANTS

★ **Anaheim Hilton and Towers**   *750-4321*
.5 mi. S at 777 W. Convention Way
  B-L-D.   *Expensive*
Pavia (D only) offers homemade pastas and updated Italian fare in a
refined Roman setting. **Hastings** (L-D) serves award-winning New
California cuisine amidst modish elegance. **The Oasis** (B-L-D)
features buffets in a neo-art deco setting by the lobby. There is also a
Sushi Bar, Lobby Bar, and **Pulse** for entertainment.

★ **Anaheim Marriott Hotel**   *750-8000*
.5 mi. S at 700 W. Convention Way
  B-L-D.   *Moderate–Very Expensive*
One of Southern California's great restaurants is **JW's** (D only. Closed
Sun.–Very Expensive). Classic and innovative Continental cuisine is
graciously presented in intimate elegant dining rooms. **La Plaza** (B-L-
D–Moderate) offers California fare and decor. **Veranda** (B-
L–Moderate) features buffets by an outdoor pool. The posh **Lobby Bar**
has a grand piano. **Gambit's Lounge** offers music for dancing.

★ **Anita's**   *525-0977*
4 mi. N at 600 S. Harbor Blvd. - Fullerton
  B-L-D.   *Moderate*
New Mexican dishes (posole, blue corn tortillas, carne adovada,
sopaipillas) distinguish this little outpost as the Southland's best
source for the cuisine of the Northern Rio Grande. Breakfasts are a
special treat in the colorful cafe/takeout with a heated shaded patio.

★ **Aurora**   *738-0272*
4.5 mi. NW at 1341 S. Euclid - Fullerton
  L-D. No L Sat. Closed Sun.   *Expensive*
In one of the region's longest-established gourmet havens, Italian
cuisine is emphasized on a Continental menu supplemented by a
nightly list of chef's specials—try the alligator, halibut cheeks or wild
game hen when available! The stylish dining room and lounge are
enlivened by colorful stained-glass windows and wall art.

Belisle's   *750-6560*
1.4 mi. S at 12001 Harbor Blvd. - Garden Grove
  B-L-D (24 hours).   *Extremely Expensive*
Jumbo-size is touted in pastries, homemade desserts, and American-
style meals coupled with some of California's highest prices for baked
goods and breakfasts. Electric fireplaces and other ersatz touches
reflect the coffee shop's mid-1950s origins.

★ **The Cellar**   *525-5682*
5 mi. N at 305 N. Harbor Blvd. - Fullerton
  D only. Closed Sun.-Mon.   *Very Expensive*
French haute cuisine, including exquisite homemade desserts, is given
a light touch in one of Orange County's most glamorous restaurants.
Dining rooms and a lounge are located in catacombs with irregular
ceilings and brimming wine racks. The romantic setting is further
enhanced by tables set with candles, crystal, china and floral bouquets.

★ **Disneyland Hotel**   *778-6600*
.3 mi. W at 1150 W. Cerritos Av.
  B-L-D. Sun. brunch.   *Moderate–Very Expensive*
Granville's Steak House (D only–Very Expensive), the hotel's

flagship, features steaks and chops and American regional cuisine skillfully prepared in a stylish dining room. **Monorail Cafe** (B-L-D–Expensive) serves all-American fare in a big cheerful coffee shop overlooking the monorail. The **Shipyard Inn** (L-D–Expensive) offers seafood and American fare in a large nautically-themed room overlooking the central pond. Downstairs is the **California Wine Cellar**, where premium California wine is poured in dark wood-trimmed comfort. **Caffe Villa Verde** (L-D–Expensive) is a big colorful trattoria serving rotisserie meats, pizza and pasta by the marina. More informal eateries offer everything from buffets to burgers, while nightlife ranges from piano music to live country/western bands for dancing.

★ **Felix Continental Cafe**   *633-5842*
   5 mi. SE at 36 Plaza Square - Orange
   B-L-D.   *Low*
Authentic Cuban and Spanish dishes like slow-roasted chicken are skillfully prepared as are desserts like pear tart a l'orange, pineapple bread pudding in rum sauce, and the lightest and loveliest vanilla pudding anywhere. The cozy congested dining room and charming sidewalk cafe have overseen Orange's picturesque plaza for years.

★ **The Hobbit**   *997-1972*
   7 mi. SE at 2932 E. Chapman Av. - Orange
   D only. Closed Mon.   *Extremely Expensive*
Seven course gourmet dinners are described on a changing menu which reflects the freshest ingredients and the chef's inspirations. Feasts start promptly at 7:30 p.m. with champagne and appetizers in the well-stocked wine cellar. At a later intermission guests can leave the intimate, informal dining rooms to explore the cottage.

La Palma Chicken Pie Shop   *533-2021*
   3.8 mi. NW at 928 N. Euclid St.
   L-D. Closed Sun.   *Low*
Here you can get a baked chicken pie in a flaky crust with soup or salad, baked potato with cheese sauce, homemade rolls and fruit pie for less than the cost of an omelet at most coffee shops! And, it is good, as are other American dishes and bakery goodies made here. The big bustling dining room, outfitted with padded booths and backlighted photo murals, has been a local landmark since the 1960s.

★ **La Vie en Rose**   *529-8333*
   9 mi. NE at 240 S. State College Blvd. - Brea
   L-D. No L Sat. Closed Sun.   *Very Expensive*
Classic and lighter French cuisine including luscious housemade pastries has won uniform approval by critics and natives alike. Decor in the style of a French country inn distinguishes numerous dining areas and an eight-sided multilevel romantic lounge.

★ **Luigi's D'Italia**   *533-1300*
   3 mi. N at 1287 E. Lincoln Av.
   L-D. Closed Mon.   *Moderate*
Southern Italian dishes—pizzas, pasta, veal (eight ways), chicken and seafoods—are terrific here. So are desserts like rum cake and cannoli in a family operation where everything is made from scratch with real talent. Don't be put off by the mundane shopping center facade and pizza parlor decor. Luigi's is one of the best informal dining experiences in Southern California.

★ **Mr. Stox**   *634-2994*
   1.8 mi. SE at 1105 E. Katella Av.
   L-D. No L Sat. & Sun.   *Expensive*
Some of the finest contemporary American cuisine in the Southland is
served at Mr. Stox, along with selections from one of the West's great
wine cellars. Steak, seafood, and specialties like venision and rabbit
are skillfully prepared, graciously served, and accompanied by grand
piano stylings nightly. Plush dining rooms and a firelit lounge recall
the area's early Spanish heritage.

★ **P.J. Mead Books & Coffee**   *007-5036*
   4.5 mi. SE at 135 S. Cambridge St. - Orange
   B-L-D.   *Moderate*
A handsome cottage in a quiet neighborhood has become one of the
region's most appealing coffee houses. Baked goods made here like the
orange-cranberry muffin and apple crumb cake and gourmet coffees
served in the charming cottage and garden patio are worth a trip.

★ **Rutabegorz**   *738-9339*
   5 mi. N at 211 N. Pomona Av. - Fullerton
   L-D. Closed Sun.   *Low*
Cockie Leeky soup (chicken, mushrooms, leeks, and cream) and sky-
high apple pie star on a long, eclectic menu of California classics. All
feature fresh ingredients and bountiful portions. Homespun dining
areas are an artful carryover of a 1960s coffeehouse.

★ **Sea Food Paradise**   *893-6066*
   6.5 mi. SW at 8602 Westminster Blvd. - Westminster
   L-D.   *Moderate*
Crustaceans, fish and unusual seafood like sea cucumber and elephant
clams are all featured in hundreds of delightful Chinese dishes
ranging from mild to hot and spicy. The cavernous dining hall with a
lot of mirrors, high-tech chandeliers, and monumental Oriental art is
often busy and noisy. The authentic cuisine is worth it.

Summit House   *671-4111*
   8 mi. N at 2000 E. Bastanchury Rd. - Fullerton
   L-D. Closed Mon.   *Expensive*
This vast clublike restaurant high on a hill opened in the early 1990s
with a city view beyond big spiffy dining rooms. Slow-roasted prime rib
and house-smoked double pork chops highlight American standards.
A well-played piano and a display of desserts also appeal.

★ **Thee White House Restaurant**   *772-1381*
   1.5 mi. NE at 887 S. Anaheim Blvd.
   L-D. No L Sat. & Sun.   *Expensive*
In one of Orange County's sophisticated bastions of haute cuisine,
classic Northern Italian dishes are made from scratch with an assured
light touch—including a cart full of luscious desserts. A handsome
Victorian-style white mansion has become a romantic haven of
candlelit table settings in intimate dining rooms.

Tlaquepaque   *528-8515*
   6.5 mi. NE at 111 W. Santa Fe Av. - Placentia
   B-L-D. Sun. brunch.   *Moderate*
Dishes ranging from machaca con huevos to shrimp four ways have
displayed authentic Mexican flavor for decades. Corn tortillas and
other baked goods made here are served to go, at a counter, or in a big
dining hall/cantina with mariachi music on weekends.

Tulsa Rib Company   *633-3760*
5.5 mi. E at 954 N. Tustin Av. - Orange
L-D. No L Sat. & Sun.   *Moderate*
Baby back pork and beef ribs are tender and flavorful highlights
served with delicious cornbread, Tulsa (round and deep-fried) taters
and other fixins' in a casual Q-parlor, or to go.
★ **Yen Ching Restaurant**   *997-3300*
    4 mi. SE at 574 S. Glassell St. - Orange
    L-D.   *Moderate*
Generous, flavorful Szechwan and Mandarin cuisine has made this an
award-winning landmark. Full linen and a choice of overstuffed booths
or chairs enhance three large genial dining areas.

LODGING

More lodgings are clustered near Disneyland than anyplace in the
Southland. No bargains are close by, but many are within easy driving
distance. Summer is prime time. Rates are usually at least 20% less
from fall through springs apart from holidays and weekends.
Anaheim Desert Inn & Suites   *772-5050*
.3 mi. E at 1600 S. Harbor Blvd. - 92802
Disneyland adjoins this new motel with an indoor pool and whirlpool.
Each well-furnished room has a refrigerator, microwave, phone and
color TV with movies and VCR. Toll-free in CA: (800)433-5271 .
    "Spa Suite" (5 of these)—1 BR, in-bath whirlpool,   K bed...$119
    regular room—   2 Q or K bed...$79
Anaheim Desert Palm Suites   *535-1133*
.4 mi. S at 631 W. Katella Av. - 92802
This four-story motel has an outdoor pool, whirlpool, sauna, exercise
room, and gift shop. Each well-furnished room has a refrigerator,
microwave, phone, and remote control color TV with movies and VCR.
Toll-free in CA: (800)521-6420; elsewhere: (800)635-5423.
    "mini-suite"—request 4th floor, private balcony with
        fine view of Matterhorn & summer fireworks,   2 Q beds...$89
    "spa suite"—large in-bath whirlpool,   K bed...$89
    regular room—   2 Q or K bed...$64
★ **Anaheim Hilton and Towers**   *750-4321*
    .5 mi. S at 777 W. Convention Way - 92802
Orange County's largest lodging (1,600 rooms) is a convention-oriented
complex with a modern fourteen-story tower next to the Convention
Center. Amenities include a large roof garden pool and four whirlpools;
restaurants and lounges (see listing); a night club; numerous specialty
shops; (fee) fitness center and pay garage. Each well-furnished room
has a window wall, phone and remote control color TV with movies.
Toll-free in CA: (800)233-6904; elsewhere: (800)222-9923.
    "Concierge floor"—14th floor, spacious, extras, 2 D or K bed...$195
    regular room—   2 D or K bed...$130
★ **Anaheim Marriott Hotel**   *750-8000*
    .5 mi. S at 700 W. Convention Way - 92802
Marriott is well-represented by a contemporary convention-oriented
hotel on beautifully landscaped grounds by the Convention Center.
The 1,042-room sixteen-story complex includes two large pools (one
indoor/outdoor); two whirlpools; an exercise center; sauna; video game
room; restaurants and lounges (see listing); shops; and pay parking.

Each well-furnished room has a large private balcony, phone, and remote control color TV with movies. Toll-free: (800)228-9290.

    regular room—request N side 14-16th floor
      with private balcony for fine cityscapes,   2 D or K bed...$180

Anaheim Plaza Hotel   *772-5900*
.4 mi. E at 1700 S. Harbor Blvd. - 92802

Disneyland adjoins this low-rise 300-room motor hotel on landscaped grounds with an Olympic-sized pool, whirlpool, restaurant, piano bar and gift shops. Each nicely decorated room has a phone and color TV with movies. Toll-free: (800)228-1357.

    regular room—request private balcony or patio, 2 D or K bed...$99

Castle Inn & Suites   *774-8111*
.4 mi. E at 1734 S. Harbor Blvd. - 92802

This castle-derived fantasy-facade motel opened in 1989 with an outdoor pool and whirlpool. Each spacious, well-furnished room has a refrigerator, phone and color TV with VCR. Toll-free: (800)521-5653.

    "Jacuzzi suites"—large whirlpool in view of   K bed...$98
    regular room—   2 D or K bed...$78

Convention Center Inn   *740-2500*
.6 mi. S at 2017 S. Harbor Blvd. - 92802

A modern motel with an outdoor pool and whirlpool. Each comfortable room has a phone and color TV with movies. Toll-free: (800)521-5628.

    #333,#233,#133—spacious, refr./wet bar,
      mirrored whirlpool with skylight in view of   K bed...$88
    regular room—   2 Q or K bed...$58

★ **Crown Sterling Suites**   *632-1221*
6 mi. NE (at CA 91) at 3100 E. Frontera St. - 92806

A New Orleans theme distinguishes one of Anaheim's most luxurious lodgings, opened in 1987. The seven-story hotel has 224 suites around a seventy-foot atrium with jungle greenery, a stream and waterfall. Amenities include an indoor pool, whirlpool, sauna, steam room, restaurant, lounge, and gift shop. Full breakfast and afternoon drinks are complimentary. Each beautiful suite has a living room, microwave oven and refrigerator, small private balcony, two phones, and two color TVs (one remote control) with movies. Toll-free: (800)433-4600.

    regular room—1 BR suite,   2 D or K bed...$140

★ **Disneyland Hotel**   *778-6600*
.3 mi. W at 1150 W. Cerritos Av. - 92802

Orange County's most famous lodging is a newly refurbished 1,130-room hotel with three twelve-story towers around a large sculptured pond in a sixty acre garden complex. The Disneyland Monorail's only stop outside the Park is here. In addition to a major convention center, amenities include an Olympic-sized pool in a tropical garden, two small pools by a sandy beach backed by banana palms, whirlpool, exercise room; (fee) pedal boats and miniature tugboats and race car games, and ten tennis courts; a dozen dining and drinking facilities (see listing); arcades of specialty shops; assorted live entertainment; the dancing waters choreographed fountains; a delightful walk-under waterfall grotto complex and pay parking. Each comfortable room has a phone, stocked (honor) bar, and color TV with movies.

    #2368,#2268—1 BR, big, corner parlor, large
      balcony, great view of Matterhorn from   K bed...$425
    regular room—   2 D or K bed...$170

Doubletree Hotel - Orange County   *634-4500*
2.4 mi. SE (near I-5) at 100 The City Dr. - Orange 92668
Here is one of Orange County's tallest lodgings. The contemporary nineteen-story convention hotel with 454 rooms has an outdoor pool and whirlpool in a fountain court, two lighted tennis courts, dining room, coffee shop, lounge, and gift shop. Each attractive room has a phone and color TV with pay movies. Toll-free: (800)222-TREE.
   regular room—request NW side from 20th to
      10th floor for best cityscapes,   2 D or K bed...$120

Econo Lodge   *952-0898*
5 mi. W at 837 S. Beach Blvd. - 92804
This modern motel is a real **bargain** with a small outdoor pool. Each spacious, nicely furnished room has a phone and remote control color TV. Toll-free: (800)424-4777.
   regular room—   K bed...$35

Friendship Inn Sunrise Motel   *761-4200*
5 mi. W at 705 S. Beach Blvd. - 92804
An indoor/outdoor pool and whirlpool are features of this modern **bargain** motel. Each nicely furnished room has a refrigerator, phone and color TV with movies. Toll-free: (800)453-4511.
   regular room—large in-bath whirlpool for extra $15,   Q bed...$30

Fullerton Suites   *579-7400*
7.5 mi. NE (by CA 57) at 2932 E. Nutwood Av. - Fullerton 92631
Here is a 1990s adult retreat. The four-story post-modern inn has an outdoor pool and exercise room. But, the real feature is the 96 beautifully decorated suites. Each has a large in-room spa in view of the bed, plus phone, and color TV with remote control and movies. Toll-free: (800)79-SUITE.
   deluxe suite—spacious, heart-shaped whirlpool,   K bed...$139
   regular room—   2 Q or K bed...$79

Hilton Suites - Anaheim/Orange   *938-1111*
2.3 mi. SE (near I-5) at 400 N. State College Blvd. - Orange 92668
Hilton's 1989 all-suites hotel has 230 units around a stark ten-story atrium. Amenities include a small indoor pool, whirlpool, sauna, exercise room, and gift shop. Full breakfast, and beverages in the lounge, are complimentary. Each well-furnished suite has a living room, microwave, refrigerator, two phones, and two color TVs (one remote control) with movies. Toll-free: (800)HILTONS.
   regular room—one-bedroom suite,   2 D or K bed...$119

Howard Johnson Hotel   *776-6120*
.4 mi. E (by I-5) at 1380 S. Harbor Blvd. - 92802
Howard Johnson has a handsome contemporary motor hotel near Disneyland's main entrance. Amenities in the 320-room seven-story complex include two large landscaped pools, a whirlpool, video game room, coffee shop, lounge, and gift shop. Each spacious, well-furnished room has a small private balcony or patio, phone and color TV with (fee) movies. Toll-free in CA: (800)422-4228; elsewhere: (800)854-0303.
   #703 & odd #s thru #717—peerless Matterhorn view,   2 D beds...$78
   regular room—request non-freeway side,   2 D or Q bed...$65

★ **Hyatt Regency Alicante**   *750-1234*
1.5 mi. S at 100 Plaza Alicante (at Harbor) - 92803
Hyatt has a "new wave" classic in this 400-room convention/resort hotel. Hundreds of date palms, and columns topped by succulents, line

the road to a sixteen-story tower built around a 160-foot-tall atrium court. Giant pink ceramic flamingos play in a fountain nearby. Amenities include a big rooftop pool, whirlpool, two lighted tennis courts, exercise room, game room, restaurant, atrium coffee shop and piano bar, specialty shops, and pay parking. Each well-furnished room has a phone and remote control color TV with (pay and free) movies. Toll-free: (800)972-2929.

    regular room—request 16th to 14th fl. N side for Disney-
      land views or atrium side for greenery,   2 D or K bed...$154

Jolly Roger Inn   772-7621
.4 mi. S at 640 W. Katella Av. - 92802
This centrally located 234-room motor hotel has two landscaped pools and a whirlpool, restaurant, lounge, and gift shop. Each comfortable room has a phone and color TV. Toll-free: (800)446-1555.

    Honeymoon Suite—refrigerator/wet bar,
      small tiled mirrored pool in view of   K bed...$200
    regular room—   2 Q or K bed...$60

Motel 6
5 mi. W at 7450 Katella Av. - 90680   891-0717
2 mi. E (at CA 91) at 1440 N. State College Blvd. - 92806 956-9690
2.5 mi. SE (by I-5 & CA 57) at 2920 W. Chapman Av.-92668 634-2441
4.5 mi. NW (near CA 91) at 1415 S. Euclid St. - 92632 992-0660
Each of these modern **bargain** motels has an outdoor pool and compact plain rooms with a phone and color TV with movies.

    regular room—(request Q bed at latter three),   D bed...$34

National Inn   636-5110
5 mi. SW at 9797 Garden Grove Blvd. - Garden Grove 92644
"Little Saigon"—a major Southeast Asian commercial strip—surrounds this 1988 **bargain** motel with a small outdoor pool. Each plain room has a phone and color TV with movies. Toll-free:(800)761-7291.

    "Spa room"—large tiled in-bath whirlpool,   K bed...$40
    regular room—   K bed...$32

Pan Pacific Hotel   999-0990
.4 mi. W at 1717 S. West St. - 92802
The Disneyland Monorail is a short stroll from this newly refurbished 503-room twelve-story convention hotel. Features include a large outdoor pool and whirlpool, Japanese dining room, coffee shop, entertainment lounge, and gift shop, plus pay garage. Each well-decorated room has a phone and remote control color TV with movies. Toll-free in CA: (800)321-8976; elsewhere: (800)821-8976.

    regular room—request Disneyland views,   2 D or K bed...$125

Peacock Suites   735-8255
.7 mi. E (near I-5) at 1745 S. Haster St. - 92802
New in 1993, this 140-suite complex has a small outdoor pool, two whirlpools, fitness center, video game room and gift shop. Each well-furnished suite includes a compact living room and bedroom, two remote control color TVs with movies and VCR, refrigerator and microwave, and three phones. Toll-free: (800)522-6401.

    regular room—   K bed...$109

Quality Hotel Maingate   750-3131
.6 mi. S at 616 Convention Way - 92802
The Convention Center is a short walk from this conference-oriented 284-room hotel. The modern nine-story complex includes a large pool,

video game room, restaurant, coffee shop, entertainment lounge, gift shop, and pay parking. Each nicely furnished room has a sliding glass door to a small private balcony, phone and remote control color TV with pay movies. Toll-free: (800)231-6215.

regular room—request 9th floor N side for best view,   K bed...$89
regular room—   2 D beds...$69

Rainbow Inn   *995-6800*
5.3 mi. NW at 831 S. Beach Blvd. - 92804
A small pool and whirlpool are features of this modern **bargain** motel. Each simply furnished room has a phone and color TV with movies.

regular room—   Q or K bed...$25

Ramada Maingate Anaheim   *772-6777*
.3 mi. E at 1460 S. Harbor Blvd. - 92802
Ramada's largest (467 rooms) hotel in the area opened across from the main entrance to Disneyland in 1988. The California-contemporary nine-story complex has a landscaped pool and whirlpool, game room, coffee shop, and gift shop. Each attractively furnished room has a phone and color TV with (fee) movies. Toll-free: (800)447-4048.

regular room—   2 D or K bed...$99

★ **Residence Inn by Marriott**   *533-3555*
.7 mi. E (near I-5) at 1700 S. Clementine St. - 92802
Marriott's all-suites motel has an outdoor pool, three whirlpools, and a sports court. Breakfast buffet and afternoon social hour (weekdays) are free. Each spacious, well-furnished suite has a kitchen with microwave, phone, and remote control color TV. Toll-free: (800)331-3131.

"Jacuzzi Penthouse" (5 of these)—2 BR, 2 baths, fireplace
in LR, large private patio with whirlpool,   2 Q beds...$250
"Penthouse Suite"—as above but no whirlpool,   2 Q beds...$149
regular room—studio,   Q bed...$94

Sheraton Anaheim Hotel   *778-1700*
1 mi. N (by I-5) at 1015 W. Ball Rd. - 92802
Sheraton's castle-themed complex alongside the freeway is a 500-room convention-oriented hotel. The modern facility has a large pool in a courtyard, restaurant, lounge, deli and gift shop. Each large, well-furnished room has a phone and remote control color TV with free and pay movies. Toll-free: (800)325-3535.

regular room—   2 Q or K bed...$130

Tropicana Inn   *635-4082*
.3 mi. E at 1540 S. Harbor Blvd. - 92802
Disneyland is across a street from this modern motel with a large outdoor pool and whirlpool, and shops. Each nicely furnished room has a phone and color TV with pay movies. Toll-free: (800)828-4898.

#366—private balcony, in-bath whirlpool,
fine Matterhorn view from   K bed...$120
regular room—   K bed...$68

Woodfin Suites   *579-3200*
11 mi. NE at 3100 E. Imperial Hwy. - Brea 92621
This 1987 all-suites hotel has a landscaped pool and whirlpool. Full breakfast, afternoon drinks and appetizers (except on weekends) and a film library are complimentary. Each well-furnished suite has a kitchen with a microwave, two phones, and two color TVs with movies (one with remote control), and a VCR. Toll-free: (800)237-8811.

"two bedroom suite"—2 BR, (request fireplace),   Q & K bed...$119
regular room—1 BR, (request fireplace),   K bed...$89

Beverly Hills

Beverly Hills is the most glamorous community in Southern California. The six-square-mile enclave, entirely surrounded by Los Angeles, is a few miles from the ocean on gentle slopes by the Santa Monica Mountains. Incorporated in 1914 with Will Rogers the first mayor, celebrity was assured from the beginning.

Today, it is a nonpareil home of the rich and famous and a renowned hallmark of fashion and style. Sightseers follow maps to the stars' manicured mansions on curving palm-lined streets. City Hall, renewed and expanded for the 1990s, remains an ultimate expression of Southern California panache. Adjoining is "the Golden Triangle," a shopper's paradise epitomized by chic boutiques and galleries along Rodeo Drive. Numerous showcase restaurants and several acclaimed hotels also contribute to a mystique that seems only to get more lustrous as time goes by.

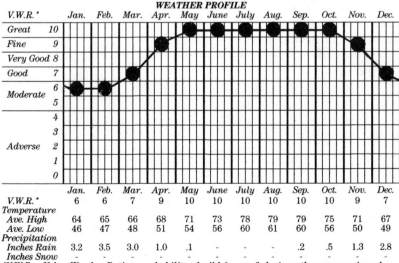

WEATHER PROFILE

V.W.R. *		Jan.	Feb.	Mar.	Apr.	May	June	July	Aug.	Sep.	Oct.	Nov.	Dec.
Great	10												
Fine	9												
Very Good	8												
Good	7												
Moderate	6												
	5												
	4												
	3												
Adverse	2												
	1												
	0												

	Jan.	Feb.	Mar.	Apr.	May	June	July	Aug.	Sep.	Oct.	Nov.	Dec.
V.W.R. *	6	6	7	9	10	10	10	10	10	10	9	7
Temperature												
Ave. High	64	65	66	68	71	73	78	79	79	75	71	67
Ave. Low	46	47	48	51	54	56	60	61	60	56	50	49
Precipitation												
Inches Rain	3.2	3.5	3.0	1.0	.1	-	-	-	.2	.5	1.3	2.8
Inches Snow	-	-	-	-	-	-	-	-	-	-	-	-

*V.W.R. = Vokac Weather Rating: probability of mild (warm & dry) weather on any given day.

23

Population: 31,971   Area Code: 310
Elevation: 268 feet
Location: 9 miles West of Los Angeles
Beverly Hills Visitors Bureau   271-8174   (800)345-2210
.4 mi. S at 239 S. Beverly Dr. - 90212

ATTRACTIONS

Greystone Park   550-4868
2 mi. N at 905 Loma Vista Dr. & Doheny Rd.
Stone walkways give strollers a free opportunity to enjoy nearly
twenty acres of elegant terraced gardens. The grounds showcase a
massive fifty-five-room mansion. The building, a star in many TV and
feature films, is closed to the public, except for occasional tours.

★ **Rodeo Drive and the "Golden Triangle"**
  downtown
The "golden triangle" (formed by Canon Drive, Wilshire Blvd., and
Little Santa Monica Blvd.) features an abundance of internationally
renowned art galleries, clothing and jewelry boutiques, and posh
eateries. Opulent facades line famed Rodeo Drive and nearby streets
further distinguished by manicured trees and vibrant plots of flowers.
The remarkably tidy and luxurious enclave appeals to shoppers,
strollers, stargazers, and diners alike.

RESTAURANTS

★ **The Beverly Hilton**   274-7777
  .7 mi. W at 9876 Wilshire Blvd.
  B-L-D. Sun. brunch.   *Expensive—Extremely Expensive*
L'Escoffier (D only. Closed Sun. & Mon.—Extremely Expensive)
presents classic New California cuisine in an opulent aerie. After 7:30,
live music and dancing enliven the capacious dining room with a
panoramic view of Beverly Hills. Coat and tie are required. **Trader
Vic's** (D only—Very Expensive) features updated Polynesian-themed
cuisine (they use macadamia nut oil only) with an exotic setting to
match. **Mr. H** (B-L-D. Sun. brunch—Very Expensive) offers buffets at
all meals. **Cafe Beverly** (B-L-D—Expensive) serves casual American
fare in a contemporary coffee shop. There is also a plush lobby lounge.

★ **Beverly Prescott Hotel**   772-2999
  1 mi. S at 1224 S. Beverwil Dr. - Los Angeles
  B-L-D.   *Very Expensive*
Sylvie is the stylish young hotel's dining room. Imaginative, carefully
prepared entrees are created from the freshest seasonally available
ingredients. The New California cuisine with a Mediterranean topspin
is complemented by a handsome dining room with a choice of
overstuffed booths or armchairs overlooking an exhibition kitchen, a
tony bar, and a heated enclosed tropical patio.

★ **The Bistro Garden**   550-3900
  downtown at 176 N. Canon Dr.
  L-D. Closed Sun.   *Very Expensive*
International specialties including unusual treats like ox tongue
marsala, and a tempting array of desserts are made here. An
enchanting garden patio with heat lamps and umbrellas adjoins. Full
linen, candles, flowers and a well-played grand piano (even at lunch)
contribute to the romantic ambiance of a cozy dining room.

★ **Celestino**   *859-8601*
  .4 mi. S at 236 S. Beverly Dr.
  L-D. No L Sat. & Sun.   *Very Expensive*
Rabbit, veal, lamb, chicken, and fish are each represented by a masterful creation on a well-thought-out menu of Northern Italian cuisine. Fine meals can be accompanied by luscious pastries made here, and displayed in an intimate, elegant dining room/bar with contemporary artistic accents.

★ **Chez Helene**   *276-1558*
  .5 mi. S at 267 S. Beverly Dr.
  L-D. No L Sun.   *Expensive*
Roast leg of lamb or poached chicken capture the authentic essence of French Canadian cuisine. Attention to details carries over to the lovely little dining rooms and shaded patio of a transformed cottage.

★ **Da Pasquale**   *859-3884*
  .5 mi. W at 9749 Little Santa Monica Blvd.
  L-D. No L Sat. & Sun.   *Expensive*
First-rate pizza and calzone and a distinctive selection of pastas have made this congested little trattoria with an expo kitchen one of Beverly Hills' most popular dining destinations for casual dining.

★ **David Slay's La Veranda**   *274-7246*
  .4 mi. S at 225 S. Beverly Dr.
  L-D. No L Sat. & Sun.   *Very Expensive*
One of LA's master chefs offers New California cuisine from a well-thought-out grazing menu of innovative dishes that change frequently. The small, simply mod dining room keeps the focus on the food.

★ **Four Seasons Hotel**   *273-2222*
  .5 mi. E at 300 S. Doheny Dr. - Los Angeles
  B-L-D. Sun. brunch.   *Extremely Expensive*
Gardens offers classic New California cuisine in luxuriously appointed dining rooms and a garden patio with heat lamps and umbrellas for alfresco dining. Adjoining is **Windows**, a plush contemporary lounge where a grand piano is well-played each evening.

★ **The Grill on the Alley**   *276-0615*
  downtown at 9560 Dayton Way
  L-D. Closed Sun.   *Very Expensive*
Some of the finest steaks and chops in Beverly Hills are featured on an all-American menu. A polished wood-toned bar and grill adjoin a high-ceilinged room with booths or armchairs at tables awash in linen. Tucked away, it is a deservedly popular celebrity refuge.

★ **Il Cielo**   *276-9990*
  .6 mi. E at 9018 Burton Way
  L-D. Closed Sun.   *Very Expensive*
You can tell that the Northern Italian cuisine featured here will be excellent just by glancing at the splendid desserts on display near the entrance. Meals are perfectly complemented by the charming setting of a cottage transformed into romantic, genteel dining areas. Both a garden patio and fountain court are ideal for alfresco dining.

★ **Jimmy's**   *552-2394*
  1 mi. SW at 201 Moreno Dr.
  L-D. No L Sat. Closed Sun.   *Extremely Expensive*
Classic and updated Continental cuisine are skillfully prepared in

Beverly Hills' paean to power and prominence. Expansive dining rooms convey an opulent air with crystal chandeliers, lavish table settings, and luxuriant greenery and flowers. Near the entrance, by a posh piano bar, is a luscious array of desserts made here.

★ **Lawry's the Prime Rib**   *652-2827*
   1.5 mi. E at 100 N. La Cienega Blvd.
   D only.   *Expensive*
The Southland's best dry aged quality beef roasted on a bed of rock salt stars at Lawry's. In fact, four cuts of prime rib are the only entrees—accompanied by a spinning salad bowl, big baked potatoes, and Yorkshire pudding. Recently relocated across the street, there is a cavernous dining room and several similarly baronial anterooms. All are informally elegant. Attention is focused on silver-domed serving carts filled with prime rib being cut to order at tableside.

★ **The Mandarin**   *859-0638*
   downtown at 430 N. Camden Dr.
   L-D. No L Sat. & Sun.   *Expensive*
Traditional and innovative Chinese cuisine are co-equally treated with flair and finesse in Beverly Hills' finest Chinese restaurant. The sophisticated blending of East and West is also reflected in the decor of the dining rooms and lounge where diners at tables set with crisp white linen can watch activity in an exhibition kitchen.

★ **Maple Drive**   *274-9800*
   1 mi. E at 345 N. Maple Dr.
   L-D. No L Sat. Closed Sun.   *Extremely Expensive*
The menu changes daily for trendy dishes like grilled salmon with lime butter sauce and fresh tomato salsa, or classic American dishes like meatloaf with spinach and mashed potatoes. Both appeal to visiting Hollywood glitterati. The talented staff is on display in a high-tech kitchen by a tony dining room. An ultra-mod lounge adjoins.

★ **Matsuhisa**   *659-9639*
   1.4 mi. E at 129 N. La Cienega Blvd.
   L-D.   *Expensive*
Halibut cheeks in pepper sauce typifies unusual seasonal specialties. Year-round, delicious sushi, tempura, and other traditional Japanese dishes and gourmet improvisations are available in great diversity. Some of the finest culinary talent in the Southland usually assures a full house at the vibrant sushi bar with distinctive accents and at tables set with crisp white linen.

Nate 'n Al's   *274-0101*
   downtown at 414 N. Beverly Dr.
   B-L-D.   *Expensive*
Deli standards at Beverly Hills' oldest breakfast place (apart from hotels) ranges from good to mediocre. Unfortunately, there is little local competition for this big prosaic California-style deli.

★ **The Peninsula Beverly Hills**   *551-2888*
   .6 mi. W at 9882 Little Santa Monica Blvd.
   B-L-tea-D. Sun. brunch.   *Very Expensive*
The Belvedere (B-L-D. Sun. brunch) features gourmet New California cuisine in an opulent setting and on a garden terrace. A harpist lends tranquility to traditional afternoon tea served daily in **The Living Room**. Decorated with museum-quality art, **The Club Bar** is a sophisticated haven for premium libations.

★ **R.J.'s the Rib Joint**   *274-RIBS*
downtown at 252 N. Beverly Dr.
L-D.   *Expensive*
Prime rib is only one feature at R.J.'s, where food as fun is the theme.
"The green grocery" with about eighty items is the best salad bar for
miles, and humongous desserts are on display. A splendiferous
backbar sports a fine selection of tap and bottled beer. Solid wood
booths and tables, sawdust on the floor, Tiffany glass and fans, brick
and plants decorate the capacious dining room/bar.

★ **The Regent Beverly Wilshire**   *275-5200*
downtown at 9500 Wilshire Blvd.
B-L-tea-D. Sun. brunch.   *Expensive–Very Expensive*
The Dining Room (B-L-D. Sun. brunch–Very Expensive) presents
fine New California cuisine in an expansive split-level room with
opulent decor that conveys the hotel's illustrious heritage. Across a
hall is a plush clubby lounge with a grand piano and lovely floral
accents. **The Cafe** (B-L-D–Expensive) has traditional American fare
in a posh coffee shop with marble floors and a picture-window view of
downtown. **The Lobby Lounge** (L-tea-D–Expensive) offers luscious
LA cuisine and beverages along with a well-played grand piano in a
luxurious tranquil setting.

LODGING

Accommodations aren't numerous, but several world-class hotels
contribute to the city's glamorous image. Rates remain about the same
year-round, but may be reduced by 10% or more on weekends.

★ **The Beverly Hilton**   *274-7777*
.7 mi. W at 9876 Wilshire Blvd. - 90210
The city's largest (nearly 600 rooms) hotel was extensively remodeled
for the 1990s. The nine-level complex now appeals to executives and
upscale conventions with an Olympic-sized pool, exercise room,
gourmet restaurants and lounges (see listing), specialty shops, and
(pay) valet parking. Each of the beautifully furnished rooms has a
refrigerator/(honor) bar, two phones, and color TV with movies. Toll-
free: (800)HILTONS.
      regular room—request balcony on
         7th or 6th floor west end for best views,   2 D or K bed...$210

★ **The Beverly Prescott Hotel**   *277-2800*
1 mi. S at 1224 S. Beverwil Dr. (at Pico Blvd.) - Los Angeles 90035
One of the Beverly Hills area's best lodgings opened in 1993 after a
multi-million dollar upgrade of a small hotel just south of the city. The
luxurious 140-room twelve-story complex has a landscaped pool and
whirlpool, exercise room, gourmet restaurant and lounge (see listing),
and (pay) valet parking. Each beautifully furnished room has a private
view balcony, (honor) bar/refrigerator, a phone and remote control
color TV with (pay) movies. Toll-free: (800)421-3212.
      "King Jacuzzi" (6 of them)—VCR, large in-bath
         whirlpool, fine Beverly Hills view from   K bed...$225
      "1 BR Jacuzzi Suite" (several)—VCR,
         spacious parlor, large in-bath whirlpool,   K bed...$525
      regular room—request north side for views,   2 D or K bed...$175

Beverly Hills
★ **Four Seasons Hotel**   *273-2222*
.5 mi. E at 300 S. Doheny Dr. - Los Angeles 90048
The "Beverly Hills feeling" is quintessentially captured in Four Seasons' only hotel in the Los Angeles basin. The sixteen-story 285-unit hotel on tropically landscaped grounds includes an extra-large pool and whirlpool in a city-view garden setting, an exercise room, gourmet restaurant and lounge (see listing), and (pay) valet or (free) self-parking. There is also a resort shop. Each luxuriously appointed room includes a small private view balcony, refrigerator/(honor) bar, two phones, and a remote control color TV with (pay and free) movies. Toll-free: (800)332-3442.

  #929,#829,#729—3 phones, 2 TVs, corner with
   large balcony with superb pool/Beverly hills view,   K bed...$330
   regular room—   2 D or K bed...$310
★ **The Peninsula Beverly Hills**   *551-2888*
.6 mi. W at 9882 Little Santa Monica Blvd. - 90212
The first California property of a legendary hotel chain opened in 1991. The 200-room, four-story complex has already earned critical acclaim for a classically elegant design in a garden setting; cabana-lined rooftop view pool and whirlpool; health club with exercise room, sauna, steam room and (for a fee) beauty and health services. There is also a gourmet restaurant (see listing), a posh haven for afternoon tea, and a sophisticated bar; pay (valet) parking; and a convenient gift shop. Each spacious room is luxuriously appointed and has an (honor) bar/ refrigerator, standing balcony, two phones, and color TV with movies and VCR. Toll-free: (800)462-7899.

  #125,#128—spacious 1 BR, pvt. patio with
   whirlpool, LR with gas fireplace   K bed...$650
   regular room—   2 D or K bed...$280
Radisson Beverly Pavilion   *273-1400*
downtown at 9360 Wilshire Blvd. - 90212
By the heart of town is a modern 110-room eight-story hotel with a rooftop view pool and garden, gourmet restaurant, bar, gift shop, and (pay) valet parking. Each well-appointed room has a tiny balcony, phone, and color TV with movies. Toll-free: (800)441-5050.

  "Deluxe Room"—refrigerator, 2 phones,
   request 8th floor for best cityscapes,   K bed...$180
   regular room—compact, request 8th floor,   K bed...$130
★ **The Regent Beverly Wilshire**   *275-5200*
downtown at 9500 Wilshire Blvd. - 90212
Downtown Beverly Hills' premier grand-luxe hotel is at the beginning of Rodeo Drive. The fourteen-story 300-room complex has a large landscaped rooftop pool; health club with saunas, whirlpool, exercise equipment, and (for a fee) massage and spa services; plus gourmet restaurants and lounges (see listing); specialty shops; and (pay) valet parking. Each spacious, luxuriously appointed unit has a refrigerator, three phones, and two remote control color TVs with movies. Toll-free in CA: (800)427-4354; elsewhere: (800)421-4354.

  regular room "Wilshire Wing"—in renovated
   landmark building, extra-large tub,   2 D or K bed...$355
   regular room "Beverly Wing"—private balcony,
   request 6th floor for best cityscapes,   K bed...$295

Big Bear Lake

Big Bear Lake is the premier mountain playground of Southern California. Only two hours by car from the coast, the village is almost 7,000 feet above sea level in a luxuriant pine forest along the high country's largest reservoir. Nearby, the San Bernardino Mountains top out in the Southland's highest peak, San Gorgonio (elevation: 11,500 feet). Furs, gold, lumber and cattle all played a part in the area's development. But, it was the completion of a concrete dam in 1912 for irrigation that opened the area to its ultimate role as an alpine recreation center.

Today, Big Bear Lake is a four-season destination with many family-oriented water and mountain sports and attractions, shops, restaurants, night spots and lodgings sprinkled along the shore. The surrounding woodlands draw campers, hikers, backpackers, and horseback riders, while major ski areas line slopes south of town.

WEATHER PROFILE

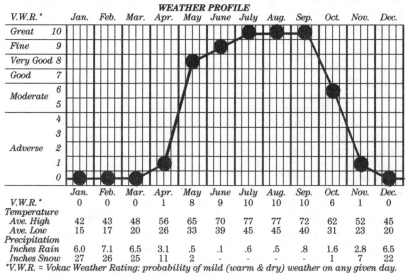

V.W.R.*		Jan.	Feb.	Mar.	Apr.	May	June	July	Aug.	Sep.	Oct.	Nov.	Dec.
Great	10												
Fine	9												
Very Good	8												
Good	7												
Moderate	6 5												
	4												
	3												
Adverse	2												
	1												
	0												

	Jan.	Feb.	Mar.	Apr.	May	June	July	Aug.	Sep.	Oct.	Nov.	Dec.
V.W.R.*	0	0	0	1	8	9	10	10	10	6	1	0
Temperature												
Ave. High	42	43	48	56	65	70	77	77	72	62	52	45
Ave. Low	15	17	20	26	33	39	45	45	40	31	23	20
Precipitation												
Inches Rain	6.0	7.1	6.5	3.1	.5	.1	.6	.5	.8	1.6	2.8	6.5
Inches Snow	27	26	25	11	2	-	-	-	-	1	7	22

*V.W.R. = Vokac Weather Rating: probability of mild (warm & dry) weather on any given day.

Big Bear Lake

Population: *5,351*   *Area Code: 909*
Elevation: *6,750 feet*
Location: *96 miles Northeast of Los Angeles*
Big Bear Lake Visitors Authority   866-7000
  downtown at 630 Bartlett Rd. (Box 2860) - 92315

ATTRACTIONS

★ *Bicycling*

A paved scenic highway circles the lake, and there are many miles of mostly dirt roads into the forested hills beyond. Mountain bikes and cruisers are available by the hour or day at:

Big Bear Bikes *1.3 mi. NE at 41810 Big Bear Blvd. 866-2224*
Skyline Ski & Sport *downtown at 653 Pine Knot Av. 866-3500*
Team Big Bear *1.8 mi. SE at 800 Summit Blvd. 866-4565*

★ **Big Bear Cannery**   585-1060
3.7 mi. NE at 1108 W. Big Bear Blvd. - Big Bear City

A cornucopia of fruit jams and jellies and flavored honeys opened in 1993. The jam-packed little roadside shop offers generous samples of almost all of their products. Closed Mon.-Thurs. in off-season.

★ *Boat Rentals*

Pine-forested slopes and picturesque boulder formations near the west end make six-mile-long Big Bear Lake a prime destination for boating as well as fishing from spring through fall. Row, speed, sail, fishing, pontoon, and water ski boats, plus canoes, jet skis and windsurfing gear can be rented by the hour or longer at:

Big Bear Marina *.3 mi. W at Paine Rd. & Lakeview Dr. 866-3218*
Hollaway's Marina *2 mi. W at 398 Edgemoor Rd. 866-5706*
Pine Knot Landing *downtown at 439 Pine Knot Av. 866-2628*
Pleasure Point Landing *2.5 mi. W on Big Bear Blvd. 866-2455*

Boat Ride
Pine Knot Landing   866-2628
downtown at 439 Pine Knot Av.

A little excursion boat takes passengers for a 75-minute narrated tour around the lake. It is a leisurely way to learn about the area's history and see points of interest close-up.

Horseback Riding
Magic Mountain Stables   878-4677
1 mi. W at 40355 Big Bear Blvd.

You can explore forest hills near the lake on one-hour guided rides.

★ **Magic Mountain**   866-4626
1 mi. W on Big Bear Blvd.

Year-round, Southern California's only twin alpine slides hustle solo riders on plastic toboggans down winding fiberglass chutes. It's as exhilarating as the chairlift to the top of the chutes is scenic. In summer, two waterslides provide exciting ways to cool off. In winter, a groomed snow play area with inner tube rentals becomes one of the most popular places for family fun in town.

★ **Rim of the World Drive**
30 mi. of CA 18 between Crestline & Big Bear Lake

Grand vistas abound along the main highway (more than a mile above the Los Angeles basin) that provides access to the area's high country lakes, sky forests, and major winter sports areas.

★ **San Bernardino National Forest**   *866-3437*
  surrounding town
  Many miles of trails extend into pine-forested mountains from trail-
  heads located along the loop highway around Big Bear Lake. Part of
  the Pacific Crest Trail parallels the lake two miles to the north.
  Scenic Flights
    Aero Haven   *585-9663*
    4.5 mi. NE at airport - Big Bear City
  Scenic flights above the high country can be arranged here any day.
  Warm Water Feature
    Meadow Park Swim Beach   *866-0135*
    .7 mi. NE at Park Av. & Mountainaire Lane
  A small sandy beach is, surprisingly, the only public swimming beach
  on the lake. The fenced (fee) park, open in summer, has lifeguards,
  restrooms, a grassy area with picnic tables, and a pool.
  Winter Sports
★   **Bear Mountain Ski Resort**   *585-2519*
    3.6 mi. SE on Club View Dr.
  Skiers enjoy the eastern San Bernardino Mountains' greatest vertical
  rise (over 1,400 feet from a base at 7,100 feet), longest run (about 2
  miles), and most complete snowmaking equipment. There are now
  eleven chairlifts including triples and quads. A half-mile
  "snowboarders only" trail has its own chairlift. All services, facilities
  and rentals are available at the base for downhill skiing. Restaurant
  and lounge facilities have been provided at the area, and lodgings are
  nearby. Skiing season is from before Thanksgiving into April.
★   **Snow Summit**   *866-5766*
    1.8 mi. SE at S end of Summit Blvd.
  One of Southern California's two most popular ski areas tops out at
  8,200 feet. The vertical rise is almost 1,200 feet and the longest run is
  1¼ miles. There are eleven chairlifts, including two triples and three
  quadruple chairs. A specialized park with a permanent half-pipe (a
  banked, U-shaped course) appeals to snowboarders. All services,
  facilities and rentals are available at the base for downhill skiing and
  for lighted skiing most nights, as are restaurants, lounges, and
  lodgings. Skiing season is from late November to early April. The
  Scenic Sky Chair gives sightseers, hikers and bikers a quick and
  comfortable trip to the top in summer.
★   **Snow Valley**   *867-2751*
    11 mi. W on CA 18 - Running Springs
  The vertical drop from 7,840-foot Slide Peak is about 1,100 feet, and
  the longest run is 1.2 miles. There are thirteen chairlifts, including
  five triples. All facilities, services and rentals are available at the base
  for downhill skiing daily, and for night-lighted skiing Wednesday
  through Sunday. Food service, but no lodgings, are near the base. The
  skiing season is from late November into April.
★   **Snowdrift Tube-boggins**   *867-2640*
    12 mi. W on CA 18 - Running Springs
  Fun-loving adults enjoy exhilarating rides down snowpacked slopes as
  much as kids. The big rubber inner tubes with belly straps and
  handles rented here by the hour are perfect for controlled careens
  down groomed slopes of various difficulty. Open daily in winter...snow
  and weather permitting.

★ **Belotti's Bakery and Pizzeria**   *866-9686*
.6 mi. E at 41248 Big Bear Blvd.
Belotti's is the most comprehensive bakery in the mountains. Cases overflow with a remarkable array of German, Austrian, Italian, and American pastries, pies, pizzas and breads, plus innovative adaptations. Quality can be awesome, but it is uneven. Best of all, for 14 years this has been the mother lode of breakfast pastries (don't miss the bear claws, raspberry roll-ups and citrus swirls).

Big Bear Prospectors   *866-6696*
downtown at 40771 Lakeview Dr.
D only. Sun. brunch.   *Moderate*
Hearty uncomplicated American fare is served with a lake view. Rough log walls and a massive stone fireplace lend relaxed ranchhouse rusticity to the dining room/bar/entertainment lounge.

Blue Whale   *866-5771*
.3 mi. NE at 350 Alden Rd.
D only. Sun. brunch.   *Expensive*
A contemporary American menu is featured along with a salad bar in a large split-level dining room with a picture window view of the lake. A lounge has live entertainment for dancing and a lakeside patio.

Boo Bear's Den   *866-2932*
downtown at 572 Pine Knot Av.
B-L-D.   *Moderate*
All-American dishes are served in a wood-toned dining room with a salad bar and fireplace or in a large umbrella-shaded garden patio.

Captain's Anchorage   *866-3997*
1.8 mi. E at 42148 Moonridge Rd.
D only.   *Moderate*
Prime ribs, steaks and seafoods are accompanied by a soup and salad bar in this high-country favorite. Both the wood and rock-trimmed dining room and lounge have a big stone fireplace.

★ **George & Sigi's Knusperhauschen**   *585-8640*
4 mi. NE at 829 W. Big Bear Blvd. - Big Bear City
D only. Closed Mon.-Thurs. off-season.   *Expensive*
Some of the best food in the mountains ranges from classic German dishes through lively contemporary adaptations of Continental cuisine to an ethereal array of desserts including strudel, Black Forest cake and bourbon cake. The Hansel-and-Gretel-themed alpine cottage decor is a whimsical counterpoint to the sophisticated cuisine.

Hansel's Restaurant   *866-9497*
downtown at 40701 Big Bear Blvd.
B-L-D. No B Mon.-Fri.   *Moderate*
German standards are featured at all meals, but breakfast is the best bet with dishes like potato pancakes and humongous German beer bratwurst. Wood-trimmed alpine chalet decor and umbrella-shaded sidewalk patio complement the wholesome hearty fare.

The Iron Squirrel   *866-9121*
downtown at 646 Pine Knot Av.
D only. Sun. brunch.   *Expensive*
A limited selection of Continental specialties is served amid casual decor and faux foliage in a long-established restaurant on main street.

La Montana   *866-2606*
1.8 mi. E at 42164 Moonridge Rd.
L-D. Sun. brunch.   *Low*
Appealing California-style Mexican dishes are served in colorful south-of-the-border-themed dining rooms and a convivial cantina.
Log Cabin Restaurant   *866-3667*
1.5 mi. W at 39976 Big Bear Blvd.
B-L-D.   *Moderate*
American and German dishes are complemented by homemade breads, biscuits, cinnamon rolls, and pies. A fireplace lends cheer to the knotty-pine decor of this long-established roadside coffee shop.
Old Country Inn   *866-5600*
.5 mi. E at 41126 Big Bear Blvd.
B-L-D.   *Moderate*
Innovative breakfast omelets star among American and German dishes served amidst ersatz alpine chalet decor festooned with faux foliage.

LODGING

Several dozen relatively small hotels, motels, bed-and-breakfast inns, and cabin clusters share the forest along Big Bear Blvd. (CA 18). However, only a few are near the lake or ski areas. Prime time is Friday and Saturday in summer and winter. Most places reduce their rates at least 10% during the week, while those near the mountain are at least 30% less than the rates shown apart from the ski season.
Bavarian Lodge   *866-2644*
.9 mi. E at 41421 Big Bear Blvd. (Box 34) - 92315
A pool, indoor whirlpool, two lighted tennis courts, and ping pong are features of this complex of cabins and motel rooms in the pines. Each comfortable unit has a refrigerator, phone, and color TV.
    motel—well-furnished, corner rock fireplace,   K bed...$65
    cabin—knotty-pine decor, kitchen, fireplace,   D or K bed...$65
    regular room—motel or cabin, request fireplace,   D or K bed...$65
Big Bear Inn   *866-3471*
1.9 mi. E at 42200 Moonridge Rd. (Box 1814) - 92315
This Vegas-in-the-pines hotel features flamboyant faux foliage, sculptures, antiques, marble halls and glitzy chandeliers. Amenities include an outdoor pool and whirlpool, restaurant, and lounge. Each well-furnished room has a gas fireplace, phone, and color TV. Toll-free: (800)BEAR-INN.
    "Jacuzzi Suite"—spacious, in-bath whirlpool,   K bed...$175
    regular room—   D bed...$100
★ **Cathy's Country Cottages**   *866-7567*
4.4 mi. NE at 600 W. Big Bear Blvd. - Big Bear City 92314
These Victorian-inspired cottages were built in 1988 exclusively for romantic getaways. Each spacious unit has a kitchenette with microwave, a large double-headed shower, gas fireplace and raised whirlpool (both in view of the king bed), phone and remote control color TV. Toll-free: (800)544-7454.
    regular room—   K bed...$199
Club View Chalet   *866-5753*
3.6 mi. SE at 1302 Clubview Dr. (Box 2817) - 92315
Bear Mountain Ski Resort is across a parking lot from these modern apartments in the pines. Each attractively furnished unit has a

refrigerator and color TV. Many have fine ski slope views.

1 BR—kitchen, fireplace,   Q bed...$155
regular room—ask for kitchenette,   Q bed...$75

★ **Cozy Hollow Lodge**   *866-9694*
.8 mi. W at 40409 Big Bear Blvd. (Box 1288) - 92315
Some of the high country's finest contemporary woodcrafted cabins share tree-shaded grounds with a whirlpool and outdoor recreation facilities. Each attractively furnished unit has a gas or woodburning fireplace, kitchenette, phone and color TV. Toll-free: (800)882-4480.

#1,#9,#10—private porch with forest view by creek,
kitchenette, whirlpool & fireplace visible from   K bed...$130
regular room—bungalow,   Q bed...$69

Fireside Lodge   *866-2253*
.3 mi. W at 40666 Lakeview Dr. (Box 635) - 92315
New in 1994, this neo-Victorian motel with a pool and whirlpool is near the lake. Each well-furnished unit has a phone and remote control color TV with movies.

#11,#15,#16—1 BR, room with gas fireplace by
whirlpool, partial lake view from   Q bed...$170
#6,#3—whirlpool and raised gas fireplace in view of   Q bed...$170
regular room—(gas fireplace extra $10),   Q bed...$80

★ **Forest Shores Estates**   *866-6551*
downtown at 40670 Lakeview Dr. (Box 946) - 92315
All of the condos in this contemporary three-story wood-trimmed complex front on the lake (and a sandy beach except at high water). Other amenities include a private marina, whirlpool, sauna, game room and ski lockers. Each spacious, attractively decorated unit has a gas fireplace, private balcony or patio, a fine floor-to-ceiling window view of the lake, phone, and color TV. Toll-free: (800)341-8000.

#201-#204—2-level, 2 BR, 2 bath, full kitchen, lakeview
windows on 2 sides, gas fireplace in LR,   2 Q beds...$195
#101—end, studio, kitchenette, patio above beach,   K bed...$120
regular room—studio,   K bed...$120

★ **Frontier Lodge & Motel**   *866-5888*
.7 mi. W at 40472 Big Bear Blvd. (Box 687) - 92315
Guests can choose refurbished cabins in the pines or a modern motel complex by the lodge's private sandy beach and boat dock. There is also a pool. Each rustic cabin or comfortably furnished motel room has a fireplace, phone and color TV. Toll-free in CA: (800)457-6401.

#29—1 BR cabin, kitchen, lakefront, small
deck by lake, fireplace & whirlpool in view of   Q bed...$180
#111, #112A—whirlpool & fireplace in view of   K bed...$105
#129—lakeview window, fireplace in view of   K bed...$78
regular room—in motel,   K bed...$73

Gold Mountain Manor Bed & Breakfast   *585-6997*
5.5 mi. NE at 1117 Anita Av. (Box 2027) - Big Bear City 92314
A historic three-story mansion has become one of the most charming bed-and-breakfast inns on the mountain. The artistically refurbished wood-trimmed building is now a romantic hideaway featuring complimentary full breakfast and afternoon wine and appetizers.

"Ted Ducey Room"—private half bath, pvt. entrance,
fireplace & whirlpool in separate room from   Q bed...$180
regular room—shared bath, small,   D bed...$75

The Knickerbocker Mansion Bed & Breakfast   866-8221
.6 mi. S at 869 S. Knickerbocker Rd. (Box 3661) - 92315
A 1920s four-story log mansion is now a handsome bed-and-breakfast inn on a forested hillside with a sundeck with a whirlpool. Breakfast and afternoon repast are complimentary. Each of ten units is comfortably furnished with country accents.

"suite"— windows on 3 sides, microwave/refr.,
   big screen TV with VCR, in-bath whirlpool,   Q bed...$225
"Carriage House room"—private bath,   Q bed...$145
regular room—in main house, shared bath,   Q bed...$110

★ **Marina Riviera Resort**   866-6705
downtown at 40770 Lakeview Dr. (Box 979) - 92315
One of Big Bear's best lodgings is this modern three-story motel. A private sandy beach and dock and a lakeview pool and whirlpool are highlights, and there are pool and ping pong tables. Each well-furnished room has a large private balcony, a floor-to-ceiling lakeview window, a phone, and remote-control color TV.

"Honeymoon Suite"—kitchen, LR, lakeview balcony,
   gas fireplace, mirrored whirlpool in view of   Q bed...$200
#102,#103—refr., gas fireplace, in-bath whirlpool,   Q bed...$145
regular room—   Q bed...$120

Motel 6   585-6666
3.7 mi. NE at 1200 Big Bear Blvd. (Box 132806) - Big Bear City 92315
The only **bargain** on the mountain is a big modern motel in the pines with an outdoor pool. Each compact, plain room has a phone and color TV.
regular room—   D bed...$37

★ **Sleepy Forest Cottages**   866-7444
.8 mi. E at 426 Eureka Dr. (Box 3706) - 92315
Some of the most romantic bedrooms in town are in this cozy cabin complex in the pines. Each comfortably furnished unit has a refrigerator, phone and color TV, plus free use of a nearby athletic club. Toll-free in CA: (800)544-7454.

#9—honeymoon cottage, microwave oven, private porch,
   gas fireplace, raised mirrored whirlpool by   K bed...$179
#4—as above, but kitchenette & less private locale,   K bed...$169
regular room—   K bed...$119

★ **Snow Summit Townhouses**   866-2223
1.8 mi. SE at 861 Thrush Dr. #40 (Box 208) - 92315
Snow Summit Ski Area adjoins this landscaped condo complex with an outdoor pool, game room and saunas. You can ski to your door in most cases. Each comfortable unit has a kitchen, living room with fireplace, and color TV. Toll-free: (800)445-2223.

#85—2 BR, large whirlpool in master BR,   2 T & Q bed...$160
#77,#76,#72,#57—2 BR, fine private slope view, Q or K bed...$160
regular room—2 bedrooms,   2 T & Q or K bed...$150

The Thundercloud Resort   866-7594
.3 mi. W at 40598 Lakeview Dr. (Box 1773) - 92315
This big motel complex includes an indoor and an outdoor pool and a whirlpool. Each spacious, simply furnished unit is decorated in pecky cedar, and has a phone and color TV. Toll-free: (800)REAL-FUN.

"efficiency"—1 BR, kitchenette, metal fireplace,   K bed...$109
regular room—   2 D or Q bed...$59

Borrego Springs

Borrego Springs is California's desert hideaway. It is a placid village sprinkled across the vastness of a broad sunbaked valley abutting rocky mountains. The site was so isolated and inhospitably hot that it was seldom visited before settlement began around 1912. Today, California's largest state park attracts increasing numbers of visitors to natural palm-lined oases and scenic gorges. So do a couple of resorts and golf courses. Otherwise, places to eat, shop and sleep are scarce and old-fashioned. Most villagers seem to like it that way.

Population: 3,000   *Area Code: 619*
Elevation: 590 feet
Location: 88 miles Northeast of San Diego
Borrego Springs Chamber of Commerce   767-5555
    downtown at 622 Palm Canyon Dr. (Box 66) - 92004

WEATHER PROFILE

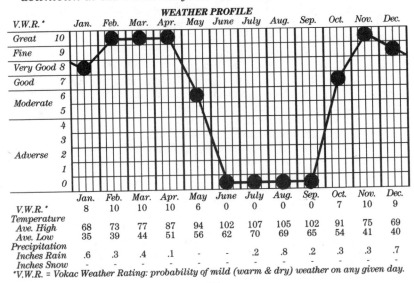

		Jan.	Feb.	Mar.	Apr.	May	June	July	Aug.	Sep.	Oct.	Nov.	Dec.
V.W.R.*		8	10	10	10	6	0	0	0	0	7	10	9
Temperature													
Ave. High		68	73	77	87	94	102	107	105	102	91	75	69
Ave. Low		35	39	44	51	56	62	70	69	65	54	41	40
Precipitation													
Inches Rain		.6	.3	.4	.1	-	-	.2	.8	.2	.3	.3	.7
Inches Snow		-	-	-	-	-	-	-	-	-	-	-	-

*V.W.R. = Vokac Weather Rating: probability of mild (warm & dry) weather on any given day.

ATTRACTIONS

★ **Anza-Borrego Desert State Park**   *767-5311*
   2 mi. W on Palm Canyon Dr. (Box 299)
   One of America's biggest state parks sprawls across 600,000 acres of massive rocky mountains and torrid deserts around town. The highlight is Borrego Palm Canyon. Natural palm-shaded oases along a stream in a narrow rugged gorge are reached by a well-marked mile-long path. Many other hiking and riding trails lead to overlooks, Indian pictographs, historic sites, waterholes and spring wildflowers. Dancing phantom lights said to look like balls of fire have been described. Does the bizarre landscape trick your eyes? The distinctive underground Visitor Center has detailed information and maps, plus exhibits portraying the area's history and geology, desert climate, vegetation and wildlife. Picnic areas and full-service campgrounds with ramadas are nearby. For toll-free reservations, call (800)444-7275.

★ *Golf*
   Rams Hill   *767-5125*
   6.3 mi. SE at 1881 Rams Hill Rd.
   The area's preeminent golf course is an 18-hole championship course on gently rolling slopes overlooking the valley and surrounding mountains. Amenities include a driving range, putting green, pro shop, club and cart rentals, restaurant, and lounge.
   The Roadrunner Club   *767-5374*
   .9 mi. E at 1010 Palm Canyon Dr.
   This 18-hole palm-lined golf course offers dramatic mountain views and lush fairways. A putting green and cart rentals are available.

RESTAURANTS

The Coffee and Book Store   *767-5080*
   downtown at 590 Palm Canyon Dr., Suite 202
   Borrego's only baker and bookstore are combined in a nifty little shop where you can browse and enjoy assorted cinnamon rolls, pastries and desserts made here with a variety of coffee and other drinks.
Kendall's Cafe   *767-3491*
   downtown at 528 The Mall
   B-L-D. No D Wed.   *Moderate*
   American standards get a boost from a half-pound buffalo burger in a cheerful coffee shop by a fountain in Borrego's shopping center.
La Casa Del Zorro Desert Resort   *767-5323*
   5.6 mi. SE at 3845 Yaqui Pass Rd.
   B-L-D. Sun. brunch.   *Expensive*
   Borrego's best-known restaurant serves updated Continental dishes overshadowed by the dramatic decor of the large Southwestern-style dining room with a tranquil garden view, Old West paintings, and a large gas fireplace. The **Fox Den** features fine whimsical wall art in a posh firelit lounge/piano bar overlooking the pool.
Palm Canyon Resort   *767-5341*
   1.1 mi. W at 221 Palm Canyon Dr.
   B-L-D. Sun. brunch.   *Moderate*
   American and Mexican dishes are served in a large neo-territorial dining room with desert views. The adjoining **Big Horn Lounge** has fine stained-glass windows and occasional live entertainment.

LODGING

In the entire isolated valley, there are only a few motels in town and a resort nearby. Winter is prime time. Rates are reduced as much as 50% off-season.

Hacienda del Sol   767-5442
  downtown at 610 Palm Canyon Dr. (Box 366) - 92004
Acres of exotic vegetation surround this older motel/cottage complex with an outdoor pool. Each plain room has a color TV.

#2,#3—cabin with kitchenette,	K bed...$60
regular room—	2 D, Q, or K bed...$47

★ **La Casa Del Zorro Desert Resort**   767-5323
  5.6 mi. SE at 3845 Yaqui Pass Rd. (Box 127) - 92004
Borrego's premier resort has been delighting guests for almost half a century. The renowned getaway has been expanded and improved over the years into a handsome complex of tile-and-stucco buildings in a luxuriant oasis. Amenities include three garden court pools and whirlpools, a putting green, exercise room, six lighted tennis courts, rental bicyclies, plus a casually elegant restaurant (see listing), distinctive bar and entertainment lounge. There is also a resort shop. Each spacious, beautifully decorated unit has a private balcony or patio, refrigerator, phone, and remote-control color TV with movies. Toll-free: (800)824-1884.

#162,#152—1 BR townhouse, baby grand piano, wet bar,	
2 fireplaces, pvt. patio & balc., in-bath whirlpool,	K bed...$330
"Pepper Tree"—3 BR, 3 baths, small pool in private	
patio, wet bar in LR, DR, fireplace,	Q & 2 K beds...$495
"Fern"—1 BR, kitchenette, LR, DR,	
private patio with whirlpool,	Q bed...$285
deluxe suite—several of these, fireplace in BR,	
private balcony or patio overlooking pool,	Q or K bed...$200
regular room—	Q or K bed...$98

Oasis Motel   767-5409
  .9 mi. W at 366 Palm Canyon Dr. (Box 221) - 92004
A fountain in a cactus garden and a landscaped outdoor pool and whirlpool with a mountain view are features of this tiny, single-level motel. Each modern, nicely furnished room has a color TV.

regular room—(kitchen available for extra $7),	Q bed...$58

Palm Canyon Resort   767-5341
  1.1 mi. W at 221 Palm Canyon Dr. (Box 956) - 92004
Borrego's newest lodging is an Old-West-themed motor hotel with a large view pool and whirlpool, restaurant (see listing), saloon and country store. Each spacious, well-furnished room has a phone and color TV. Toll-free in CA: (800)242-0044.

#106—2 rooms, raised tiled whirlpool overlooking	K bed...$130
regular room—	2 Q or K bed...$90

Buena Park

Buena Park is the home of Knott's Berry Farm—California's first themed amusement park. The city, a few miles from the ocean in a broad valley, was established a century ago as a farming center. During the Depression, Walter Knott and his neighbor Rudolph Boysen created a new berry by crossing the blackberry, raspberry, and loganberry. When his friend passed away during the development, Knott named the berry after him, and opened a roadside stand to sell boysenberries. A chicken dinner restaurant followed. Because of his interest in history, it was soon surrounded by Early California ghost town buildings and replicas.

Today, the still-growing attraction is one of the most popular amusement parks in America. Thanks to Knott's and a burgeoning array of nearby attractions, Buena Park is firmly established as a major year-round destination for family fun.

WEATHER PROFILE

V.W.R. *		Jan.	Feb.	Mar.	Apr.	May	June	July	Aug.	Sep.	Oct.	Nov.	Dec.
Great	10												
Fine	9												
Very Good	8												
Good	7												
Moderate	6												
	5												
	4												
	3												
Adverse	2												
	1												
	0												

	Jan.	Feb.	Mar.	Apr.	May	June	July	Aug.	Sep.	Oct.	Nov.	Dec.
V.W.R. *	7	7	8	9	10	10	8	8	8	10	9	7
Temperature												
Ave. High	67	68	70	73	76	79	84	86	85	79	75	69
Ave. Low	38	40	43	47	51	55	58	59	56	51	43	40
Precipitation												
Inches Rain	2.8	3.0	2.4	1.3	.3	.1	-	-	.2	.6	1.3	3.0
Inches Snow	-	-	-	-	-	-	-	-	-	-	-	-

*V.W.R. = Vokac Weather Rating: probability of mild (warm & dry) weather on any given day.

Population: 68,784   Area Code: 714
Elevation: 74 feet
Location: 20 miles Southeast of Los Angeles
Buena Park Convention & Visitors Office   562-3560   (800)541-3953
1.7 mi. N at 6280 Manchester Blvd., Suite 103 - 90621

ATTRACTIONS

★ **Knott's Berry Farm**   *220-5200*
  1 mi. S of CA 91 at 8039 Beach Blvd.
The Granddaddy of Western theme parks has been delighting visitors
for sixty years. It has grown (a lot) since 1934, and now occupies 150
luxuriant tree-shaded acres. Well-maintained grounds contain six
theme areas: re-created **Ghost Town** (don't miss the "Log Ride");
Fiesta Village; **Roaring '20s** including a ride back in time to the
"Kingdom of the Dinosaurs"; **Camp Snoopy** (with a High Sierra
theme); **Indian Trails**; and **Wild Water Wilderness**; plus a full-size
reproduction of Independence Hall with the Liberty Bell. Among
dozens of thrill rides, "Bigfoot Rapids" is a wet and wild
superstar—California's longest manmade whitewater river. "Mystery
Lodge" (opened in 1994) is a wonderful multimedia theater experience
that uses high-tech effects to present legends of Pacific Northwest
Indians. Live shows and entertainment happen continuously at
various locations—highlighted by the Good Time Theatre, where
performances by major stars are regularly scheduled. Three dozen
shops surrounded by gardens are in the **California Marketplace**,
along with sit-down restaurants (see listing) and takeout eateries.

McDonald's   *521-2303*
  .4 mi. N at 7861 Beach Blvd.
McThriller couples a small wide-angle screen showing exciting outdoor
rides with motion-simulation seating. Elsewhere, you can eat fast food
(B-L-D—Low) amidst model McTrains running on tracks overhead and
in mini-villages. Assorted McTrinkets are sold up front.

★ **Medieval Times**   *521-4740*
  .6 mi. N at 7662 Beach Blvd.
A jousting tournament is the dramatic highlight of one of Southern
California's most fanciful dining and entertainment venues. Complete
dinners (from appetizers through chicken or spare ribs to pastries)
plus beer, wine or sodas are served by costumed staff, who also
entertain with medieval pageantry, sword play, and horsemanship.
Seating is behind tiered counters around a vast dirt arena where the
action takes place. The mock castle also houses a bar and gift shop,
and stables where you can view some of the horses up close. Dinner
(expensive) is served nightly, and there is a Sunday matinee. Toll-free
in CA: (800)899-6600.

★ **Movieland Wax Museum**   *522-1154*
  .5 mi. N at 7711 Beach Blvd.
Nearly three hundred wax figures of movie and TV stars are posed in
more than one hundred sets that re-create memorable scenes from
films and TV shows. California's largest wax museum also houses
major collections of early-day movie machines, mementos from vintage
westerns, and Hollywood memorabilia. The "Chamber of Horrors" lets
you experience horror movies through scary special effects. A
Hollywood souvenir shop and a gift shop are also here.

★ **Wild Bill's**   *522-4611*
.7 mi. N at 7600 Beach Blvd.
A Wild West extravaganza of fun for the whole family is the theme of the area's newest dining and entertainment complex. Four-course dinners (stew, salad, chicken & ribs, and apple pie) plus beer, wine or soda pop are served in a cavernous dining hall. Long tables encircle a big thrust stage where the West meets Hollywood in trick roping, whip cracking, juggling, Indian dances, can cans, cowboy skits, folk and bluegrass songs. All are rousing crowd-pleasers. Out front are a saloon and engaging Western memorabilia. Dinner (expensive) is served nightly, and there are matinees Sat. and Sun. Toll-free: (800)883-1547.

RESTAURANTS

★ **Gourmet Pie & Cafe**   *995-8930*
5.7 mi. SW at 4139 Ball Rd. - Cypress
B-L-D.   *Moderate*
Delectable baked goods displayed up front are all made here from scratch. So are specialty omelets, surprises like banana-pecan pancakes, and other contemporary California fare served in the comfortable coffee shop and on a shaded patio.

Katella Deli & Bakery   *594-8611*
6 mi. SW at 4470 Katella Av. - Los Alamitos
B-L-D.   *Moderate*
Here is a classic "California deli" where corned beef and cabbage competes with chicken cashew. Other enticements include fountain treats, and tantalizing displays of bagels, cakes, cookies and other baked goods made here. Several wood-and-live-greenery-trimmed dining areas and a lounge adjoin a full-line bakery and deli.

★ **Knott's Berry Farm**   *827-1776*
1 mi. S of CA 91 at 8039 Beach Blvd.
B-L-D. Sun. brunch.   *Moderate*
Visitors can dine at classic American family-oriented restaurants in the **California Marketplace** without paying to park or to enter the rides area. The vast **Chicken Dinner Restaurant** (B-L-D) has featured its namesake meals for sixty years in big country-style dining rooms. The **Knott's Family Steak House** (L-D) specializes in steaks and prime rib in a large dining room with Old West decor. Knotts' own baked goods and desserts are featured at both restaurants, and throughout the park.

Ming's Palace Restaurant   *522-8355*
.4 mi. N at 7880 Beach Blvd.
L-D.   *Moderate*
Cantonese, Mandarin and Szechwan styles are all well-represented. Cloth napery enhances large comfortable dining rooms.

★ **The Original Fish Company**   *594-4553*
7 mi. SW at 11061 Los Alamitos Blvd. at Katella - Los Alamitos
L-D.   *Moderate*
In one of Southern California's best fish houses, both the Boston and Manhattan-style clam chowders are excellent starters on a menu augmented by a daily listing of authentically fresh selections. Every dish is carefully prepared in an exhibition kitchen amidst several intimate dining areas with live greenery and flowers and casual Victorian decor. A fish market up front displays the day's catch.

LODGING

Most area lodgings are clustered around Knott's Berry Farm. A surprising number are bargains, even during summer and on weekends. Fall through spring rates are often reduced at least 15%.

Buena Park Hotel   *995-1111*
   by Knott's Berry Farm at 7675 Crescent Av. - 90620
Knott's Berry Farm adjoins Buena Park's largest lodging. The 350-room, conference-oriented hotel is a nine-story complex with a landscaped courtyard pool and whirlpool; video game room; restaurant and lounge; and a gift shop. Each nicely furnished room has a phone and remote-control color TV with (pay) movies. Toll-free in CA: (800)422-4444; elsewhere: (800)854-8792.

"Executive Club"—special amenities,	2 D or K bed...$85
regular room—	2 D or K bed...$64

Covered Wagon Motel   *995-0033*
   .3 mi. S at 7830 Crescent Av. (at Beach Blvd.) - 90620
Knott's Berry Farm is across a street from this single-level **bargain** motel with an outdoor pool. Each compact, simply furnished room has a phone and color TV.

   regular room—   Q or K bed...$30

★ **Embassy Suites Hotel**   *739-5600*
   .4 mi. N at 7762 Beach Blvd. - 90620
The city's finest lodging is a contemporary hotel with 203 suites within walking distance of Knott's and all major attractions. Pepper, avocado and palm trees shade a large courtyard pool in the four-story complex. Other amenities include a whirlpool, game room, restaurant, lounge, and gift shop. Breakfast and afternoon cocktails are complimentary. Each attractively furnished two-room suite has a kitchenette with microwave oven and refrigerator, two phones, and two remote-control color TVs with movies. Toll-free: (800)EMBASSY.

   regular room—   2 D or K bed...$109

Farm De Ville Motel   *527-2201*
   .3 mi. S at 7800 Crescent Av. (at Beach Blvd.) - 90620
A large **bargain** motel across from Knott's has two outdoor pools and saunas. Each plain room has a phone and color TV with movies.

   regular room—   Q or K bed...$30

Gaslite Motel   *522-8441*
   .4 mi. N at 7777 Beach Blvd. - 90620
This modern **bargain** motel has an outdoor pool. Each simply furnished room has a phone and color TV with movies.

   regular room—   Q or K bed...$30

Holiday Inn   *522-7000*
   1 mi. N (by CA 91) at 7000 Beach Blvd. - 90620
This modern five-story hotel has a large landscaped pool and whirlpool, video game room, restaurant, lounge and gift shop. Each of the 246 nicely refurbished rooms has a phone and color TV with movies. Toll-free: (800)HOLIDAY.

   regular room—   2 D or K bed...$69

Motel 6   *522-1200*
   2.8 mi. NW (by CA 91) at 7051 Valley View Av. - 90622
The chain's big modern **bargain** motel has a courtyard pool. Each compact, plain room has a phone and color TV with movies.

   regular room—   Q bed...$32

Carlsbad

Carlsbad is an inviting beach town at the center of San Diego's North County coast with several miles of shoreline between two picturesque lagoons. It was named more than a century ago because of similarities to renowned Karlsbad, Czechoslovakia.

The mineral water spa is being restored and the beaches are more popular than ever. Nearby, work continues on the first American Legoland theme park. Elaborate inland resorts, a picturesque downtown, and an improving selection of beach-oriented lodgings are expanding the city's role as a major year-round tourist destination.

Population: *63,126*   *Area Code: 619*
Elevation: *39 feet*
Location: *36 miles North of San Diego*
Carlsbad Convention & Visitors Bureau 434-6093   (800)227-5722
  downtown at Old Train Depot, P.O. Box 1246 - 92018

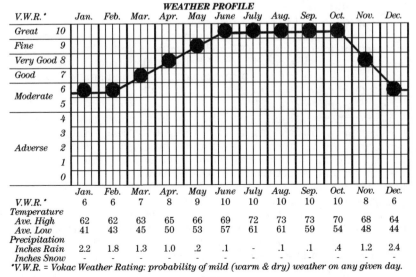

WEATHER PROFILE

V.W.R. *		Jan.	Feb.	Mar.	Apr.	May	June	July	Aug.	Sep.	Oct.	Nov.	Dec.
V.W.R. *		6	6	7	8	9	10	10	10	10	10	8	6
Temperature													
Ave. High		62	62	63	65	66	69	72	73	73	70	68	64
Ave. Low		41	43	45	50	53	57	61	61	59	54	48	44
Precipitation													
Inches Rain		2.2	1.8	1.3	1.0	.2	.1	-	.1	.1	.4	1.2	2.4
Inches Snow		-	-	-	-	-	-	-	-	-	-	-	-

*V.W.R. = Vokac Weather Rating: probability of mild (warm & dry) weather on any given day.

ATTRACTIONS

Bicycling
  Carlsbad Cyclery   *434-6681*
  downtown at 2796 Carlsbad Blvd.
  To enjoy many miles of bikeways along the scenic coast, you can rent bikes here by the hour or day. Closed Mon.-Tues.
★ **Carlsbad State Beach**   *729-8947*
  1 mi. S via Carlsbad Blvd. at Tamarack Av.
  Conditions are good for swimming, surfing and skin diving off a long sandy strand accented by patches of pebbles. At the south end by Agua Hedionda Lagoon, North County's grossest landmark thrusts skyward above an S.D.G.& E. power plant. Surf fishing from nearby rocks is popular. Lifeguards, restrooms, and picnic areas are available. The city oversees a mile-long beach north to Buena Vista Lagoon.
★ **Mission San Luis Rey de Francia**   *757-3651*
  7 mi. N via CA 76 at 4050 Mission Av. - Oceanside
  The "King of the Missions," founded in 1798, reigns again in a brilliant white reconstruction of the largest of California's twenty-one early Spanish missions. The handsome interior with lofty beamed ceilings has been fully restored, and includes some original Indian decorations. The well-tended historic complex also has a museum with Spanish artifacts, an Indian cemetery, cloister gardens, and a gift shop.
★ **Oceanside City Beach**   *439-7145*
  3 mi. NW at W end of Mission Av. - Oceanside
  Oceanside's major attraction is a broad, fine-sand beach which extends for four miles. Normally gentle surf works for swimming as well as body and board surfing. Fishing is popular on **Oceanside Pier**. Miniparks and walkways of the adjoining palm-shaded **Pacific Street Linear Park** attract picnickers and strollers. Charter and pleasure boats fill **Oceanside Harbor** to the north where a small complex has a New England theme for specialty shops and harbor-view eateries. Birders flock to **Buena Vista Lagoon Bird Sanctuary** at the city's southern boundary.
  Snug Harbor Marina   *434-3089*
  1.7 mi. SE (near I-5) at 4215 Harrison St.
  Agua Hedionda Lagoon, a natural saltwater inlet, provides a usually calm setting for enjoying motorized water recreation. Jet skis, waterbikes, and waterskis (complete with driver and instruction) are rented by the hour. There are also picnic tables, a shop and snack bar.
★ **South Carlsbad State Beach**   *438-3143*
  4 mi. S along Carlsbad Blvd.
  This long narrow strand, backed by low bluffs, appeals to swimmers, surfers, and skin divers in spite of the pebbly beach. Lifeguards, a picnic area, and restrooms are available. The large year-round blufftop campground (no hookups) is extremely popular. Many sites have ocean views. Camping reservations: (800)444-PARK.
Sportfishing
★   **Helgren's Sportfishing**   *722-2133*
  4.5 mi. NW at 315 Harbor Drive South - Oceanside
  Deep sea fishing can be chartered year-round. Special tours in winter give everyone a chance to get close to great gray whales during their annual southern migration. Trips leave from here daily.

Warm Water Feature

★ **The Wave**   940-9283
9 mi. NE at 161 Recreation Dr. - Vista
San Diego County's best water park features a high-tech surfing wave simulator; four waterslides (for individuals or two-person tubes); a circular lazy river; a large lap pool; and a children's play pool area—all amidst tropical vegetation. Open Memorial Day to Labor Day.

RESTAURANTS

The Chart House   722-1345
4.7 mi. NW at 314 Harbor Dr. South, Oceanside Marina - Oceanside
D only.   *Expensive*
Prime rib, steak, and fish are favored in Oceanside's most romantic restaurant. Hardwoods and greenery artistically divide a big upstairs room into intimate dining areas backed by an upscale salad bar, skylit waterfalls of hanging plants, and a window wall above the harbor. A plush prow-shaped lounge juts over the water.

★ **Coyote Bar & Grill**   729-4695
downtown at 300 Carlsbad Village Dr.
L-D.   *Moderate*
North County's most exciting "new concept" restaurant, tucked into a stylish shopping complex, is off to a great start. California-style Southwestern cuisine ranges from crab enchiladas in blue corn crepes to spit-turned smoke-roasted chicken, and key lime pie for dessert. Rough-wood, adobe, copper lamps and cacti accent dining areas overlooking an exhibition kitchen, an island bar, kiva fireplaces, and a shaded patio with gas-heated conversation firepits. Cactus margaritas are an unusual treat with frequent live entertainment.

★ **Debbi Ann's Kitchen & Pie Shop**   758-1549
9.5 mi. NE at 868 E. Vista Way - Vista
B-L-D.   *Low*
Big homemade cinnamon rolls and pecan rolls are delicious when they are fresh. Pies (the lemon meringue is mile-high) also star among all-American fare generously served at all meals in this cheerful homespun coffee shop on the main road north from Vista.

Don's Country Kitchen   729-2274
downtown at 2885 Roosevelt St.
B-L.   *Moderate*
Breakfast is featured all day among hearty all-American dishes served in this convivial coffee shop. You have a choice of a counter, table and chairs with an intimate view of downtown, or sidewalk tables.

Fidel's Norte   729-0903
.3 mi. W at 3003 Carlsbad Blvd.
L-D. Sat. & Sun. brunch.   *Moderate*
California-style Mexican standards are featured in a branch of the Solana Beach original with a large wood-trimmed cantina and a balmy patio. A few of the padded booths have an ocean view.

Jay's Gourmet Restaurant   720-9688
.3 mi. W at 2975 Carlsbad Blvd. #B
L-D.   *Moderate*
A wide ranging menu of Southern Italian dishes features seafood and creations like sausage rolls or pepperoni bread with meat sauce. The good food offsets the casually congested beach shack decor.

Jolly Roger   *722-1831*
5 mi. NW at 1900 Harbor Dr. North, Oceanside Marina - Oceanside
B-L-D. Sun. brunch.   *Moderate*
A choice location by Oceanside Harbor is the claim to fame of this
large link in an over-burgeoned chain offering standard American fare.
There is also an entertainment lounge in a New England-themed
building outfitted with gas fireplaces, real greenery, and marina views.
Kahala Cafe   *729-5448*
downtown at 795 Carlsbad Village Dr.
B-L.   *Moderate*
Hawaiian specialties like pureed banana pancakes or macadamia nut
waffles highlight a good selection of all-American cafe fare served in
a cheerful little dining room with a choice of padded booths or counter.
Tables are delightfully accented by live orchids.
★ **La Costa Resort & Spa**   *438-9111*
8 mi. SE on Costa del Mar Rd. at El Camino Real
B-L-D.   *Very Expensive–Extremely Expensive*
Pisces (D only–Very Expensive) has for years featured some of the
county's finest fresh seafoods amidst swank decor. Jackets are
requested. **Ristorante Figaro** (D only–Extremely Expensive)
presents Northern Italian classics in an opulent setting of crystal,
silver and fine china. Jackets are appropriate. **Brasserie La Costa**
(B-L-D–Very Expensive) serves upscale California fare in a refined
dining room, or in a garden terrace by fairways. The **Tournament of
Champions Lounge** offers live entertainment and dancing, while the
posh **Lobby Lounge** shares golf course views.
Neimans   *729-4131*
.3 mi. W at 2978 Carlsbad Blvd.
B-L-D. Sun. brunch.   *Expensive*
Contemporary American fare is served in a distinctive eight-sided
dining room of Carlsbad's most historic building. The century-old
complex also includes a wood-and-plant-trimmed brasserie with
lighter portions, and an entertainment/dancing lounge.
Old California Restaurant Row
11 mi. E at 1020 San Marcos Blvd. - San Marcos
B-L-D.   *Moderate*
A dozen distinctive restaurants share a sprawling complex which has
been decorated with an Early California motif. Collectively, they
provide a very wide range of family dining possibilities.
★ **The Quails Inn Dinnerhouse**   *744-2445*
11 mi. E at 1025 La Bonita Dr. - Lake San Marcos
L-D. Sun. brunch.   *Moderate*
A seafood/salad bar highlights fresh California cuisine in this very
popular lakeside restaurant at Lake San Marcos Resort. The
downstairs lounge shares the lovely waterfront view and features a
renowned happy hour buffet, and live entertainment for dancing.
★ **Tip Top Meats**   *438-2620*
3.6 mi. SE (near I-5) at 6118 Paseo del Norte
B-L-D.   *Low*
All kinds of flavorful meats from their own butcher shop distinguish
otherwise-conventional American fare in one of North County's best
bargain eateries. Family-oriented country-themed dining rooms adjoin
the meat market, gourmet deli, and wine shop. Next door, **California
Ranch Market** is a source of fresh local fruits and vegetables.

LODGING

Nearly two dozen lodgings are sprinkled in and around Carlsbad including a famed resort and a choice beachfront motel. Summer is the peak season. Rates are usually reduced at least 15% at other times.

Andersen's Inn - Best Western   *438-7880*
3.6 mi. SE (by I-5) at 850 Palomar Airport Rd. - 92008
This modern motor hotel has some **bargain** rooms, a large pool and whirlpool in a landscaped courtyard, restaurant, bakery, lounge and gift shop. Each nicely furnished room has a small private patio or balcony, phone, and color TV. Toll-free: (800)266-7880.
　regular room—quiet, remote control TV,　　　2 Q or K bed...$89
　regular room—by freeway,　　　　　　　　　2 Q or K bed...$49
★ **Beach Terrace Inn - Best Western**   *729-5951*
.4 mi. W at 2775 Ocean St. - 92008
North County's finest beachfront lodging is a contemporary four-story motel that juts out to the tide line. Amenities include a glassed oceanview pool, whirlpool, and sauna. Each large attractive unit has a refrigerator, phone, and remote control color TV with movies and VCR. Toll-free in CA: (800)ON-BEACH; elsewhere: (800)433-5415.
　#10,#16—1 BR on corner, kitchenette, extra window,
　　glass door to big pvt. balc. by waves, gas fireplace,　K bed...$168
　"Royal Garden Suite" (#61)—separate whirlpool;
　　gas fireplace, window wall and large private
　　balcony with grand ocean view shared by　raised K bed...$210
　"Coral Suite" (#51)—kitchen, gas fireplace, window
　　wall, large pvt. balcony, grand ocean view from　K bed...$175
　"Sunset Suite" (#56)—gas fireplace, window wall,
　　large private balcony, grand ocean view from　K bed...$175
　#11,#12,#14,#15—1 BR, kitchenette, gas fireplace,
　　window wall & large pvt. balc. next to waves,　Q or K bed...$168
　#18,#24,#23,#29—as above, but corner
　　with extra window; higher above waves,　　Q or K bed...$168
　regular room—gas fireplace, kitchenette, no view, Q or K bed...$99
Carlsbad Inn Beach Resort   *434-7020*
.3 mi. W at 3075 Carlsbad Blvd. - 92008
Lawns and gardens surround a sprawling complex near the ocean that includes a modern three-story hotel, time-share condos, a garden pool and whirlpool, sauna, exercise room, ping pong table, restaurants and shops. Each attractively decorated unit has a phone and remote control color TV with VCR. Toll-free: (800)235-3939.
　#369,#367—spacious, kitchenette, in-bath whirlpool,
　　small private balcony with garden/ocean views,　K bed...$175
　#361,#363—kitchenette, floor-to-ceiling windows
　　& small private balcony with garden/ocean view,　Q bed...$135
　regular room—　　　　　　　　　　　　　　　Q bed...$115
★ **La Costa Resort & Spa**   *438-9111*
8 mi. SE on Costa del Mar Rd. at El Camino Real - 92009
La Costa is one of America's largest and most complete resorts. It includes nearly five hundred rooms and suites on gentle hills above Batiquitos Lagoon two miles inland from the ocean. Recreational amenities set amidst carefully tended landscaping include two large pools surrounded by gardens, a jogging track; plus (for a fee) two

championship 18-hole golf courses, 21 tennis courts (6 lighted), and a world famous men's and women's health spa and fitness center. Leisure amenities include five restaurants (including three for fine dining—see listing), two lounges with live entertainment, and resort shops and salons. Each beautifully furnished unit has a stocked (honor) refrigerator, phone, and remote control color TV with free and pay movies. Toll-free: (800)854-5000.

"Executive Homes"—2 BR, extra large, posh,   2 Q & K bed...$1050
"Golf Units"—spacious, request fairway view, 2 Q or K bed...$310
   regular room—in main building,   2 Q beds...$225

Motel 6
.5 mi. E (by I-5) at 1006 Carlsbad Village Dr. - 92008   434-7135
3.6 mi. SE (by I-5) at 6117 Paseo del Norte - 92009   438-1242
5 mi. SE (by I-5) at 750 Raintree Dr. - 92009   431-0745
Each of these **bargain** motels has an outdoor pool. All offer simply furnished small rooms with a phone and color TV with movies.
   regular room—   D or Q bed...$35

★ **Olympic Resort Hotel & Spa**   438-8330
7 mi. SE at 6111 El Camino Real - 92009
A full-service health and fitness center is the centerpiece of this contemporary resort-style motor hotel. Other amenities include a 25-meter lap pool, plus a recreation pool and whirlpool in a landscaped courtyard; steam and sauna rooms; plus (for a fee) five night-lighted tennis courts; and an elaborate golf putting and driving facility. A casually elegant restaurant and lounge are in the main building. Each spacious well-furnished room has a private patio or balcony, phone and remote control color TV with movies. Toll-free: (800)522-8330.
   regular room—   2 Q or K bed...$85

★ **Pelican Cove Inn**   434-5995
.4 mi. S at 320 Walnut Av. - 92008
The ocean is only 200 yards from this appealing bed-and-breakfast inn, although you can't see it. Full breakfast is complimentary. Each of the eight rooms has an artistic blend of period and contemporary furnishings, including a feather bed and down comforter, a private bath, a gas fireplace, and remote control color TV.

"La Jolla"—round vaulted ceiling, private,
   many windows, large in-bath whirlpool,   Q bed...$175
"Coronado"—large in-bath whirlpool,   4-poster K bed...$175
"Newport"—round vaulted ceiling,   Q bed...$125
   regular room—compact,   2 T beds...$85

★ **The Quails Inn at Lake San Marcos Resort**   744-0120
11 mi. SE at 1025 La Bonita Dr. - Lake San Marcos 92069
Lovely mile-long Lake San Marcos borders this affable conference resort hotel with two landscaped pools, whirlpool, exercise room, three tennis courts, paddleball courts, and (for a fee) boats and two nearby 18-hole golf courses. A handsome dining room and lounge (see listing) share a lakefront view. Each beautifully furnished room has a private patio or balcony, phone and remote control color TV with movies. Toll-free: (800)447-6556.

#132,#130,#128,#126—spacious split-level, refr./wet bar,
   in-bath whirlpool, private balc. with fine lake view, K bed...$125
#410—end, top (2nd) floor lakefront, spacious,
   refrigerator, in-bath whirlpool,   K bed...$125
   regular room—   2 D or K bed...$85

Catalina Island

Catalina is California's only island resort. The mainland is twenty-two miles from the rugged twenty-by-eight-mile isle with peaks rising nearly 2,000 feet. Spaniards discovered it in 1542, named it Santa Catalina in 1602 (ironically, the "island of romance" is named for the patron saint of spinsterhood!) and left it and the local Indians alone. Much later, sporadic smuggling, mining and ranching continued until 1919 when William Wrigley, Jr. bought the island.

The compact village of Avalon is now the single major urban enclave on an island that remains mostly off-limits to visiting drivers and bicyclists. But, some of the warmest and clearest waters and one of the balmiest climates of California lure shiploads of visitors daily for all kinds of saltwater recreation: notably glass-bottom boat tours and flying-fish trips. Avalon's numerous attractions, shops, restaurants, and lodgings all emphasize fun-for-the-whole-family.

WEATHER PROFILE

V.W.R. *		Jan.	Feb.	Mar.	Apr.	May	June	July	Aug.	Sep.	Oct.	Nov.	Dec.
Great	10												
Fine	9												
Very Good	8												
Good	7												
Moderate	6 5												
	4												
	3												
Adverse	2												
	1												
	0												

	Jan.	Feb.	Mar.	Apr.	May	June	July	Aug.	Sep.	Oct.	Nov.	Dec.
V.W.R. *	6	6	7	8	10	10	10	10	10	10	9	6
Temperature												
Ave. High	62	63	64	65	68	69	72	73	72	71	68	64
Ave. Low	47	48	49	51	54	56	60	61	60	56	51	49
Precipitation												
Inches Rain	2.5	3.0	1.9	1.0	.1	.1	-	.1	.2	.8	1.0	3.0
Inches Snow	-	-	-	-	-	-	-	-	-	-	-	-

*V.W.R. = Vokac Weather Rating: probability of mild (warm & dry) weather on any given day.

Catalina Island

Population: 2,918   Area Code: 310
Elevation: 20 feet
Location: 44 mi. South of Los Angeles by land & sea
Chamber of Commerce & Visitor's Bureau   510-1520
    downtown on the Green Pleasure Pier (Box 217) - Avalon 90704
Transportation Information—Catalina Express   (800)995-4386

ATTRACTIONS

★ **Avalon**
Most of the island residents live in Avalon, a village in a natural
amphitheater sheltered by steep hills. A picturesque jumble of homes
and businesses tumbles down to a tiny crescent of sand by a little bay
chuck-full of boats. Beyond the beach and harbor, some of the West's
clearest waters abound with game fish and colorful sea life. The
Avalon Pleasure Pier serves strollers and would-be aquanauts.
Crescent Avenue, the island's main shopping street, extends along the
bayfront for half a mile to the Avalon Casino.

★ **Avalon Casino**   510-2444
    .4 mi. N via Crescent Av. on Casino Way (Box 737)
Host to most famous groups of the big band era, the island's largest
and most renowned landmark was built in 1929. The circular structure
with a red tile roof is an art deco treasury containing a theater with
remarkable acoustics near the center of the auditorium, dramatic
murals, and a pipe organ; the world's largest circular ballroom; and a
small history museum. For tours, call 510-2000.

Bicycling
Unlike the natives, visitors are not permitted to drive cars anywhere
on the island. In mid-1989, the interior was put off-limits to rental
vehicles and even to bicyclists. Bicycles and tandems can be rented
downtown by the hour or longer for use in the village. So can
ubiquitous gasoline-powered golf carts (unfortunately, rental mopeds
have been disallowed).
    Brown's Bikes *(bicycles)   107 Pebbly Beach Rd.   510-0986*
    Catalina Rentals *(golf carts, bicycles) Crescent/Metropole 510-1600*
    Island Rentals *(golf carts)   125 Pebbly Beach Rd.   510-1456*

★ *Boat Rentals*
    Joe's Rent-a-Boat   510-0455
    downtown on Avalon Pleasure Pier
For sailors lured by the clear water of Avalon Bay, Joe's is perfectly
situated on the pier with paddleboards, pedal and row boats and
runabouts (but no sailboats), plus fishing tackle.

★ *Boat Rides*
Glass-bottom boat tours take visitors out to a nearby cove. Catalina's
"undersea gardens" are luxuriant kelp beds rich in marine plant life
and fish. Night tours offer glass-bottom views of sea life attracted by
floodlights. The summer highlight is watching aerial antics of
phosphorescent flying fish which are seasonal denizens of these
waters. Toll-free in CA: (800)4-AVALON.
    Catalina Adventure Tours   510-2888
    downtown on Avalon Pleasure Pier
    Santa Catalina Island Company   510-2500
    downtown on Avalon Pleasure Pier (Box 737)

★ *Diving*
For exploring the crystal-clear depths, you can rent snorkeling and scuba equipment—even underwater cameras—at:
Catalina Divers Supply   *510-0330*
downtown on Avalon Pleasure Pier (Box 126)
Hiking
Hikers, outside Avalon, must have a permit to visit Catalina's rugged outback. The shrub and cactus-covered slopes and hills give way on all sides to rocky cliffs, secret coves and sandy beaches. In the interior, bison still roam rugged terrain little changed since they were imported in the 1920s by a movie company filming a western. Shuttles and drop-off services can be arranged to many remote scenic locales. For maps, permits and information, contact:
LA County Parks Dept. *downtown at 213 Catalina Av.* *510-0688*
★ *Parasailing*
Fly over water with a parachute—take off and land in the boat.
Island Cruzers   *510-1777*
downtown at 107 Pebbly Beach Rd. (Box 2275)
★ *Sportfishing*
Surrounding waters offer sea bass, swordfish, and other sportfishing prizes. Avalon is home port to several charters. Deep sea fishing and diving are popular year-round, while whale watching in winter and flying fish in summer lend excitement to nautical excursions. All equipment is provided for trips of various lengths at:
Boat Stand Charters   *(Box 1449)* *510-2274*
Catalina Island Charter Boat Co.   *(Box 2350)* *510-2720*
Catalina Island Sportfishing   *(Box 1912)* *510-9669*
Ice Breaker Charters   *(Box 2716)* *510-1073*
Keeper Charters   *(Box 467)* *510-1624*
★ Two Harbors and the Island Interior
Tour buses and excursion boats leave daily to provide the only access via the interior or along the coastline to Twin Harbors. Catalina's only other community is a tiny village on a half-mile-wide isthmus where lush palms frame large beaches and two sheltered harbors. Upland hiking trails provide scenic views of crystal-clear waters known for snorkeling, skin diving and fishing. Oceanview campgrounds are nearby. So is the **Banning House**, a historic ranch-style home on a rise above the isthmus. It is now a picturesque bed-and-breakfast where the "Crows Nest" and "Cliff House East" have splendid private views of the harbors. By the beach, **Doug's Harbor Reef** is the sole restaurant, but the bar and patio come alive at night with visitors enjoying "buffalo milk," the Island's specialty drink. For information and reservations, contact:
Santa Catalina Island Company   *510-2500*
downtown at Island Plaza on Catalina Av. (Box 737)
Wrigley Memorial and Botanical Garden   *510-2288*
1.7 mi. SW on Avalon Canyon Rd.
Native trees, succulents and flowering shrubs surround an imposing memorial to William Wrigley, Jr. near the head of Avalon Canyon. Colorful local tiles adorn a tower with a spiral staircase. The thirty-seven-acre garden can be reached by a tram that leaves from downtown several times daily in summer (infrequently at other times).

Catalina Island
RESTAURANTS

★ **Armstrong's Seafood Restaurant**   *510-0113*
downtown at 306 Crescent Av.
L-D.   *Moderate*
Mesquite-broiled fish is simply but carefully prepared on a short list
of American standards, and there is an oyster bar. The comfortable
little dining room has an exhibition kitchen and a window-wall
waterfront view which is shared with a spacious heated deck.
Busy Bee   *510-1983*
downtown at 306 Crescent Av.
B-L-D.   *Moderate*
Buffalo—in a sausage omelet, in burgers, or as a steak—and hearty
breakfasts are specialties. However, the wood-trimmed waterfront
deck with Avalon's most idyllic view is the reason to bee here.
Channel House   *510-1617*
downtown at 205 Crescent Av.
D only. Closed Mon.-Tues.   *Expensive*
Traditional Continental and seafood entrees get careful attention in
the Island's newest dinner house. A handsome hardwood bar overlooks
several large casual dining areas festooned with faux greenery. Sliding
glass doors open to a lush patio by the promenade.
Ristorante Villa Portofino   *510-0508*
downtown at 111 Crescent Av.
D only.   *Expensive*
Authentic Neapolitan cuisine is the feature of Avalon's most elaborate
restaurant. Full linen encircles closely spaced tables in a large post-
modern bistro with a piano bar.
Solomon's Landing   *510-1474*
downtown at 101 Marilla Av. & Crescent Av.
L-D.   *Moderate*
A contemporary California menu offers Mexican-style specialties or
mesquite-broiled dishes in the island's most colorful restaurant and
cantina. The big dining room shares a bay view with a bar featuring
entertainment and dancing. Outside, terraces and garden patio
seating provide romantic panoramas of the waterfront and town.

LODGING

Lodgings are numerous, mostly small, and relatively expensive.
Summer is the high season, and weekends are busy year-round. Fall
through spring rates on weekdays are usually reduced 20% or more.
Catalina Canyon Hotel   *510-0325*
.5 mi. W at 888 Country Club Dr. (Box 736) - 90704
The island's largest lodging is an older Spanish-Colonial style hotel
with 80 rooms, a big pool and whirlpool in a garden court, sauna,
restaurant and lounge. Each comfortable room has a private balcony
or patio, phone, and color TV. Toll-free in CA: (800)253-9361.
     regular room—   2 Q or K bed...$135
Glenmore Plaza Hotel   *510-0017*
downtown at 120 Sumner Ave. (Box 155) - 90704
Parts of this restored four-story landmark are more than a century old.
Light breakfast and evening wine and cheese are complimentary. Each
comfortable room has a few nostalgic touches, a private bath, phone,

and color TV with movies. Toll-free: (800)748-5660.
#401–bar/refr., microwave, round in-bath whirlpool, spiral
   staircase to pvt. deck overlooking entire harbor, & ten-
   sided cupola with village's best private view from   K bed...$400
#407–pvt. mtn. views from 2 loveseats, small
   in-bath whirlpool,   K bed...$150
   regular room–compact,   D or Q bed...$120

★ **Hotel Metropole**   *510-1884*
   downtown at Crescent Av. & Whitley (Box 1900) - 90704
Avalon's most posh hotel opened in 1990 in the heart of town. The 47-
unit three-level complex includes a rooftop whirlpool and sundeck with
a spectacular bay view and the Channel House restaurant (see listing).
Each beautifully furnished unit has a phone, stocked (honor) bar, and
remote control color TV with movies. Toll-free in CA: (800)541-8528.
   #320,#321,#215,#216–spacious corner suite, gas
   fireplace, fine ocean view from private balcony,
   big whirlpool and   K bed...$275
   #301–private bay view balcony, gas fireplace,
   skylight over whirlpool tub,   K bed...$225
   #408–gas fireplace, whirlpool, private
   bayview balcony,   K bed...$179
   regular room–balcony with courtyard view,   K bed...$149
Hotel St. Lauren   *510-2299*
   downtown at 231 Beacon St. (Box 497) - 90704
This Victorian-style hotel, a multi-angled pink confection with six
levels, opened in 1987 on a slope above town. Each well-furnished
room has neo-Victorian decor, a phone, and color TV.
   #501–big, in-bath whirlpool, grand village/bay view, K bed...$250
   regular room–the pipes may be noisy,   Q bed...$125

★ **Hotel Vista Del Mar**   *510-1452*
   downtown at 417 Crescent Av. (Box 1979) - 90704
The beach, harbor, and pier surround the island's newest and most
luxurious little inn, opened in 1988 upstairs in a historic building in
the heart of town. Most of the beautifully decorated Mediterranean-
style rooms have a gas fireplace, wet bar with refrigerator, phone and
remote control color TV/VCR and movies.
   "Ocean View Suite" (2 of them)–private balcony
   with romantic beach/bay view, large in-room
   bay-view whirlpool, raised gas fireplace in view of K bed...$275
   regular room–adjoining atrium garden courtyard,   Q bed...$165
   regular room–smaller, in back, no fireplace or wet bar, D bed...$95

★ **Zane Grey Hotel**   *510-0966*
   .4 mi. N at 199 Chimes Tower Rd. (Box 216) - 90704
In 1926, famed Western author Zane Grey built a pueblo-style home
at the crest of a hill high above Avalon Bay. The hotel retains the
Western spirit of his residence, and also sports a small garden view
pool and bay-view sunning decks. Each compact room is nostalgically
decorated in a simplified Southwestern motif and has a private bath.
   "Tonto Rim"–split-level, top of complex, great private
   harbor/casino view,   Q bed...$125
   "Purple Sage," "Desert Wheat", "Call of the Canyon"–
   picture window view of the bay,   Q bed...$110
   regular room–no view,   Q bed...$75

Claremont

Claremont is the hidden gem of the Los Angeles area. The ocean is less than an hour by car. Yet, downhill skiing is closer to this tranquil community than to any other subtropical city in America, thanks to the majestic San Gabriel Mountains which rise abruptly to the north. Nearby Mt. San Antonio (Old Baldy) is 10,064 feet above sea level.

Claremont was established as a college town more than a century ago with the opening of Pomona College. Today, six distinctive Claremont Colleges share some facilities on a campus of expansive lawns, colorful gardens, and streets and walkways overhung by noble shade trees. Luxuriant landscaping similarly enhances the delightful village center and neighborhoods accented by handsome Victorian homes. A gracious blend of cultural facilities, distinctive shops, and excellent restaurants in a setting of quiet beauty makes Claremont an idyllic destination for conferences, retreats, or simply relaxing.

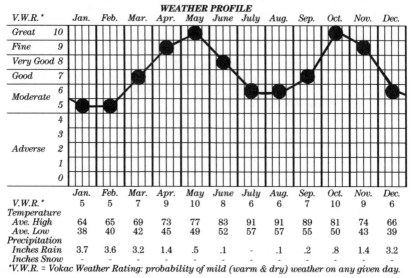

WEATHER PROFILE

V.W.R.*		Jan.	Feb.	Mar.	Apr.	May	June	July	Aug.	Sep.	Oct.	Nov.	Dec.
Great	10												
Fine	9												
Very Good	8												
Good	7												
Moderate	6 5												
	4												
	3												
Adverse	2												
	1												
	0												

	Jan.	Feb.	Mar.	Apr.	May	June	July	Aug.	Sep.	Oct.	Nov.	Dec.
V.W.R.*	5	5	7	9	10	8	6	6	7	10	9	6
Temperature												
Ave. High	64	65	69	73	77	83	91	91	89	81	74	66
Ave. Low	38	40	42	45	49	52	57	57	55	50	43	39
Precipitation												
Inches Rain	3.7	3.6	3.2	1.4	.5	.1	-	.1	.2	.8	1.4	3.2
Inches Snow	-	-	-	-	-	-	-	-	-	-	-	-

*V.W.R. = Vokac Weather Rating: probability of mild (warm & dry) weather on any given day.

Population: 32,539   Area Code: 909
Elevation: 1,150 feet
Location: 32 mi. East of Los Angeles
Claremont Chamber of Commerce   624-1681
downtown at 205 Yale Av. - 91711

ATTRACTIONS

★ **Angeles National Forest**   982-3816
   starts 6 mi. N via Mt. Baldy Rd.
   Mt. San Antonio (Old Baldy Peak—elevation 10,064 feet) is the high
   point of a vast forest that covers more than one thousand square miles
   of the rugged northern rim of the Los Angeles Basin. The towering
   peak is a destination for skiers in winter (see listing) while hikers and
   backpackers enjoy many miles of trails in summer. There are
   numerous trailheads and picnic areas, plus complete campgrounds far
   below Old Baldy and at Crystal Lake Recreation Area.

★ **The Claremont Colleges**   621-8000
   .5 mi. NE at 747 N. Dartmouth Av.
   One of California's most distinguished enclaves of higher education is
   comprised of six independent colleges in a park-like campus.
   Expansive lawns and mature shade trees surround a handsome mix
   of early twentieth century and contemporary buildings. Art galleries,
   museums, and four performing arts centers serve the public.

★ **Frank G. Bonelli Regional Park**   599-8411
   6 mi. SW at 120 Via Verde Park Rd. - San Dimas
   The region's most complete county park is a 2,200-acre facility with
   fishing, boat rentals, a beach on Puddingstone Reservoir, hiking and
   equestrian trails, an 18-hole golf course, picnic areas, and a full service
   campground. **Raging Waters** (see listing) is also here.

★ **Rancho Santa Ana Botanic Garden**   625-8767
   1 mi. N at 1500 N. College Av.
   Near the foothills of the San Gabriel Mountains is an eighty-six-acre
   preserve dedicated exclusively to native plants of California. Visitors
   are free to wander along nature trails past lush, well-marked stands
   of conifer, oak woodland, chaparral, coastal shrubs, and wildflowers.
   Riparian vegetation along an arroyo, a cactus garden, and a native
   palm-fringed oasis are highlights. There are also experimental gardens
   and an interpretive center. Admission is free.

Warm Water Feature
★ **Raging Waters**   592-6453
   6 mi. SW at 111 Raging Waters Dr. - San Dimas
   Southern California's ultimate water park is this forty-five-acre
   aquatic playground. Wildly wet experiences are assured on "The
   Vortex," two enclosed spiral body flumes distinguished by fog, wind
   and other special effects; the "Dark Hole," America's first two-man raft
   adventure through total darkness; and "Thunder Rapids," a six-man
   raft flume. There are also gentle surfing waves; a sunbathing beach;
   a lazy river; many serpentine waterslides; and speed flumes. For
   assured thrills and spills, passengers in inner tubes navigate a series
   of rapids, dams and waterfalls on a quarter-mile-long "whitewater"
   river. Refreshment stands, video game arcades, and a gift shop have
   also been provided. Open weekends early April to Memorial Day; daily
   through mid-September; weekends only until late October close.

Winter Sports

★ **Mt. Baldy**   *981-3344*
  16 mi. NE at the end of Mt. Baldy Rd.
Southern California's largest ski area has 400 skiable acres, the highest vertical rise (2,100 feet) and the longest run (2.5 miles). It also has the unique distinction of being America's closest ski area to subtropical cities. Elevation in the pines at the top is 8,600 feet, yet skiers are only a few miles from palm-shaded pools enjoyed by swimmers year-round. There are four chairlifts. All essential services, facilities, and rentals are available at the base for downhill skiing. Several restaurants, lounges, and lodges are near the base. The skiing season is December through mid-April.

RESTAURANTS

★ **Buffalo Inn**   *981-5515*
  2.9 mi. NE at 1814 W. Foothill Blvd. - Upland
  L-D.   *Low*
Buffalo burgers are featured among casual American fare served along with a dozen premium tap beers in a delightfully funky mining-shaft-modern complex of multilevel dining/drinking areas, and on a tree-shaded firelit patio.

The Danson   *621-1818*
  downtown at 109 Yale Av.
  L-D.   *Moderate*
A comprehensive selection of flavorful American and Mexican dishes can be washed down with an outstanding choice of tap beer. The pleasant coffee shop also features tree-shaded sidewalk tables and a lounge/patio that is a distinctive 1930s gas station redo.

★ **Griswold's Inn**   *626-2411*
  .8 mi. N at 555 W. Foothill Blvd.
  B-L-D. Sun. brunch.   *Low—Very Expensive*
The **Candlelight Pavilion Dinner Theatre** (D only. Closed Mon.-Tues.—Very Expensive) earns the star by artfully combining American cuisine with Broadway shows and musical revues in a posh, multilevel dinner theater. **Griswold's Indian Hill** (D only. Only brunch on Sun. Closed Mon.—Moderate) serves American and Continental dishes in a comfortable firelit dining room. **Griswold's Smorgasbord** (B-L-D—Low) offers abundant American fare amidst family-oriented decor.

★ **Harvard Square Cafe**   *626-7763*
  downtown at 206 W. Bonita Av.
  L-D.   *Expensive*
New American cuisine is the hallmark of Claremont's best young restaurant. Everything from designer pizzas and pastas to entrees like chicken breast with raspberry vinaigrette sauce and enoki mushrooms reflects freshness and the flair of a talented chef. Guests have a choice of a casual modish dining room or a heated, shaded sidewalk patio overlooking downtown's trees and gardens.

★ **Las Cazuelitas**   *985-1339*
  4 mi. E at 134 N. 2nd Av. - Upland
  B-L-D. No B Tues-Fri. No D Sun. Closed Mon.   *Low*
Chicken mole, pork in tomatillo sauce, and big shrimp in ranchero sauce typify the authentic California-style Mexican fare that make this colorful casual dining room worth finding.

★ **Molly's Souper**   *982-1114*
4 mi. E at 388 N. 1st Av. - Upland
B-L.   *Low*
Molly's super breakfasts are among the best in Southern California.
Omelets, cottage-fried potatoes, and biscuits and gravy are abundant,
fresh from scratch, and delicious. First-rate all-American cuisine is
coupled with boarding house decor in homespun little dining rooms. A
tree-and-umbrella-shaded patio adjoins.

Oliver Duvall's   *626-6770*
downtown at 102 Harvard Av.
L-D. Closed Sun.   *Moderate*
New California cuisine is featured in an appealing selection of dishes
served in a stylish contemporary dining room and bar. One of the
village's newest gourmet havens is off to a good start.

★ **Some Crust Bakery**   *621-9772*
downtown at 119 Yale Av.
The Some Crust Bakery is one of the best in Southern California.
Pastries, cookies, cakes, scones and breads are all as delicious as they
look. (Don't miss the sample plate on top of the display case.) The
humongous cheddar cheese/chile croissant is a stellar New California
update of the French classic.

★ **Walter's Restaurant**   *624-2779*
downtown at 308 Yale Av.
B-L-D. Sun. brunch.   *Moderate*
Toothsome, unusual baked goods displayed near the entrance herald
good things to come. Carefully prepared contemporary American
cuisine and some Afghani specialties are served in several cheerful
dining rooms and in a trellis-covered patio and heated umbrella-
shaded garden court of the deservedly popular restaurant.

★ **Yianni's**   *621-2413*
downtown at 238 Yale St.
L-D. Sun. brunch. Closed Mon.   *Moderate*
Authentic full-course Greek dinners including soup, salad, baklava,
and an after-dinner drink are the specialty. Lunches highlighting such
dishes as flaming Greek cheese are similarly distinctive. Full linen
and fresh flowers are used at each table in a cozy colorful taverna that
complements the robust cuisine.

LODGING

Most of Claremont's surprisingly scarce lodgings are clustered near
the freeway. More and newer hotels and motels adjoin nearby Ontario
Airport. With no high season, rates remain the same year-round.

Doubletree Club Hotel   *391-6411*
8 mi. SE (near I-10) at 429 N. Vineyard Av. - Ontario 91764
This newly remodeled 300-unit six-story motor hotel has a big outdoor
pool, whirlpool, exercise room, dining room and lounge. Full breakfast
is complimentary. Each well-furnished room has two phones and
remote control color TV with movies. Toll-free: (800)528-0444.
    regular room—request 6th floor mtn. side for view,   Q bed...$79

Griswold's Inn   *626-2411*
.8 mi. N at 555 W. Foothill Blvd. - 91711
Claremont's biggest and best lodging is a conference-oriented 280-room
motor hotel on seventeen tree-shaded acres. Amenities include a large

pool and whirlpool in a tropical court; dinner theater, dining room, smorgasbord restaurant, and bakery (see listing); and a specialty shop complex. Each nicely furnished room has a phone and remote control color TV with (fee) movies. Toll-free: (800)854-5733.

#176 & even #s thru #188—small private
  balconies with fine mountain view, 2 D beds...$109
  regular room—request private balcony, 2 D, Q, or K bed...$109
Marriott Ontario Airport Hotel *986-8811*
8.5 mi. SE (near I-10) at 2200 E. Holt Blvd. - Ontario 91764
This 300-unit contemporary hotel includes a near-Olympic-sized courtyard pool and whirlpool and (fee) health club with racquetball and one lighted tennis court. There is also a restaurant, entertainment lounge, piano bar, and gift shop. Each spacious, attractively furnished room has two phones, and remote control color TV with (free and pay) movies. Toll-free: (800)284-8811.
  regular room— 2 D or K bed...$124
Motel 6 *986-6632*
4 mi. SE (by I-10) at 1515 N. Mountain Av. - Ontario 91762
The chain's nearest modern **bargain** motel has an outdoor pool. Each plain room has a phone and color TV with movies.
  regular room— D bed...$35
Ramada Inn *621-4831*
1 mi. S (by I-10) at 840 S. Indian Hill Blvd. - 91711
Amenities in this modern motor hotel by the freeway include a large outdoor pool, whirlpool, saunas, eight lighted tennis courts, and a restaurant. Each large, comfortable room has a refrigerator, phone, and remote control color TV with movies. Toll-free: (800)322-6559.
  regular room—request pool side for quietest room, 2 Q or K bed...$55
Red Lion Inn *983-0909*
8 mi. SE (by I-10) at 222 N. Vineyard Av. - Ontario 91764
The area's largest lodging is a 340-room motor hotel. The contemporary complex includes a big pool and whirlpool in a landscaped courtyard, plus exercise facilities, restaurant, entertainment lounge, and gift shop. Each well-furnished room has a sliding glass door to a tiny private balcony, phone, and remote control color TV with movies. Toll-free: (800)547-8010.
  #348,#248,#148—spacious, refr./wet bar, 3 phones,
    large mirrored whirlpool in bathroom, K bed...$375
  regular room— Q bed...$79
Residence Inn by Marriott *983-6788*
8 mi. SE (near I-10) at 2025 E. D St. - Ontario 91764
This 200-unit all-suites motel has a pool and whirlpool in a courtyard. Breakfast and afternoon appetizers are complimentary. Each spacious, attractively furnished unit has a living room, kitchen, phone, and color TV with movies. Toll-free: (800)331-3131.
  penthouse suite—extra-large, fireplace, loft with Q bed...$119
  regular room—request away-from-freeway for quiet, Q bed...$89
Travelodge Claremont *626-5654*
1 mi. S (by I-10) at 736 S. Indian Hill Blvd. - 91711
A 1988 motel with a small pool. Each compact, nicely furnished room has a phone and color TV with movies. Toll-free: (800)255-3050.
  #215,#210,#101—big mirrored whirlpool in view of K bed...$75
  regular room— K bed...$45

Coronado

Coronado is a genteel getaway highlighted by California's premier coastal hotel. The village is surrounded on three sides by the ocean and bay a few miles from San Diego. It was a sand spit with nothing but sagebrush until 1888 when the grandiose Hotel Del Coronado opened with an electrical system by Thomas Edison. Coronado prospered, thanks to a subtropical climate and the incomparable resort. Transition from a quiet backwater to a vibrant year-round vacation destination happened quickly when the graceful San Diego-Coronado bridge replaced ferry service in 1969.

The "Hotel Del" still reigns over an expanding array of lodgings ranging from historic bed-and-breakfast inns to two world-class bayfront hotels for the 1990s. Yet, downtown remains one of the Southland's most strollable, with many distinctive shops and restaurants amid luxuriant subtropical flowers and greenery.

WEATHER PROFILE

V.W.R.*		Jan.	Feb.	Mar.	Apr.	May	June	July	Aug.	Sep.	Oct.	Nov.	Dec.
Great	10												
Fine	9												
Very Good	8												
Good	7												
Moderate	6 / 5												
	4												
	3												
Adverse	2												
	1												
	0												

	Jan.	Feb.	Mar.	Apr.	May	June	July	Aug.	Sep.	Oct.	Nov.	Dec.
V.W.R.*	7	7	8	9	10	10	10	10	10	10	9	7
Temperature												
Ave. High	64	65	66	67	69	70	73	75	74	71	68	65
Ave. Low	44	45	47	51	54	59	62	63	61	55	50	45
Precipitation												
Inches Rain	2.1	2.2	1.6	1.0	.2	-	-	.1	.1	.6	1.0	2.1
Inches Snow	-	-	-	-	-	-	-	-	-	-	-	-

*V.W.R. = Vokac Weather Rating: probability of mild (warm & dry) weather on any given day.

Coronado

Population: 26,540   Area Code: 619
Elevation: 25 feet
Location: 5 mi. Southwest of San Diego
Coronado Visitor Information Center   437-8788, (800)622-8300
downtown at 1111 Orange Av., Suite A - 92118

ATTRACTIONS

★ *Bicycling*

Flat terrain, picturesque neighborhoods, and spectacular oceanfront and bayside streets and a separated bikeway on the Silver Strand make Coronado one of the best locales for easy bicycling in California. Bicycles can be rented by the hour or longer at:

Bikes & Beyond   *1 mi. NE at 1201 First St., Suite 122*   435-7180
Holland's Bicycle Shop   *downtown at 977 Orange Av.*   435-3153

★ *Boat Rentals*

Catamarans, sailboats, pedal-boats, jet skis, fishing skiffs, and windsurfer rentals and lessons are offered on Glorietta Bay. The sheltered waters of the inner bay are tranquil and scenic. Beyond, San Diego Bay offers exciting reaches and grand nautical vistas.

Coronado Boat Rentals   *.5 mi. SE at 1715 Strand Way*   437-1514
Glorietta Bay Marina   *.5 mi. SE at 1715 Strand Way*   435-5203

★ *Boat Ride*

San Diego Harbor Excursions   234-4111
1 mi. NE at 1201 First St. at Ferry Landing Marketplace
A passenger ferry service operates once again, as it did for decades before the bridge was built between Coronado and San Diego. The short ride—a quick, comfortable way to experience the beauty of the bay and its surroundings—leaves on the half-hour each day & evening.

★ **Coronado City Beach**   522-7342
.3 mi. W along Ocean Blvd.
Lush vegetation and imposing homes punctuate the inland view from a broad white sandy beach with distinctive dunes along the village's western border. Sunbathing, body surfing and surfboarding are popular. For great seascapes and people-watching, don't miss strolling on a mile-long promenade between the beach and the Hotel Del.

★ **Coronado Tidelands Park**   522-7342
1 mi. NE at Glorietta Blvd. & Mullinix Dr.
Sea-blue supports of the gently curving San Diego-Coronado Bay Bridge complement the lush greenery of this delightful bayfront park. Palm-shaded picnic areas and play equipment are strategically located to maximize bay views of shipyards and San Diego's skyscrapers.

Golf

★   **Coronado Municipal Golf Course**   435-3121
.8 mi. E at 2000 Visilia Row
One of Southern California's prettiest 18-hole public courses has subtropical landscaping and grand views of the bay and dramatic blue bridge. A pro shop with club and cart rentals, a driving range, and a snack bar/lounge are available.

Silver Strand State Beach   435-5184
5 mi. S on CA 75 at Coronado Cays Blvd.
A wide beach extends for two miles along a treeless strand. At the north end is a parking lot campground for RVers. Near the park entrance is **Loews Coronado Bay Resort** (see listing).

RESTAURANTS

Beach Bay Cafe   *435-4900*
1 mi. NE at 1201 First St.
B-L-D.   *Expensive*
Updated American dishes are served in a casual dining room with a window wall view shared by a shaded deck of a palm-lined walkway, the bay and San Diego skyline beyond the ferry landing.
The Chart House   *435-0155*
.5 mi. SE at 1701 Strand Way
D only.   *Expensive*
Seafood, steaks, and prime rib are served in the century-old Del Coronado Hotel boathouse. The splendid over-the-water building retains its nautical spirit with historic pictures, art objects, and bay-view windows on three sides of the dining room and upstairs lounge.
★ **Chez Loma**   *435-0661*
downtown at 1132 Loma Av.
L-D. Sun. brunch. No L Sat. Closed Mon.   *Expensive*
French classics are given a light fresh California topspin in dishes like venison with lingonberry sauce. Desserts made here are similarly distinctive. Crisp white linen and fresh flowers enhance the intimate dining areas and glassed-in porch of a converted Victorian cottage.
★ **Hotel Del Coronado**   *435-6611*
.4 mi. S at 1500 Orange Av.
B-L-D. Sun. brunch.   *Expensive–Very Expensive*
In the new **Prince of Wales** (D only–Very Expensive), contemporary California cuisine complements opulent moderne decor and an ocean view. The **Crown/Coronet Dining Room** (B-L-D. Sun. brunch– Expensive) offers American fare at richly appointed tables in two of America's most spectacular dining rooms. The Crown Room is an ellipsoid of epic proportions with sugar pine paneling across a thirty-foot-high vaulted ceiling. Parquet paneling distinguishes the graceful Coronet Room which adjoins. **Ocean Terrace** (L only–Expensive) has casual meals and drinks in a dark club room or (better yet) on a terrace overlooking the sea. The **Palm Court** offers light fare by a palm court. **The Promenade Deck Bar & Grill** is the place for drinks and snacks at umbrella-shaded tables with nonpareil beach and pool views. The **Del Deli** is open 24 hours.
Kensington Coffee Company   *437-8506*
1 mi. NE at 1106 First St. by Orange Av.
B-L-D.   *Moderate*
Gourmet coffees complement pastries, cakes, cookies and gelato served to go, or on a sidewalk patio with a peek-a-boo bay view.
★ **Le Meridien San Diego at Coronado**   *435-3000*
1.1 mi. NE at 2000 Second St.
B-L-D. Sun. brunch.   *Very Expensive–Extremely Expensive*
At **Marius** (D only–Extremely Expensive), French classics receive New California cuisine enhancements in expert presentations like roasted rack of lamb in a crust of nuts and dried fruit or sauteed buffalo tenderloin with cranberries served in intimate, formally elegant dining rooms. **L'Escale** (B-L-D. Sun. brunch–Very Expensive) features New California cuisine in a large refined dining room with a skyline view shared by a poolside terrace. The Sunday brunch is memorable. Nearby is **La Provence**, a plush entertainment lounge.

Coronado

★ **Loews Coronado Bay Resort**   *424-4000*
5 mi. S on CA 75 at 4000 Coronado Bay Rd.
B-L-D. Sun. brunch.   *Expensive–Very Expensive*
Azzura Point (D only–Very Expensive) is a new landmark for some
of the Southland's best Pacific Rim cuisine. The freshest seafoods,
vegetables and fruits are transformed into innovative flavorful fare
that combine California and Asian cultures in dishes like crispy whole
sea bass with a black bean sauce. Culinary delights, presented in a
casual yet urbane setting with a picture-window view across the bay,
distinguish this as one of the West's great hotel dining experiences. In
RRRs Cafe (B-L-D. Sun. brunch–Expensive), New California cuisine
is served in a large semicircular dining room with a picture window
view of the marina.

Mandarin Cafe   *435-2771*
downtown at 1330 Orange Av., Suite 280
L-D. No L Sun.   *Moderate*
Mandarin and Szechwan specialties and full linen table service
enhance this upstairs dining room with a peek-a-boo surf view.

McP's Irish Pub   *435-5280*
downtown at 1107 Orange Av.
L-D.   *Moderate*
Irish dishes like corned beef or Mulligan stew are highlighted with all
kinds of libations in a lively little pub where wood trim, brass, a
fireplace, and greenery capture the Irish spirit. An umbrella-shaded
patio is also popular. Live entertainment happens nightly.

★ **Peohe's**   *437-4474*
1 mi. NE at 1201 First St.
L-D. Sun. brunch.   *Very Expensive*
Hawaiian seafood is featured in creative dishes like coconut crunchy
shrimp served with three sauces. The big bayfront restaurant is a
showplace of post-modern decor. Simulated rock walls are festooned
with live tropical greenery and vibrant orchids. Multilevel dining areas
separated by waterfalls and sculptured ponds offer posh banquettes or
wicker chairs with a window-wall view of San Diego's bay and skyline.

Prima Vera Pastry Caffe   *435-4191*
downtown at 956 Orange Av.
B-L.   *Moderate*
Assorted Continental and American pastries and desserts plus light
fare are served with all kinds of coffees and teas. A counter and a few
tables overlook display cases and there is a sidewalk patio.

★ **PrimaVera Ristorante**   *435-0454*
downtown at 932 Orange Av.
L-D. No L Sat. & Sun.   *Expensive*
The rich flavors, textures and colors of Northern Italian cuisine are
complemented by fine housemade baked goods and desserts–the
tiramisu is a knockout. The handsome split-level dining room and
lounge are among the village's most sophisticated.

Rhinoceros Cafe & Grill   *435-2121*
downtown at 1166 Orange Av.
L-D. No L Sun.   *Moderate*
Contemporary California cuisine is featured in flavorful dishes like
tequila lime chicken and meatloaf with jalapeno peppers. Crisp linen
napery enhances white bright post-modern decor.

LODGING

Three of California's finest lodgings anchor the dozen places sprinkled near the main street (Orange Av.). There are no bargains in the village. While summer is the busiest season, rates remain about the same year-round.

Best Western Suites Coronado Island   *437-1666*
.7 mi. NE at 275 Orange Av. - 92118
This newer motel has a small pool and whirlpool. Each well-furnished room has a wet bar/refrigerator, microwave, phone, and remote control color TV with movies. Toll-free: (800)528-1234.

#110—2 phones, 2 TVs, in-bath whirlpool,	K bed...$129
regular room—	Q bed...$87

Glorietta Bay Inn   *435-3101*
.4 mi. SE at 1630 Glorietta Blvd. - 92118
A turn-of-the-century mansion is the centerpiece for a modern 100-room motel across the road from the Hotel Del and the bay. Tropically landscaped grounds include a bay-view pool and rental bikes. Each attractively appointed unit has a refrigerator, phone, and remote control color TV with movies. Toll-free: (800)283-9383.

"Penthouse Suite"—top floor of mansion, in-bath	
whirlpool, spacious, elegant, view of Del & bay,	K bed...$275
"bay-view rooms"—small, pvt. balc., bay view,	2 Q or K bed...$124
regular room—garden view,	2 Q or K bed...$99

★ **Hotel Del Coronado**   *435-6611*
.4 mi. S at 1500 Orange Av. - 92118
The "Hotel Del" is one of the world's renowned lodgings, and one of only a few California resorts fronting on the ocean. The spectacular Victorian landmark, on the National Register, has served as an ultimate seaside resort for more than a century. The tropically landscaped 33-acre complex includes the giant whitewashed 1888 hotel with its red-trimmed towers and roofs, plus a seven-story "Ocean Towers" and "Poolside Addition." In addition to a broad white sand public beach, there are two vast outdoor pools, and (for a fee) six lighted tennis courts by the sea, plus a complete health spa. Dining possibilities are abundant including one of America's most spectacular dining rooms (see listing). There are also elaborate convention facilities and an arcade of specialty shops. All 700 comfortably updated rooms include a refrigerator, phone, and color TV with (pay) movies. Toll-free: (800)HOTEL-DEL.

#3481—spacious, great private oceanfront & Pt. Loma	
view, extra window, wet bar/refr., pvt. balcony,	K bed...$325
#3560—great pvt. ocean & Pt. Loma view, extra window,	K bed...$249
#3544—great ocean view, extra window,	K bed...$249
#3462—fine courtyard & ocean view, private balcony,	K bed...$299
#4224,#4222—newer, spacious, private balcony	
& floor-to-ceiling oceanfront view,	K bed...$299
#6727—top floor, 1 BR apt., corner, kitchenette,	
pvt. balcony, fine floor-to-ceiling oceanfront view,	2 D beds...$550
"Lanai"—request private oceanfront balcony,	2 D or K bed...$359
regular room—ocean view, in historic hotel,	2 T, D or K bed...$209
regular room—in historic hotel, garden view,	2 T, D or K bed...$149

Coronado

★ **Le Meridien San Diego at Coronado**   435-3000
1.1 mi. NE at 2000 Second St. - 92118
Coronado's second grand-luxe resort opened in 1988. The low-profile 300-room complex in a manicured tropical garden with terraced ponds and fountains extends for a quarter-mile along San Diego Bay. The view of San Diego's skyline is enchanting. Amenities include a huge freeform outdoor pool by the bay; plus two other landscaped pools, two whirlpools, a lighted waterfront promenade and dock, and gift shops. In addition (for a fee), there are bicycles, six lighted tennis courts, a complete health and beauty spa, and valet or self (covered) parking, along with fine dining and lounge facilities (see listing). Each luxuriously appointed room has a floor-to-ceiling sliding glass door to a private bougainvillea-strewn balcony (most with unobstructed bay views), stocked (honor) refrigerator, phone, and remote control color TV with free and pay movies. Toll-free: (800)543-4300.

#347,#330—top floor end unit, large balcony, in-bath
whirlpool, great private view of bay & skyline,   K bed...$475
#331,#332,#334,#335—top floor, small, private
balcony, great bay/skyline view across lily ponds,   K bed...$225
#233,#235,#236,#237—as above, but one floor down, K bed...$225
regular room—garden view,   2 D or K bed...$165

★ **Loews Coronado Bay Resort**   424-4000
5 mi. S on CA 75 at 4000 Coronado Bay Rd. - 92118
Coronado's newest grand-luxe resort opened in 1991 on its own fifteen-acre gated peninsula in San Diego Bay. An ocean beach is just a short stroll across the narrow strand to the west. Enticements at the exclusive 477-unit enclave include an 80-slip private marina, three tropically landscaped large pools and whirlpools overlooking the bay, ping pong and game rooms, and putting green, plus (for a fee) five lighted tennis courts, a full-service fitness center, rental bicycles and various watercraft, and valet or self parking. In addition, there are two fine restaurants (see listing), a market/gift shop, and a live entertainment lounge. Each of the luxuriously appointed rooms and suites has some water view, a balcony or terrace, two phones, an (honor) stocked mini-bar, and a remote control color TV with pay and free movies. Toll-free: (800)23-LOEWS.

#7106,#7101—bayfront suite, kitchen, LR,
in-bath whirlpool, pvt. over-water deck
shares grand view of bay/bridge with   K bed...$495
#1325,#1326—top floor, large room & private
balcony with fine ocean/bay view from   K bed...$225
#2324,#2323—large room with private balcony
and fine bay/bridge view,   K bed...$195
regular room—overlooking pool and marina, K bed...$175

Village Inn   435-9318
downtown at 1017 Park Place - 92118
Coronado's first bed-and-breakfast serves a light complimentary breakfast. The remodeled apartment near everything sports Early California touches. Each simply comfortable room has a phone and color TV.

#206—corner, windows with streetscape view,   Q bed...$70
regular room—   Q bed...$60

Dana Point

Dana Point is a classic contemporary collaboration between man and nature. The "point," a ragged sandstone bluff towering above a manmade oceanfront harbor, was named for Richard Henry Dana, who noted it in his 1830s classic **Two Years Before the Mast**.

The born-again sailing center with a mild year-round climate is now home port to more than 2,500 pleasure craft. The picturesque little harbor also offers boat rentals, sportfishing and whale watching cruises, plus waterfront shops and restaurants, a safe swimming beach, and luxuriant sea-view parks that extend to a fine ocean beach backed by a manicured state park and campground. Three miles inland is San Juan Capistrano, the most romantic of California's chain of Spanish missions. It was founded more than two centuries before the current renaissance added two world-class ocean-view resort hotels to Dana Point during the 1980s.

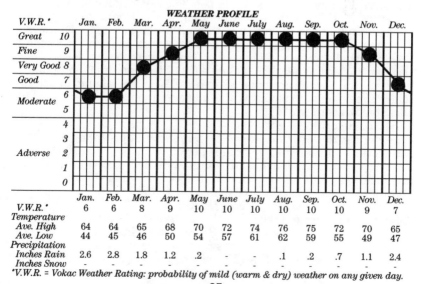

WEATHER PROFILE

V.W.R. *		Jan.	Feb.	Mar.	Apr.	May	June	July	Aug.	Sep.	Oct.	Nov.	Dec.
V.W.R. *		6	6	8	9	10	10	10	10	10	10	9	7
Temperature													
Ave. High		64	64	65	68	70	72	74	76	75	72	70	65
Ave. Low		44	45	46	50	54	57	61	62	59	55	49	47
Precipitation													
Inches Rain		2.6	2.8	1.8	1.2	.2	-	-	.1	.2	.7	1.1	2.4
Inches Snow		-	-	-	-	-	-	-	-	-	-	-	-

*V.W.R. = Vokac Weather Rating: probability of mild (warm & dry) weather on any given day.

Population: 31,896   *Area Code: 714*
Elevation: 10 feet
Location: 56 miles Southeast of Los Angeles
Dana Point Chamber of Commerce   496-1555
downtown at 24671 La Plaza #2 - 92629

ATTRACTIONS

★ **Dana Point Marina**   *496-6137*
.3 mi. S along Dana Point Harbor Dr.
A natural cove backed by high sandy bluffs has become a major manmade marina that can accommodate nearly 3,000 boats. Other attractions include lovely seaview parks, a sandy beach, and two nautically-themed villages on the waterfront that feature shopping and dining with a view. Whale watching cruises leave daily in winter.

★ **Doheny State Beach Park**   *496-6172*
.7 mi. E at 25300 Dana Point Harbor Dr.
One of the region's most complete seaside parks includes an expansive lawn with palm trees, well-spaced picnic tables, food concessions, restrooms, and rentals. Swimming and surfing are excellent off a wide sandy beach at the mouth of San Juan Creek, and snorkelers can explore the offshore underwater park. A small sea life interpretive center is new with several aquariums, an indoor tidepool, and gift shop. A full service campground is a highlight of the premium location. Some tree-shaded sites have ocean views. All share the sound of the surf. Camping reservations: (800)444-PARK.

★ **Mission San Juan Capistrano**   *248-2049*
4 mi. NE at Camino Capistrano & Ortega Hwy. - San Juan Capistrano
The "jewel of the missions" is one of California's most captivating historical sites. Founded in 1776 by Father Junipero Serra, the complex includes three churches. The Great Stone Church, built by Indians between 1797 and 1806, was nearly destroyed by an earthquake in 1812. The building remains a picturesque ruin surrounded by peaceful gardens. The Serra Chapel decorated with primitive designs and art is still in use. The restored adobe structure, dedicated in 1778, is the oldest building in California. Nearby is an imposing young parish church with multiple domes and a belltower. For more than 200 years, cliff swallows have returned on St. Joseph's Day, March 19, to rear their young. They depart on St. John's Day, October 23, for the nearly 6,000-mile flight to Argentina. Self-guided tours of the lovely grounds also include padres' living quarters, soldiers' barracks, a cemetery, and museum rooms exhibiting Indian and Spanish artifacts.

O'Neill Museum   *493-8444*
3.6 mi. NE at 31831 Los Rios St. - San Juan Capistrano
A restored Victorian cottage houses period furnishings, artifacts, and historic photographs. Nineteenth century buildings are within walking distance along this oldest residential street in Orange County.

Orange County Marine Institute   *496-2274*
.7 mi. SW at 24200 Dana Point Harbor Dr.
A full-sized replica of Richard Henry Dana's ship **Pilgrim**, which he described in 1835 in **Two Years Before the Mast**, adjoins a small museum and gallery with a good selection of nautical books and gifts. Visitors can go on board the 120-foot brig on Sundays.

Ronald W. Caspers Regional Park   *831-2174*
12 mi. NE on CA 74 - San Juan Capistrano
Orange County's largest park extends for nearly five miles along the
Ortega Highway (CA 74). Rugged mountains and narrow canyons are
interconnected by miles of hiking and riding trails, and even more in
the adjoining Cleveland National Forest. A complete campground,
picnic areas, and a nature center have been provided.

★ **Salt Creek Beach Park**   *661-7013*
1.5 mi. NW on CA 1
A lofty headland topped by the Ritz-Carlton Hotel subdivides a
splendid mile-long strand backed by sandstone bluffs. On a clear day,
Catalina Island shimmers in the distance. Swimming and surfing are
popular, and lifeguards serve all sections in summer.

★ **San Juan Capistrano Regional Library**   *493-1752*
4.2 mi. NE at 31495 El Camino Real - San Juan Capistrano
The area's most inspiring contemporary building (circa 1983) is a post-
modern charmer by Michael Graves. The library surrounding an
arcaded courtyard with a fountain, stream and reflecting pools is a
modish amalgam of Egyptian, Spanish, and even pre-Columbian
American architectural styles. Furnishings range from traditional
hardwood tables to overstuffed sofas, and nooks with posh chaise
lounges. Both the library and art exhibits are free. Closed Sun.

★ *Sportfishing*
Dana Wharf Sportfishing   *496-5794*
.5 mi. S at 34675 Golden Lantern
Coastal and deep sea fishing are seasonally popular. All equipment is
provided for trips of various lengths. Cruising, whale watching and
para-sailing can also be arranged. The association has information and
makes reservations on any of a dozen boats.

Warm Water Feature
★ **San Juan Capistrano Hot Springs**   *728-0400*
15 mi. NE at 35501 Ortega Hwy. (Box 58) - San Juan Capistrano
Since 1846, visitors have sought out this sybaritic sylvan idyll. You
can relax in natural hot mineral water in an outdoor pool. Better yet,
rent one of the the twenty-five private hot tubs sprinkled along a little
tree-shaded stream. They are available 24 hours daily.

RESTAURANTS

★ **A Tavola Ferrantelli**   *493-1475*
.3 mi. SE at 25001 Dana Point Harbor Dr. in the Pavilion
L-D. No L Sat. & Sun.   *Expensive*
Classic California/Italian grazing fare is given the kind of trendy
treatment that has made this young restaurant one of the most
popular in the area. The handsome dining room, awash in crisp white
linen, has a comfortable contemporary feeling. So does the adjoining
lounge. Both seem right for Dana Point.

Beach Street Diner   *496-2434*
.6 mi. E at 34242 Del Obispo St.
B-L-D.   *Moderate*
Sticky buns, croissants and other baked goods made here are
displayed, and served with American short order fare and soda
fountain treats. A bright circular room has been retrofitted with 1950s
diner decor including chrome juke boxes at each booth.

★ **Cannons**   *496-6146*
.7 mi. W at 34344 Street of the Green Lantern
L-D. Sun. brunch.   *Expensive*
The fresh fish and well-thought-out selection of updated American dishes are first-rate in this blufftop landmark perched high above the marina. Both the large casually elegant dining room and downstairs lounge have an awesome window-wall view. So does the popular garden terrace, with heat lamps and shaded or sunny tables.

★ **Chart House**   *493-1183*
.8 mi. W at 34442 Street of the Green Lantern
D only.   *Expensive*
Seafood is featured, along with an excellent salad bar. The view of the harbor and coast from this blufftop eyrie is magnificent. A dramatic circular staircase leads to two curvilinear dining rooms and an angular lounge where natural woods, concrete, greenery, and picture windows are artistically combined in quintessential California decor.

★ **Dana Point Resort**   *661-5000*
.7 mi. E at 25135 Park Lantern
B-L-tea-D. No D Sun. Sun. brunch.   *Very Expensive*
Watercolors features New California cuisine like roast rack of lamb with zucchini pancake and rosemary dijon sauce, and spa items like poached salmon with asparagus sauce. The refined tri-level room is enhanced by monumental floral sprays and greenery, brass-and-glass wine storage/display walls, and a wraparound view. **Lantern Bay Lounge** offers ultra-plush seating, an ocean view, and grand piano entertainment, and afternoon tea (usually Wed.-Sun.). **Burton's Lounge** features live entertainment in a posh setting.

★ **El Adobe de Capistrano**   *830-8620*
3.8 mi. NE at 31891 Camino Capistrano - San Juan Capistrano
L-D. Sun. brunch.   *Moderate*
The area's premier Mexican restaurant has both traditional and contemporary dishes. All of the sauces are especially appealing, as is the decor. Big tri-level dining rooms, a cantina, and a lounge by a garden patio reflect the site's centuries-long heritage.

★ **Luciana's**   *661-6500*
downtown at 24312 Del Prado
D only.   *Expensive*
Traditional Italian cuisine is given careful attention in a wide assortment of robust pastas and meat dishes, and desserts like cannoli that look as good as they taste. The romantic firelit dining areas and bar have the warm spirit of an Italian country inn. Grand piano stylings contribute to the tranquil mood most evenings.

Paul's Pantry   *364-1088*
8 mi. N (near I-5) at 27409 Bellogente - Mission Viejo
B-L.   *Moderate*
The area's best breakfast features generous, fresh California fare. Extras like big homemade cinnamon rolls are served with your omelet at comfy booths in the coffee shop or on an umbrella-shaded patio.

Rio Grande Bar & Grill   *496-8181*
3.9 mi. NE at 26701 Verdugo St. - San Juan Capistrano
L-D. Only brunch on Sun.   *Expensive*
Steak and prime rib highlight contemporary California fare served in tasteful dining areas built into an old Spanish-revival brick depot.

★ **The Ritz-Carlton**   *240-2000*
1.6 mi. NW at 33533 Ritz-Carlton Dr.
B-L-tea-D. Sun. brunch.   *Very Expensive–Extremely Expensive*
The Dining Room (D only. Closed Sun.-Mon.–Extremely Expensive) showcases creative Continental cuisine prepared with the best ingredients of the season in exquisite entrees and desserts. Crystal chandeliers and dramatic paintings contribute to the thoroughly opulent setting. Jackets are required for gentlemen. Next door **The Bar** has the ambiance of a posh club. **The Club Grill & Bar** (D only. Closed Tues.-Wed.–Extremely Expensive) presents contemporary California cuisine in an elegant supper club with lavish equine art and live music for dancing. Jackets are required. **The Terrace** (B-L-D. Sun. brunch–Very Expensive) serves fresh and tasty California cuisine in a light and lovely room with a grand piano accompaniment, and alfresco on a handsome garden court terrace. **The Lounge** (L only. Sat. & Sun. brunch–Very Expensive) offers buffets, and peerless brunches on weekends. In the elegant room, widely spaced tables by the expansive windows provide a superb ocean view. In **The Library** (tea daily–Very Expensive) afternoon tea, evening desserts and liqueurs can be enjoyed in baronial splendor enhanced by fine art and an ocean view.

★ **Sunset Grille & Bar**   *661-5220*
downtown at 34150 Pacific Coast Hwy.
L-D. Sun. brunch.   *Moderate*
This fine source of New California cuisine opened in 1994 with standouts like roasted poblano chiles stuffed with cheese on a smoked corn cream sauce, and grilled swordfish with papaya mango salsa. Housemade desserts like apple-banana crisp with crumb top a la mode change daily and are extraordinary (people come from miles just for dessert). The comfortably modish dining room is enhanced by whimsical fish art and flamboyant wooden flowers.

Swallows Inn   *493-3188*
3.9 mi. NE at 31786 Camino Capistrano - San Juan Capistrano
L-D.   *Low*
Burgers and border Mexican dishes are okay as an excuse for a tall one in the area's funkiest saloon. No place has a more uneven wood floor or more signs and pictures on walls and ceilings. When live music happens, the joint jumps with California cowboys and cowgirls.

Walnut Grove Restaurant   *493-1661*
4.2 mi. NE at 26871 Ortega Hwy. - San Juan Capistrano
B-L-D.   *Moderate*
Hearty all-American dishes are accompanied by pastries, biscuits, breads, and desserts made here. The comfortable coffee shop has been a family favorite for fast, fair and friendly meals since 1946.

Wind and Sea Restaurant   *496-6500*
.5 mi. SE at 34699 Golden Lantern at Dana Wharf
L-D. Sun. brunch.   *Expensive*
Fresh seafood is featured on a contemporary American menu while short order fare and appetizers are served in the adjoining grill with an umbrella deck overlooking the harbor. The big contemporary dining room has a wraparound waterfront view shared by a popular entertainment lounge.

LODGING

Several lodgings, including two grand hotels, take advantage of Dana Point's seaside locale. While the coast is popular year-round, rates are often reduced by 10% or more apart from summer and weekends.

★ **Blue Lantern Inn**   *661-1304*
.7 mi. W at 34343 Street of the Blue Lantern - 92629
One of the Southland's most romantic bed-and-breakfast lodgings is the Blue Lantern Inn. This elegant young Cape Cod-style hideaway amidst manicured gardens is perched on a bluff high above the marina. Gourmet breakfast and afternoon wine and appetizers are complimentary. Each of the twenty-nine spacious, luxuriously appointed guest rooms has a gas fireplace, oversized bathroom with whirlpool tub, stocked refrigerator, and color TV with movies. Many rooms have a private sundeck.

#301,#201—extra-large end room, oversized in-bath whirlpool, private deck & corner window view of harbor/ocean, 4-poster	K bed...$350
#302,#202—fine ocean view from pvt. deck &	K bed...$200
#306,#206—fine harbor view,	K bed...$150
regular room—	2 D beds...$135

Dana Point Hilton   *661-1100*
1 mi. E at 34402 Pacific Coast Hwy. - 92629
Hilton's local all-suites hotel opened in 1991 with 200 units across a highway from the beach. Amenities in the post-modern four-story complex include a courtyard pool and whirlpool, sauna, exercise room, rental bicycles, and (for a fee) parking, plus a dining room and lounge. Light breakfast and evening beverages are complimentary. Each well-furnished suite has a sitting room and bedroom, microwave oven, refrigerator/wet bar, two remote control color TVs with VCR and two phones. Toll-free: (800)HILTONS.

#406—gas fireplace, in-bath whirlpool, balcony with fine stream & beach view,	K bed...$250
regular room—ocean view (request balcony),	2 Q or K bed...$165
regular room—non-ocean view (by highway),	2 Q or K bed...$125

★ **Dana Point Resort**   *661-5000*
.7 mi. E at 25135 Park Lantern - 92629
Crowning a bluff above the harbor is a young Cape-Cod-style resort and conference hotel with 350 rooms in a four-level complex surrounded by lawns and gardens. The luxurious facility has two large garden court pools; two whirlpools; steam room, sauna, exercise equipment, and (for a fee) massage, bicycles, and three lighted tennis courts; plus a gourmet restaurant (see listing), lounge, and nightclub with live entertainment; and a resort shop. Each spacious, beautifully decorated room has an ocean view, stocked (honor) bar, phone and remote control color TV with pay and free movies. Toll-free in CA: (800)533-9748.

#1016,#1011,#1041—grand harbor/coast view from large private deck & from	K bed...$280
"Concierge" (many)—comp. breakfast & afternoon repasts, private balcony with fine harbor view,	K bed...$260
regular room—	K bed...$190; 2 D beds...$170

Holiday Inn Express - Dana Point Edgewater   *240-0150*
1.9 mi. SE at 34744 Pacific Coast Hwy. - *Capistrano Beach 92624*
A long sandy beach is across the highway from this newly remodeled
motel with a whirlpool and sauna. Most well-furnished rooms have a
kitchenette, phone and remote control color TV with movies. Toll-free:
(800)HOLIDAY.
#201 "Bridal Suite"—gas fireplace, private balcony
   & corner windows with fine ocean view from   K bed...$135
#301,#306—spacious, raised in-room whirlpool,   K bed...$135
regular room—   Q or K bed...$85
Marina Inn - Best Western   *496-1203*
.3 mi. S at 24800 Dana Point Harbor Dr. - *92629*
The only lodging on the harbor is a contemporary motel with a large
pool in a landscaped courtyard and an exercise room. Each nicely
furnished room has a refrigerator, phone and remote control color TV
with free and pay movies. Toll-free: (800)255-6843.
"King Deluxe"—private balcony, harbor view from   K bed...$102
regular room—   K bed...$83; Q bed...$70
Ramada Limited Suites   *248-1000*
.4 mi. E at 34280 Pacific Coast Hwy. - *92629*
The area's first "spa motel" opened by the highway in 1988 with a
small outdoor pool, sauna and exercise room. The beach is a stroll
away. Each spacious, well-furnished room has a whirlpool, phone and
color TV with movies. Toll-free: (800)272-6232.
"Theme Suite" (8 of these)—spacious, individual
   decor, private balcony, large whirlpool in view of   K bed...$120
"King Spa Suite" (9 of these)—spacious, private
   balcony, kitchenette, large in-bath whirlpool,   K bed...$79
   regular room—   Q or K bed...$59
★ **The Ritz-Carlton**   *240-2000*
1.6 mi. NW at 33533 Ritz-Carlton Dr. - *92629*
Ritz-Carlton has proved that contemporary opulence can be as
enchanting as the timeless grandeur found in Southern California's
ultimate coastal resorts. The region's newest beachfront superstar
crowns a high bluff overlooking a fine sandy beach and popular surfing
area. Vibrant gardens surround a classic Spanish-Colonial-style
complex of 393 rooms. Museum-quality art is used throughout the
four-story buildings. Amenities include two garden court pools (one
extra-large), two whirlpools, plus (for a fee) a championship 18-hole
golf course, four tennis courts, and a fitness center with exercise room,
sauna, steam room, and massage and beauty treatments. There are
also exquisite dining and drinking facilities (see listing), pay parking,
and resort shops. Each luxuriously appointed, spacious room has a
large private balcony or patio, a refrigerator/(honor) bar, two phones,
and remote control color TV with movies. Toll-free in CA: (800)287-
2706; elsewhere: (800)241-3333.
#3022—extra-large 1 BR, fireplace, in-bath whirlpool,
   private balconies with grand beach/ocean view,   K bed...$1600
"Ritz-Carlton Club Floor"—top floor, concierge,
   delightful food/drink amenities, ocean view,   K bed...$475
#3524 and even #s to #3502, #3020 & even #s to #3002—
   superb ocean view,   2 D or K bed...$415
   regular room—   2 D or K bed...$215

Del Mar

Del Mar is a seaside village with a wealth of natural attractions. A splendid beach defines the two-mile-long western boundary. Forests of rare Torrey pines are sprinkled among canyons and mesas to the east. As a result, Del Mar has served as a coastal destination from its beginning in 1885. Development of a racetrack in the 1930s attracted the rich and famous. Downtown Del Mar, above a beachfront park, includes a plush sea-view hotel and popular specialty shopping complexes. Beyond, tree-shaded streets wind past fashionable homes and gardens to the increasingly popular beach and pine preserve.

Population: *4,900*   *Area Code: 619*
Elevation: *120 feet*
Location: *21 miles North of San Diego*
Del Mar Chamber of Commerce   *755-4844*
    downtown at 1104 Camino Del Mar - 92014

WEATHER PROFILE

V.W.R.*		Jan.	Feb.	Mar.	Apr.	May	June	July	Aug.	Sep.	Oct.	Nov.	Dec.
Great	10												
Fine	9												
Very Good	8												
Good	7												
Moderate	6												
	5												
	4												
	3												
Adverse	2												
	1												
	0												

	Jan.	Feb.	Mar.	Apr.	May	June	July	Aug.	Sep.	Oct.	Nov.	Dec.
V.W.R.*	7	7	8	9	10	10	10	10	10	10	9	7
Temperature												
Ave. High	64	65	66	67	69	70	73	75	74	71	68	65
Ave. Low	42	43	45	50	54	58	62	63	60	54	49	44
Precipitation												
Inches Rain	2.1	1.8	1.6	.9	.2	-	-	.1	.1	.6	1.0	2.4
Inches Snow	-	-	-	-	-	-	-	-	-	-	-	-

V.W.R. = Vokac Weather Rating: probability of mild (warm & dry) weather on any given day.

ATTRACTIONS

★ **Ballooning**
Passengers on sunrise or sunset champagne flights experience the sights and sounds of the coast and valleys from a unique and tranquil vantage. These hour-long adventures are so popular that several companies downtown offer manned hot-air balloon rides, including:
A Beautiful Morning Balloon Co. *1342 Camino Del Mar 481-6225*
A Skysurfer Balloon Co. *1221 Camino Del Mar (800)660-6809*
★ **Del Mar Beach**   *755-1556*
downtown at W end of 15th St.
Del Mar is bordered along its entire west side by a fine sandy beach backed by bluffs that give way to lagoons at either extremity. North of pretty little Seagrove Park, the beach is at its widest and busiest. Lifeguards oversee swimming, surfing, and surf fishing, while the warm sand attracts beachcombers, joggers, and sunbathers.
★ **Del Mar Fairgrounds**   *793-5555*
1 mi. NE (near I-5) on Jimmy Durante Blvd.
From late June to early July, expansive grounds host one of the West's largest fairs. Festivities include name entertainment, a giant carnival and midway, trade and hobby exhibits, and a floral extravaganza. All facilities were lavishly improved and upgraded in 1994. From late July through mid-September, a fast track surrounding a beautifully land-scaped infield hosts thoroughbred horse racing.
Solana Beach Park   *755-1569*
2.4 mi. N at W end of Lomas Santa Fe Dr. - Solana Beach
This mile-long corridor includes a mini-park at a manmade break in sandstone cliffs that back most of the beach. Lifeguards look after swimmers, surfers, skin divers, surf fishermen, and sunbathers.
★ **Torrey Pines State Beach**   *755-2063*
1.5 mi. S along US 101
A narrow, sandy beach abuts a highway where Los Penasquitos Lagoon empties into the ocean. Southward, the road climbs into the Torrey Pines Reserve above a beach at the base of massive, multicolored cliffs. With easy highway access and a spectacular backdrop, the strand is extremely popular, especially in summer when swimming and surfing are overseen by lifeguards along the northern half-mile. Sunbathing and surf fishing are also enjoyed year-round. Scenic hiking trails extend to lagoon overlooks and into rare forests of Torrey Pines. **Black's Beach**, California's renowned destination of surf-loving skinny-dippers, begins beyond a rocky headland about two miles south of the parking lot.
★ **Torrey Pines State Reserve**   *755-2063*
2 mi. SE at N end of Del Mar Scenic Parkway
The world's rarest pine tree (Pinus Torreyana) is protected in a 1,750-acre reserve that includes almost all of its natural habitat on the mainland. Several thousand Torrey Pines are clustered on bluffs and in ravines on either side of Los Penasquitos Lagoon. Extra-long needles and unexpected shapes distinguish these trees which grow up to eighty feet tall. From a small interpretive museum on the south bluff, well-marked trails (most between half and 1½ miles in length) extend into picturesque forests and beyond to ocean vistas. The unique attraction is free to bicyclists and pedestrians.

RESTAURANTS

Baja Grill & Cantina   *792-6551*
downtown at 1342 Camino Del Mar
L-D.   *Moderate*
Mexican coastal cuisine is featured. Specialties like seafood tortilla soup are fine, but the overall quality is uneven. A charming deck by the sidewalk and a lower patio are heated and enhanced by luxuriant trees and vines.

Bully's North   *755-1660*
downtown at 1404 Camino Del Mar
L-D.   *Moderate*
The area's best prime rib highlights American standards served at comfortable red-vinyl booths in a cozy, casual dining room and in the ever-popular lounge—the focal point of the restaurant.

Carlos & Annie's Cafe   *755-4601*
downtown at 1454 Camino Del Mar
B-L-D.   *Moderate*
One of the area's most popular breakfast places features California and Mexican egg dishes, biscuits and gravy, and tasty baked goods (made elsewhere). Innovative burgers and light fare prevail later. Both the modish dining room enhanced by succulents and the sidewalk cafe offer scenic townscapes and great people-watching.

★ **Fidel's Little Mexico**   *755-5292*
3.5 mi. N at 607 Valley Av. - Solana Beach
L-D.   *Moderate*
North County's favorite Mexican restaurant has, for a third of a century, featured a showstopping tostada suprema and other California-style Mexican dishes that emphasize fresh produce. Mexican arts and crafts are displayed in several comfortable dining rooms, two cantinas, and a dining patio. Fidel's is the premier restaurant in the "Eden Gardens" Mexican dining enclave.

★ **French Pastry Cafe**   *481-8622*
.3 mi. S at 1140 Camino Del Mar
B-L.   *Moderate*
Tantalizing French and American pastries and desserts are making this 1994 bakery a favorite, especially for breakfast when locals flock here for pastry and coffee on the delightful garden deck or patio.

★ **Jake's**   *755-2002*
.3 mi. NW at 1660 Coast Blvd.
L-D. Sun. brunch. No L Sat. Closed Mon.   *Expensive*
Nightly fresh seafood specials highlight contemporary American fare. The adjoining beach is delightfully scenic and surf can reach nearly to a picture-window wall surrounding a long, romantic dining room and lounge. The high-ceilinged interior is artistically decorated with luxuriant greenery and dramatic dark wood trim.

L'Auberge Del Mar Resort & Spa   *755-4940*
downtown at 1540 Camino Del Mar at 15th St.
B-L-D Plus tea on Fri. & Sat..   *Expensive*
The 15th Street Grille offers contemporary California cuisine in a casually elegant dining room and on an umbrella-shaded garden terrace. The firelit **Durante Pub** is warmly nostalgic with many pictures of the actor. In **St. Tropaz Bakery-Bistro-Cafe** (B-L), French-style baked goods are served to go or on a garden patio.

★ **Pacifica Del Mar**   *792-0476*
downtown at 1555 Camino Del Mar, Suite 321
L-D. Sun. brunch.   *Expensive*
An eclectic fusion of skillfully prepared New California cuisine and
Pacific Rim fare has won critical and popular acclaim. Crowds often fill
a big boisterous dining room/lounge and a congestion of tables on a
heated shaded deck with a distant ocean view.
Poseidon   *755-9345*
.3 mi. NW at 1670 Coast Blvd.
L-D. Also B on weekends.   *Expensive*
American standards play second fiddle to panoramic surf views from
the big, gussied-up bar and dining room of this beachfront landmark.
A terrace on the sand is even more popular on sunny days.
Scalini   *259-9944*
3 mi. NE at 3790 Via de la Valle
D only.   *Very Expensive*
Italian cuisine gets a light touch on a comprehensive grazing menu.
An antipasti side bar, exhibition kitchen with wood-fired oven, cushy
lounge, and greenery enhance a large, plush dining room.
★ **Solana Donuts**   *755-9148*
2.3 mi. N at 124 Lomas Santa Fe Dr. - Solana Beach
A diversity of delicious donuts includes unique treats like a crumb-
frosted apple fritter—the Southland's most delectably decadent
morning delight. All are served 24 hours daily to go or at coffee tables.

LODGING

Among the few lodgings, only one is by a beach, but there are several
fine ocean-view lodgings. Summer is prime time. Rates are usually
reduced about 10% during the remainder of the year.
Del Mar Hilton North San Diego   *792-5200*
1.4 mi. NE (by I-5) at 15575 Jimmy Durante Blvd. - 92014
The area's largest hotel (245 rooms) opened by the freeway near the
fairgrounds/racetrack in 1989 with a large courtyard pool and
whirlpool, restaurant, firelit lobby lounge, and gift shop. Each well-
furnished room has a stocked (honor) bar, two phones and remote
control color TV with movies. Toll-free: (800)HILTONS.
       regular room—   2 D or K bed...$115
Del Mar Inn - A Clarion Carriage House   *755-9765*
.7 mi. S at 720 Camino Del Mar - 92014
A pool and whirlpool in a lovely garden enhance this modern half-
timbered three-story motel. Afternoon tea and cakes are free on
weekdays. Each compact, well-furnished room has a tiny private patio
or balcony, a phone, and remote control color TV with movies. Toll-free
in CA: (800)453-4411; elsewhere: (800)451-4515.
       regular room—request 3rd fl. oceanside for view, 2 D or K bed...$99
       regular room—poolside,   Q bed...$85
Del Mar Motel   *755-1534*
.3 mi. NW at 1702 Coast Blvd. - 92014
The area's only seaside lodging is a remodeled older motel with few
beachfront rooms. Each spacious, plain room has a refrigerator, phone
and color TV. Toll-free: (800)223-8449.
       #48,#49—extra windows, beach beyond walkway,   K bed...$120
       regular room—   K bed...$95

Del Mar

★ **L'Auberge Del Mar Resort & Spa**   *259-1515*
downtown at 1540 Camino Del Mar at 15th St. (Box 2889) - 92014
Since 1989, Del Mar once again has a luxury hotel as the major
downtown landmark. The 123-room three-story complex overlooks the
nearby coast. Amenities include a garden court pool and whirlpool; and
(for a fee) two lighted tennis courts; a full-service spa with exercise,
sauna and steam rooms, massage and beauty services; plus (see
listing) a handsome restaurant, friendly pub, nostalgic lobby lounge,
and French bakery; pay parking and specialty boutiques. Each
beautifully decorated room has a private patio or balcony, (honor)
refrigerator/wet bar, two phones and remote control color TV with free
and pay movies. Toll-free: (800)553-1336.
"Valentino Suite"—spacious, in-bath whirlpool,
   gas fireplace, fine ocean view from private balcony, K bed...$525
"Directors Suite"—as above, but no whirlpool,   K bed...$450
   regular room—courtyard view,   2 D or K bed...$209
★ **Ramada Inn**   *792-8200*
1.5 mi. N at 717 S. Hwy. 101 - Solana Beach 92075
The best Ramada Inn in San Diego County opened in 1991 within easy
walking distance of a beach (but with no ocean views). The motel has
a large pool and two whirlpools in a landscaped courtyard, and an
exercise room. Continental breakfast buffet is complimentary. Each
spacious, well-furnished room has a private balcony or patio,
refrigerator, phone and remote control color TV with movies. Toll-free:
(800)BEACH-07.
   #202,#203,#232,#233—private balcony above
   pool/courtyard, kitchenette with microwave,
   large raised whirlpool in view of   K bed...$125
   regular room—   2 Q or K bed...$85
Rock Haus Inn   *481-3764*
downtown at 410 15th St. - 92014
A bungalow-style turn-of-the-century landmark has become Del Mar's
finest bed-and-breakfast inn. It is set in a garden on a rise by the heart
of town. Elaborate Continental breakfasts are served on a glass-
enclosed ocean-view veranda. Ten comfortable rooms are tastefully
decorated with period pieces. Some share baths.
   "Huntsman's"—private bath, spacious rock fireplace, K bed...$150
   "Wicker Garden","Cabana"—ocean view, share bath, Q bed...$100
   regular room—some ocean view, share bath,   2 T or Q bed...$90
★ **The Stratford Inn of Del Mar**   *755-1501*
.7 mi. S at 710 Camino Del Mar - 92014
Del Mar's finest motel has many rooms with ocean views, although the
beach is a long walk away. Amenities of the sprawling well-landscaped
complex include two large courtyard pools and a whirlpool. Each
attractively appointed, spacious unit has a phone and remote control
color TV with movies. Toll-free: (800)446-7229.
   "Camelot Suite"—LR with kitchenette, windows on
   3 sides, big private balcony with fine ocean view,
   raised whirlpool in room with   K bed...$300
   #401,#403,#405,#407,#437—vaulted room, kitchenette,
   big pvt. balc., ocean view windows on 3 sides, K bed...$149
   regular room—poolside,   2 Q or K bed...$99

El Centro

El Centro is the heart of one of the richest farming areas in the world and America's biggest town below sea level. In 1940, America's largest irrigation ditch, the All-American Canal, brought river water to one of the hottest and driest places on earth. The real feature for visitors to El Centro is the fact that it is the heartland of Cal-Mex cuisine which blends year-round fresh local produce with the culinary heritage of generations of Californians of Mexican descent. It is also a base in warm winter months for exploring nearby attractions like the Salton Sea, sand dunes, or a Mexican provincial capital.

Population: *31,405*   *Area Code: 619*
Elevation: *52 feet below sea level*
Location: *121 miles East of San Diego*
Chamber of Commerce & Visitors Bureau   *352-3681*
  downtown at 1100 Main St. (Box 3006) - 92243

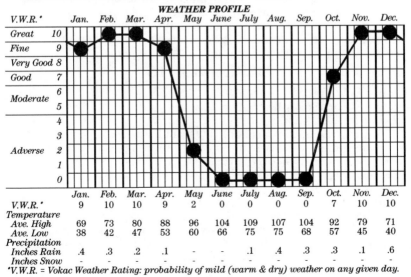

WEATHER PROFILE

V.W.R.*		Jan.	Feb.	Mar.	Apr.	May	June	July	Aug.	Sep.	Oct.	Nov.	Dec.
Great	10												
Fine	9												
Very Good	8												
Good	7												
Moderate	6												
	5												
	4												
	3												
Adverse	2												
	1												
	0												

	Jan.	Feb.	Mar.	Apr.	May	June	July	Aug.	Sep.	Oct.	Nov.	Dec.
V.W.R.*	9	10	10	9	2	0	0	0	0	7	10	10
Temperature												
Ave. High	69	73	80	88	96	104	109	107	104	92	79	71
Ave. Low	38	42	47	53	60	66	75	75	68	57	45	40
Precipitation												
Inches Rain	.4	.3	.2	.1	-	-	.1	.4	.3	.3	.1	.6
Inches Snow	-	-	-	-	-	-	-	-	-	-	-	-

V.W.R. = Vokac Weather Rating: probability of mild (warm & dry) weather on any given day.

ATTRACTIONS

Mexicali
12 mi. S via I-8 & CA 111
Mexicali, the capital of the Mexican state of Baja California, is a sprawling young city with about half a million residents. Only a fence separates it from little Calexico on the American side of the border. Surrounded by vast, flat farmlands, Mexicali lacks the hustle of Tijuana or the quaintness of Tecate. But, there are some distinctive governmental buildings and monuments. Many unassuming restaurants and shops are within walking distance of the border.

The Salton Sea   *393-3052*
34 mi. N via CA 86 or CA 111
California's largest lake is at the lowest point in the Imperial Valley (230 feet below sea level). The vast waterway (thirty miles long and twelve miles wide) is uniformly shallow. It was created over a two-year period beginning in 1905 when floods on the Colorado River caused a breakthrough in an irrigation canal serving the valley. Although saltier than the ocean, the sea is both a fishery and a national wildlife refuge. A sprinkling of houses (mostly for sale) that punctuate a vast grid of decaying streets and little-used waterways along the desolate western shore give mute testimony to the failed dreams of post-war visionaries who touted the sea as California's inland Riviera. Today, tiny communities with limited supplies, campgrounds, primitive beaches with swimming areas, and boating facilities are sprinkled along an ever-changing shoreline that ranges from lush (citrus orchards) to ugly (expanses of alkali deposits). Summer is torrid. As a result, most visitors come between November and May.

★ *Sand Dunes*
38 mi. E on I-8
One of America's largest dune systems, as much as six miles wide, extends from the southeastern corner of California northwest for more than fifty miles. Some dunes are nearly 300 feet high. For years, movie producers have used these sand piles in Sahara-type epics. More recently, they were featured in "Star Wars." Motorists on Interstate 8 can park at a rest stop midway in the dunes for a picnic or a hike. Nearby, more adventurous visitors can rent (or use their own) dune buggies to put some excitement into a sandy sojourn.

RESTAURANTS

Camacho's Place   *352-5810*
8 mi. SW at 796 W. Wahl Rd.
L-D. Closed Sun.-Mon.   *Low*
California-style Mexican cuisine has been featured by generations of the same family in this homespun little dining room/cantina—in a roadhouse miles from anywhere.

★ **El Sombrero**   *353-8118*
downtown at 841 Main St.
B-L-D.   *Low*
For Mexican breakfasts, this is the valley's best source. It is predictably open for all meals, served in an unaffected dining room with a few south-of-the-border flourishes and a picture window view of landscaped municipal buildings.

★ **La Fonda**   *353-6450*
.3 mi. N at 832 Adams Av. (CA 86)
L-D. Only brunch on Sun.   *Low*
Beef, pork, chicken, shrimp, and even goat and lamb are skillfully
prepared for homestyle Mexican dishes. Authentic, flavorful specialties
like beef with cactus are uniformly delicious and excitingly different.
The colorful little dining room in a converted cottage has long been one
of the best restaurants in the valley. Giant shrimp and other goodies
from the nearby Gulf of California highlight "seafood only" Sundays.

★ **La Hacienda**   *355-1640*
5 mi. N at 999 S. Imperial Av. (CA 86) - Imperial
L-D. Closed Sun.-Mon.   *Low*
Here is a premier source of California-style Mexican specialties like
fluffy empanadas de queso or tender carne asada with guacamole
prepared with consistent skill from fresh local products. Aficionados
of the robust cuisine, served in an unassuming brick-and-tile-trimmed
dining room and cantina, have made the roadhouse a landmark.

La Mexicana   *352-3913*
downtown at 488 Broadway
L-D.   *Low*
Jumbo shrimp and steaks are among classic California-style Mexican
dishes served in a big dining room outfitted with hand-wrought highbacked wood chairs by rustic tables on floor tiles. Live music draws
crowds to the adjoining cantina on weekends.

LODGING

Lodgings in town are all standard motels. Several are bargains. Prime
time is fall-to-spring. Rates are at least 10% less in summer.

Barbara Worth Country Club   *356-2806*
8.5 mi. E at 2050 Country Club Dr. - Holtville 92250
Imperial Valley's only resort has a palm-studded (fee) 18-hole golf
course with a putting green and driving range, plus an outdoor pool
and whirlpool, restaurant, lounge, and golf shop. Each spacious, plain
room has a phone and color TV. Toll-free: (800)356-3806.
   "Executive"—refr., private balcony, in-bath whirlpool,   Q bed...$64
   regular room—shared patio or balcony,   Q bed...$54

E-Z 8 Motel   *352-6620*
2 mi. SE (near I-8) at 455 Wake Av. - 92243
This single-level **bargain** motel has an outdoor pool and whirlpool.
Each compact, no-frills room has a phone and color TV with movies.
Toll-free: (800)32-MOTEL.
   regular room—   Q bed...$30

Motel 6   *353-6766*
1.8 mi. SE (near I-8) at 395 Smoketree Dr. - 92243
The chain's modern **bargain** motel has an outdoor pool and compact,
plain rooms with a phone and color TV with movies.
   regular room—   D bed...$32

Ramada Inn   *352-5152*
1.8 mi. SW (by I-8) at 1455 Ocotillo Dr. - 92243
Ramada has remodeled this modern motor hotel with a large garden
court pool and whirlpool, a coffee shop and an entertainment lounge.
Each well-furnished room has a phone and remote control color TV
with movies. Toll-free: (800)272-6232.
   regular room—   K bed...$58

Encinitas

Encinitas is a jaunty beach town with some of the finest sand and surf in the Southland. A six-mile-long coastline between two lagoons is the western boundary for a town that was founded in 1882, grew up around a railroad depot, and incorporated four diverse local communities in 1986. Today, ocean beaches backed by palm-shaded parks are still the major attractions. Shops, while abundant, are prosaic, as are lodgings (which are surprisingly scarce). But, there is a major concentration of notable dining opportunities.

Population: 55,406   Area Code: 619
Elevation: 92 feet
Location: 27 miles North of San Diego
Encinitas Chamber of Commerce   753-6041
* downtown at 345-H First St. - 92024*

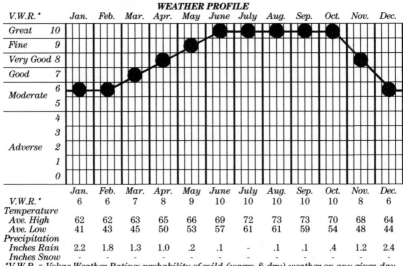

WEATHER PROFILE

V.W.R. *		Jan.	Feb.	Mar.	Apr.	May	June	July	Aug.	Sep.	Oct.	Nov.	Dec.
Great	10						●	●	●	●	●		
Fine	9					●							
Very Good	8				●								
Good	7			●									
Moderate	6	●	●										●
	5												
	4												
	3												
Adverse	2												
	1												
	0												

	Jan.	Feb.	Mar.	Apr.	May	June	July	Aug.	Sep.	Oct.	Nov.	Dec.
V.W.R. *	6	6	7	8	9	10	10	10	10	10	8	6
Temperature												
Ave. High	62	62	63	65	66	69	72	73	73	70	68	64
Ave. Low	41	43	45	50	53	57	61	61	59	54	48	44
Precipitation												
Inches Rain	2.2	1.8	1.3	1.0	.2	.1	-	.1	.1	.4	1.2	2.4
Inches Snow	-	-	-	-	-	-	-	-	-	-	-	-

*V.W.R. = Vokac Weather Rating: probability of mild (warm & dry) weather on any given day.

ATTRACTIONS

★ *Bicycling*
Cycles by the Sea   *753-0737*
1.4 mi. S at 2185 San Elijo Av. - Cardiff
Scenic separated bikeways extend for miles along the coast. Inland, paved scenic byways beckon bicyclists to explore the luxuriant rolling hills of Rancho Santa Fe and beyond. This well-located full-service shop rents mountain bikes by the hour or day.

★ **Cardiff State Beach**
2.4 mi. S along Old Highway 101 - Cardiff
This sandy beach at the mouth of San Elijo Lagoon is backed by a collection of upscale restaurants with splendid marine views. Lifeguards in summer, tidepools, and big breakers make it a popular destination for surfers and swimmers, surf-fishers, beachcombers, and sunbathers.

★ **Moonlight Beach**   *729-8947*
.3 mi. W at W end of Encinitas Blvd.
One of the county's finest beaches is a broad sandy corridor that extends for nearly three miles between Leucadia and Cardiff State Beach. Most of the action is concentrated by a picturesque natural break in the sandstone bluffs. Gentle surf pleases swimmers and boogie boarders—and lifeguards. Above the usually crowded beach are volleyball and tennis courts, rental equipment, a snack bar, and palm-shaded picnic tables. About a mile south is a renowned surfing beach called "Swami's" named for the Indian guru who founded the Self-Realization Fellowship Center on the blufftop in the 1940s. A tiny palm-shaded park just south of the center offers bird's-eye views of surfers, and a long staircase to the beach.

★ **Quail Botanical Gardens**   *436-3036*
1.4 mi. NE via Encinitas Blvd. at 230 Quail Gardens Dr.
Self-guided trails provide access to all sections of this free thirty-acre garden. The highlight is a waterfall in a lush tranquil setting shaded by giant tree ferns and banana palms. Rare tropical and subtropical palms, cacti and America's largest collection of bamboos flourish because of the frost-free climate in this sheltered locale near the coast. A gift shop has a map and information, and sells specimens.

★ **San Elijo State Beach**   *(800)444-7275*
1.6 mi. S along Old Hwy. 101 at W end of Chesterfield Dr. - Cardiff
The mile-long beach at the base of sandstone bluffs north of San Elijo Lagoon has abundant offshore rock formations that make it a major tide-pooling and surf-fishing spot. Surfing and swimming are also popular. The most popular feature, however, is a well-landscaped full-service campground paralleling the blufftop. San Diego County's only oceanfront campsites are always full in the summer.

RESTAURANTS

Beach House   *753-1321*
2 mi. S at 2530 S. Highway 101 - Cardiff
L-D. Sun. brunch.   *Expensive*
Contemporary California seafood is offered, but it is the dramatic freeform decor and seaside views that make this the best of a small chain. Upstairs, a lounge and deck share the memorable surf view.

★ **Charlie's Grill**   *942-1300*
2 mi. S at 2526 S. Highway 101 - Cardiff
L-D. Sun. brunch.   *Expensive*
Charlie's Grill is one of the best seaside restaurants in Southern California. New California cuisine is showcased on a well-thought-out grazing menu. Fresh seafood stars in creative possibilities like sauteed sea bass rolled in creole mustard and cracker crumbs topped with grilled corn salsa. Surf splashes against boulders by a window wall surrounding tables set with full linen and candles. A stylish lounge and sunny deck share the spectacular scene.

★ **Christina's**   *634-0057*
downtown at 315 First St. (Old Highway 101)
Christina's makes the finest specialty breads in San Diego County. Soudough basil with parmesan, apple pecan, potato herb and others are superb. So are the pecan rolls and fruit danish sold with coffee or to go. (They may be in a new location on First St.–Old Highway 101.)

Country Inn   *942-9166*
2.4 mi. E at 1486 Encinitas Blvd.
B-L-D;   *Moderate*
Generous portions of all-American fare have made this big comfortable restaurant a favorite of hungry families in North County.

★ **DB Hacker's Seafood Cafe**   *436-3162*
.3 mi. N at 101 N. Highway 101
L-D.   *Moderate*
Some of North County's finest fried seafood, fish and chips, Mexican fish soup, and other casual foods come from this little fish shack. It's all served to go, in a tiny dining room, or on an enclosed patio.

The Encinitas Cafe   *632-0919*
downtown at 531 First St. (Old Highway 101)
B-L-D.   *Moderate*
Breakfasts featuring many omelets plus oatmeal pancakes and homemade cinnamon rolls, and low-cost dinners of California comfort foods, explain this spiffy coffee shop's popularity.

Hideaway Cafe   *943-8651*
1 mi. SE (near I-5) at 582 Santa Fe Dr.
B-L.   *Moderate*
Traditional American fare, including housemade cinnamon rolls, is generously served in a comfortable contemporary coffee shop.

La Bonne Bouffe   *436-3081*
.8 mi. E at 471 Encinitas Blvd.
D only. Closed Sun.-Mon.   *Expensive*
Robust renditions of country French cuisine are served amidst cozy congestion in a candlelit bistro tucked away in a shopping center.

La Especial Norte   *942-1040*
1.2 mi. N at 664 N. Highway 101 - Leucadia
B-L-D. No B in winter.   *Low*
Machaca and chorizo are put to good use in tasty Mexican breakfasts offered in a simply cheerful little dining room and enclosed patio.

★ **Las Olas**   *942-1860*
2.2 mi. S at 2655 S. Highway 101 - Cardiff
L-D.   *Low*
Shrimp-stuffed chile rellano, fish tacos, and charbroiled fish burritos distinguish the authentic Baja-style dishes at this cheerful shaped-up beach cantina across a highway from the surf.

★ **The 101 Diner**   *753-2123*
downtown at 552 First St. (Old Highway 101)
B-L.   *Moderate*
Baked apple or german pancakes served on weekends are classic diner delights. A room with padded booths and 1950s pics was added recently next to the counter/short order kitchen.

★ **Potato Shack Cafe**   *436-1282*
.3 mi. S at 120 W. I St.
B-L.   *Moderate*
California breakfast classics are accompanied by homemade muffins, superb biscuits and skin-on potatoes with sausage gravy. The little wood-toned coffee shop with hardwood tables, stained glass and memorabilia is deservedly popular. Outside, a pleasant tree-shaded sidewalk is used for year-round alfresco dining.

St. Germains Cafe   *753-5411*
.3 mi. S at 1010 First St. (Old Highway 101)
B-L.   *Moderate*
Light American fare and pastries (made elsewhere) are served in a casual contemporary coffee shop with an airy cafe and a shaded patio.

★ **Taco Auctioneer**   *942-TACO*
1.9 mi. S at 1951 San Elijo - Cardiff
L-D.   *Moderate*
Authentic Mexican coastal specialties and well-prepared beef, pork, and chicken dishes are the best in the county. Here is a delightful alternative to ubiquitous California-style Mexican eateries. Mexican beach shack decor includes a congested little dining room/bar, a shaded porch, a distant ocean view, and a fun-loving staff.

★ **VG Donuts & Bakery**   *753-2400*
1.8 mi. S at 106 Aberdeen Dr. - Cardiff
B-L-D.   *Low*
A full line of donuts, pastries, breads and desserts includes some real winners. The buttercake squares are outstanding. It's all served to go or with coffee at a few tables. The area's most popular bakery has been here for twenty years.

★ **When in Rome**   *944-1771*
.3 mi. S at 1108 First St. (Old Highway 101)
L-D. No L Sun.   *Expensive*
Fresh homemade pastas, sauces, and assorted rich desserts made on the premises complement first-rate Northern Italian cuisine. Sauteed salmon with a creamy cognac/peppercorn sauce is a fine house specialty. The stylish restaurant sports fresh flowers, candles and linen on well-spaced tables in a firelit dining room and lounge.

LODGING

Less than a dozen accommodations are in the area. While none is by the ocean, the best offers good views within walking distance. Apart from the busy summer season, rates are usually reduced at least 15%.

Budget Motels of America   *944-0260*
.5 mi. NE (by I-5) at 133 Encinitas Blvd. - 92024
The ocean is half a mile from this modern motel by the freeway. Each compact, comfortable room has a phone and color TV with movies. Toll-free: (800)795-6044.
      regular room—   Q bed...$45

★ **The Cardiff-by-the-Sea Lodge**   *944-6474*
1.8 mi. S at 142 Chesterfield - Cardiff 92007
The area's most elegant bed-and-breakfast lodging opened in 1991.
Guests can enjoy a spectacular ocean view from a whirlpool in a roof
terrace garden. An extended Continental breakfast is complimentary.
Each of seventeen rooms is beautifully custom-furnished and includes
an oversized bathtub or shower and remote control color TV.

#209—spacious circular room with scrolled beam
   ceiling, refr./wet bar, big heart-shaped whirlpool
   near double-sided fireplace that is visible from   Q bed...$250
#208—panoramic ocean view, big deep tile tub,
   flagstone fireplace in view of   Q bed...$180
#206—sea captain's chambers theme, some
   ocean view, in-bath whirlpool,   Q bed...$190
   regular room—   Q bed...$105

Country Side Inn   *944-0427*
1.7 mi. SE (by I-5) at 1661 Villa Cardiff Dr. - Cardiff 92007
The area's first bed-and-breakfast motel opened in 1985 with a
landscaped pool and whirlpool. Buffet breakfast and afternoon repast
are free. Each well-furnished room has a refrigerator, phone, and
remote control color TV with movies. Toll-free: (800)322-9993.
   regular room—   2 Q or K bed...$74

Friendship Inn   *436-4999*
.9 mi. N at 410 N. Highway 101 - 92024
In this 1988 motel, each comfortable room has a refrigerator, phone,
and remote control color TV with movies. Toll-free: (800)424-4777.
   regular room—   Q or K bed...$45

Moonlight Beach Motel   *753-0623*
.3 mi. N at 233 Second St. - 92024
The area's finest beach is a short stroll from this modern apartment
motel. Spacious, plain units have a kitchenette, small private view
patio or balcony, and color TV. Toll-free: (800)323-1259.
#308-#305—top floor, balcony with fine ocean view,   Q bed...$75
   regular room—   Q bed...$60

Ocean Inn   *436-1988*
2 mi. N at 1444 N. Highway 101 - Leucadia 92024
All-suite rooms are the feature of this 1990s motel, and there is a trail
to the nearby beach. Each comfortable room has a kitchenette with
microwave, phone and remote control color TV with movies. Toll-free:
(800)546-1598.
#210—quiet, large whirlpool,   Q bed...$69
   regular room—   Q bed...$59

Radisson Inn Encinitas   *942-7455*
.4 mi. NE (near I-5) at 85 Encinitas Blvd. - 92024
Encinitas' finest motor hotel tops a bluff overlooking the ocean half a
mile to the west. Amenities of the contemporary four-level complex
include a tropically landscaped pool and whirlpool and an ocean-view
restaurant and lounge. Each well-furnished, spacious unit has a
refrigerator, large private balcony, phone and remote control color TV
with movies. Toll-free: (800)333-3333.
#302—2 rooms, 2 phones, 2 TVs, huge private balc. with ocean
   view, bogus fireplace in LR, mirrored whirlpool by   K bed...$220
regular room—(kitchenette for extra $20),   2 Q or K bed...$89

Idyllwild

Idyllwild is a mile-high alpine village. Only two hours by car from the Southland's major cities, it is nestled in a big, relatively dry pine forest. Nearby to the east the skyline is crowned by San Jacinto Peak, 10,804 feet above sea level. Clear pine-scented air and a four-season climate started luring flatlanders up the mountain a century ago. Hordes now trek here on weekends to escape heat and smog. The village also serves as a gateway for hikers, rock climbers, and campers. Eateries and lodgings are mostly prosaic and family-oriented. A growing number of shops downtown display local arts and crafts.

Population: *2,500*   *Area Code: 909*
Elevation: *5,394 feet*
Location: *112 miles East of Los Angeles*
Idyllwild Chamber of Commerce   *659-3259*
    downtown at 54274 N. Circle Dr. (Box 304) - 92549

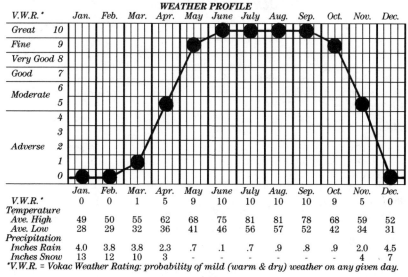

WEATHER PROFILE

V.W.R.*		Jan.	Feb.	Mar.	Apr.	May	June	July	Aug.	Sep.	Oct.	Nov.	Dec.
Great	10												
Fine	9												
Very Good	8												
Good	7												
Moderate	6 5												
	4												
	3												
Adverse	2												
	1												
	0												

	Jan.	Feb.	Mar.	Apr.	May	June	July	Aug.	Sep.	Oct.	Nov.	Dec.
V.W.R.*	0	0	1	5	9	10	10	10	10	9	5	0
Temperature												
Ave. High	49	50	55	62	68	75	81	81	78	68	59	52
Ave. Low	28	29	32	36	41	46	56	57	52	42	34	31
Precipitation												
Inches Rain	4.0	3.8	3.8	2.3	.7	.1	.7	.9	.8	.9	2.0	4.5
Inches Snow	13	12	10	3	-	-	-	-	-	-	4	7

*V.W.R. = Vokac Weather Rating: probability of mild (warm & dry) weather on any given day.

Idyllwild
ATTRACTIONS

Idyllwild County Park   *659-3850*
1 mi. W at end of County Park Rd.
Forested hiking trails, picnic areas, and a campground are features, plus a visitor center with exhibits.
Lake Hemet   *659-2680*
8.4 mi. S via CA 243 on CA 74
In a meadow surrounded by forested hills is a narrow, two-mile-long reservoir, the area's largest. It is a popular fishing site with rental boats. The Forest Service provides free access to shore fishing and picnics. **Hurkey Creek County Park** (half a mile east) and **Lake Hemet Campground** (near the northeastern shore) are complete campgrounds in the pines.
★ **Mt. San Jacinto State Park**   *659-2607*
borders town on north
Crowned by 10,804-foot Mt. San Jacinto, this alpine park and adjoining wilderness area offer a wealth of granite outcroppings, meadows and a clean, dry forest that extends from Idyllwild to ridgetops overlooking Palm Springs. It is a favorite of rock climbers. Backpackers enjoy miles of well-marked trails including strenuous hikes to the mountaintop. The visitor center (closed Mon.-Tues.) has a small display and some marked walks. Picnic areas, and developed and hike-in campgrounds, are nearby.
★ **San Bernardino National Forest**   *659-2117*
around town
All of the San Jacinto Mountains beyond Mt. San Jacinto State Park are part of this large forest. Small reservoirs and some intermittent streams are features, along with meadowlands and rocky outcroppings along ridgetops. Complete and primitive campgrounds and picnic areas are well positioned at trailheads that serve as gateways to the wilderness. The Ranger District office downtown has trail maps, information and permits.

RESTAURANTS

The Chart House
.7 mi. NE at 54905 North Circle Dr.
D only. Sun. brunch. Closed Mon.-Wed. except summer.   *Expensive*
Steaks, prime rib and assorted seafood highlight contemporary American fare served with a salad bar in a dark wood-toned dining room or on a pleasant rear deck built around an enormous pine.
Gastrognome   *659-5055*
downtown at 54381 Ridgeview Dr.
D only.   *Expensive*
An eclectic array of much-touted, but uninspired fare is served amid restful mountain lodge decor, in the lounge, or on a patio.
Granny's Pies   *659-6344*
downtown at 54225 N. Circle Dr., Suite G-10 (in "The Fort")
Good french apple crumb and other pies, cinnamon rolls, cookies, and other goodies are made in a sidewalk-fronting exhibition kitchen. They're served to go, in little homespun dining areas, and on a shaded patio overlooking downtown and Tahquitz Rock.

★ **Idyllwild Cafe**   *659-2210*
.6 mi. SW at 26600 CA 243
B-L.   *Moderate*
Wild Willy's hobo eggs with diced ham, cheddar, mushrooms, and bell peppers scrambled together plus sausage gravy and home fries is a big-eater breakfast bonanza. Humongous biscuits and cinnamon rolls also display the skill and generosity that make this big homespun roadside cafe the best bet for breakfast in the mountains.

★ **River Rock Cafe**   *659-5047*
.3 mi. SW at 26290 CA 243
D only. Closed Mon.-Tues.   *Moderate*
The River Rock Cafe is the best restaurant on the mountain. A grazing menu of contemporary Italian fare ranges from gourmet pizzas and calzone through a selection of chicken, beef, and seafood. Portions are uniformly well-prepared, generous, fresh and flavorful. For dessert, try the grand double layer chocolate cake, or bananas Foster with homemade vanilla ice cream. The pleasant little dining room has a choice of padded booths or tables, and a forest view.

LODGING

Lodgings in the Idyllwild area are relatively numerous. All are small, most are rustic and family-oriented, and surprisingly few have pools or whirlpools. On Friday and Saturday night year-round, the better lodgings will be full. Rates are often reduced by 20% and more during the week apart from summer.

★ **Cedar Street Inn**   *659-4789*
downtown at 25880 Cedar St. (Box 627) - 92549
Idyllwild's newest lodging is a delightful neo-Victorian complex of artfully upgraded cabins in a sylvan garden. Each unit is individually, romantically themed, and beautifully decorated including quality antiques. Most have a fireplace. All have a tucked-away refrigerator and remote control color TV with movies.

"Victorian Suite"—spacious, corner brick fireplace,
    large Roman tub in dramatic bathroom,   Q bed...$93
"Captains Quarters"—spacious, secret door, big
    river rock fireplace, clawfoot tub & shower,   Q bed...$93
"Idyllwild"—unique knotty pine decor, fireplace,
    whirlpool tub in bathroom,   Q bed...$82
"Carriage House"—cozy split-level charm,
    antique iron fireplace,   Q bed...$88
"Attic"—cozy, private spiral staircase & deck in trees,   Q bed...$68
regular room—fireplace,   Q bed...$78

Fern Valley Inn   *659-2205*
1.2 mi. NE at 25240 Fern Valley Rd. (Box 116) - 92549
This red-trimmed cabin complex in the pines surrounds an outdoor pool by a lovely rose garden.   Homemade bread highlights a complimentary Continental breakfast.   Each of the eleven units is nicely furnished with antiques and a fireplace, refrigerator, and private bath.

"The Bungalow"—individual 1 BR cottage, kitchen,   Q bed...$85
"The Loft"—A-frame cottage, full kitchen,   in-loft Q bed...$85
regular room—duplex cottage,   Q bed...$65

Idyllwild Inn   *659-2552*
downtown at 54300 Village Center Dr. (Box 515) - 92549
In the heart of town is a pine-studded cabin complex. Each nicely furnished unit has a kitchen, fireplace, and color TV.

cabin (studio)–	Q bed...$70
regular room–theme room, distinctive decor,	Q bed...$62

Quiet Creek Inn   *659-6110*
1.3 mi. SW at 26345 Delano Dr. (Box 240) - 92549
Five contemporary wood-trimmed duplexes line a gentle slope in a secluded pine forest above Strawberry Creek. Each comfortably furnished unit has a river-rock fireplace, a deck facing the creek, kitchenette, and color TV.

"1 BR"–separate bedroom,	Q bed...$81
"studio"–	Q bed...$70

★ **Strawberry Creek Inn**   *659-3202*
.4 mi. SW at 26370 CA 243 (Box 1818) - 92549
The area's premier bed-and-breakfast inn captures the essence of Idyllwild in a rambling wood-trimmed complex set off by a flower garden in the pines. A full breakfast is complimentary. Each compact, beautifully decorated room has a private bath and some antiques and mementos that are also evident throughout the appealing inn. Toll-free: (800)262-8969.

"The Cottage"–kitchen, two baths, TV & VCR,	
LR with fireplace, glassed-in porch, big whirlpool,	K bed...$125
"courtyard rooms" (4 of these)–refr., skylight, fireplace,	Q bed...$90
regular room–in the main house,	Q bed...$80

Tahquitz Motel   *659-4554*
.3 mi. N at 25840 CA 243 (Box 1290) - 92549
The only pool (small) and whirlpool for guests in the area (summer only) are features of this rustic motel in the pines. Each compact, simply furnished unit has a refrigerator and color TV.

"fireplace unit" (6 of these)–1 BR,	
kitchen, fireplace in tiny living room,	Q bed...$60
regular room–	Q bed...$52

Woodland Park Manor   *659-2657*
1 mi. NE at 55350 S. Circle Dr. (Box 86) - 92549
This modern cabin complex in the pines has an outdoor pool (summer only) with a slide and a ping pong table. Each comfortable wood-trimmed unit has a floor-to-ceiling window with a forest view, a fireplace, refrigerator, and color TV.

"cottage in the woods"–secluded studio cottage	
with kitchen, private sun deck,	Q bed...$89
"cottage"–duplex studio, kitchen, private sun deck,	D & Q bed...$84
regular room–	Q bed...$64

Julian

Julian is the heart of San Diego County's high country. The picturesque village is tucked into folds of low mountains 4,200 feet above sea level. Gold was discovered here in 1870 and the town boomed for a decade. Today, the tiny community is smaller and quieter . . . except on weekends. Then, carloads of families drive up to enjoy cool clear air, alpine scenery, and a strollable little downtown where authentic and reproduced Victorian buildings house numerous prosaic eateries and gift shops. Apples are the other feature in pies and cider in cafes downtown and at roadside stands.

Population: *2,500*   *Area Code: 619*
Elevation: *4,230 feet*
Location: *57 miles Northeast of San Diego*
Julian Chamber of Commerce   *765-1857*
  Box 413 - 92036

WEATHER PROFILE

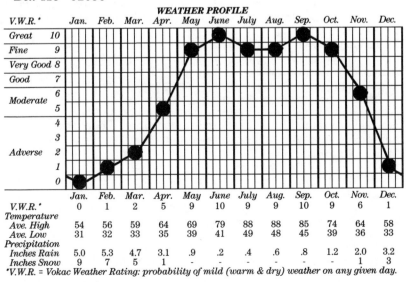

V.W.R.*		Jan.	Feb.	Mar.	Apr.	May	June	July	Aug.	Sep.	Oct.	Nov.	Dec.
Great	10												
Fine	9												
Very Good	8												
Good	7												
Moderate	6 / 5												
	4												
	3												
Adverse	2												
	1												
	0												

	Jan.	Feb.	Mar.	Apr.	May	June	July	Aug.	Sep.	Oct.	Nov.	Dec.
V.W.R.*	0	1	2	5	9	10	9	9	10	9	6	1
Temperature												
Ave. High	54	56	59	64	69	79	88	88	85	74	64	58
Ave. Low	31	32	33	35	39	41	49	48	45	39	36	33
Precipitation												
Inches Rain	5.0	5.3	4.7	3.1	.9	.2	.4	.6	.8	1.2	2.0	3.2
Inches Snow	9	7	5	1	-	-	-	-	-	-	1	3

*V.W.R. = Vokac Weather Rating: probability of mild (warm & dry) weather on any given day.

ATTRACTIONS

★ **Apple Country**
Sprinkled along the highway and byways west of town for several miles are apple orchards and stands. A few are open year-round. The best time to buy fruit and cider here is during the fall harvest.
Apple Bar Ranch   *3.9 mi. NW at 3767 Wynola Rd.   (fall only)*
Farmer's Fruit Stand   *3.9 mi. NW at 4510 CA 78   765-0335*
Manzanita Ranch   *3.9 mi. NW at 4470 CA 78*
Meyer Orchards   *2.8 mi. W at 3962 CA 78   (fall only, closed Wed.)*

★ **Cuyamaca Rancho State Park**   765-0755
10 mi. S on CA 79
San Diego County's best mountain park has dense stands of pine, plus live oak and sycamore along streams etched into rugged hills. The high point is **Cuyamaca Peak**—6,512 feet above sea level. From the top—reached by a strenuous eleven-mile trail—the ocean, Mexico, and the Salton Sea are (often) visible. Desert views reward an easy two-mile hike to the 5,730-foot summit of **Stonewall Peak**. Miles of trails thread backcountry rich in vistas and wildlife. The most distinctive campground is **Green Valley**, where tiny Sweetwater River runs through a rocky little gorge with waterfalls and deep pools. At park headquarters is a local history museum.

Julian Cider Mill   765-1430
downtown at 2103 Main St.
Here is downtown's primary source of apple and other ciders, and gourmet nuts, dried fruit, honeys, and produce. Samples are offered.

Julian Drug Store
downtown on Main St.
You can still enjoy an old-timey ice cream soda or malted milk at the picturesque marble counter in Julian's well-maintained original drug store. It is also a good source of reading material. Closed Sun.

Julian Pioneer Museum   765-0227
downtown at Washington & 4th Sts.
The old brewery has become a capacious storehouse of pioneer memorabilia. Out front are tree-shaded picnic tables. Closed Mon. and weekdays in winter.

Lake Cuyamaca   765-0515
8 mi. S on CA 79
A highway skirts most of this mile-long reservoir in a forest-backed meadow, providing easy access for fishermen. The **Lake Cuyamaca Store** has provisions and a rustic cafe overlooking the lake, which reached its highest level in decades in 1993. Boats (with or without motors) are rented for panfish and trout fishing. There is also a bait and tackle shop. A complete campground is nearby.

★ **Mount Laguna**
19 mi. SE via CA 79 on County Highway S-1
Nearly 6,000 feet above sea level is a popular pine-forested recreation area with numerous picnic areas, campgrounds and a tiny cluster of businesses. The Sunrise Highway and many miles of trails lead to sylvan hideaways and panoramic desert vistas. Occasional winter storms provide snow that lasts just long enough to draw hordes of lowlanders intent on experiencing a "winter wonderland" only an hour away from their flower-filled backyards. The **Visitor Center** has trail

maps, information, books about the area, and some local exhibits (open Fri.-Sun.). **Blue Jay Lodge** (B-L-D. Only open Fri. 3:00 p.m. through Sun. 5:00 p.m.–Moderate) is a rustic roadside restaurant/saloon serving casual American fare since 1926. Huge hand-hewn log booths and tables, a great stone fireplace, and a wood-trimmed bar surrounded by tractor seats plus occasional live music make it well worth a stop. The **Laguna Mountain Lodge** (445-2342) has groceries and gifts, plus plain wood-trimmed motel units and cabins with a wood-stove fireplace and kitchenette.

RESTAURANTS

Dudley's Bakery   765-0488
7 mi. W on CA 78 - Santa Ysabel
Dudley's has grown from a boffo boondock baker to an industrial-strength supplier of more than a dozen kinds of bread. Pastries, cookies and pies are also served here, or to go. Closed Mon.-Tues.

★ **The Julian Fondue & Cheesecake**   765-2817
downtown at 1921 Main St.
L-D. Closed Mon.-Thurs.   *Moderate*
Julian's most beguiling gourmet experience is an authentic fondue parlor and Swiss bakery opened in 1993. The fondue, fresh farmer bread, and superb cheesecakes are made here with genuine European know-how. Samples are generously offered of the best breads in the region. Whole loaves and cheesecakes are sold.

The Julian Grille   765-0173
downtown at 2224 Main St.
L-D. No L Thurs. No D Mon.   *Moderate*
Contemporary American dishes are featured in a cottage converted into several homespun little dining rooms.

Julian Pie Company   765-2449
downtown at 2225 Main St.
During the fall harvest, apples star in two-crust, crumb, or sugarless pies, plus cherry-apple crunch, and apple cider. The appealing treats are served in the cottage, in the shade of a big apple tree out back, on a sunny front deck, or as slices or whole pies to go.

Romano's Dodge House   765-1003
downtown at 2718 B St.
L-D. Closed Tues.-Wed.   *Moderate*
Pastas, pizzas and other Italian fare attract a loyal following to a cozy dining room and lounge in a rustic side street cottage.

★ **Ysabel Inn Family Restaurant and Bakery**   765-1366
7 mi. W at 30270 CA 78 - Santa Ysabel
B-L-D.   *Low*
The best breakfast in the San Diego outback features humongous homemade cinnamon rolls and blueberry coffee cake. Later, buffalo burgers and fruit pies star among generous old-fashioned fare that has made this big young coffee shop a family favorite in the foothills.

LODGING

Area lodgings are relatively scarce and uniformly small. Most are rustic reflections of Julian's bucolic background. There are no bargains in summer or on weekends year-round. At other times, prices are usually at least 20% less than those shown.

Julian Hotel   765-0201
downtown at Main & B Sts. (Box 1856) - 92036
The town's century-old landmark hotel has been refurbished. A complimentary full breakfast is served daily to guests. Each tiny, quaint room has some antique furniture. Toll-free: (800)734-5854.
"Honeymoon House"—separate cottage with fireplace, Q bed...$145
    room with private bath—   Q bed...$94
    regular room—shared bath,   2 T or D bed...$82

Julian Lodge   765-1420
downtown at 4th & C Sts. - 92036
This contemporary motel was patterned after a century-old hotel. An expanded Continental breakfast is free to guests. Each comfortably furnished room has antique accents and color TV.
    deluxe room—spacious, refrigerator,   Q bed...$85
    regular room—   Q bed...$72

★ **Orchard Hill Country Inn**   765-1700
downtown at 2502 Washington St. (Box 425) - 92036
Julian's best in-town lodging opened on a hill by downtown in 1994 with nine units surrounded by gardens and pines. A lodge and ten more units were constructed in 1995. A full breakfast and afternoon appetizers and beverages are complimentary. Beautiful American-country decor prevails throughout. Each spacious room has a refrigerator/wet bar, gas fireplace, remote control color TV and VCR.
"Sweet Bough Room"—pvt. garden views, in-bath
    whirlpool shares view of 2-sided gas fireplace with K bed...$138
"Bellflower Room"—loveseat, big in-bath whirlpool, K bed...$138
    regular room—(request "Cortland" for private patio), K bed...$130

★ **Shadow Mountain Ranch**   765-0323
3.4 mi. SW via Pine Hills Rd. at 2771 Frisius Rd. (Box 791) - 92036
Here is one of the Southland's most extraordinary lodgings. Enchanting cabins, decorated with comfortable country furnishings and surrounded by lush gardens and greenery, offer fine views across a pond and meadow to distant mountains. An indoor lap pool, a whirlpool, a well-stocked library, and a pool table are other features. Full breakfast and afternoon tea are complimentary.
"Tree House"—unique contemporary cottage in
    the arms of a giant oak, tranquil private view
    from 3 sides, private toilet, commute to bath,   Q bed...$80
"Gnome's Home"—like a giant tree stump built into a slope,
    a cave leads to a skylit BR with splendid wood handcrafts,
    the rock waterfall shower is a tour-de-force,   Q bed...$90
"Enchanted Cottage"—storybook cabin with fireplace
    and mountain/meadow views from   Q bed...$90
"Grandma's Attic"—wooden bridge leads to upstairs
    room with fireplace and mountain/meadow views, Q bed...$90
    regular room—in main bldg., fireplace, views from Q bed...$80

Villa Idaleen Bed & Breakfast   765-1252
.3 mi. E at 2609 D St. (Box 190) - 92036
A contemporary Victorian replica on a hill above town is now a bed-and-breakfast inn with a (seasonal) swimming pool in a garden. Full breakfast is complimentary. Each attractively decorated room has some antiques and cable color TV.
    regular room—private bath,   Q bed...$85
    regular room—shared bath, (fireplace room add $10), Q bed...$65

Laguna Beach

Laguna Beach is Southern California's pre-eminent seaside artists colony. Resplendent mansions and quaint cottages amidst flamboyant subtropical gardens line bluffs above sandy coves sprinkled along seven miles of photogenic coastline. Inland, luxuriant foliage and sea-view homes cover lower canyons and ridges of hills that rise steeply more than 1,000 feet above the sea. A resort settlement developed here more than a century ago. Artists began arriving soon afterwards drawn by spectacular seascapes and a benign year-round climate.

Today, the city still draws artists and vacationers from all over the world. Many visitors are here to enjoy surfing, swimming, snorkeling and other sports in some of the warmest and clearest ocean water in California. Others are here to relax on the beaches and enjoy breathtaking displays of the latest swimwear. All spend some time downtown—a heavy contender for the Southland's most strollable space, with its vibrant commercial district adjoining an idyllic beach park. The artistry of the residents is apparent everywhere. Outdoors, it is displayed in details of human-scaled architectural craftsmanship; in a superabundance of flowers and carefully tended landscapes; and in memorable public sculptures. Inside handsome buildings, many studios and galleries display first-rate locally handcrafted products and artwork inspired by the setting. Restaurants are plentiful. Many have stunning picture window views while others display culinary talents as compelling as the lovely surroundings. As a final beguilement, Laguna offers more beachfront accommodations than anywhere in Southern California.

Population: 23,170   *Area Code: 714*
Elevation: 25 feet
Location: 49 miles Southeast of Los Angeles
Laguna Beach Chamber of Commerce   494-1018
   downtown at 357 Glenneyre St. - 92651   (800)877-1115

Laguna Beach

V.W.R. *		Jan.	Feb.	Mar.	Apr.	May	June	July	Aug.	Sep.	Oct.	Nov.	Dec.

Great	10
Fine	9
Very Good	8
Good	7
Moderate	6
	5
	4
	3
Adverse	2
	1
	0

	Jan.	Feb.	Mar.	Apr.	May	June	July	Aug.	Sep.	Oct.	Nov.	Dec.
V.W.R. *	6	6	8	9	10	10	10	10	10	10	9	7
Temperature												
Ave. High	64	64	67	68	71	73	76	78	77	73	70	65
Ave. Low	44	45	47	50	53	56	60	60	58	54	49	47
Precipitation												
Inches Rain	2.5	2.6	2.0	1.0	.3	.1	-	-	.2	.6	1.1	2.2
Inches Snow	-	-	-	-	-	-	-	-	-	-	-	-

*V.W.R. = Vokac Weather Rating: probability of mild (warm & dry) weather on any given day.

ATTRACTIONS

★ **Aliso Beach County Park**   567-6206
  2.8 mi. SE on Coast Hwy. (CA 1)
A fishing pier juts into the clear water beyond a mile-long narrow sandy beach. Homes are sequestered in garden settings on steep hills above. Fishing, swimming, body surfing, and sunbathing are popular. Lifeguards, restrooms, showers and a concession are available.

★ **Crescent Bay Point Park**
  1.4 mi. NW at W end of Crescent Bay Dr.
Competition for California's loveliest pocket park must include this luxuriant headland overlooking a sandy beach in a sheltered cove. There are tidepools and rocks to explore at either end; and offshore is Seal Rock—complete with raucous residents. Fans intent on skin diving, swimming, body surfing, fishing, or sunbathing occasionally overcrowd the enchanting setting, especially in summer.

★ **Crystal Cove State Park**   494-3539
  3 mi. NW on Coast Hwy.
The state has provided a three-mile-long park on natural grass terraces between the highway and a narrow sandy beach at the base of sandstone bluffs. Offshore is an underwater preserve popular with snorkelers. Swimming and surfing are also good.

★ **Festival of Arts and Pageant of the Masters**   494-1145
  .4 mi. N at 650 Laguna Canyon Rd.
The Pageant at the Irvine Bowl nightly in July and August has been the city's cultural highlight annually since 1933. In a brilliant blend of art and technical wizardry, local residents dressed as figures from famous paintings and sculptures remain motionless against tableaus that (with the live models) look remarkably like the original artwork. The presentation is enriched by a narrator backed by a full orchestra. It is usually sold out in advance—but ask about cancellations. The adjoining festival showcases works of well over 100 of the best local artisans. Toll-free: (800)487-3378.

The Greeter
.7 mi. SE at jct. of Coast Hwy. & Brooks St.
For many years, until he died in 1975, Eiler Larsen stood by the highway and called his cheerful welcome to arriving visitors and waved goodbye to those leaving. He is now immortalized in a bigger-than-life technicolor sculpture in front of the **Pottery Shack**, itself a landmark since 1936 with an alluring labyrinth of housewares.

★ **Heisler Park**   *497-0706*
downtown west along the coast for .5 mi.
Laguna's most photographed park features subtropical landscaping and meandering walkways along a blufftop punctuated by rocky headlands above tiny white sand coves and colorful tidepools. Beyond are panoramic seascapes. Water in an offshore preserve is often among the West Coast's clearest. Sunbathing, people-watching, fishing, swimming, and skin diving are enjoyed year-round.

Laguna Art Museum   *494-6531*
.3 mi. NW on Coast Hwy. at 307 Cliff Dr.
The county's oldest cultural institution (circa 1918) is now housed in a handsome contemporary building. Exhibits highlight Southern California art since before the turn of the century. Closed Mon.

★ **Main Beach**   *497-0716*
downtown at Coast Hwy. & Broadway
Here is the quintessential California beach scene. Gentle waves lap a white-sand beach backed by a palm-studded lawn with curving pathways, playgrounds, and ball courts. Adjoining the half-mile strand are handsome shops and tree-lined streets of downtown. If major crowds aren't your thing, go on a weekday apart from summer.

★ **Ruby Street Park**
1.5 mi. SE via Coast Hwy. at W end of Diamond St.
Sandy coves indent the base of bluffs in both directions from this pocket park. Some offer tidepools and photogenic rock forms. Others have perfect breaks for body surfing or clear calm water for skin diving. All are more secluded and less crowded than most local beaches.

Sawdust Festival   *494-3030*
.5 mi. N at 935 Laguna Canyon Rd.
Behind a block-long "village" facade, sawdust-covered walkways in a eucalyptus grove lead past a myriad of arts and crafts for sale in an informal setting. Open in July and August, the exhibition has grown since 1966 to include works by hundreds of local artisans.

RESTAURANTS

A La Carte   *497-4927*
1.3 mi. SE at 1915 S. Coast Hwy.
L-D.   *Moderate*
Gourmet picnics can be assembled from an eclectic mix of light contemporary cuisine displayed in this convenient takeout. The cheese rolls made here are especially notable.

★ **Aegean Cafe**   *494-5001*
downtown at 540 S. Coast Hwy.
L-D. Closed Mon. No L Tues.-Thurs.   *Expensive*
Traditional and innovative Greek cuisine has clearly delighted full houses of diners since the restaurant opened in 1991. So have belly dancers and live music nightly in this lively upscale taverna.

Beach House Inn   *494-9707*
.4 mi. SE at 619 Sleepy Hollow Lane
B-L-D. Sun. brunch.   *Expensive*
An appealing selection of contemporary American dishes is offered.
But, the real feature is the lovely beach view from an enclosed plant-
filled patio. "Early Laguna" objects of art and fresh flowers grace
dining areas and a sea-view bar in the oceanside cottage.

Ben Brown's   *499-2663*
2.8 mi. SE at 31106 Coast Hwy. - South Laguna
B-L-D. Sun. brunch.   *Expensive*
Traditional American fare is served at all meals in a country-club-like
restaurant with several dining rooms, a trellis-shaded terrace
overlooking the golf course, and a dark wood-toned lounge.

★ **Cafe Zinc & Market**   *494-6302*
downtown at 350 Ocean Av.
B-L. No L on Mon.   *Moderate*
Raspberry-almond muffins and scones and light egg dishes are notable
morning delights among creative fare (including pizettes for lunch)
that is both delicious and nutritious. Patrons can dine in a tiny,
spotless cafe or on a sidewalk patio bordered by a honeysuckle hedge.
The outdoor dining area is shared by a little market with a big
selection of gourmet foods to go, and tastes of new products.

The Cottage Restaurant   *494-3023*
.3 mi. NW at 308 N. Coast Hwy.
B-L-D.   *Moderate*
Fresh juices, fruits, and many egg dishes enhance an American menu
with some tasty variations like cranberry-orange pancakes. The classic
Laguna cottage with artsy little dining rooms and a garden patio has
been popular for casual dining for many years.

Coyote Grill   *499-4033*
3.3 mi. SE at 31621 S. Coast Hwy.
B-L-D.   *Moderate*
Breakfast features California and Baja creations like beer-batter
banana pancakes, chicken machaca, or green chile and cheese omelet.
Innovative dinners like tequila-cooked chicken or shrimp in beer and
coconut batter are also served in two colorful dining rooms, a bar, or
on an umbrella-shaded deck with a distant ocean view.

★ **Dexter's**   *497-8912*
2 mi. SE at 2892 S. Coast Hwy.
D only. Sun. brunch. Closed Mon.   *Expensive*
Since opening in early 1994, Dexter's has already become one of the
region's favorite sources for truly creative cuisine. Smoked chicken
spinach salad tossed with warm citrus vinaigrette, quail eggs, and
pancetta bacon; or a taco trio of souvlaki lamb, mu shu duck and
Cajun fish typify offerings. All are skillfully prepared in an exposition
kitchen of the sophisticated little bistro.

★ **Dizz's As Is**   *494-5250*
1.9 mi. SE at 2794 S. Coast Hwy.
D only. Closed Mon. except in summer.   *Expensive*
Contemporary American dishes with an emphasis on freshness and
homemade quality (including some unusual desserts) are served in a
clapboard cottage artistically converted into intimate dining rooms and
an island bar. A garden patio shaded by giant ferns adjoins.

★ **Five Feet Restaurant**   *497-4955*
downtown at 328 Glenneyre St.
D only.   *Very Expensive*
"Contemporary Chinese cuisine" served here is some of the most
exciting in California. Lamb, veal, chicken and beef woked with scal-
lions and wild mushrooms in a red wine hoisin sauce, and salmon with
almond herb crust, blackberry merlot sauce and baby leeks, typify the
extraordinary creations. Post-modern decor is similarly distinctive.
Bare wooden rafters, exposed metal ducts, and textured concrete walls
in a high-ceilinged room with a semi-exhibition kitchen may not sound
like much, but it works. So does the greenery and artwork, and flowers
in designer pots on tables with sleek place settings.

★ **Hotel Laguna**   *494-1151*
downtown at 425 S. Coast Hwy.
B-L-D. Sun. brunch.   *Expensive*
Claes' (B-L-D. Sun. brunch. No D Mon.) does justice to a breathtaking
beachfront location. California contemporary dishes with a seafood
emphasis, plus homemade desserts and sorbets, are served in a spiffy
dining room with a panoramic window-wall view of the main beach in
the heart of town. **The Terrace** (L-D) features light grazing fare
inside or on an umbrella-shaded garden patio by the surf. **Le Bar**
offers live entertainment with an ocean view.

★ **Kachina**   *497-5546*
downtown at 222 Forest Av.
D only. Sun. brunch.   *Expensive*
Southwestern-style cuisine gets a New California topspin in dishes
like three-cheese rellano with papaya salsa. Skillfully prepared
flavorful adaptations and appealing post-modern decor touches have
made this a major success since opening in 1989.

★ **Laguna Village Cafe**   *494-6344*
.3 mi. SE at 577 S. Coast Hwy.
B-L-D.   *Moderate*
Tasty light fare is served along with a wide range of beverages
including cool fruit-flavored icy drinks like guava champagne. Fresh
flowers grace picnic-style tables in a courtyard cafe and on a sunny
cliffside terrace with a wondrous view of the coast.

★ **Las Brisas**   *497-5434*
.3 mi. NW at 361 Cliff Dr.
B-L-D. Sun. brunch.   *Expensive*
Traditional and innovative seafoods and other Mexican adaptations
cannot compete with one of the great coastal views in America. The
handsome multilevel restaurant is constantly full of patrons enjoying
a spellbinding panoramic seascape beyond a lavish flower garden and
an umbrella-shaded dining patio.

★ **Mark's**   *494-6711*
.6 mi. SE at 858 S. Coast Hwy.
D only.   *Expensive*
Light, bright New California dishes, including designer pizzas and
pastas, have a new showcase. Consider papaya and brie quesadilla,
mixed baby greens with grapefruit sections, and filet mignon with
roquefort shallot sauce. Luscious desserts like tiramisu and chocolate
souffle are made here. Living palms and flamboyant wall art lend
drama to the whitewashed dining room, lounge and heated deck.

★ **Orange Inn**   *494-6085*
.4 mi. SE at 703 S. Coast Hwy.
   B-L.   *Moderate*
Orange, peach and other seasonally fresh tasty muffins and cinnamon
rolls are made here daily and served to go or at a few tables with fresh
juice (including orange, lemon, and grapefruit squeezed here) and
coffees. Date, banana, fig and other exotic milkshakes are available
later. So are smoothies and sandwiches.

★ **Partners Bistro & Terrace**   *497-4441*
downtown at 448 S. Coast Hwy.
   L-D. No L Sun.   *Expensive*
Creative Continental cuisine includes dishes like chicken en papillote.
Closely spaced tables are set with full linen and fresh flowers in a
dining room with a view of a splendid whale mural across the street.
The upstairs terrace is a posh little greenhouse showcasing a tree.

★ **Romeo Cucina**   *497-6627*
downtown at 249 Broadway
   L-D. No L Mon.   *Expensive*
Italian classics have been updated to emphasize fresh light
ingredients. The trattoria decor is similarly sophisticated with a
woodburning oven with avant garde tile trim, a post-modern heraldic
nude painting, a handsome bar and a covered sidewalk patio.

★ **Senor Lico's Mexican Restaurant & Cantina**   *858-0724*
18 mi. NE at 20722 Rose Canyon Rd.
   L-D.   *Moderate*
Their carnitas, chicken mole and other Mexican classics are among
Orange County's best. If you prefer freshness and subtlety to border-
Mexican heat, this ranch-style roadhouse with colorful wood-trimmed
dining rooms and a cantina in a remote canyon is worth finding.

★ **Sorrento Grille**   *494-8686*
downtown at 370 Glenneyre St.
   D only. Closed Mon.   *Expensive*
Since opening in 1988, New California cuisine has been showcased in
fresh innovative dishes like Dungeness crab-stuffed squash blossoms,
or homemade vanilla bean ice cream. The split-level neo-Spanish-
Colonial restaurant sports an exhibition kitchen and stylish earth-tone
and wood decor.

★ **Surf & Sand Hotel**   *497-4477*
1.1 mi. SE at 1555 S. Coast Hwy.
   B-L-D. Sun. brunch.   *Expensive–Very Expensive*
In **Splashes** (B-L-D. Sun. brunch–Expensive) fusion food stars in
novel dishes like roasted salmon with pistachio crust and champagne
sauce that reflect complex flavors, textures and colors of the freshest
and best seasonal ingredients. The menu changes daily with the
whims of the gifted chef. The firelit dining room lives up to the name
with spiffy Southwestern decor and an intimate sea view. Below is a
romantic lounge with picture windows just over the surf. New
California cuisine is featured in **The Towers Restaurant** (D
only–Very Expensive), a glittering neo art deco aerie perched nine
floors above a beach. Floor-to-ceiling windows, mirror walls, and a
mirrored ceiling in a plush, spacious dining room and adjoining piano
bar (the **Fireside Lounge**) reveal glorious panoramic seascapes. The
ambiance and view are among the most compelling in California.

Ti Amo Ristorante   *499-5350*
3.4 mi. SE at 31727 Coast Hwy. - South Laguna
D only.   *Expensive*
Light and lively Northern Italian cuisine is given a New California
topspin in a dinner house that opened in spring 1994. Complementing
the food is an intimate firelit dining room and a heated garden court.
Tortilla Flats   *494-6588*
1.2 mi. SE at 1740 S. Coast Hwy.
L-D. Sun. brunch.   *Moderate*
Conventional Mexican-style seafoods and other specialties have been
served here for more than forty years. The multiroom extravaganza
includes a jungle of greenery and wealth of Mexican art objects.
★ **Trabuco Oaks Steak House**   *586-0722*
17.7 mi. NE at Trabuco Oaks Dr. & Trabuco Canyon Rd.
D only.   *Moderate*
Cowboy-style steak dinners are featured. Two-pound sirloins, filets,
and other hunks of choice beef are hand-cut, mesquite-broiled and
accompanied by traditional Western fixin's. Rustic little dining rooms
and a bar in the remote roadhouse are festooned with fallout from
management's fetish on snipped ties and business cards.
★ **242 Cafe**   *494-2444*
downtown at 242 N. Coast Hwy.
B-L-D. Closed Tues.   *Moderate*
This classy contemporary charcuterie uses fresh quality ingredients
for innovative dishes. Displays often include strawberry and banana
scones, flavorful pastas, and several kinds of delicious brownies. All
are served at half a dozen high blond-wood tables, and to go.
The White House   *494-8088*
downtown at 340 S. Coast Hwy.
B-L-D.   *Moderate*
Traditional American fare has been served in Laguna's oldest coffee
shop for more than seventy years. Diners have a choice of comfortable
booths or closely spaced tables in a skylit room adjoining a wood-
trimmed firelit bar with live entertainment nightly.

LODGING

Lodgings are not plentiful, but are diverse, including many of the
Southland's scarce oceanfront accommodations. There are no bargains.
Summer weekends are prime time. Summer weekday rates and fall-to-
spring weekend rates are often reduced about 10%, while weekday
rates apart from summer may be reduced another 10%.
★ **Aliso Creek Inn**   *499-2271*
2.8 mi. SE at 31106 Coast Hwy. - South Laguna 92677
Hidden away in a coastal canyon one-third-mile from a beach is a
ranch-style apartment hotel by a luxuriant 9-hole (fee) golf course. The
sprawling complex also includes a large pool in a garden court,
whirlpool, and **Ben Brown's** (see listing). Each well-furnished unit
has a kitchen, private patio or balcony, phone and color TV with
movies. Toll-free: (800)223-3309.
"one-bedroom suite"—1 BR, large pvt. patio,   2 D or Q bed...$128
regular room—studio with private balcony over creek,Q bed...$112

Capri Laguna   *494-6533*
1 mi. SE at 1441 S. Coast Hwy. - 92651
A private staircase leads to the beach at the base of this hillside apartment motel with a courtyard pool and sauna. Each nicely furnished room has a kitchenette, phone and color TV with movies. Toll-free: (800)225-4551.

#101,#102,#103—1 BR, large private
deck with great beach/ocean view,   K bed...$190
regular room—   2 Q or K bed...$115

The Carriage House   *494-8945*
1.3 mi. SE at 1322 Catalina St. - 92651
The ocean is a stroll away from this delightful bed-and-breakfast inn with a tropical garden court. Breakfast and fresh fruit are complimentary. Each of six spacious units is beautifully decorated with antiques and memorabilia, and has a private bath.

"Home Sweet Home"—kitchen, windows on
three sides, calico & gingham extravaganza,   Q bed...$150
regular room—kitchen,   Q or K bed...$125
regular room—   old brass D bed...$95

Hotel Laguna   *494-1151*
downtown at 425 S. Coast Hwy. - 92651
The seventy-room three-story beachfront hotel has been a landmark in the heart of town since 1930. It has been refurbished to include a tropical garden, restaurant and lounge (see listing). Continental breakfast is complimentary. Each compact, nicely furnished room has a phone and color TV with movies. Toll-free in CA: (800)524-2927.

#204—3rd floor, grand corner view of beach/ocean,   Q bed...$130
regular room—view of hills/town,   2 T or D bed...$90

★ **Inn at Laguna Beach**   *497-9722*
downtown at 211 N. Coast Hwy. - 92651
Laguna's best downtown lodging, new for the 1990s, is a three-story motel on a low bluff by the beach. Tropical landscaping surrounds a sheltered pool and whirlpool. Many of the beautifully furnished rooms have private ocean-view balconies. All have a refrigerator/(honor) bar, phone and remote control color TV with movies and VCR. Toll-free: (800)544-4479.

#507,#514—spacious, corner windows, big
private balcony with grand village/ocean view,   2 Q beds...$299
#406,#305—as above,   K bed...$299
regular room—   Q bed...$139

★ **Irvine Suites Hotel**   *380-9888*
8 mi. N (near I-5) at 23192 Lake Center Dr. - Lake Forest 92630
The best all-suites motel inland from Laguna opened in late 1988. The contemporary four-story complex has a large pool and whirlpool in a courtyard. Full breakfast and (on weekdays only) afternoon beverages are complimentary. Each well-furnished two-room suite has a small private balcony, living room with refrigerator/wet bar, microwave, two phones and remote control color TV with pay and free movies and VCR. Toll-free: (800)34-SUITE.

"Tower Suite" (two)—spiral stairs to
loft Q bed, raised whirlpool in view of   K bed...$149
"Executive Suite" (several)—raised whirlpool in view of Q bed...$129
regular room—   2 D or Q bed...$89

Laguna Brisas Spa Hotel - Best Western   *497-7272*
1.1 mi. SE at 1600 S. Coast Hwy. - *92651*
The area's first "spa" motel is a four-story contemporary structure with
an outdoor pool, one block across the highway from a fine ocean beach.
Each compact, well-furnished room has a large in-bath whirlpool,
refrigerator, phone and remote control color TV with movies. Toll-free:
(800)624-4442.

> #305,#306,#307—partial ocean view, private balcony, Q bed...$149
> regular room—by highway, Q bed...$99

★ **Laguna Riviera**   *494-1196*
.6 mi. SE at 825 S. Coast Hwy. - *92651*
This long-established apartment hotel is terraced down a bluff to a
fine sandy beach. Other amenities include an indoor garden pool,
whirlpool and sauna. Each nicely furnished unit has a refrigerator,
phone and color TV with movies. Toll-free: (800)999-2089.

> #201—private balcony and window-wall view
> of beach & ocean, in-bath whirlpool, K bed...$148
> #508—gas fireplace, kitchen, private deck
> & superb three-sided view of beach/ocean, Q bed...$142
> regular room— Q bed...$89

★ **Surf & Sand Hotel**   *497-4477*
1.1 mi. SE at 1555 S. Coast Hwy. - *92651*
Laguna's consummate contemporary resort is a 160-room, nine-story
tower that extends down a bluff to a sandy beach. The newly upgraded
complex is now one of California's quintessential oceanfront hotels.
Amenities include a large well-landscaped ocean-view pool, gourmet
restaurants and lounges (see listing), (pay) valet parking, and
specialty shops. Each spacious, beautifully furnished room has a
balcony, stocked (honor) bar/ refrigerator, phone, and remote control
color TV with movies. Toll-free: (800)524-8621.

> #280,#270,#260,#250,#240—in-bath whirlpool,
> corner windows & sliding glass door to private
> balcony, nonpareil oceanfront views, K bed...$295
> "one bedroom penthouse" (2 of these)—1 BR, separate
> parlor with fireplace, in-bath whirlpool, large
> private balcony with great pool/ocean view from K bed...$475
> #224,#234—in-bath whirlpool, intimate surf view, K bed...$240
> regular room—private ocean-view balcony, 2 Q or K bed...$215
> regular room—shared balcony, partial ocean view, K bed...$200

★ **Vacation Village**   *494-8566*
.4 mi. SE at 647 S. Coast Hwy. - *92651*
One of Laguna's largest and finest on-the-beach resorts is a five-story,
130-room complex with a wide range of modern lodgings, plus two
landscaped pools, a whirlpool and the **Beach House Inn** (see listing).
Each well-furnished room has a phone and color TV with movies. Toll-
free: (800)843-6895.

> #115,#112,#109—kitchenette, corner window wall &
> sliding glass door to large pvt. balc. with
> awesome beachfront view shared by K bed...$205
> "The Reef" (12 of these)—refr., floor-to-ceiling sliding
> glass door to pvt. balc. with fine beachfront view, K bed...$145
> regular room—studio apartment with kitchenette, T & Q bed...$95
> regular room—hotel room by street, 2 D beds...$80

Lake Arrowhead

Lake Arrowhead is a popular lakeside village in the pines. Although less than two hours from the coast by car, it is a mile above sea level in a luxuriant pine forest along the shore of a little reservoir. While development started a century ago, the dam and village weren't completed until the 1920s. A spire-top dance pavilion from those days is now the centerpiece for an alpine-style shipping complex that opened in 1981. The tiny downtown also includes several family-oriented restaurants, privately controlled beach and dock facilities, and a resort hotel.

Population: 6,539   *Area Code: 909*
Elevation: *5,150 feet*   *Lodging Info: (800)550-5253*
Location: *82 miles Northeast of Los Angeles*
Lake Arrowhead Communities Chamber of Commerce   *337-3715*
   downtown at Lake Arrowhead Village Building F-280 (Box 155) - 92352

WEATHER PROFILE

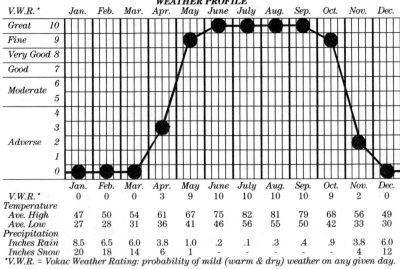

V.W.R. *		Jan.	Feb.	Mar.	Apr.	May	June	July	Aug.	Sep.	Oct.	Nov.	Dec.
Great	10												
Fine	9												
Very Good	8												
Good	7												
Moderate	6 / 5												
	4 / 3												
Adverse	2 / 1												
	0												

	Jan.	Feb.	Mar.	Apr.	May	June	July	Aug.	Sep.	Oct.	Nov.	Dec.
V.W.R. *	0	0	0	3	9	10	10	10	10	9	2	0
Temperature												
Ave. High	47	50	54	61	67	75	82	81	79	68	56	49
Ave. Low	27	28	31	36	41	46	56	55	50	42	33	30
Precipitation												
Inches Rain	8.5	6.5	6.0	3.8	1.0	.2	.1	.3	.4	.9	3.8	6.0
Inches Snow	20	18	14	6	1	-	-	-	-	-	4	12

V.W.R. = Vokac Weather Rating: probability of mild (warm & dry) weather on any given day.

ATTRACTIONS

★ **Boat Rentals**
Three area reservoirs are boating destinations. Only Silverwood Lake (the largest) allows private boats, but each has a marina with rentals.
Lake Arrowhead Marina *downtown at 870 Hwy. 173* 337-2553
Lake Gregory Regional Park *8 mi. W on Lake Dr.* 338-2233
Silverwood Lake Marina *19 mi. NW on Cleghorn Rd.* 389-2320
Boat Ride
Arrowhead Queen *336-6992*
downtown on waterfront at Lower Village
View the alpine scenery aboard a sixty-passenger paddlewheeler. On the hour each afternoon, 50-minute tours are offered daily in summer and on weekends (weather permitting) the rest of the year.
★ **Ice Castle** *33-SKATE*
1.4 mi. W at 27307 Hwy. 189 near North Bay Rd. - Blue Jay
This Olympic-sized covered ice rink has a special feature. It is open to a lush pine forest on three sides. Rentals, warming area, pro shop, snacks and public sessions are offered daily year-round.
★ **Lake Arrowhead and the Village**
downtown
Southern California's prettiest lake is surrounded by a dense pine forest and exclusive homes one mile above sea level in the mountains. The 740-acre reservoir is private, but you can rent boats (see listing) and swim off a (fee) beach with lifeguards by the South Shore Marina. Nearby, an alpine-style shopping complex is at the heart of the village.
★ **Lake Gregory** *338-2233*
8 mi. W via CA 189 at 24171 Lake Dr. - Lake Gregory
Pine-shaded slopes surround a tiny 86-acre mile-long reservoir with a (fee) swimming beach backed by two 300-foot-long waterslides. You can fish from shore, or from small rental boats (see listing).
★ **Santa's Village** *337-2481*
2.2 mi. SE on CA 18 - Skyforest
Kids love this Santa-themed park with a puppet theater; monorail, pony and train rides; and other amusements; plus toy and gift shops, and eateries in gingerbread houses. Open daily in summer and mid-Nov. through Dec. (weekends at other times). Closed Mar.-late May.
★ **Silverwood Lake Recreation Area** *389-2303*
19 mi. NW via CA 189 on CA 138
Swimming is popular in summer (there are lifeguards) at this 1,000-acre reservoir in the foothills. So are fishing (trout, panfish); boating (see listing); sailing; and waterskiing. Miles of hiking trails and bike paths have been provided, and there is a complete campground.

RESTAURANTS

★ **Antlers Inn** *337-4020*
4.6 mi. SW at 26125 Hwy. 189 - Twin Peaks
L-D. No L Sun.-Thurs. *Moderate*
Buffalo burgers and chili highlight Old Western grub showcased in a perfect setting—a massive turn-of-the-century log lodge with a great stone fireplace and a couple of trophy-antlered elk heads presiding over all-wood decor right down to the armchairs. Reopened in 1993, the fully restored landmark is once again a mealtime mother lode.

The Chef's Inn and Tavern   *336-4487*
2 mi. E at 29020 Oak Terrace - Cedar Glen
L-D. Sun. brunch. Closed Mon.   *Moderate*
A thoughtful selection of Continental and American dishes is served
in several small rooms outfitted with eclectic antiques in a building
dating back to Victorian times when it was a logger's bordello.
Downstairs is a rustic Old West barroom.

The Cliffhanger Restaurant   *338-3806*
5.8 mi. SW at 25187 Hwy. 18
L-D.   *Expensive*
The American and international fare is okay. But, the panorama of
mountains and basins beyond a window wall around the big casual
dining room and adjoining lounge is astounding.

La Casita   *338-6488*
8 mi. W at 633 Forest Shade Dr. - Lake Gregory Village
L-D. Closed Mon.-Tues. No L Sat.-Wed.   *Low*
Steak picados is the house specialty among California-style Mexican
dishes served in a cozy cottage with a fireplace and sundeck.

Lake Arrowhead Resort   *336-1511*
downtown in Lake Arrowhead Village
B-L-D. Sun. brunch.   *Moderate–Expensive*
Beau Rivage (D only. Sun. brunch–Expensive) offers New American
cuisine in a posh, romantic lakeside restaurant. The **Lobby Cafe** (B-
L–Moderate) offers family fare, while the **Lakeview Lounge** is a
nightclub with live entertainment on weekends.

★ **The Royal Oak**   *337-6018*
2 mi. W at 27187 Hwy. 189 - Blue Jay
D only. Sun. brunch.   *Expensive*
Continental and American cuisine is skillfully prepared in one of the
area's most popular dinner houses. The wood-trimmed dining room
provides a choice of plush highback armchairs or booths, and tables
are set with linen, flowers and candles. A cozy lounge adjoins.

LODGING

Both lakes (Arrowhead and Gregory) feature an appealing lodging by
the water, and a few others tucked away in nearby forests. None are
bargains. Summer is prime time, along with weekends year-round.
Most places reduce their rates by at least 20% at other times.

★ **Chateau Du Lac Bed & Breakfast Inn**   *337-6488*
3 mi. NE via CA 173 at 911 Hospital Rd. (Box 1098) - 92352
One of the mountain's most romantic bed-and-breakfasts crowns a
bluff overlooking Lake Arrowhead. Handsome public rooms with fine
lake and forest views are used for complimentary full breakfast and
afternoon tea. The Tower view room and the library are other special
places for all guests. Each of six beautifully decorated guest rooms has
a phone and color TV with remote control.

"Lakeview Room"—large private balcony and
whirlpool tub with grand lake views, spacious
bedroom with gas fireplace in view of   Q bed...$250
"Loft Room"—private bath with
whirlpool, gas fireplace,   Q bed...$195
#4—window seats, private bath with whirlpool,   Q bed...$185
regular room—shared bath,   Q bed...$95

★ **Lake Arrowhead Resort**   *336-1511*
   downtown in Lake Arrowhead Village (Box 1699) - 92352
The area's largest and most complete lodging is a conference/resort hotel on a sylvan slope by the lake. The contemporary alpine chalet has 261 units, a private beach and dock, a big view pool, whirlpools, and (for a fee) a complete fitness club and two lighted tennis courts, plus restaurants and a nightclub (see listing), and a gift shop. Each beautifully furnished unit has a stocked (honor) bar, phone and remote control color TV with pay movies. Toll-free in CA: (800)800-6792.
   #356,#256—extra-large 1 BR corner; LR/DR w. gas f'place;
      wet bar/refr.; wraparound view balc.; in-bath whirlpool;
      grand lake view & raised gas fireplace visible from K bed...$399
   #770,#774,#780,#784—big 1 BR, wet bar/refr.,
      in-bath whirlpool, private balcony with grand
      lake view, raised marble gas fireplace in view of   K bed...$279
   regular room—pine view,   2 D or K bed...$159

North Shore Motel   *338-5230*
   8 mi. W at 24202 Lake Dr. (Box 3057) - Crestline 92325
Lake Gregory is 100 yards from this newer chalet-style motel. Each attractive, spacious unit has a private balcony with a fine lake/mountain view and color TV. Toll-free: (800)300-5230.
   #8—lake view on 2 sides, raised stone fireplace by   K bed...$70
   #9—1 BR suite, kitchen, stone fireplace, big view deck, K bed...$95
   regular room—   K bed...$52

Saddleback Inn - Arrowhead   *336-3571*
   downtown at 300 S. CA 173 (Box 1890) - 92352
This elaborate little lodge-and-cottages complex in the pines has a restaurant and lounge. Each attractive unit has a bath, refrigerator, phone, and remote control color TV. Toll-free: (800)858-3334.
   "inn double" or "cottage suite"—stone (gas)
      fireplace, in-bath whirlpool,   Q or K bed...$140
   regular room—   Q or K bed...$110

★ **Storybook Inn - Bed & Breakfast**   *336-1483*
   2 mi. SE at 28717 Hwy. 18 (Box 362) - Sky Forest 92385
The high country's most dramatic bed-and-breakfast is on the rim of a mountain overlooking much of Southern California. A big older home has been transformed to include a valley-view whirlpool and ten rustic comfortable units, each with a private bath. Full breakfast, and wine, appetizers and dessert in the evening are complimentary.
   cabin—big 2 BR, 2 baths, loft, kitchen, fireplace,
      private deck with barbeque and awesome view, D & K bed...$200
   #4—wet bar, solarium, superb tree & panoramic view,   2 Q beds...$175
   regular room—   D bed...$98

Willow Creek Inn   *336-2008*
   4 mi. N via CA 173 at 1176 N. CA 173 (Box 479) - 92352
The mountain's most immaculate bed-and-breakfast opened in 1991 in a forest near the lake. Public rooms including an exercise/game room, and four beautiful guest rooms, are furnished with heirloom antiques and a wealth of memorabilia. Full breakfast and afternoon appetizers and beverages are complimentary. Toll-free: (800)241-0354..
   "Honeymoon Suite"—pvt. entrance, pvt. deck, double
      powder-blue whirlpool in elegant bathroom,   Q bed...$185
   regular room—   Q bed...$105

Long Beach

Long Beach is California's reborn coastal metropolis. Southern California's third largest city sprawls for miles along a broad sandy beach. Development began in the 1870s. The pace quickened after a colossal oil boom in the 1920s, but by the 1960s, the fabled coastline had become a tattered eyesore. In 1975, multibillion-dollar redevelopment of the waterfront began.

The renaissance continues in full bloom. Fountains, sculptures, and gardens surround dramatic skyscrapers and hotels downtown. The splendid beach is backed by manicured parks and promenades. Major tourist attractions, plus convention and entertainment facilities line the waterfront. Offshore, several surrealistic islands disguise oil derricks with palms and other distractions. Specialty shopping complexes and gourmet restaurants are proliferating. And—Long Beach has become the gourmet breakfast capital of the Southland.

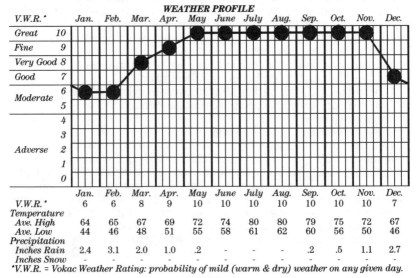

WEATHER PROFILE

V.W.R.*		Jan.	Feb.	Mar.	Apr.	May	June	July	Aug.	Sep.	Oct.	Nov.	Dec.
Great	10												
Fine	9												
Very Good	8												
Good	7												
Moderate	6 5												
	4												
	3												
Adverse	2												
	1												
	0												

	Jan.	Feb.	Mar.	Apr.	May	June	July	Aug.	Sep.	Oct.	Nov.	Dec.
V.W.R.*	6	6	8	9	10	10	10	10	10	10	10	7
Temperature												
Ave. High	64	65	67	69	72	74	80	80	79	75	72	67
Ave. Low	44	46	48	51	55	58	61	62	60	56	50	46
Precipitation												
Inches Rain	2.4	3.1	2.0	1.0	.2	-	-	-	.2	.5	1.1	2.7
Inches Snow	-	-	-	-	-	-	-	-	-	-	-	-

*V.W.R. = Vokac Weather Rating: probability of mild (warm & dry) weather on any given day.

Population: 429,321   Area Code: 310
Elevation: 32 feet
Location: 24 mi. South of Los Angeles
Long Beach Convention & Visitors Council 436-3645 (800)4-LB-STAY
    downtown at One World Trade Center, Suite 300 - 90831

ATTRACTIONS

★ **Alamitos Bay Beach**   594-0951
  3.8 mi. E along Ocean Blvd.
Saltwater swimming and windsurfing are excellent off a small bayside strand sheltered from the ocean by a long narrow peninsula. Sunbathers have a fine view of Naples across the lovely little bay.

★ **Belmont Pier**   434-6781
  2.5 mi. E via Ocean Blvd. at 39th Pl.
This quarter-mile-long pier gives strollers views of the shoreline, nearby surreal "oil islands," and a miles-long walking and bike path along the beach. A bait shop and tackle rental serves anglers. Onshore is **Belmont Plaza Olympic Pool**.

★ *Bicycling*
  Belmont Heights Cyclery *2 mi. E at 3350 E. Broadway 434-4991*
Flat terrain, picturesque neighborhoods and a separated bikeway on the beach make Long Beach a choice locale for easy touring. Bicycles can be rented by the hour or longer.

★ **The Gondola Getaway**   433-9595
  3.8 mi. E at 5437 E. Ocean Blvd.
For a relaxing and romantic respite, a one-hour cruise in a gondola rowed Venetian-style through the picturesque waterways of Naples Island can't be beat. Bring your own bottle to accompany the ice bucket, glasses, appetizers, and Italian music they'll supply. Sunset cruises are especially popular. For this California classic, reservations are necessary.

★ *Harbor Cruises*
Harbor cruises get close to the palm-clad "oil islands," and whale watching excursions depart daily in winter. Contact:
  Shoreline Village Cruises   495-5884

★ **Long Beach City Beach**
  .5 mi. E between 1st & 72nd Pls.
The city's namesake is a broad silver strand that extends for more than four miles eastward from downtown. It's all inside the Long Beach Breakwater. There isn't much surf, so swimming is safe. Nearby, several tiny manmade islands conceal oil drilling apparatus behind elaborate landscaping and surreal structures. Picnic areas, concessions, lifeguards, and restrooms are available.

★ **Long Beach Convention and Entertainment Center**   436-3661
  downtown at 300 E. Ocean Blvd.
Following major expansion completed in 1994, Long Beach has one of the West's best complexes for public gatherings, including a convention/exhibition center (tripled in size in 1994), a sports arena (with the world's largest mural), concert hall and traditional theater. Ballet, opera, symphonies, and live theater performed by professional resident companies share the busy calendar with everything from rock concerts and road shows to rodeos.

Long Beach Museum of Art   *439-2119*
1.5 mi. E at 2300 E. Ocean Blvd.
A 1912 mansion on a bluff by the sea is the setting for a notable collection of permanent and changing contemporary art exhibitions, while landscaped grounds showcase modern sculpture. The carriage house serves as a museum store. Closed Mon.-Tues.

★ **Naples Island**
4 mi. E via Ocean Blvd. & Livingston Dr. on 2nd St.
During the early years of this century, a half-square-mile community was developed on an island dredged from Alamitos Bay. Today, the upscale neighborhood captures the spirit of its namesake. Whimsical footbridges span narrow canals. Picturesque homes and gardens line curving streets. A walkway along the island's perimeter overlooks the bay and marina, and connects nicely landscaped pocket parks. While its true charm is best enjoyed on foot, you can access the island by car via a bridge at either end of 2nd Street. This main thoroughfare is a delightful melange of specialty shops and distinctive restaurants.

The Promenade
downtown from 3rd St. to the bay
A seven-block-long stone walkway gives pedestrians access between glittering post-modern skyscrapers in the heart of downtown and a subtropically landscaped waterfront park and Shoreline Village.

★ **Queen Mary**   *435-3511*
1.7 mi. S via Queensway Bridge at E end of Queens Hwy.
Easily the biggest attraction in Long Beach is the Queen Mary. The largest passenger liner still afloat is permanently moored in the bay. The majestic ship includes a unique hotel (see listing), restaurants and lounges (see listing), convention facilities, and specialty shops. A tour is a must, with facilities refurbished to their original 1930s art deco splendor. In addition to posh salons, staterooms, and officers' quarters, you'll see the bridge, engine room, and an enormous propeller, plus museum exhibits and model ships.

Rancho Los Alamitos   *431-3541*
6 mi. E via 7th St. at 6400 Bixby Hill Rd.
An adobe ranch house, enlarged several times since it was built in 1806, has been restored and furnished with antiques. Visitors can take a free guided tour of the adobe, outbuildings, and a garden of native California succulents. Closed Mon.-Tues.

★ **Seal Beach**
6 mi. SE via CA 1 at S end of Main St. - Seal Beach
Tucked between jetties at the mouths of the San Gabriel River and Anaheim Bay is a mile-long strand of fine sand. A pier that bisects the broad beach is a popular promenade with terrific views of surfers and sunbathers. In addition to fishing from the pier and jetties, there is swimming and some of the area's best surfing. Lifeguards, restrooms, picnic areas and snack bars are available. Inland the pier becomes Main Street, a colorful collection of shops and eateries.

Shoreline Village
.4 mi. S via Pine Av. at 407 Shoreline Dr.
A turn-of-the-century Western coastal village is the theme of this popular bayside complex. Specialty shops, water-view restaurants, both in-lounge and outdoor live entertainment venues and an antique carousel are interconnected by brick walkways.

★ *Sportfishing*

Long Beach is home port to several sportfishing charters. You can troll for halibut, bass, and more during trips of various lengths. Whale watching trips are regularly scheduled in winter. Contact:

Belmont Pier Sportfishing *Ocean Blvd. / 39th Pl.* 434-6781
Long Beach Sportfishing *555 Pico Av.* 432-8993

RESTAURANTS

Andiamo 435-1225
5.2 mi. E at 6509 E. Pacific Coast Hwy.- Marketplace Shopping Ctr.
L-D. No L Sat. & Sun. Expensive
Contemporary Italian dishes including cannolis and other desserts made here are served in a smart dining room by a heated garden patio overlooking a pond. A new clone is downtown.

August Moon 493-2377
5.2 mi. E at 6417 E. Pacific Coast Hwy.- Marketplace Shopping Ctr.
L-D. Moderate
Tea-smoked duck and asparagus beef suggest the appealing variety of Mandarin and Szechwan specialties served in several dining areas with glass-topped tables and contemporary Chinese decor.

Belmont Brewing Company 443-3891
2.5 mi. E at 25 39th Pl.
B-L-D. No B Mon.-Fri. Moderate
Contemporary California classics accompany an assortment of brews made here in giant kettles and served at blondwood tables amidst greenery in the dining room and bar. The umbrella-shaded dining patio abutting the hike/bike path and beach competes for the best place in Long Beach to enjoy shoreline scenery up-close.

★ **Brogino's** 434-4479
4.5 mi. E at 5760 E. 2nd St. - Naples Island
D only. Moderate
Italian cuisine is skillfully prepared in veal, chicken and seafood dishes, and in fresh-made pasta for cannelloni and a wide range of pizzas. Even the cannolis are made here. Full linen contributes to the appeal of the cozy wood-toned dining rooms.

★ **Buon Gusto** 439-5096
3.8 mi. E at 5316 E. 2nd St. - Belmont Shore
6.3 mi. NE at 5755 E. Pacific Coast Hwy. (498-1135)
L-D. Moderate
The humongous calzone customized to your choice of fillings is peerless. Pizza is also made fresh daily with homemade dough and sauce, and there are flavorful homemade pastas and a fine assortment of veal and chicken dishes. A larger and similarly lively new clone is on Pacific Coast Highway.

★ **Cafe Piccolo** 438-1316
2.3 mi. E at 3222 E. Broadway
L-D. No L Sat. & Sun. Moderate
Italian cuisine is given a delightful New California topspin in dishes like sauteed chicken in raspberry sauce with chambord and spicy shrimp in cucumber-mint dressing. A loyal local following often causes a wait for the cozy congested dining room or the glass-enclosed courtyard with lush greenery.

Cannon's   *436-2247*
1.2 mi. S at 600 Queensway Dr.
L-D. Sun. brunch. Closed Mon.   *Expensive*
Updated American standards accompany one of the city's better soup-and-salad bars. The large split-level restaurant offers cushy seating and a window-wall view of the harbor and skyline.

★ **Dominick's East Village**   *437-0626*
downtown at 555 E. Ocean Blvd.
L-D. No L Sat. & Sun.   *Expensive*
Most of the fare in this 1994 addition to the culinary scene is Italian, but there are also prime steaks. Generous portions of carefully prepared dishes (many available family-platter-style) are served at tables set with linen in spacious dining areas with lots of polished hardwoods and a well-played grand piano.

Grandma's Sugarplums   *439-3363*
3.5 mi. E at 4908 E. 2nd St. - Belmont Shore
The suicide cake and the angel food torte are as humongous as they are decadent. The cakes, cheesecakes, brownies and candies brought in daily from their inland shop make this a "must" destination for anyone with a sweet tooth.

★ **Hotel Queen Mary**   *432-6964*
1.7 mi. S at 1126 Queensway Hwy.
B-L-D. Sun. brunch.   *Moderate–Very Expensive*
Sir Winston's (L-D. No L Sat. & Sun.–Very Expensive) features French classics in an informally elegant dining room with a splendid skyline view. The Sunday brunch served in the **Grand Salon** (Expensive) is worth a special trip to experience the largest fine dining salon ever built on a ship. Lavish art deco murals and other decor touches have been lovingly maintained. The **Chelsea** (D only–Expensive) for seafood and the **Promenade Cafe** (L-D–Moderate) also offer fine harbor views, as does the **Observation Bar**, a great place to top off an evening with live music in a snazzy art deco setting.

★ **Hyatt Regency Long Beach**   *491-1234*
downtown at 200 S. Pine Av.
B-L-D. Sun. brunch.   *Moderate–Expensive*
The Beacon (L-D. No L Sat. Sun. brunch–Expensive) features New California cuisine showcased in dishes like venison medallions marinated in cabernet with dried cherries and mushrooms. The namesake light is centered at one end of a large split-level plush dining room/lounge with the city's best window-wall view of the Queen Mary and shoreline park. The **Emerald Cafe** (B-L-D–Moderate) is a California-contemporary coffee shop with a fine view. The **Lobby Bar** offers posh armchairs with a waterfront view and a baby grand piano.

★ **Jongewaard's Bake 'n Broil**   *595-0396*
4 mi. N at 3697 Atlantic Av.
B-L-D.   *Moderate*
Consistent freshness and homestyle quality are hallmarks of one of Southern California's best coffee shops. Everything is made here daily, from the cinnamon rolls, muffins and coffee cake, through the peach/pineapple jam, to the seasonal fruit pies. Careful attention to details is also apparent in the cheerful decor of dining rooms with padded booths, chairs, or counter, fresh flowers, and tantalizing displays of luscious baked goods.

★ **Kelly's**   *433-4983*
4.4 mi. E at 5716 E. 2nd St. - Naples Island
D only.   *Expensive*
For more than a third of a century, Kelly's has been pleasing patrons
with an outstanding array of prime rib, steaks and chops. Now there
is even more. Fresh seafood is included on a menu that changes daily
with splendid dishes like whitefish with a pecan mustard crust, or
warm scallop salad. For dessert, the creme brule is a knockout. Posh
booths, warm wood tones and live greenery and flowers distinguish a
refined dining room tastefully separated from the handsome and
popular bar in one of the Southland's great dinner houses.

Kinda Lahaina Broiler   *596-3864*
6.2 mi. E at 901 Ocean Av. & Main St. - Seal Beach
B-L-D.   *Moderate*
For an unusual morning delight, take a pass on the American
standards and try the banana-nut pancakes with coconut syrup served
in a wood-trimmed bar, cafe and patio by the pier and beach.

★ **L'Opera Ristorante**   *491-0066*
downtown at 101 Pine Av.
L-D. No L Sat. & Sun.   *Expensive*
Updated Italian classics prepared with fresh quality ingredients
distinguish one of the city's loveliest restaurants. The sophisticated
redo of a large historic building has picture windows overlooking the
main walking street downtown, heraldic paintings, floral sprays, live
greenery and contempo lighting, plus a dramatic bar.

The Library - A Coffee House   *433-2393*
2.5 mi. E at 3418 E. Broadway
B-L-D.   *Moderate*
Different coffees can be enjoyed with assorted muffins, fruit and nut
bars and other light fare in rooms decorated with hundreds of books
and an appealing array of overstuffed old furniture.

★ **Long Beach Hilton**   *983-3400*
.5 mi. W at Two World Trade Center
B-L-D. Sun. brunch.   *Expensive*
Ascari (B-L-D. Sun. brunch) features contemporary California and
Italian fare. Full linen enhances the light and lively decor. At **City
Grill** (L only. Closed Sat.-Sun.) contemporary fare is served in a big
snazzy dining pub with a sunny dining patio. Lush vegetation and
overstuffed furnishings lend appeal to the **Lobby Bar.**

★ **Morry's of Naples**   *433-0405*
4.5 mi. E at 5764 E. 2nd St. - Naples Island
One of the finest selections of premium California wines in the state
is the hallmark of a gastronomic showplace that's been here since
1938. A cozy wine tasting bar is in back. Gourmet deli items and gift
baskets round out the selection.

★ **Mum's**   *437-7700*
downtown at 144 Pine Av.
L-D.   *Expensive*
A classic California grazing menu can be topped off with a variety of
fresh and flavorful desserts made here. The large split-level dining
room is surrounded by a mesquite grill, exhibition kitchen, sleek bar,
a wealth of colorful contemporary art and live plants. Flowers grace
each table. There is also a sidewalk cafe and occasional live music.

Long Beach
Naples Rib Company   *439-7427*
4.5 mi. E at 5800 E. 2nd St. - Naples Island
D only.   *Moderate*
The barbecued baby back ribs and other meats are first-rate. So are
supporting dishes like cornbread served in wood-trimmed split-level
dining rooms and a bar with half a dozen tap beers.
★ **Omelette Inn**   *437-5625*
downtown at 108 W. 3rd St.
B-L-D. No D Sun.-Thurs.   *Moderate*
Downtown's best bet for breakfast lives up to its namesake with a vast
selection of first-rate omelets accompanied by assorted tasty muffins
made here, and fresh juices. The cheerful coffee shop with a gallery of
paintings and historic photos opened in 1992.
Panama Joe's   *434-7417*
3.6 mi. E at 5100 E. 2nd St. - Belmont Shore
L-D.   *Moderate*
Contemporary Mexican fare is popular, but the real appeal is in the
capacious wood-toned barroom with its multitude of stained-glass
lampshades, greenery, and a resplendent backbar.
★ **Papaluccis Ristorante**   *434-4454*
3.4 mi. E at 4611 E. 2nd St. - Belmont Shore
L-D.   *Moderate*
Fresh flavorful Southern Italian dishes include unusual pizzas and
pastas. There are also some terrific specialties topped by "Supremo
Bread"—pizza dough stuffed with mortadella, salami, pepperoni,
cheeses and bell peppers baked with poppy seeds. The cozy congested
dining room is deservedly popular.
★ **Park Pantry**   *434-0451*
1.6 mi. E at 2104 E. Broadway
B-L-D.   *Moderate*
Cinnamon twists, sticky buns, banana-macadamia muffins and a
wealth of other morning glories, plus first-rate fruit and cream pies are
coupled with California classics made with tender loving care and
fresh quality ingredients. Padded chairs and booths surround polished
hardwood tables set with fresh flowers. The large dining areas offer
picture window views of floral borders and a park.
Pine Avenue Fish House   *432-7463*
downtown at 100 W. Broadway
B-L-D. No B Mon.-Fri.   *Expensive*
Seafood is emphasized among contemporary California fare served in
an attractively restored older building with San Francisco style decor.
★ **The Pizza Place & Garden Cafe**   *432-6000*
1.2 mi. E at 1431 E. Broadway
L-D.   *Moderate*
Tender thick-crust pizza with delicious toppings along with eight
chicken specialties and assorted pastas highlight a cheerful little
parlor outfitted with greenery and flowers. Heat lamps warm a garden
patio that is a sensory delight when the honeysuckle is in bloom.
★ **The Potholder Cafe**   *433-9305*
2.7 mi. E at 3700 E. Broadway
B-L.   *Low*
Hearty helpings of classic California breakfast fare are served amidst
beach/funky decor at a counter or in dining rooms with padded booths
in one of the natives' favorite breakfast places.

★ **Ruth's Country Kitchen**   *494-1763*
3.5 mi. NE at 3720 E. Anaheim St.
B-L.   *Low*
Omelets and scramblers highlight an appealing selection of American
and Mexican favorites. Everything is carefully prepared from scratch
in this comfortable cheerful little coffee shop.

★ **Shenandoah Cafe**   *434-3469*
3.4 mi. E at 4722 E. 2nd St. - Belmont Shore
D only.   *Moderate*
Southern regional dishes start with homemade apple fritters, and
range from Florida beer-battered shrimp thru Louisiana seafood
gumbo to Texas-fired chicken in this folksy, venerable dinner house.

★ **Simon & Seafort's**   *435-2333*
.8 mi. W at 340 Golden Shore Dr.
L-D. No L Sat. & Sun.   *Moderate*
Seasonal fresh seafood stars on a menu of traditional and innovative
American regional cuisine, along with staples like baked crab and
artichoke heart appetizer, housemade rosemary pan bread, luscious
key lime pie, and ten premium tap beers. Polished hardwood
armchairs, posh booths, live greenery and many paintings lend
sophistication to a capacious split-level dining room with a fine harbor
view. The lounge has a grazing menu and city view.

★ **Sweet Jill's**   *438-4945*
3.7 mi. E at 5224 E. 2nd St. - Belmont Shore
B-L-D.   *Moderate*
They really live up to their name here in giant cinnamon rolls and
sticky buns, apple and cherry coffee cakes, macadamia nut chocolate
brownies, fruit cobbler, and outrageously decadent cakes. Coffees,
Italian sodas, fresh lemonade and frappes round out the delights
served at several tables or to go.

★ **Yankee Doodles**   *439-9777*
2.5 mi. E at 4100 E. Ocean Blvd.
L-D.   *Moderate*
Southern California's most complete sports and recreation hall
features a sea of pool tables, ping pong, foozball, air hockey, darts,
shuffleboard, and pinball games. A couple of bars and lots of tables
overlook the frenetic fun, and pizza and American bar chow are served.

LODGING

The ongoing renaissance has added several major hotels overlooking
the vibrant waterfront. Rates vary little year-round.

Golden Sails Hotel - Best Western   *596-1631*
5.7 mi. E at 6285 E. Pacific Coast Hwy. - 90803
A marina backwater adjoins this 175-room four-story hotel with a
landscaped courtyard pool, whirlpool, restaurant and entertainment
lounge. Each nicely furnished room has a balcony or patio,
refrigerator, phone and remote control color TV with movies. Toll-free:
(800)762-5333.

#145,#137,#141—spacious, whirlpool in view of   K bed...$130
regular room—   2 Q or K bed...$100

Holiday Inn - Convention & World Trade Center   *435-8511*
downtown at 500 E. 1st St. - 90802
This newly renovated 220-room hotel is close to the Convention
Center, and has a courtyard pool, saunas, coffee shop and lounge. In

the nine-story tower, each nicely refurbished room has a floor-to-ceiling sliding glass door to a tiny balcony, two phones and color TV with movies and remote-control. Toll-free: (800)HOLIDAY.

#926,#924,#922—fine view of
Queen Mary & harbor from   K bed...$99
regular room—   2 Q or K bed...$84

★ **Hotel Queen Mary**   *432-6964*
  1.7 mi. S at 1126 Queensway Hwy. (Box 8) - 90801
The largest and one of the most luxurious passenger ships ever built is berthed in a choice site overlooking downtown Long Beach and the inner harbor. The ship, with refurbished art deco fixtures, now includes 365 rooms, fine dining (see listing), a coffee shop, lounge with music for dancing, a tour and museum, plus gift shops. Each compact stateroom includes a private bath, phone and color TV with (fee) movies. Toll-free: (800)437-2934.

"Royalty Staterooms"—original "first class"
cabin, polished wood & metal, 2 portholes,   2 T or K bed...$160
regular room—Starboard (harbor view),   2 T or K bed...$130
regular room—Portside, (no original furnishings), 2 T or K bed...$90

★ **Hyatt Regency Long Beach**   *491-1234*
  downtown at 200 S. Pine Av. - 90802
Hyatt's sixteen-story complex is a 531-room convention-oriented hotel adjacent to both the harbor and Convention Center. The post-modern landmark is surrounded by ponds and luxuriant tropical greenery. Amenities include a well-landscaped pool and whirlpool, exercise room, gourmet dining (see listing), entertainment, and a gift shop. Each beautifully furnished room has a stocked (honor) bar, phone and color TV with movies. Toll-free: (800)233-1234.

#1706,#1606,#1701,#1601—corner windows on top floors
with grand beach/city/harbor panorama from   K bed...$189
"Regency Club"—comp. light breakfast, appetizers &
beverages, request harbor side for fine view, 2 D or K bed...$189
regular room—request 12th & 14th floor
harbor side,   2 D or K bed...$164

Long Beach Airport Marriott   *425-5210*
  6 mi. NE (near I-405) at 4700 Airport Plaza Dr. - 90815
The largest (311 rooms) and finest hotel near the Long Beach Airport is a convention-oriented eight-story complex with an indoor pool, a large pool in a tropical courtyard with waterfalls, whirlpool, saunas, exercise room, restaurant, coffee shop, and entertainment lounge. Each well-decorated room has a phone and remote control color TV with movies. Toll-free: (800)321-5642.

#724,#702—corner window, fine mountain view,   K bed...$129
"Concierge Floor"—extra amenities,   2 D or K bed...$139
regular room—request 8th floor golf course side
for quiet, airport side to watch planes land, 2 D or K bed...$129

★ **Long Beach Hilton**   *983-3400*
  .5 mi. W at Two World Trade Center
The city's newest lodging landmark is a modernistic fifteen-story 398-room complex with a rooftop pool and whirlpool, steam room and (fee) fitness center, bicycles, valet parking, plus gourmet dining (see listing) and entertainment, and a gift shop. Each beautifully furnished room

Long Beach

has an (honor) bar, two phones, and remote control color TV with pay and free movies. Toll-free: (800)HILTONS.

#1515,#1513—balcony, fine ocean view,	K bed...$170
regular room—	K bed...$160

★ **Long Beach Renaissance Hotel**   *437-5900*
downtown at 111 E. Ocean Blvd. - 90802
The Convention Center and harbor are walking distance from this post-modern twelve-story hotel. The 374-room convention-oriented complex has a rooftop landscaped pool, whirlpool and exercise room, plus a gourmet dining room, coffee shop, deli, entertainment lounge, plush lobby piano bar, gift shop, and (pay) parking. Each beautifully decorated room has a stocked (honor) bar, phone, and remote control color TV with movies. Toll-free: (800)228-9898.

"Renaissance Club"—11th & 12th floors,	
extra amenities, request harbor side,	2 D or K bed...$140
regular room "Deluxe"—high floors, bay view,	2 D or K bed...$125
regular room—lower floors,	K bed...$95

Marriott Residence Inn   *595-0909*
5.2 mi. NE (by I-405) at 4111 E. Willow St. - 90815
Long Beach Airport is near this all-suites motor hotel with two outdoor pools and two whirlpools. A light breakfast and afternoon drinks are complimentary. Each spacious, well-furnished suite has a kitchen, two phones and remote control color TV with movies and VCR. Toll-free: (800)331-3131.

"Penthouse Suite" (many)—fireplace, 2 baths,	loft Q bed...$145
regular room—studio, (request fireplace),	Q bed...$119

★ **Sheraton Long Beach**   *436-3000*
downtown at 333 E. Ocean Blvd. - 90802
The Convention Center and harbor are across the street from this convention-oriented fifteen-story hotel. The curved post-modern complex opened in 1988 with 460 rooms above a capacious atrium lobby and interior gardens, a large landscaped pool and whirlpool, exercise room, restaurant, coffee shop, lobby lounge, nightclub, gift shop, and (pay) parking. Each beautifully furnished room has a stocked (honor) refrigerator, phone and remote control color TV with free and pay movies. Toll-free: (800)325-3535.

regular room—request 16th thru 12th	
floors for fine city/harbor views,	2 D or K bed...$165
regular room—city view from lower floors,	2 D or K bed...$139

★ **Travelodge Hotel Resort & Marina**   *435-7676*
1.4 mi. S at 700 Queensway Dr. - 90802
An idyllic setting in a lush shoreline park by the harbor is the major feature of this five-story, 200-room conference hotel. In addition to splendid views across the water to downtown and the nearby Queen Mary, there is a garden pool, boat dock, two lighted tennis courts, a waterfront restaurant and lounge, and gift shop. Each comfortable room has a phone and color TV with free and pay movies. Toll-free: (800)255-3050.

#504,#404,#304—spacious, sliding glass door to	
big pvt. balc. with grand view of harbor/city,	K bed...$89
regular room—request 5th & 4th floor	
harborside for fine views,	2 Q or K bed...$89

Los Angeles

Los Angeles is one of the world's most celebrated cities. The West's largest (and America's second largest) metropolis sprawls across 460 square miles of floodplains and foothills from the Pacific Ocean to the San Gabriel Mountains. Several cities (like Beverly Hills) are completely engulfed by the potpourri of communities (Hollywood, Bel Air, etc.) that comprise Los Angeles. All are linked by a vast system of freeways. The dramatic setting is complemented by a mild subtropical climate. Flowery landscapes flourish and outdoor activities are enjoyed year-round, notwithstanding some of the nation's worst smog.

"El Pueblo de Nuestra Senora la Reina de Los Angeles" (town of our lady the queen of the angels) was established by a tiny band of Spanish soldiers, friars, and families from nearby Mission San Gabriel in 1781. Seventy years later, there were only 1,600 residents. The population didn't reach 100,000 until 1900. Shortly afterward, however, the new "movie" industry began to centralize here. Coupled with tourism and a phenomenal oil boom, the city's population exploded—to almost two million by 1950. Among the half dozen cities that were America's largest at mid-century, only LA is larger today. This is true in spite of the cataclysmic riot, fire storms, earthquake, and floods that beset the city in recent years.

The tallest skyscraper in the West opened in 1990, crowning a downtown skyline that finally belies the notion of a lot of communities, but no heart of town. Moreover, Los Angeles still lives up to its billing as the cinema capital of the world. Artists of all kinds, and even larger numbers who aspire to stardom, continue to contribute to the city's unsurpassed creative vitality. The combination of fresh local produce year-round and an influx of talented chefs from all over the world has made LA the quintessential source of New California cuisine, and home to some of the world's great restaurants. Lodgings are similarly diverse and increasingly cosmopolitan, ranging from exquisitely rehabilitated historic hotels to grand luxe post-modern architectural showplaces. The variety and numbers of urban diversions are remarkable. Cultural and amusement complexes, historic sites, museums, golf courses, parks and beaches, plus several urbane business districts assure something for every whim and wallet.

Los Angeles

Population: 3,485,398	Area Codes:	primary: 213
Elevation: 320 feet	parts of:	310 & 818
Location: Southern Coastal California		

Greater Los Angeles Visitors & Convention Bureau   624-7300
downtown at 515 Figueroa St. - 90071

WEATHER PROFILE

V.W.R.*		Jan.	Feb.	Mar.	Apr.	May	June	July	Aug.	Sep.	Oct.	Nov.	Dec.
Great	10												
Fine	9												
Very Good	8												
Good	7												
Moderate	6 / 5												
	4												
	3												
Adverse	2												
	1												
	0												

	Jan.	Feb.	Mar.	Apr.	May	June	July	Aug.	Sep.	Oct.	Nov.	Dec.
V.W.R.*	6	6	7	10	10	10	8	8	8	10	10	7
Temperature												
Ave. High	65	66	68	70	73	76	83	84	83	77	74	67
Ave. Low	45	46	48	51	54	57	61	61	60	56	49	46
Precipitation												
Inches Rain	3.0	3.1	3.1	1.1	.3	-	-	-	.2	.5	1.3	2.9
Inches Snow	-	-	-	-	-	-	-	-	-	-	-	-

*V.W.R. = Vokac Weather Rating: probability of mild (warm & dry) weather on any given day.

ATTRACTIONS

★ *Bicycling*

Many miles of separated and designated bikeways interconnect the sprawling metropolis. Nearly everyone's favorite route parallels the beach through Venice. For rentals in Venice, contact:

Skatey's Sports Inc.   102 Washington St.   (310)823-7971
Venice Pier Bike Shop   21 Washington St.   (310)823-1528

★ **Bradbury Building**   500-2291
downtown at 304 S. Broadway

In 1893 a silver magnate commissioned an extraordinary five-story brick office building. Behind the inconspicuous facade of LA's oldest restored historic landmark, a glass-canopied roof filters light into a multilevel court. Open corridors and stairways are embellished with wood paneling, brick and polished stone, ornamental grillwork, and see-through metal-cage elevators.

★ **Cabrillo Beach**   (310)548-7562
25 mi. S at 3720 Stephen M. White Dr. - San Pedro

The San Pedro Breakwater and a fishing pier subdivide a half-mile-long beach between calm water in the harbor and ocean surf. On the bluff above, majestic Moreton Bay fig trees shades **Point Fermin Park**. At **Cabrillo Beach Marine Museum**, sea life is imaginatively presented in aquariums, interpretive displays, and tidepool tours. The delightful free museum is closed Mondays.

★ **California Museum of Science and Industry**   744-7400
3 mi. SW at 700 State Dr. in Exposition Park

One of LA's best free museums offers innovative hands-on exhibits that get visitors involved with computers, health, communications, energy, geography, and other aspects of contemporary culture. The Aerospace Building, dedicated to the history of manned flight, displays historic aircraft and a recently used space capsule. In the IMAX Theater, high-tech films are shown on a huge screen. Science-related crafts, toys and books are sold in a first-rate gift shop.

★ **Chinatown**
1 mi. NE around Broadway/Alpine
Chinese have been here for well over a century, but "New Chinatown" (with its themed entrance gate and pagoda) only dates back to 1938. Fresh produce markets, Oriental restaurants, import shops, and frequent festivals make the compact district a visitors' favorite. It also serves as a cultural center for well over 100,000 Orientals who now live throughout the Los Angeles basin.

★ **Civic Center**
.5 mi. NE between Grand, 1st, Spring St. & US 101
City, county, state and federal offices are all clustered into one of the nation's largest government centers. **City Hall** became the first true skyscraper in Southern California when the distinctive 454-foot landmark was completed in 1928. Across Spring Street, the **Los Angeles Mall** is a multilevel complex of shops, restaurants, and a landscaped plaza with a triforium—high-tech music and light presentations. The **Music Center**, at the other end of the complex, is the city's premier performing arts center, with four theaters sized for performances ranging from grand opera to intimate drama. Sweeping lawns, subtropical trees, gardens, fountains, and sculpture surround the monumental buildings.

Dockweiler State Beach
16 mi. SW at W end of Culver Blvd.
A broad sandy beach extends for four miles south from Marina Del Rey. Unfortunately, it's backed by the runways of Los Angeles International Airport and a huge sewage treatment plant. It's seldom crowded, even though the waves are right for surfing and swimming, and there are plenty of picnic, play, and parking areas.

★ **El Pueblo de Los Angeles Historic Monument**   *628-1274*
1 mi. NE at 622 N. Main St.
The original pueblo was founded here in 1781, and some historical landmarks have been restored. **The Plaza**, a small park with century-old Moreton Bay fig trees and an ornate hexagonal bandshell, is the scene of several annual fiestas. **Olvera Street** is a block-long re-creation of a Mexican street market lined with sidewalk vendors, restaurants, cantinas, and shops selling Mexican foods, drinks, and handicrafts. **Avila Adobe** is the city's oldest (1818) house. The restored single-level structure is now a free museum, furnished as it was during the Mexican era (closed Mon.). The **Old Plaza Catholic Church** was completed in 1822. Substantially modified over the years, the restored building is still in use. Nearby, the **Pico House** was built by Pio Pico (the last Mexican governor of California) in 1870. The partially restored three-story building was once the region's finest hotel. The **Masonic Temple** (1884) has been restored and outfitted with free historical exhibits. **Sepulveda House**, a partially restored 1887 boarding house, now serves as the **Visitor Center** (closed Sun.).

118

★ **Exposition Park**   *747-7111*
3 mi. SW along Figueroa St. S of Exposition Blvd.
Several of LA's major recreational and cultural facilities lie within a
big park adjoining the University of Southern California. The **Los
Angeles Memorial Coliseum** (damaged by a recent earthquake) is
the home field for the USC football teams. The 92,000-seat stadium
was the focal point of both the 1932 and 1984 Olympics. Next door, the
16,000-seat **Sports Arena** hosts indoor sports and entertainment
events. The **Los Angeles Swimming Stadium** hosts water sports
competitions. It is open daily year-round. The sunken **Rose Garden**
has almost 200 varieties. The **California Museum of Science and
Industry** and the **Natural History Museum of Los Angeles
County** (see listings) are the park's top cultural attractions.

★ **Farmer's Market**   *933-9211*
7 mi. W at 6333 W. 3rd St. & Fairfax Av.
From humble origins as a farmer's co-op during the Depression, the
site has grown into a maze of market stalls, food stands, restaurants,
and shops featuring fresh produce and gourmet goodies from around
the world. Exotic sights, smells, touches and tastes delight the senses
of huge crowds who arrive daily year-round to browse, shop and eat.
Try **The Gumbo Pot** (B-L–Low) for New Orleans specialties like
beignets, or **Kokomo** (B-L–Moderate) for unusual breakfasts like
turkey hash or three-grain molasses flapjacks.

★ **Forest Lawn Memorial Park**   *254-3131*
6 mi. N at 1712 S. Glendale Av. - Glendale
America's most talked-about cemetery covers half a square mile. It is
a superbly landscaped resting place where fans can pay their respects
at the graves of Hollywood legends–if they can find them. (Staff never
disclose exact locations.) Only real flowers are allowed. Major bronzes
and large marble reproductions of famous statuary were crowned by
a dazzling copy of Michelangelo's "David" until the 1994 earthquake
destroyed it. (It will be replaced.) Nearby are a stained glass version
of Da Vinci's "The Last Supper," and gigantic paintings of the
"Crucifixion" and the "Resurrection." **Forest Lawn Memorial Park -
Hollywood Hills** (9 mi. NW at 6300 Forest Lawn Dr.) is
distinguished by the "Birth of Liberty," America's largest historical
mosaic (with more than ten million pieces of Venetian glass);
"Abraham Lincoln," a sixteen-foot bronze by Augustus Saint-Gaudens;
and a sixty-foot bronze and marble Washington Memorial. Visitors are
welcomed in both of the remarkable free attractions.

Frederick's of Hollywood   *466-8506*
7 mi. NW at 6608 Hollywood Blvd. - Hollywood
LA's most provocative museum occupies the back of a lavender-colored
building full of libidinous lingerie. On display are the foundation
finery of famous females from Mae West through Madonna.

★ **Gene Autry Western Heritage Museum**   *667-2000*
7.5 mi. N (by I-5) at 4700 Western Heritage Way
A long-held dream of the famed Western star became a reality in 1988.
The expansive facility in Griffith Park is a blend of California
architectural styles with one of the most comprehensive collections of
Western Americana anywhere. Fine art by Charles Russell, Frederic
Remington, Albert Bierstadt and others are among permanent

collections along with historic firearms, vehicles, equipment, clothing, and furnishings. In addition to the "real" West, the West of the imagination is depicted in extensive permanent and changing exhibits of Autry's and other's films, recordings, and videos. A museum theater, special effects theater, library, cafe, and Western specialty store are other aspects of a museum that is already one of America's half dozen leaders in the field of Western history. Closed Mon.

Grand Central Public Market   *624-2378*
downtown at 317 S. Broadway
This cavernous fresh food bazaar is a long-established landmark, albeit with the feeling of a Mexican marketplace in recent years. Hoards of cost-conscious shoppers swarm a labyrinth of fruit and vegetable stalls, butcher shops, fresh fish markets, bakeries, fast foods and juice stands. It's frenzied fun for the senses.

★ **Griffith Observatory and Planetarium**   *664-1191*
7 mi. NW at 2800 E. Observatory Av.
An Observatory, planetarium and scientific museum crown a knoll overlooking the city in Griffith Park. You can use the small refracting telescope for free on clear nights in the refurbished observatory. All major celestial phenomena visible to the naked eye are reproduced in the Planetarium theater. Mankind's relationship with outer space is examined through participatory exhibits in the Hall of Science. Closed Mon. except summer.

★ **Griffith Park**   *665-5188*
6 mi. NW at 4730 Crystal Springs Dr.
One of America's largest city parks sprawls across more than 4,000 acres of flatlands, canyons and hills topping out at Mt. Hollywood (elev. 1,625 feet). A visitor center has free road and trail maps and information about the park. Undeveloped rugged highlands have more than fifty miles of hiking and horseback riding trails. Recreation facilities include four golf courses; tennis courts; an Olympic-sized swimming pool; ball fields; an antique carousel; and playgrounds. The best picnic areas are at **Fern Dell**—a spring-fed stream lined with native and exotic ferns, and at the **Bird Sanctuary**—ponds and a stream in a picturesque little canyon. At **Travel Town** is a Victorian railroad station, a free transportation museum, and a tiny train pulled by a miniature steam locomotive. The famed **Greek Theatre** offers a wide range of musical programs from June into October in a natural amphitheater. The **Griffith Observatory and Planetarium** and **Los Angeles Zoo** (see listings) are also here.

Hollyhock House   *662-7272*
5 mi. NW at 4800 Hollywood Blvd. - Hollywood
Frank Lloyd Wright's first Los Angeles house was completed in 1921 in what is now Barnsdall Park. The city has restored it, including original Wright furnishings, and offers guided tours. Closed Mon.

★ **Hollywood Bowl**   *850-2000*
7 mi. NW (near US 101) at 2301 N. Highland Av. - Hollywood
A natural amphitheater in the foothills plays host to nearly 18,000 people at summer concerts by the LA Philharmonic, and performances by renowned visiting artists. The **Hollywood Studio Museum** is nearby in the restored barn where Cecil B. De Mille shot "The Squaw Man"—the first feature-length Hollywood movie. Early films, gear, and star memorabilia are displayed, and there is a related gift shop.

Los Angeles

★ **J. Paul Getty Museum** *(310)458-2003*
19 mi. W at 17985 Pacific Coast Hwy.
A re-creation of a palatial Roman villa houses the world's most richly endowed art museum, thanks to the multibillion-dollar Getty bequest. Extraordinary permanent collections feature Greek and Roman antiquities and pre-twentieth-century Western European paintings, sculpture, decorative art, and illuminated manuscripts. Formal gardens surround the imposing free museum, which also has an excellent book-and-gift store and a lunch room. Parking reservations are required. Closed Mondays and holidays. (A monumental new Getty museum is currently under construction crowning a hill overlooking the LA basin from Brentwood.)

★ **La Brea Tar Pits** *936-2230*
6 mi. NW at 5801 Wilshire Blvd. in Hancock Park
One of the world's greatest sources of ice age fossils are these tar ("la brea" in Spanish) pits. Innumerable prehistoric animals, plants and reptiles became trapped and preserved in the sticky beds. Continuing excavations have yielded hundreds of thousands of specimens since work began near the turn of the century. A free viewing area and observation pit display how specimens appeared when found, and there are dramatic life-size statues of some of the huge beasts. The **George C. Page La Brea Discoveries Museum** features color murals and reconstructed life-size skeletons of saber-toothed tigers, horses, wolves and other animals that roamed the area thousands of years ago. Documentary films describe the site's evolution. Visitors can watch ongoing work with fossils. In the most arresting high-tech display, holograms give flesh to the bones of a woman and a tiger found here. Equally effective is a hands-on demonstration of how sticky tar is. There is also a fine gift shop.

★ **Little Tokyo** *680-3361*
.8 mi. E around 1st & Main Sts.
Since 1970, Little Tokyo has emerged as the focal point of one of the largest Japanese communities outside Japan. First settled a century ago, the district now includes the **New Otani Hotel** (see listing), specialty shopping complexes, dozens of restaurants, a cultural and community center, galleries, theaters, temples and gardens.

★ **Los Angeles County Museum of Art** *857-6000*
6 mi. W at 5905 Wilshire Blvd.
One of America's great art collections is housed in five buildings. The **Ahmanson Building** houses permanent (and some changing) collections of international art through the ages in galleries around an atrium. Major changing exhibits are shown in the **Hammer Building**, while the **Anderson Building** (1986) is a great wedge of limestone and glass-brick well-suited to displays of twentieth century paintings and sculpture. The **Bing Center** has a theater for concerts, lectures, and films. The **Pavilion for Japanese Art** opened in 1988 as a showcase for renowned Japanese artworks. Meals are served in the indoor/outdoor **Plaza Cafe**, and quality art and gifts are sold in an excellent museum store. Closed Mon.-Tues.

★ **Los Angeles Zoo** *666-4090*
7.5 mi. NW at 5333 Zoo Dr.
One of America's biggest and best zoos covers eighty landscaped acres

in Griffith Park. Dozens of endangered mammals, birds and reptiles are included among over 2,000 creatures. Animals are grouped into five Continental areas. They live in naturalistic habitats separated from visitors by surrounding moats. Several koalas and white tigers star among rare species. The Children's Zoo, Animal Nursery, camel and elephant rides, animal shows, tram rides and food concessions are other features.

★ **Mann's Chinese Theater**   *464-8111*
   6.5 mi. NW at 6925 Hollywood Blvd. - Hollywood
Hollywood's most famous landmark is a well-preserved movie theater that resembles a fanciful Chinese pagoda. The forecourt is renowned for its collection of concrete impressions of the hand- and footprints of movie stars. The world's first gala movie premiere with celebrities and searchlights took place here in 1927.

★ **Museum of Contemporary Art**   *626-6222*
   downtown at 250 S. Grand Av.
A striking Post-Modern building, the first in America by famed Japanese architect Arata Isozaki, opened in 1986. Galleries around a sunken courtyard provide a fitting showcase for a major collection of international post-war artworks. The au courant complex also has a stylish cafe and shop, plus an intimate theater. Closed Mon.

★ **Natural History Museum of Los Angeles County**   *744-3466*
   3 mi. SW at 900 Exposition Blvd.
Exposition Park has been the site of one of America's largest treasuries of antiquities for three-quarters of a century. The mammoth Spanish Renaissance building has more than thirty halls and galleries. Permanent exhibits include detailed habitats for exotic animals, plus extensive displays of mammals, birds, insects, and marine life. Dinosaurs and other extinct creatures are also presented, along with outstanding collections of cut gems and minerals. Halls of history depict 400 years of life in California, American life from Colonial times through 1914, and pre-Columbian cultures. The Discovery Center features hands-on artifacts. Other facilities include a bookstore, specialty shops and a cafeteria. Closed Mon.

★ **Ports O'Call Village**   *(310)831-0287*
   24 mi. S via I-110 E of Front & 9th Sts. - San Pedro
In the region's first themed shopping complex, buildings recalling early California and nineteenth century New England share a nautical setting by the main channel of Los Angeles Harbor. Cobblestone streets lead to waterfront restaurants and a lively assortment of specialty shops featuring regional and imported arts, crafts, and gifts. Sportfishing and cruises of any length can be arranged at:
   Eurosail Boat Rentals *(310)831-2363*
   Los Angeles Harbor Cruise *(310)831-0996*
   Los Angeles Harbor Sportfishing *(310)547-9916*
   Scenic Drive

★ **Mulholland Drive**
   8 mi. NW via US 101 (Hollywood Fwy.)
Breathtaking panoramas of the entire LA basin, and close-up glimpses of elegant aeries of the rich and famous, reward sightseers who take this road that hugs the crest of the Santa Monica Mountains for fifty miles between the Hollywood Freeway and the ocean.

Los Angeles

★ **Six Flags Magic Mountain**   *(805)255-4111*
35 mi. NW via I-5 at 26101 Magic Mountain Pkwy. - Valencia
Some of the world's fastest and most exhilarating rides highlight more than 100 features in this prodigious amusement park. Luxuriant vegetation covers the hilly 260-acre fun-factory, and softens scary headliners like "Batman - the Ride"—a suspended looping mega-tech theme coaster; "Viper"—a metal coaster with an initial drop of nearly 200 feet followed by vertical loops, corkscrews and a boomerang turn; "Colossus"—the highest and fastest dual-track wooden roller coaster in the world; "Shock Wave"—the first stand-up looping roller coaster; and "Revolution" with its giant 360° vertical loop. Then (not for the fainthearted) there is a "Free Fall," (the world's first) where you can simulate a leap from a ten-story building—and live to tell about it. For a wet-and-wild time, "Roaring Rapids" is an exciting whitewater raft ride, while "Log Jammer" puts you up a creek without a paddle in a hollowed-out log that goes down the mountain in America's largest waterflume. In "Tidal Wave," you'll get drenched in a wall of water. For a more sedate overview, an elevator goes nearly 400 feet to the observation deck of the "Sky Tower." "Bugs Bunny World" features Looney Tunes characters and kids' rides, and there is an animal farm and petting zoo. "Spillikin Junction" resembles a pioneer village where artisans demonstrate and sell their crafts. Live music, water shows, and name entertainment are also presented daily. Food is abundant, ranging from fast-food stands to view restaurants. Open daily in summer, and on weekends and holidays the rest of the year.

Television Studio Tours

★ **NBC Television Studios**   *(818)840-4444*
10 mi. NW at 3000 W. Alameda Av. - Burbank
The "Tonight Show" starring Jay Leno is filmed in Studio 1 of America's largest complex of color TV facilities. It's part of a 90-minute guided backstage tour that also includes a sound and special effects center; huge prop warehouse; wardrobe department; and an opportunity to see yourself on camera. Free tickets are available for standby seating for TV shows by writing well in advance.

★ **Universal Studios**   *(818)508-9600*
10 mi. NW at 100 Universal City Plaza - Universal City
The world's largest motion picture and television studio is the best place to see Hollywood in action. In 1993, "Back to the Future" opened. The most expensive amusement ride ever created offers a new generation of thrills (and an unforgettable introduction to "virtual reality") through eye-filling cinema, surround-sound, hypertech seating, and a show with real mass appeal. Witty, well-informed guides escort visitors on a two-hour tram and walking tour of much of the 420-acre complex where movies and television series are in continuous production. Visitors experience the parting of the Red Sea; survive an avalanche, a collapsing bridge, a flash flood, and an encounter with a runaway train; get attacked by Jaws; meet face-to-face a thirty-foot-tall King Kong; get trapped in a blazing inferno in "Backdraft"—and more. You'll also get to visit a star's dressing room, participate in demonstrations of special effects, see costumes and props, and glimpse hundreds of outdoor sets including a New England village; ancient European town; the streets of New York; and a frontier settlement. After the tram ride, visitors should allow several more

hours for a self-guided tour of the Entertainment Center. Five live action shows are presented throughout the day; a western Stunt Show; Animal Actors Theater; Comedy Screen Test Theater (where you might be filmed as an extra and watch the instant replay); the Adventures of Conan (a sword and sorcery extravaganza complete with fire-breathing dragon); and the Miami Vice Action Spectacular (with all sorts of thrilling stunts, pyrotechnics and special effects). As an added attraction, The Incredible Hulk, The Phantom of the Opera, and other talented star look-alikes roam the grounds. There are also plenty of refreshment stands and gift shops. Next door is **Universal City Walk**, an elaborate new Hollywood-themed shopping and enter-tainment promenade with whimsical architecture, live performers and an array of casual dining and gift emporiums. Open daily year-round.

★ **University of California, Los Angeles (UCLA)**   *(310)825-4321*
11 mi. NW at 405 Hilgard Av. - Westwood
More than 35,000 students give UCLA the largest enrollment of any University of California campus. The 411-acre site in the foothills above Westwood opened in 1929. Today, the parklike campus has nearly 100 buildings in a wealth of architectural styles. **Royce Hall**, one of the original 1929 brick buildings (designed in Romanesque style) presents concerts by famed performers year-round. Nearby, an imposing rotunda and staircase grace another original building, **Pavell Library**, the main undergraduate library for one of the world's largest book collections. **Dickson Art Center** includes changing exhibits of historic and modern artworks. In front is a sculpture garden with outstanding twentieth century works by Moore, Miro, and others. The centrally located **Ackerman Student Union** has a wealth of restaurants, recreation and leisure areas, and shops, including a huge bookstore. **Pauley Pavilion** seats 13,000 for basketball and other indoor games. The **Mildred Mathias Botanical Gardens** fill an eight acre canyon with a superb collection of native trees, subtropical and exotic plants. The **Visitor Center** has information, maps and schedules of sports and cultural events.

★ **University of Southern California (USC)**   *740-2311*
2.5 mi. SW at Exposition Blvd. & Figueroa St.
The West's largest independent university was founded in 1880. Today, more than 27,000 students are enrolled on a landscaped 150-acre campus surrounded by problematic neighborhoods. USC's first building, an 1880 clapboard, now serves as the **Widney Alumni House**. Furnished with period antiques, it is the state's second oldest school building. The **Norris Cinema Theater** is part of a state-of-the-art production center endowed by George Lucas and Steven Spielberg, alumni of the oldest film studies program. Drama is offered year-round at **Bing Theater**. The (1984) **Olympic Swimming Stadium** and the **Tennis Stadium** host major competitions. **University Art Galleries** present (free) rotating exhibits.

★ **Venice**
16 mi. SW at W end of Washington St. - Venice
LA's flamboyant coastal community borders the ocean for three miles north of the entrance channel to Marina Del Rey. A broad sandy beach paralleled by the region's most notorious promenade is a kaleidoscopic meeting place for a prodigious potpourri of people of all persuasions. Lifeguards, picnic and play areas line the sand, while funky shops,

food stalls and restaurants line the walkway. Swimming and surfing are popular, as is fishing from Venice Pier.

★ ***Walking Districts***
   Hollywood Boulevard *6.5 mi. NW around Hollywood Blvd. / Vine*
   Melrose Avenue *7.5 mi. NW around Melrose & Fairfax Avs.*
   Westwood Village *11 mi. W around Westwood Blvd. & Weyburn*
The world's most auto-oriented city has three unique commercial districts with real pedestrian appeal. **Hollywood** still boasts movie palaces, hotels and other vestiges from when this was the heart of the movie colony. In spite of elaborate new street furniture and lighting, and major developments and restorations, it has a seamy edge. Vibrant wall murals; pink marble stars embedded in the sidewalk ("Walk of Fame"); shops displaying sexy bikinis, lingerie, and makeup; and wacky tourist attractions are worth a light-hearted look. Native passers-by can be notably outlandish, too. **Melrose Avenue** is LA at its trendiest. Radical fashion shops, galleries and design stores are interspersed with many of the city's au courant eateries. You may have to park blocks away on evenings and weekends. **Westwood Village** is a dynamic extension of UCLA with an abundance of specialty shops, eateries, and first-run movie theaters on tree-shaded streets.

★ **Watts Towers** *847-4646*
   10 mi. S at 1727 E. 107th St.
Over a thirty-three-year period from 1921 to 1954, Simon Rodia worked alone to create the quintessential masterpiece of American folk art. Web-like spires made of salvaged steel rods and pipes covered with cement rise as much as 107 feet above the yard. A myriad of seashells and bits of bottles, tiles, and plates embellish the conical creations. Public access is limited, but upper portions of the towering treasures are visible from the adjoining art center. Closed Mon.

Wells Fargo History Museum *253-7166*
   downtown at 333 S. Grand Av.
Wells Fargo Bank was founded in 1852 and grew up with the West. This free tribute to the rambunctious history of the region and the bank features a two-pound gold nugget, a stagecoach, and other nineteenth century relics, maps, and photos. Closed Sat.-Sun.

★ **Will Rogers State Beach** *(310)394-3266*
   17 mi. W along Pacific Coast Hwy.
Swimming and surfing are popular beyond a wide sandy beach that parallels a huge parking lot and the highway for nearly three miles.

★ **Will Rogers State Historic Park** *(310)454-8212*
   16 mi. NW at 1501 Will Rogers State Park Rd. - Pacific Palisades
Will Rogers' home during the 1920s and 1930s is now a museum filled with the cowboy-humorist's possessions. Nearby is a visitor center with a short film and a gift shop. Matches are still played on Rogers' polo field on weekends. Riding and hiking trails extend into the mountains of adjoining Topanga State Park.

Winery
   San Antonio Winery/Maddalena Vineyard *223-1401*
   2.5 mi. NE at 737 Lamar St.
Los Angeles' oldest winery still produces many (primarily bulk) wines. You can take a free self-guided tour and visit the picnic area, restaurant, and gift shop. The tasting room is open daily.

RESTAURANTS

The Apple Pan   *475-3585*
10.5 mi. W at 10801 W. Pico Blvd. - West Los Angeles
L-D. Closed Mon.   *Low*
A couple of burgers plus a few sandwiches can be topped off with pies
baked here. That's it. Since 1947, simple fare quickly prepared with
quality ingredients has made this plastic-and-paper diner with a
horseshoe counter a timeless favorite of fast food fans.

★ **Art's Delicatessen & Restaurant**   *(818)762-1221*
11 mi. NW at 12224 Ventura Blvd. - Studio City
B-L-D.   *Expensive*
Art's is back. LA's best deli is bigger (and maybe better) than ever. It
was reborn quickly after being destroyed in the 1994 earthquake.
Housemade pastries, bread, and meats once again fill display cases,
and the deli sandwiches are still "works of art."

★ **Authentic Cafe**   *939-4626*
6.8 mi. W at 7605 Beverly Blvd.
L-D.   *Moderate*
Blue corn chile rellano, chicken dumplings with cilantro sauce, or
designer pizzas and pastas are possibilities among New Southwestern
and New California cuisines available in one of LA's most hip
hideaways. A nondescript storefront marks the entrance to the tiny,
ever-crowded cafe backed by a bustling exhibition kitchen.

★ **Bel Age (Wyndham) Hotel**   *(310)854-1111*
10 mi. NW at 1020 N. San Vicente Blvd. - West Hollywood
B-L-D. Sun. brunch.   *Very Expensive–Extremely Expensive*
Diaghilev Restaurant (D only. Closed Sun.-Mon.–Extremely
Expensive), Southern California's premier source of "New Russian"
cuisine, features dishes like sturgeon fillet with caviar, and other
masterful adaptations. Haute cuisine, from the selection of caviars and
Russian appetizers to exquisite pastries made here, is presented in an
opulent, romantic setting, replete with splendid wall hangings and
museum-quality art objects. Nearby is a luxurious contemporary
lounge. **La Brasserie** (B-L-D. Sun. brunch–Very Expensive), one of
the plushest and prettiest coffee shop/lounges in the city, offers first-
rate New California cuisine.

★ **The Biltmore Los Angeles**   *624-1011*
downtown at 506 S. Grand Av.
B-L-tea-D.   *Expensive–Extremely Expensive*
Bernard's (L-D. No L Sat. Closed Sun.–Extremely Expensive), the
hotel's flagship restaurant, formally presents New California cuisine
expertly prepared with seasonally fresh quality ingredients in a split-
level dining room where a harpist contributes to tranquil wood-
panelled elegance. **Sai Sai** (L-D. No L Sat. & Sun.–Very Expensive),
a beautifully rendered Tokyo transplant, features a full range of
superb Japanese classics in an exquisite contemporary setting,
including many private dining areas. **Rendezvous Court** (L-tea. No
L Sat. & Sun.–Expensive) is a grandiose hall with spectacular
entryways, a vaulted ceiling festooned with raised relief murals, and
a fountain centered on the marble floor. Museum-quality furniture and
art, and a grand piano amidst a jungle of greenery and flowers, are
perfect for high tea. A baronial lounge, live entertainment bar, and
bakery/deli are also available.

★ **Ca' Brea**   *938-2863*
5.6 mi. W at 346 S. La Brea Av.
L-D. No L Sat. Closed Sun.   *Expensive*
A half-roasted air-dried duck with honey balsamic vinegar sauce and grilled lamb chops with black truffle and mustard sauce suggest LA cuisine at its best on a menu that also features traditional Italian classics. The cozy congested trattoria has an appealing contemporary ambiance on two levels beyond a handsome hardwood bar.

★ **Campanile**   *938-1447*
5.7 mi. W at 624 S. La Brea Av.
B-L-D. No L Sat. Only brunch on Sun.   *Very Expensive*
New wave LA cuisine is featured in creative dishes made with fresh quality ingredients. A cozy congestion of simply outfitted tables fill an airy skylit front room and soft-toned modish dining room. The adjoining bakery showcases breads, pastries, and desserts that contribute to the restaurant's continuing popularity.

★ **Century Plaza Hotel & Tower**   *(310)277-2000*
10 mi. W at 2025 Av. of the Stars - Century City
B-L-D. Sun. brunch.   *Expensive*
The Terrace (L-D. Sun. brunch. No D Mon. & Tues.) offers innovative international cuisine in an informally elegant dining room overlooking a lovely garden. **Cafe Plaza** (B-L-D) has updated American fare and a full delicatessen in a handsome coffee shop. **The Living Room** features wine by the glass in an intimate firelit lounge with plush sofas, while the stylish **Lobby Court** provides an expansive picture window view of pools and gardens. A pianist contributes to the tranquility nightly.

★ **Chaya Brasserie**   *(310)859-8833*
9.8 mi. W at 8741 Alden Dr.
L-D. No L Sat. & Sun.   *Very Expensive*
Pacific Rim cuisine like duck and mango salad or mustard-coated sea bass has earned critical acclaim. When crowded, the airy, informal dining room/bar can be noisy. But, it is enhanced by striking wall hangings, floral sprays, and a central atrium with a luxuriant bamboo thicket.

★ **Chez Nous**   *(818)761-2050*
10 mi. NW at 10550 Riverside Dr. - Toluca Lake
B-L-D. No D Sun.   *Expensive*
A lavish display of fine pastries, breads and delectable desserts is served with fresh light fare at all meals in several bright cheerful dining areas, a lounge, on a shaded sidewalk cafe, or to go. This is one of LA's best bets for breakfast.

★ **Chianti Ristorante and Cucina**   *653-8333*
6.9 mi. NW at 7383 Melrose Av.
L-D. No L Sun.   *Very Expensive*
LA's most popular trattoria may well be **Chianti**. Impeccable Northern Italian cuisine is matched by the easy elegance of a high-ceilinged main dining room outfitted with vivid wall art, a comfortable bar, and a bright and lively back room. **Cucina** next door serves the same high quality Italian cuisine in a modish dining room with an exhibition kitchen, wine racks, and floral accents.

★ **Cicada**   *655-5559*
   8.4 mi. NW at 8478 Melrose Av. - West Hollywood
   L-D. No L Sat. Closed Sun.   *Very Expensive*
New California cuisine is emphasized on an appealing bistro menu, and there is a similarly delightful array of desserts and ice creams made here. The restaurant, which opened in 1992, is already deservedly popular for both the cuisine and the sophisticated tranquility provided by soft colors, a choice of booths or armchairs at full linened tables and vibrant greenery.

★ **Citrus** and **The Bar Bistro**   *857-0034*
   6.1 mi. NW at 6703 Melrose Av.
   L-D. No L Sat. Closed Sun.   *Expensive—Extremely Expensive*
Each season, quality, fresh ingredients become culinary works of art in **Citrus** (Extremely Expensive). New California dishes might include sauteed scallops with onion rings as an appetizer, and chicken in mushroom crust as an entree. Delectable housemade desserts are displayed between the dining room and **The Bar Bistro** (Expensive) with a shorter menu. Both offer refined table settings amidst luxuriant greenery and whimsical art objects that epitomize Southern California panache.

Dinah's Family Restaurant   *645-0456*
   11 mi. SW (by I-405) at 6521 S. Sepulveda Blvd. (at Centinella)
   B-L-D.   *Moderate*
Puffy oven-baked pancakes with fresh apples and cinnamon glaze star among many pancakes, waffles and omelets served all day. Hearty all-American fare, including low-cost dinners and housemade baked goods, are just like they were in the 1950s when this ever-popular coffee shop opened. So are the overstuffed vinyl booths and decor.

★ **El Cholo**   *734-2773*
   4.2 mi. W at 1121 S. Western Av.
   L-D.   *Moderate*
Mexican combination plates are still popular as they have been since they were first introduced here almost seventy years ago. But, they've kept up with dishes like shrimp enchiladas and fajitas. The colorful complex of dining rooms and cantina has earned its place as LA's most popular traditional Mexican restaurant.

★ **Empress Pavilion**   *617-9898*
   1.2 mi. NE at 988 N. Hill St. - Chinatown
   L-D.   *Moderate*
Some of the finest Chinese gourmet cuisine in Southern California is ensconced in this young restaurant. A remarkable range of delicacies includes unusual dishes like braised bird's nest soup with crabmeat or double-boiled fish maw and black mushroom soup or sliced abalone with sea cucumber. The vast yet tranquil upstairs dining room is enhanced by well-attended tables set with full linen.

★ **Fenix (at the Argyle)**   *654-7100*
   9.2 mi. NW at 8358 Sunset Blvd. - West Hollywood
   B-L-D.   *Very Expensive*
One of the Southland's stellar chefs—Ken Frank—opened this delightful adjunct to the Argyle hotel in 1995. Exquisite New California cuisine, typified by spinach soup with lobster or rack of lamb roasted with chipotle pepper, is served in a luxurious dining room. There is also a stylish bar with live piano music nightly.

★ **Flora Kitchen**   *931-9900*
5.7 mi. W at 460 S. La Brea Av.
B-L-D.   *Moderate*
Whole Cornish game hen with spicy citrus marinade is featured along
with assorted pastas, salad and sandwiches. The lavish display of
decadent or sugarless desserts, breads and muffins is a spellbinder in
one of Southern California's best takeouts. There is also a spiffy cafe
and sidewalk tables overlooking display cases and floral sprays.

★ **Four Oaks Restaurant**   *(310)470-2265*
14 mi. NW at 2181 N. Beverly Glen Blvd. - Bel Air
L-D. Sun. brunch. No L Mon.   *Extremely Expensive*
New California cuisine with a classic French accent is masterfully
presented in innovative dishes. Pan-seared venison fillet with black
currant brandy sauce and cinnamon spatzil and for dessert, thin
crepes with warm key lime meringue and raspberry sauce, typify the
exciting possibilities. The restaurant is a romantic hideaway in the
upper reaches of a luxuriant canyon above Bel Air. A white clapboard
house is full of candlelit tables in intimate rooms overlooking gardens.

★ **Hal's Bar & Grill**   *(310)396-3105*
14 mi. W at 1349 Abbot Kinney Blvd. - Venice
L-D. Sat. & Sun. brunch.   *Expensive*
Exciting renditions of American standards have made Hal's one of the
beach area's best bets. The pizzazz of the cuisine is matched by the
modish decor of a dining room/bar with overstuffed booths or chairs
surrounded by massive avant-garde art objects and wall hangings.

★ **Harold & Belle's**   *735-9023*
6 mi. W at 2920 W. Jefferson Blvd.
L-D. Closed Mon.   *Expensive*
Harold & Belle's has been serving some of the best down-home
Southern and creole cooking in LA for a quarter century. Meanwhile,
the surrounding neighborhood has changed so much that you are now
urged to park in their lot. Everything from fried catfish or chicken to
sauteed creole dishes is generous and first-rate. Glass-topped tables
set with candles and fresh flowers fill several pleasant dining rooms.

★ **Hotel Bel-Air**   *(310)472-1211*
12 mi. W at 701 Stone Canyon Rd. - Bel Air
B-L-D. Sun. brunch.   *Extremely Expensive*
New California cuisine is featured in **The Restaurant**, where the
finest meats and produce of each season become innovative
masterpieces. LA's most romantic hotel restaurant is a beautifully
proportioned room with: tables set with linen, crystal, silver and china;
colorful floral bouquets; a fireplace; an elegant crystal chandelier; an
enormous floral spray; plus a window-wall view of a (heated) tropical
patio that provides the region's most delightful alfresco dining. Jackets
are required for gentlemen in the evening. **The Bar** is a firelit
baronial lounge enhanced by a well-played grand piano each evening.

★ **Hotel Sofitel Ma Maison**   *(310)278-5444*
8 mi. W at 8555 Beverly Blvd. - West Hollywood
B-L-D. Sun. brunch.   *Expensive–Extremely Expensive*
Ma Maison (D only. Closed Sun.–Extremely Expensive) presents
French cuisine with New California flourishes in a posh garden
setting. **La Cajole Brasserie** (B-L-D. Sun. brunch–Expensive) serves
contemporary California cuisine in a glitzy neo-art deco bistro.

★ **Hugo's**   *654-3993*
9.3 mi. NW at 8401 Santa Monica Blvd. - West Hollywood
B-L-D.   *Expensive*
Pureed pumpkin pancakes, Italian cakebread with real maple syrup, and designer omelets are some reasons why Hugo's is deservedly popular for breakfast. Updated Italian and American grazing fare with pizzazz is served later. Happily the food transcends the din in the industrial-strength coffee shop that surrounds an exhibition kitchen.

★ **Indigo**   *653-0140*
7.5 mi. W at 8222½ W. 3rd St.
L-D. No L Sat. & Sun.   *Expensive*
International classics have been given an appealing LA topspin in light and lively dishes that pair the chef's whims with seasonal produce. Eclectic decor ranges from padded booths to lawn chairs, but the colorful comfy result complements the deservedly popular cuisine.

★ **The Ivy**   *274-8303*
8.3 mi. W at 113 N. Robertson Blvd.
L-D.   *Extremely Expensive*
California meets Louisiana in fine evocations of Cajun/creole and New California cuisines. Desserts on display were made here and are magnificent. A tucked-away cottage captures the romantic essence of Cajun country in intimate dining rooms and a heated garden patio. Alluring food and chic surroundings have made this a perennial favorite of the glitterati.

★ **JW Marriott at Century City**   *(310)277-2777*
10 mi. W at 2151 Av. of the Stars - Century City
B-L-D.   *Very Expensive*
JW's Restaurant features New California cuisine in a luxuriously appointed dining room overlooking gardens that accommodate alfresco dining. **JW's Lounge** offers soft piano medleys with drinks in an opulent setting accented by luxuriant greenery.

★ **Joe's Restaurant**   *(310)399-5811*
14 mi. W at 1023 Abbot Kinney Blvd. - Venice
L-D. Closed Mon.   *Expensive*
"LA cuisine"—rooted in classic European and Asian traditions, and with a California penchant for seasonal freshness, lightness and spices—is Joe's hallmark. Because of it, his 1990s restaurant is already acclaimed. Cozy dining areas with tables simply set in crisp white linen appropriately keep attention on the appealing cuisine.

★ **Katsu**   *665-1891*
4.5 mi. NW at 1972 Hillhurst Av.
L-D. No L Sat. Closed Sun.   *Expensive*
Grilled chicken with sesame seed or shitake salad are among tempting possibilities in addition to some of LA's best sushi and sashimi. A tony dining room/sushi bar is accented by colorful flowers and wall art.

★ **Koutoubia**   *(310)475-0729*
11 mi. W at 2116 Westwood Blvd. - Westwood
D only. Closed Mon.   *Expensive*
The Southland's premier source of Moroccan cuisine features couscous five different ways, lamb shank on brochette, some exotic dishes and tempting homemade breads and desserts. The authentic fare is served by a costumed staff amid a wealth of lavishly padded chairs and sofas and vivid tapestries, and circular brass tables with no utensils.

★ **L'Orangerie**   *(310)652-9770*
8.4 mi. NW at 903 N. La Cienega Blvd.
L-D. No L Sat. & Sun. Closed Mon.   *Extremely Expensive*
Classic French cuisine is prepared with exemplary finesse and described on a menu that changes nightly in one of California's quintessential restaurants. Culinary pleasures are presented in dining rooms where museum-quality tapestries and art objects complement formally elegant table settings. The floral centerpiece in the main dining room is probably the Southland's most grandiose. A spacious, beautifully appointed lounge shares the impeccable good taste of the dining rooms. So does the tranquil patio, where fragrant Hawaiian wedding flower vines in summer are part of the magic.

★ **La Serenata De Garibaldi**   *265-2887*
2 mi. E at 1842 E. First St. - Boyle Heights
L-D. Closed Mon.   *Moderate*
One of the best Mexican restaurants in the Southland is hidden behind a mundane storefront deep in the largest barrio outside of Mexico. Fresh fish, shrimp, beef, pork and chicken are treated with authenticity and dedication. The free cheese quesadilla appetizer; tables set with tablecloth and flowers; sophisticated wall art, music, and decor all contribute to the charm. Use fenced (free) parking in the rear and walk up.

★ **Le Chardonnay**   *655-8880*
8 mi. NW at 8284 Melrose Av. - West Hollywood
L-D. No L Sat. Closed Sun.   *Very Expensive*
Medallions of venison with pineapple fritters, spit-roasted lamb, and Peking duck suggest the range of light and lively delights in LA's finest bistro/brasserie. Exquisite desserts made here are displayed near the exhibition kitchen. Evoking turn-of-the-century Paris, the dining hall is lavishly outfitted with polished rosewood and a lot of mirrors that reflect a usually full house of sophisticated gourmets.

★ **Le Dome**   *(310)659-6919*
9.6 mi. NW at 8720 Sunset Blvd. - West Hollywood
L-D. No L Sat. Closed Sun.   *Very Expensive*
An extensive selection of contemporary Continental cuisine is featured, along with a seductive array of pastries made here. The large restaurant, subdivided into several fashionable dining rooms and a handsome circular bar, is an enduring show-biz favorite.

★ **Locanda Veneta**   *(310)274-1893*
8.2 mi. W at 8638 W. 3rd St.
L-D. No L Sat. Closed Sun.   *Very Expensive*
Locanda Veneta offers some of LA's finest Italian cuisine in both traditional and creative styles. The cozy, congested Venetian trattoria is extremely popular with cognoscenti. It can be noisy. Stars and star-gazers alike watch masterful preparation of the night's delights in the exhibition kitchen along one wall.

★ **Los Angeles Renaissance Hotel**   *(310)337-2800*
12.5 mi. SW (by LAX) at 9620 Airport Blvd.
B-L-D.   *Expensive*
In 1994, **The Library** (D only. Closed Sun.—Expensive) became one of LA's best steak and chop houses. Exclusively Black Angus beef, Wisconsin veal and New Zealand venison are showcased in entrees like a spectacular 32-oz. Porterhouse steak accompanied by gourmet

side dishes and toothsome housemade desserts. An elegant, intimate dining room perfectly matches the gourmet fare. The adjacent **Conservatory** (B-L-D—Expensive) is a large comfortable dining room with contemporary California cuisine.

★ **Lunaria**   *(310)282-8870*
10 mi. W at 10351 Santa Monica Blvd. - Century City
L-D. No L Sat. Closed Sun.-Mon.   *Very Expensive*
Fine New California cuisine with a Provencal accent is prepared in an exhibition kitchen. A posh split-level dining room complements the innovative fare. A snazzy oyster bar and jazz boite adjoin.

★ **Morton's**   *(310)276-5205*
8.6 mi. NW at 8764 Melrose Av. - West Hollywood
L-D. No L Sat. Closed Sun.   *Extremely Expensive*
In 1994, one of LA's favorite glitterati-gathering-places reopened after a move across a street. Light and lively New California cuisine is showcased in a large casually posh dining room enhanced with luxuriant greenery and fresh flowers. The bar at one end works for both gawkers and deal-closers.

★ **Musso & Frank Grill**   *467-7788*
7 mi. NW at 6667 Hollywood Blvd. - Hollywood
L-D. Closed Sun.-Mon.   *Expensive*
The oldest restaurant in Hollywood (circa 1919) not only offers a remarkable variety of traditional American favorites, it is also a great place to enjoy a dining experience that hasn't changed much in seventy-five years. You have a choice of booths, regular chairs, or an extra-long counter. The two convivial congested dining rooms still convey the spirit of Hollywood's glory days.

★ **The New Otani Hotel & Garden**   *629-1200*
.8 mi. E at 120 S. Los Angeles St. - Little Tokyo
B-L-D. Sun. brunch.   *Expensive–Very Expensive*
A Thousand Cranes (B-L-D. No L Sat. Sun. brunch–Very Expensive) presents authentic Japanese cuisine in an expansive dining room with a choice of low traditional seating or refined table settings overlooking a serene Japanese garden. **Garden Grill** (L-D. No L Sat. & Sun.–Very Expensive) features teppan-yaki dining. **Azalea** (B-L-D. Sun. brunch–Expensive) offers American dishes in a post-modern coffee shop. Drinks are served in a garden-view bar and posh lounge.

★ **Ocean Seafood Restaurant**   *687-3088*
1 mi. NE at 747 N. Broadway - Chinatown
B-L-D.   *Moderate*
Some of the city's best dim sum is a highlight (only available at lunch). A comprehensive menu of regional Chinese dishes includes outstanding fresh fish and shellfish specialties. Oriental art enhances a cavernous upstairs dining room filled with highbacked chairs surrounding tables set with pink linen.

The Original Pantry Cafe   *972-9279*
.5 mi. W at 877 S. Figueroa St.
B-L-D (24 hours).   *Low*
Generous old-fashioned American fare continues to earn a place among the city's most popular long-running eateries for this short order coffee shop. There is usually a line waiting for a choice of well-worn booths or counters. The owner, LA's Mayor Richard Riordan, is often in attendance.

★ **Papadakis Taverna**   *(310)548-1186*
20 mi. S at 301 W. Sixth St. - San Pedro
D only.   *Expensive*
Authentic Greek cuisine including gourmet items like white veal fillet
in pastry with a basil sauce, or filet of salmon with spinach and feta
in filo pastry is featured in LA's liveliest Aegean outpost. The award-
winning taverna has some colorful decor flourishes, but it's the good
food and the warm feeling of the spirited staff that makes it worth
driving out of the way for.

★ **Patina**   *467-1108*
5.5 mi. NW at 5955 Melrose Av.
L-D. No L Sat.-Mon.   *Extremely Expensive*
Patina is one of the Southland's genuine gourmet superstars. In this
prototypical source of New California cuisine, Santa Barbara shrimp
with mashed potatoes and potato truffle chips or roasted duck with
figs and pepper sauce typify the offerings. So does the selection of
delectable and creative desserts like a quartet of creme brules, or a
warm banana tart with banana sorbet. The intimate, luxuriously
contemporary dining rooms and lounge reflect the elan.

★ **Paty's**   *(818)760-9164*
10.4 mi. NW at 10001 Riverside Dr. - Toluca Lake
B-L-D.   *Moderate*
Paty's makes a beignet with whipped cream that is the most delectable
morning delight in LA. Cinnamon rolls, sticky buns, biscuits, muffins
and other baked goods made here are also worth going out of the way
for. Several New Orleans-style dishes highlight traditional American
fare that accompanies the baked goods bonanza. Diners can opt for
counter stools, padded booths, or a shaded sidewalk patio.

Philippe The Original   *628-3781*
1.1 mi. NE at 1001 N. Alameda St. - Chinatown
B-L-D.   *Low*
French-dipped beef, pork, ham, lamb or turkey sandwiches star on a
short list of American standards posted above an order counter that
also displays pies and baked goods. The big blah dining hall with long
communal tables and stools and sawdust on the floor has been here for
nearly ninety years.

★ **Pinot Bistro**   *(818)990-0500*
12.8 mi. NW at 12969 Ventura Blvd. - Studio City
L-D. No L Sat. Sun. brunch.   *Very Expensive*
Pinot Bistro is the best restaurant in the Valley. It figures, since this
is the sole offspring of **Patina**, one of California's ultimate gourmet
havens. A well-rounded grazing menu offers both classic and creative
French bistro fare, plus super desserts made here. Dark-wood
panelling, subtle artistic flourishes and elegant table settings are the
backdrop for memorable sumptuous repasts.

★ **Posto**   *(818)784-4400*
14.5 mi. NW at 14928 Ventura Blvd. - Sherman Oaks
L-D. No L Sat. & Sun. Closed Mon.   *Very Expensive*
In 1992, the owner of **Valentino** headed north intent on bringing
lusty Italian country cuisine to the Valley. Simple sensual dishes like
parmesan cheese chips and assorted housemade sausages succeed
admirably. The setting is a starkly handsome post-modern trattoria.

★ **Primi** *(310)475-9235*
10 mi. W at 10543 W. Pico Blvd.
L-D. No L Sat. Closed Sun. *Very Expensive*
This offspring of **Valentino** is one of LA's foremost grazing grounds, with a thoughtful selection of distinguished Northern Italian dishes prepared in an exhibition kitchen. The post-modern dining room is a tour de force of mirrors and glass and lacquered wood softened by greenery, wall art, and a floor-to-ceiling wine chiller by the entry bar.

★ **Rex Il Ristorante** *627-2300*
downtown at 617 S. Olive St.
L-D. No L Sat. & Mon.-Wed. Closed Sun. *Extremely Expensive*
Rex may be the most expensive and grandiose Italian restaurant in LA. The monumental two-story dining room, evoking the ultimate ocean liner's main salon, is decked out in plush neo-art deco decor. Jackets are required for dinner.

★ **Sabor** *660-0886*
5 mi. N at 2538 Hyperion Av. - Silver Lake
L-D. No L Sat. Sun. brunch. Closed Mon. *Expensive*
Sabor is one of LA's unique dining adventures. A truly "new Mexican" cuisine combining old South, Southwest, and interior Mexican flavors is artfully presented in dishes like Yucatan soup with grilled chicken, avocado, lime, chiles and corn strips; or tamales filled with chicken and chiles topped with creole sausage and chipotle sauce. All desserts are made here. Don't miss the ginger sauteed banana with a pecan pastry and vanilla ice cream. Full linen and candles, colorful folk art and greenery distinguish little dining areas.

★ **Sofi** *651-0346*
7 mi. W at 8030¾ W. 3rd St.
L-D. No L Sun. *Expensive*
From assorted filo pies to the baklava, this hideaway taverna provides some of the best authentic Greek cuisine in the city. A cozy sheltered garden patio adjoins a split-level dining room outfitted with plenty of crisp white linens and distinctive Greek accents.

★ **Spago** *(310)652-4025*
9.5 mi. NW at 1114 Horn Av. (at Sunset Blvd.) - West Hollywood
D only. *Extremely Expensive*
Spago is Southern California's most famous restaurant. It was here that Wolfgang Puck became one of the first to introduce New California cuisine to the glitterati and the masses. Emphasis was, and is, on transforming classic dishes into fresher, lighter, and zestier fare. While the price for a complete meal is high, the menu makes grazing among appetizers, pizzas, pastas, entrees and desserts easy. The casually elegant congested dining room up front has a picture window view of Hollywood, while out back is a room surrounded by luxuriant greenery. In between, you can watch the expert staff in the bustling exhibition kitchen (Puck's was first), enjoy a bar with flamboyant folk art decor, or look for celebrities.

★ **Sweet Lady Jane** *653-7145*
8 mi. NW at 8360 Melrose Av.
B-L-D. Closed Sun. *Expensive*
LA's best bakery features a delectable display of desserts and breakfast goodies in handsome glass-and-wood cases. It is served to go, or with coffee and light fare at a few tables.

★ **Talesai**   *(310)275-9724*
10 mi. NW at 9043 Sunset Blvd. - West Hollywood
L-D. No L Sat. Closed Sun.   *Expensive*
Classic and creative Thai cuisine is served in one of LA's loveliest
Asian dining rooms. Understated decor touches like orchid sprays at
tables set with full linen contribute to the urbane tranquility.

★ **Teru Sushi**   *(818)763-6201*
13.4 mi. NW at 11940 Ventura Blvd. - Studio City
L-D. No L Sat. & Sun.   *Expensive*
Happy hecticity reigns in LA's premier sushi parlor where dozens of
colorful dishes are displayed between patrons at the wood-trimmed
counter and the knife-wielding chefs beyond. There are also two wood-
toned dining areas and an enchanting Japanese tea garden where you
can enjoy first-rate traditional and innovative Japanese cuisine like
catfish strips marinated in ginger breaded with almonds and deep-
fried, or salmon teriyaki. The green tea or ginger ice cream wrapped
in tempura-styled pound cake as dessert is unforgettable.

★ **Trattoria Farfalla**   *661-7365*
4.5 mi. NW at 1978 Hillhurst Av. - Los Feliz
L-D. No L Sat. & Sun.   *Expensive*
Here is one of LA's most popular little trattorias. Pizzas and calzone
redolent of tomato sauce and mozzarella cheese and assorted other
Southern Italian dishes are given first class treatment in a bustling
kitchen adjoining the ever-crowded little dining room.

★ **Water Grill**   *891-0900*
downtown at 544 S. Grand Av.
L-D. No L Sat. & Sun.   *Very Expensive*
Favorite dishes from various American regions are well-represented
by the salt and fresh water fish and crustaceans featured in this
acclaimed young fishhouse. A tony dining room is flanked by an
exhibition kitchen and one of the city's best oyster bars.

★ **The Westin Bonaventure Hotel & Suites**   *624-1000*
downtown at 404 S. Figueroa St.
B-L-D.   *Expensive–Very Expensive*
California cuisine is showcased in **Top of Five** (L-D. No L Sat. &
Sun.–Very Expensive), an ultramodern circular dining room with a
grand overview of downtown. The plush **BonaVista Revolving
Lounge** has LA's best 360° look at the burgeoning skyline. A full
range of other dining facilities is also available.

★ **Westwood Marquis Hotel and Gardens**   *(310)208-8765*
11 mi. W at 930 Hilgard Av. - Westwood
B-L-D. Sun. brunch.   *Very Expensive*
In the **Dynasty Room** (D only), New California cuisine is masterfully
prepared and presented in an opulent dining room with dramatic wall
hangings. An innovative breakfast menu is offered in the **Garden
Terrace** (B-L. Sun. brunch), a light gazebo-themed room by a dining
courtyard. The posh **Lounge** features a grand piano.

★ **Wyndham Checkers Los Angeles**   *624-0000*
downtown at 535 S. Grand Av.
B-L-D. Sun. brunch.   *Extremely Expensive*
The hotel's dining room offers a selection of New California cuisine.
Tables are set with flowers, linen, silver, crystal and china in a
handsome room decorated with fine art. A cozy plush lounge adjoins.

LODGING

Los Angeles has been the preeminent destination for vacation and business travelers in Southern California for nearly a century. New waves of lodging construction followed arrival of the transcontinental railroad in the 1890s; the city's rise to stardom as the movie capital in the 1920s; the post-war boom of the 1950s; and LA's expanding role as the West's major metropolis in the 1980s. Today, contemporary lodgings serve every major activity center in the city. Summer is the prime season near the coast. Rates in fall through spring are often at least 20% less. Inland, weeknights are prime time year-round. Rates are usually reduced by 20% and more on weekends.

★ **The Argyle**   *654-7100*
   9.2 mi. NW at 8358 Sunset Blvd. - West Hollywood 90069
The most extraordinary art deco landmark in LA is a sixteen-story tower (circa 1931) at the heart of the famed "Sunset Strip." The plush 64-unit complex opened as a hotel in 1995 with a lap pool on a terrace overlooking the city, and (for a fee) a health/fitness center and valet parking, plus gourmet cuisine in Fenix (see listing) and a piano bar. Each spacious unit is luxuriously furnished with art deco custom reproductions, and has a minibar, phone and remote control color TV with pay and free movies. Toll-free: (800)225-2637.

"One Bedroom Penthouse"—extra-large, big in-bath whirlpool,
   panoramic cityscape from large private balcony &   K bed...$850
"One Bedroom Grand Suite"—big in-bath whirlpool,
   panoramic view from   K bed...$475
   regular room—   Q bed...$225

★ **Bel Age (Wyndham) Hotel**   *(310)854-1111*
   10 mi. NW at 1020 N. San Vicente Blvd. - West Hollywood 90069
One of the region's great executive hotels is a nine-story 200-room lodging in a tranquil neighborhood. Amenities include a rooftop view pool and mineral water whirlpool surrounded by lush gardens; saunas; exercise facilities; gourmet restaurant and lounge (see listing); salons and boutiques; and (pay) valet parking. Each spacious unit is luxuriously appointed and detailed with art objects. Furnishings include a refrigerator and wet bar, floor-to-ceiling window and large private city-view balcony, a phone, and two remote control color TVs with movies. Toll-free: (800)996-3426.

#811,#711,#611,#511,#411—extra-large 1 BR, 2 refr./wet bars,
   2 bathrooms including one with large sunken tile tub, 2 pvt.
   balc. with grand overlooks of Century City & LA, K bed...$500
#807,#707,#607,#507—as above but slightly smaller, K bed...$225
   regular room—   K bed...$195

Beverly Hills Ritz Hotel   *(310)275-5575*
   10.3 mi. W at 10300 Wilshire Blvd. - 90024
Halfway between Beverly Hills and Westwood is a lovely 100-unit garden hotel with a large pool in a tropical courtyard, a whirlpool by a jungle waterfall, exercise room, cafe/bar, gift shop, and (pay) valet parking. Each spacious, well-furnished unit features stylish neo-art deco decor, a refrigerator/(honor) bar, phone, and remote control color TV with (pay) movies. Toll-free: (800)800-1234.

#640—1 BR, top floor, 2 phones, private view balcony, Q bed...$165
1 BR (several)—full kitchen, request private balcony, K bed...$205
   regular room—studio,   Q bed...$105

★ **The Biltmore Los Angeles** *624-1011*
downtown at 506 S. Grand Av. - 90071
The largest historic-landmark lodging in the state would be a must-see museum if it wasn't a remarkable hotel. The block-square twelve-story building fronting on Pershing Square has 700 rooms and a labyrinth of facilities amidst fully restored palatial grandeur. Amenities include a full service health club with an exquisitely tiled indoor swimming pool, whirlpool, sauna, steam room and exercise equipment and (fee) massage; (pay) valet parking; restaurants and lounges (see listing); and boutiques. Each well-furnished room has a phone and remote control color TV with free and pay movies. Toll-free: (800)245-8673.

"Biltmore Club Service"—spacious, lavish
food & drink, amenities,   2 D, Q or K bed...$245
regular room—   2 D, Q or K bed...$205

Century City Inn   *(310)553-1000*
10 mi. W at 10330 W. Olympic Blvd. - 90064
This contemporary motor hotel is next to Century City, and has (pay) valet parking. Each nicely furnished room has a refrigerator, microwave oven, in-bath whirlpool, and remote control color TV with free and pay movies. Toll-free: (800)553-1005.

"Loft Suite"—spacious, Century City view,   K bed...$99
regular room—   Q bed...$89

★ **Century Plaza Hotel & Tower**   *(310)277-2000*
10 mi. W at 2025 Avenue of the Stars - Century City 90067
The west side's largest (nearly 1100 rooms) and finest convention-oriented hotel is a thirty-story complex in a parklike setting in the heart of Century City. Amenities include two garden court pools (one extra-large); two whirlpools; gourmet restaurants and lounges (see listing); specialty shops; and (pay) valet parking. Each beautifully decorated room has a floor-to-ceiling glass door to a private view balcony, refrigerator/(honor) bar, two phones, and a remote control color TV with free and pay movies. Toll-free: (800)228-3000.

"Tower-Corner King"—2 private balconies, (request NE
corner 27th to 15th floor for superb cityscapes),   K bed...$255
regular room—in original tower,   2 D or K bed...$200

Chateau Marmont   *656-1010*
9 mi. NW at 8221 Sunset Blvd. - Hollywood 90046
The gracious aura of 1929 Hollywood lingers in the well-maintained gardens and lobby of this small chateau-style hotel with a landscaped pool, fitness center, free valet parking, and cafe. Each of the landmark's well-furnished rooms and apartments has a phone and remote control color TV with movies. Toll-free: (800)CHATEAU.

#64—2 BR penthouse, kitchen, 2 baths, fireplace,
vast terrace with boffo Hollywood view,   Q & K bed...$1000
#76—top floor corner, kitchen, panorama of city,   Q bed...$210
regular room—   Q bed...$160

★ **Crown Sterling Suites**   *640-3600*
16 mi. SW (near LAX) at 1440 E. Imperial Av. - El Segundo 90245
Luxuriant vegetation is a major asset in this Spanish-Colonial-style hotel with 350 suites. Amenities include a spectacular five-story tropical atrium, an indoor garden pool, whirlpool, sauna, steam room, restaurant, lounge, garage, and gift shop. A full breakfast is complimentary. Each beautifully outfitted one-bedroom unit has a

tiny balcony, kitchen with microwave, two phones and a remote control color TV with free and pay movies. Toll-free: (800)433-4600.

regular room— 2 D or K bed...$149

★ **Doubletree Hotel Marina Del Rey** *(310)301-3000*
14 mi. SW at 4100 Admiralty Way - Marina Del Rey 90292
One of the marina's best hotels is a stylish nine-story complex with 300 rooms across a street from the marina's lovely manmade beach. Amenities include a tropically landscaped pool by a waterfall, a gourmet restaurant, coffee shop, rooftop view entertainment lounge and deck, and a posh lobby piano bar, plus gift shop and (pay) parking. Each room is beautifully contemporary, and features a sliding glass door to a tiny private balcony, phone, and remote control color TV with free and pay movies. Toll-free: (800)528-0444.

"Concierge Level"–many extra amenities,
fine marina & beach view, 2 D or K bed...$170
regular room— 2 D or K bed...$135

★ **Embassy Suites Hotel** *(310)215-1000*
12.5 mi. SW (near LAX) at 9801 Airport Blvd. - 90045
A vast landscaped eight-story atrium is the focus of this 1990s all-suites hotel. Amenities include an indoor pool, whirlpool, sauna, exercise room, restaurant, lounges and gift shop, plus (pay) parking. Breakfast buffet and evening beverages are complimentary. Each beautifully furnished two-room suite has a standing balcony, kitchen with microwave, two phones, and two remote control color TVs with free and pay movies. Toll-free: (800)EMBASSY.

regular room— 2 D or K bed...$139

Foghorn Hotel *(310)823-4626*
14 mi. SW at 4140 Via Marina - Marina Del Rey 90292
The palm-studded crescent of the marina's only beach adjoins this small motel, and the ocean and Venice pier are a stroll away. Each well-furnished room has a refrigerator, phone, and remote control color TV with movies. Toll-free in CA: (800)624-7351; elsewhere: (800)423-4940.

#201-#209–large pvt. balcony by the beach, 2 D or K bed...$110
regular room— 2 D or K bed...$80

Holiday Inn - Brentwood/Bel Air *(310)476-6411*
11.6 mi. W (by I-405) at 170 N. Church Lane (at Sunset Blvd.)- 90049
Hard by a freeway, this seventeen-story 211-room circular hotel offers spectacular panoramas. Amenities include an outdoor pool and whirlpool, exercise room, top-floor view restaurant and lounge/piano bar. Each nicely furnished room has a tiny private balcony, phone, and remote control color TV with (pay) movies. Toll-free: (800)HOLIDAY.

#1500,#1400–superb city-to-ocean panorama, K bed...$129
regular room–request Century City views, K bed...$109

Holiday Inn - Crowne Plaza *(310)642-7500*
12.5 mi. SW (near LAX) at 5985 W. Century Blvd. - 90045
Holiday Inn's largest and most complete LA lodging is a sixteen-story 612-room hotel. The contemporary complex was recently renovated. Amenities include a small pool, sauna, whirlpool, exercise room, restaurant, coffee shop, entertainment lounge, gift shop, and (pay) parking. Each well-decorated room has a phone and remote control color TV with free and pay movies. Toll-free: (800)HOLIDAY.

"Concierge floors"–top floors, many extra amenities, K bed...$154
regular room— 2 D or K bed...$99

Holiday Inn - Hollywood   *462-7181*
7 mi. NW at 1755 N. Highland Av. - Hollywood 90028
Hollywood's finest contemporary hotel is an upgraded twenty-three-story 470-room complex by the heart of the action. Amenities include an outdoor pool, coffee shop, revolving rooftop dining room/nightclub with a terrific view of downtown Hollywood, gift shop, and (pay) valet parking. Each well-furnished room has a phone and remote control color TV with movies. Toll-free: (800)HOLIDAY.

"Club Floor"—21st floor, breakfast & extra
amenities, panoramic view of Hollywood,   K bed...$149
regular room—request Hollywood view,   K bed...$125

★ **Hotel Bel Air**   *(310)472-1211*
12 mi. W at 701 Stone Canyon Rd. - Bel Air 90077
Tucked away in the foothills of Bel Air is an ultimate Southern California lodging experience. Sequestered along a meandering stream amidst a veritable arboretum of mature palms, giant ferns, and a kaleidoscope of flowers are 91 soft pink-toned villas. Amenities include an extra-large oval pool backed by a tropical garden, a gourmet dining room and lounge (see listing), and a choice of (fee) valet or self-parking. Each luxuriously appointed unit captures the essence of Southern California at its opulent best, and includes a refrigerator/stocked (honor) bar, private patio, two phones, and a remote control color TV with movies. Toll-free: (800)648-4097.

#302—spacious, large patio with whirlpool, fireplace, K bed...$550
#304—extra-large 1 BR suite, kitchen, parlor with extra
TV & fireplace, large private patio with whirlpool, K bed....$950
#326—corner windows, fireplace, small private patio,K bed....$380
regular room—   K bed...$315

★ **Hotel Inter-Continental Los Angeles**   *617-3300*
downtown at 251 S. Olive St. - 90012
Opened in 1992, this hotel has 429 rooms in a sixteen-story complex with a landscaped pool, saunas, steam room, restaurant and entertainment lounge, and (pay) valet parking. Each beautifully furnished room has a phone, (honor) bar/refrigerator, and remote control color TV with free and pay movies. Toll-free: (800)327-0200.

"Club Floor"—top 2 floors, complimentary
breakfast & afternoon cocktails,   2 D or K bed...$260
regular room—   2 D or K bed...$200

★ **Hotel Sofitel Ma Maison**   *(310)278-5444*
8 mi. W at 8555 Beverly Blvd. - West Hollywood 90048
One of the region's showiest conference hotels opened in 1988 with 311 rooms in a ten-story facility by the Beverly Center. Amenities of the post-modern chateau-style complex include a roof garden pool, saunas, exercise room, gift shop, and (fee) valet parking, plus gourmet restaurants and lounge (see listing). Each beautifully decorated room has a stocked (honor) bar/refrigerator, phone, and remote control color TV with free and pay movies. Toll-free: (800)521-7772.

#1005,#1025—parlor & BR, large private
balcony with panoramic view of Hollywood,   K bed...$300
"Executive" (many of these)—spacious, French
doors to tiny balcony & Hollywood hills view,   K bed...$230
regular room—   K bed...$185

Los Angeles
Hyatt on Sunset   *656-1234*
9.2 mi. NW at 8401 Sunset Blvd. - West Hollywood 90069
A large rooftop garden pool with a terrific view of Hollywood, the adjoining hills, and all of LA is the highlight of this twelve-story 260-room hotel with a restaurant, lounge, gift shop and (fee) valet parking. Each well-furnished room has a phone and remote control color TV with free and pay movies. Toll-free: (800)233-1234.
#919,#819,#719—spacious, wet bar/refrigerator, extra
   window & pvt. balc. with fine Hollywood/city views, K bed...$194
regular room—request Sunset Blvd. side above 6th floor
   for private balcony & fine city view,   2 D or K bed...$144
Hyatt Regency Los Angeles   *683-1234*
downtown at 711 S. Hope St. (at Broadway Plaza) - 90017
The new subway and a shopping mall adjoin this contemporary convention-oriented hotel. The refurbished 24-story 487-room facility has a whirlpool, exercise room and (fee) parking, plus a restaurant, bar, and gift shop. Each well-furnished room has a phone and remote control color TV with free and pay movies. Toll-free: (800)233-1234.
regular room—request NW corner 18-22nd fl., 2 D or K bed...$169
★ **Industry Hills Sheraton Resort/Conference Center***(818)810-4455*
20 mi. E via CA 60 at 1 Industry Hills Pkway. - Industry 91744
Sheraton's premier resort in the LA basin is a contemporary twelve-story hilltop landmark. The 294-room convention-oriented facility includes two big outdoor pools (one Olympic-sized); whirlpools; exercise room; saunas; jogging trails; and connected by a funicular (for fees) two 18-hole golf courses, seventeen lighted tennis courts and a swimming complex; plus specialty shops, a coffee shop, restaurant and entertainment lounge that share a valley view. Each well-furnished room has a tiny view balcony, phone, and remote control color TV with pay and free movies. Toll-free: (800)524-4557.
#1118,#1119—3-room suite with refr./wet bar, corner
   windows to large pvt. view balc. with big whirlpool, K bed...$325
regular room—   2 D or K bed...$125
★ **JW Marriott at Century City**   *(310)277-2777*
10 mi. W at 2151 Av. of the Stars - Century City 90067
The flagship of the Marriott chain in the West, opened in 1988, is a triumph of post-modern architecture and decor. The seventeen-story 375-unit hotel has two large pools (one indoors; one in a rooftop garden); whirlpool; saunas; steam room; exercise equipment; and (for a fee) massage or tanning bed; plus gourmet restaurant and lounge (see listing); (pay) valet parking; and specialty shops. Each spacious, luxuriously appointed suite carries out the hotel's peach and rose tones, makes lavish use of polished stone and mirrors, and includes a panorama of Century City and the LA basin, a private balcony, stocked (honor) refrigerator, phone, and remote control color TV with pay and free movies. Toll-free: (800)228-9290.
#1515,#1005—extra-large corner room, wraparound
   private balcony with superb panorama,   K bed...$275
#802,#702,#602—French doors between BR & LR,
   big deck with superb Century City view,   K bed...$175
#1510,#1410,#1408,#1004,#902,#904—extra-large
   pvt. balc. with grand view of Century City,   K bed...$165
regular room—   2 D or K bed...$165

140

Jamaica Bay Inn - Best Western   *(310)823-5333*
14 mi. SW at 4175 Admiralty Way - Marina Del Rey 90292
This small motor hotel has a pool and whirlpool in a tropical court
overlooking the adjoining marina beach, plus a restaurant and lounge.
Each spacious, well-furnished room has a private patio or balcony,
phone, and color TV. Toll-free: (800)528-1234.

"king deluxe"—refr., microwave, beach-view balc.,	K bed...$145
regular room—	K bed...$105

★ **Le Montrose**   *(310)855-1115*
10.1 mi. NW at 900 Hammond St. - West Hollywood 90069
Opened in 1988, this all-suites hotel in a residential area has 110 units
in a four-level complex that includes a rooftop garden with a
spectacular view pool and whirlpool; lighted tennis court; exercise
room; bicycles; (pay) parking; and dining room for hotel guests only.
Each beautifully furnished suite has a living room with gas fireplace;
small private balcony (some with city views); (honor) refrigerator/wet
bar; two phones; and remote control color TV with movies and VCR.
Toll-free: (800)776-0666.

"Executive Suite"—larger, has kitchenette,	K bed...$200
regular room—	Q bed...$165

Los Angeles Airport Doubletree Hotel   *(310)216-5858*
12 mi. SW (near LAX) at 5400 W. Century Blvd. - 90045
This twelve-story, 750-room convention-oriented hotel is a contemporary facility with a landscaped pool, whirlpool, sauna, exercise
facilities, gourmet restaurant, grand piano lounge, coffee shop, (pay)
parking, and specialty shops. Each attractively furnished room has a
refrigerator, phone and remote control color TV with (pay) movies.
Toll-free: (800)HOTELS-1.

"Spa Suite"(21 of these)—spacious, parlor, large private deck with whirlpool,	K bed...$325
regular room—	2 Q or K bed...$139

Los Angeles Airport Hilton   *(310)410-4000*
12.3 mi. SW (near LAX) at 5711 W. Century Blvd. - 90045
The giant among LAX lodgings is a newly refurbished seventeen-story
1240-room Hilton with a landscaped courtyard pool, and (for a fee) a
health club (whirlpool, sauna, racquetball) and garage; plus
restaurants, entertainment lounge, and gift shop. Each well-decorated
room has a phone and remote control color TV with free and pay
movies. Toll-free: (800)HILTONS.

regular room—	2 D or K bed...$149

★ **Los Angeles Airport Marriott Hotel**   *(310)641-5700*
12.4 mi. SW (near LAX) at 5855 W. Century Blvd. - 90045
The most resort-like convention-oriented hotel near LAX is this 1012-
room complex. The contemporary eighteen-story facility includes a
tropically landscaped courtyard with a vast freeform pool and
whirlpool; saunas; exercise room; restaurant, coffee shop; posh lobby
piano bar and sports bar; specialty shops; and a (pay) garage. Each
beautifully decorated room has a phone and remote control color TV
with movies. Toll-free: (800)228-9290.

regular room—request private balcony,	2 D or K bed...$144

Los Angeles Hilton   *629-4321*
.4 mi. W at 930 Wilshire Blvd. - 90017
This sixteen-floor 900-room convention-oriented landmark has a pool

in a landscaped courtyard, exercise equipment, four dining rooms, and an entertainment lounge; (pay) garage; plus a gallery of specialty shops. Each compact, well-decorated room has a phone and remote control color TV with free and pay movies. Toll-free: (800)445-8667.

"Tower Room"—(top 2 floors), spacious, extras, K bed...$229
regular room— 2 D or K bed...$169

★ **Los Angeles Renaissance Hotel** *(310)337-2800*
12.5 mi. SW (by LAX) at 9620 Airport Blvd. - 90045
One of the airport's best lodgings is an eleven-story, 505-room executive hotel that opened in 1991. Amenities include a pool, whirlpool, sauna, exercise room, two posh restaurants (see listing) and an enter-tainment lounge, plus (pay) valet parking and a gift shop. Each beautifully decorated room has two phones, refrigerator/(honor) bar, and remote control color TV with free and pay movies. Toll-free: (800)HOTELS-1

"Renaissance Club"—top 2 floors, extras,
comp. buffet breakfast, evening appetizers, K bed...$185
regular room— K bed...$145

★ **Mondrian Hotel** *650-8999*
9.3 mi. NW at 8440 Sunset Blvd. - West Hollywood 90069
LA's most beautifully situated post-modern lodging is a twelve-story 220-room hotel with spectacular cityscapes and a fine collection of modern art. The architectural gem, a stylized tribute to the colorful spirit of the Dutch artist Mondrian, houses a large outdoor view pool, fitness center with sauna, steam room, whirlpool and (fee) massage, (pay) garage, gourmet dining room and view lounge, and gift shop. Each spacious, luxuriously appointed room includes some of LA's best decor touches and has a city view, refrigerator, (honor) bar, phone, and remote control color TV with movies. Toll-free: (800)525-8029.

#1217,#1117,#1017—corner, 1 BR, kitchenette, in-bath whirl-
pool, grand window wall view of Hollywood & LA, K bed...$325
#1222,#1122,#1022,#922—corner, kitchenette,
great window wall view of Hollywood & LA, K bed...$185
regular room— 2 T or K bed...$175

Motel 6 *(818)894-9341*
21 mi. NW (by I-405) at 15711 Roscoe Blvd. - Van Nuys 91343
This modern **bargain** motel has a small outdoor pool. Each compact, simply furnished room has a phone and color TV with movies.
regular room— 2 T or Q bed...$38

★ **The New Otani Hotel & Garden** *629-1200*
.8 mi. E at 120 S. Los Angeles St. - Little Tokyo 90012
Downtown LA's most exotic hotel is a modish twenty-one-story 434-room complex with lovely Japanese gardens, and a (fee) health spa with whirlpool, sauna, steam rooms and massage; restaurants and lounges (see listing); a (pay) garage; and specialty shops. Each beautifully decorated room has a refrigerator, phone, and remote control color TV with (pay) movies. Toll-free in CA: (800)273-2294; elsewhere: (800)421-8795.

#421,#419,#417—Japanese experience suite,
balcony shares view of tranquil garden,
deep-in-bath whirlpool, futon Q bed...$395
"deluxe" room—spacious, K bed...$200
regular room— Q bed...$170

Los Angeles
Radisson Bel Air Summit Hotel   *(310)476-6571*
11.8 mi. W (near I-405) at 11461 Sunset Blvd. - Brentwood 90049
Above Brentwood is a post-modern 162-room motor hotel with a
landscaped pool, tennis court, restaurant and lounge, and a gift shop.
Each spacious, beautifully high-tech room has patio or balcony (some
private), two phones, refrigerator/(honor) bar, exercise room, and
remote control color TV with (pay) movies. Toll-free: (800)333-3333.
"Vista Suites" (4 of these)—in-bath whirlpool,
    spectacular panoramic city view,   K bed...$209
    regular room—   2 D or K bed...$139
★ **Radisson Hollywood Roosevelt Hotel**   *466-7000*
7.3 mi. NW at 7000 Hollywood Blvd. - Hollywood 90028
Hollywood's premier hostelry was restored for the 1990s to its 1927
status. The expansive lobby and other public spaces showcase art deco
decor in a twelve-story 340-room hotel with an Olympic-sized pool and
whirlpool in a tropical garden court; an exercise room; art deco dining
room, entertainment showroom; gift shop; and (fee) parking. Each
well-furnished, restored room has a phone and color TV with free and
pay movies.
"Star Suite" (#1101,#1001 to #701)—spacious parlor,
    great corner window view of Hollywood Blvd.,   K bed...$299
"Cabana Room" (80 of these)—private
    balcony or patio by tropical garden pool,   2 D or K bed...$129
    regular room—   2 D or K bed...$109
★ **Sheraton Grande Hotel**   *617-1133*
downtown at 333 S. Figueroa St. - 90071
An expansive atrium lobby gives this fourteen-story, 470-room
convention-oriented hotel a high-tech post-modern feeling. Amenities
include a large pool in a palm-shaded garden, three dining rooms, live
entertainment, a posh piano lounge, (pay) valet parking, and gift shop.
Each beautifully decorated room has a floor-to-ceiling window view of
downtown, two phones and remote control color TVs with free and pay
movies. Toll-free: (800)325-3535.
"Junior Suite"—spacious, fine downtown view,   K bed...$275
    regular room—   2 D or K bed...$200
Sheraton Los Angeles Airport Hotel   *(310)642-1111*
12.5 mi. SW (by LAX) at 6101 W. Century Blvd. - 90045
LA's biggest Sheraton was recently refurbished. The fifteen-story 800-
room contemporary hotel has a landscaped outdoor pool, whirlpool,
exercise room, restaurant, entertainment lounge, coffee shop, specialty
shops, and (pay) garage. Each well-decorated room has a phone and
color TV with movies. Toll-free: (800)325-3535.
    regular room—   2 D or K bed...$150
Sheraton Los Angeles Harbor Hotel   *(310)519-8200*
20 mi. S at 601 S. Palos Verdes St. - San Pedro 90731
The best lodgings in LA's harbor district opened in 1990 overlooking
the waterfront. The ten-story, 244-room tower includes a large
landscaped pool, whirlpool, fitness center, restaurant, night club, gift
shop, and (pay) parking. Each well-furnished room has a phone and
remote control color TV with free and pay movies. Toll-free: (800)325-3535.
"Executive level"—10th floor, comp. Continental
    breakfast & afternoon drinks & appetizers,   K bed...$125
    regular room—request harbor side,   2 D or K bed...$115

Sheraton Universal Hotel   *(818)980-1212*
9.5 mi. NW at 333 Universal Terrace Pkwy. - *Universal City 91608*
Universal Studios and Universal City Walk adjoin this convention-oriented twenty-one-story 444-room complex. Amenities include a large pool and whirlpool in a garden court, exercise room, restaurant, posh lobby lounge, gift shop, and (pay) garage. Each well-furnished room has a floor-to-ceiling view window, a stocked (honor) refrigerator, phone, and remote control color TV with free and pay movies. Toll-free: (800)325-3535.

#2028,#1928,#1828,#1728—fine corner valley view
& Universal Studio/tour area overlook,   2 D beds...$160
regular room—   2 D or K bed...$140

★ **Sunset Marquis Hotel and Villas**   *(310)657-1333*
9.4 mi. NW at 1200 N. Alta Loma Rd. - *West Hollywood 90069*
The Hollywood area's finest garden hotel is located on a tropically landscaped slope just below the Sunset Strip. Amenities include two large garden court pools, a whirlpool, sauna, exercise room, gourmet dining room, poolside cafe and grand piano bar. Each spacious suite or villa offers soft-toned traditional elegance and includes a refrigerator/wet bar, two phones, and remote control color TV with movies. Most have private balcony or patio. Toll-free: (800)858-9758.

"One Bedroom Villa"—big, kitchenette, fireplace,   K bed...$550
"5 North"—fireplace in view of   K bed...$450
regular room—1 BR, balcony or patio,   Q or K bed...$235

★ **Universal City Hilton & Towers**   *(818)506-2500*
9.6 mi. NW at 555 Universal Terrace Pkwy. - *Universal City 91608*
One of LA's best convention-oriented hotels, a blue landmark for the valley, is within walking distance of Universal Studios tours. The twenty-four-story 450-room complex is built around a spectacular post-moderne atrium that extends luxuriant landscaping into the lobby. Amenities include a large palm-shaded pool and whirlpool in a garden overlooking the Hollywood hills; exercise room; gourmet restaurant and lounge; a gift shop; and (pay) parking. Each beautifully furnished room includes two phones, (honor) refrigerator/wet bar, and remote control color TV with free and pay movies. Toll-free: (800)HILTONS.

#2269,#2169,#2069,#1969,#1869,#1769—spacious,
grand panorama of Universal Studios & valley,   K bed...$175
regular room—   2 D or K bed...$135

The Venice Beach House   *(310)823-1966*
14 mi. W at 15 30th Av. - *Venice 90291*
A large home only one hundred feet from the promenade and Venice beach has been converted into a handsome nine-room bed-and-breakfast inn. Full breakfast is complimentary. Each well-furnished room includes some antiques and hand-detailed furnishings.

"Pier Suite"—private bath, spacious, fireplace,
glassed-in porch with pier/ocean view,   K bed...$150
"James Peasgood's Room"—large in-bath
whirlpool with skylight, private balcony,   K bed...$150
regular room—shared bath,   Q bed...$90

★ **Warner Center Marriott Hotel**   *(818)887-4800*
24 mi. NW at 21850 Oxnard St. - *Woodland Hills 91367*
One of the valley's classiest convention-oriented hotels is a contemporary fifteen-story 473-room complex that was refurbished

after the 1994 earthquake. In addition to a park-like setting and a dramatic garden atrium, amenities include an extra-large indoor/outdoor pool and whirlpool surrounded by tropical greenery; saunas and exercise room; and (for a fee) massage or tanning booth; a gourmet restaurant, coffee shop, entertainment lounge and plush piano lounge; and gift shop. Each beautifully furnished room has a small balcony, two phones, and a remote control color TV with movies. Toll-free: (800)228-9290.

"Concierge level"—extra amenities, Continental
   breakfast & afternoon appetizers, fine valley views, K bed...$170
   regular room—   2 D or K bed...$160

★ **The Westin Bonaventure Hotel & Suites**   *624-1000*
downtown at 404 S. Figueroa St. - 90071
LA's premier post-modern landmark is a thirty-two-story 1474-room hotel. The convention-oriented facility has a landscaped rooftop with a big view pool, distinctive restaurants and lounges (see listing), specialty shops, and a (pay) garage, in addition to a cavernous futuristic interior. Each compact, beautifully decorated room has a stocked (honor) refrigerator, phone and remote control color TV with (pay) movies. Toll-free: (800)228-3000.

suite—parlor & bedroom, extras, request 31st to
   25th floor, blue or red towers for best city views,   K bed...$325
   regular room—   2 D or Q bed...$175

★ **Westwood Marquis Hotel and Gardens**   *(310)208-8765*
11 mi. W at 930 Hilgard Av. - Westwood 90024
Elegant Southern California style is further enhanced by recent major rejuvenation of this 258-room hotel in a garden setting by the heart of Westwood. Posh furnishings and fine art are used throughout. The sixteen-story contemporary gem includes two pools (one large) in luxuriant tropical gardens; a health spa, exercise room, and (for a fee) massage; gourmet dining rooms and lounge (see listing); a salon and gift shop; and (fee) valet parking. Each spacious, beautifully appointed one- or two-bedroom suite has a refrigerator and stocked (honor) bar, three phones, and two remote control color TVs with pay and free movies. Toll-free: (800)421-2317.

"Penthouse Suite" (several)—1 BR, top floor,
   panoramic views, posh new furnishings,   K bed...$375
#1107,#907—1 BR, awesome corner
   view of Westwood,   K bed...$325
   regular room—1 BR, pool view,   Q or K bed...$220

★ **Wyndham Checkers Los Angeles**   *624-0000*
downtown at 535 S. Grand Av. - 90071
Downtown's finest small hotel is a young 190-room charmer with sumptuous furnishings, antiques and floral sprays throughout. Amenities include a rooftop lap pool and whirlpool, saunas, steam rooms, exercise room, and (for a fee) massage and valet parking. There is also a sophisticated dining room and plush lounge (see listing). Each beautifully appointed room has a stocked (honor) minibar, three phones and remote control color TV with free and pay movies. Toll-free: (800)996-3426.

#1003-1004,#803-804—1 BR suite, spacious,
   fine corner window view of downtown,   2 T or K bed...$289
   regular room—   2 T or K bed...$189

Malibu

Malibu is a scenic coastal town renowned as a celebrity hideaway. Imposing hillside mansions and beachfront townhomes hug miles of a south-facing shoreline backed by mountains. The dramatic setting and mild year-round climate began attracting movie stars, artists and dreamers shortly after the turn of the century. In spite of major fires, floods, and mudslides in the 1990s, Malibu is more popular than ever as a celebrity haunt. So are surfing, swimming, beachcombing and other seaside pursuits. Ocean-view restaurants are plentiful. Notable shops are scarce. Seaside lodgings are (surprisingly) scarcer.

Population: 20,000   *Area Code: 310*
Elevation: *5 feet*
Location: *27 miles West of Los Angeles*
Malibu Chamber of Commerce   *456-9025*
   1.7 mi. E at 22235 W. Pacific Coast Hwy. - 90265

WEATHER PROFILE

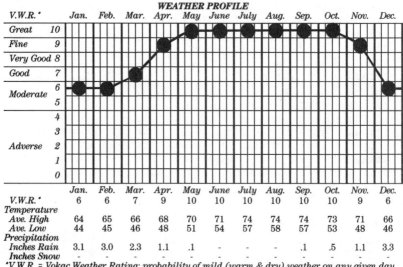

V.W.R.*		Jan.	Feb.	Mar.	Apr.	May	June	July	Aug.	Sep.	Oct.	Nov.	Dec.
Great	10												
Fine	9												
Very Good	8												
Good	7												
Moderate	6												
	5												
	4												
	3												
Adverse	2												
	1												
	0												

	Jan.	Feb.	Mar.	Apr.	May	June	July	Aug.	Sep.	Oct.	Nov.	Dec.
V.W.R.*	6	6	7	9	10	10	10	10	10	10	9	6
Temperature												
Ave. High	64	65	66	68	70	71	74	74	74	73	71	66
Ave. Low	44	45	46	48	51	54	57	58	57	53	48	46
Precipitation												
Inches Rain	3.1	3.0	2.3	1.1	.1	-	-	-	.1	.5	1.1	3.3
Inches Snow	-	-	-	-	-	-	-	-	-	-	-	-

*V.W.R. = Vokac Weather Rating: probability of mild (warm & dry) weather on any given day.

ATTRACTIONS

★ **Leo Carrillo State Beach**   *(800)444-7275*
15.4 mi. W on CA 1
The most versatile park in the area has a mile of prime sandy beach
by a rocky headland with sea caves, a tunnel, and tidepools. Bluffs
offer up-close whale-watching in winter. Swimming; scuba diving; and
board, body and wind surfing are popular. Lifeguards, restrooms, and
picnic areas are provided. Campers have a choice of sheltered sites in
a canyon or primitive sites on a beachfront parking lot.

Malibu Creek State Park   *880-0367*
7.3 mi. N via Malibu Canyon Rd.
Much of the 4,000-acre preserve in the Santa Monica Mountains is
closed to the public. However, more than a dozen miles of trails thread
oak-studded creeks and chaparral-covered highlands. From a large
dirt parking lot, it is 1.1 mile to a picturesque rock pool, 1.5 miles to a
tiny lake, and 2.5 miles to the former M*A*S*H filming site.

★ **Malibu Lagoon Museum**   *456-8432*
downtown at 23200 Pacific Coast Hwy.
Overlooking the beach and lagoon is the Adamson House, a stately
Spanish-revival dwelling adorned with colorful tiles, handcrafted wood
and ironwork. The 1929 mansion and surrounding luxuriant gardens
are free to visitors, and there is a gift shop. Closed Sun.-Tues.

★ **Malibu Lagoon State Beach**   *456-8432*
downtown on CA 1 at Cross Creek Rd.
The heart of Malibu includes a rare east-facing beach of fine sand. It's
a very popular place to swim or surf. Beachwalkers can glimpse
Malibu mansions, or check out shore birds at wetlands by the mouth
of Malibu Creek. Nearby, Malibu Pier provides good fishing and close-
up views of Surfrider Beach, famed for its surf breaks.

Paramount Ranch   *888-3770*
11.2 mi. NW via Malibu Cyn. Rd. at 2813 Cornell Rd. - Agoura Hills
This park was once a major location for movie (and later television)
westerns. Tiny "Western Town," with its false-front buildings, is still
used for commercials and TV episodes like "Dr. Quinn, Medicine
Woman." You may luck into a filming and are free to watch. Anyway,
you can explore the authentic backdrop of grassy hills, rocky defiles,
and tree-lined streams that make it an ideal movie set.

Topanga State Park   *455-2465*
12.5 mi. NE via CA 1 on CA 27 - Topanga
A 9,000-acre chunk of the Santa Monica Mountains above Malibu is
set aside for a little-known and slowly developing park. Miles of fire
roads and trails access streams, meadows bordered by ancient oaks,
and highlands more than 2,000 feet above the distant sea.

★ **Zuma County Beach/Point Dume State Beach**   *457-9891*
8.2 mi. W on CA 1
The longest Malibu beach is a superb sandy strand that extends for
more than four miles. Half of it, operated by the State, is away from
the highway and bordered by colorful sandstone bluffs. The other half
(Zuma County Beach) parallels the highway and is bordered by an
enormous linear parking lot. Swimming, surfing, and body surfing are
extremely popular and there are lifeguards, restrooms, and picnic
areas. Pirate's Cove, near Point Dume, is a notorious nude beach.

RESTAURANTS

Alice's Restaurant   *456-6646*
.5 mi. E at 23000 Pacific Coast Hwy.
L-D.   *Expensive*
New California dishes are served. A few of the closely spaced tables in a big, casual dining room share a pier/ocean view with a little bar.

★ **Beaurivage**   *456-5733*
3.3 mi. W at 26025 Pacific Coast Hwy.
D only. Sun. brunch.   *Very Expensive*
Contemporary Mediterranean cuisine is skillfully prepared in the area's longest established dinner house. The recently expanded landmark features casually elegant dining areas around a luxuriant courtyard in a building that captures the charm of the Malibu coast.

Borderline Bar & Grill   *457-5516*
10 mi. W at 30765 Pacific Coast Hwy.
L-D. No L Wed.-Fri. Closed Mon.-Tues.   *Moderate*
American standards are served in a sprawling roadhouse that is "Action Central" for the Malibu coast with several casual dining areas, a saloon, and a nightclub. A massive see-through fireplace, a tree growing through the saloon, stone and wood trim contribute to laid-back conviviality.

The Chart House   *454-9321*
6.7 mi. E at 18412 Pacific Coast Hwy.
D only. Sun. brunch.   *Expensive*
Contemporary American fare can be accompanied by a fine salad bar, but the real draw is the place and the location. A handsome wood-and-plant-trimmed dining room and lounge and cozy alfresco area each provide a surfside view of a splendid curve of coastline.

★ **Geoffrey's**   *457-1519*
5 mi. W at 27400 Pacific Coast Hwy.
L-D.   *Extremely Expensive*
New California cuisine in innovative dishes like grilled tiger prawns with papaya mint salsa and parsnip chips, and seasonal fruit sorbets served in a crisp pastry shell finds a quintessential setting at Geoffrey's. Guests have a choice of a romantic, toney dining room or a heated terrace where exotic foliage frames the sea below.

★ **Granita**   *456-0488*
downtown at 23725 W. Malibu Rd. in Malibu Colony Plaza
L-D. Sun. brunch. No L Mon.-Tues.   *Extremely Expensive*
Wolfgang Puck's latest paean to New California cuisine is off to a heady start. Fresh innovative dishes are showcased amid florid decor in a capacious dining room/lounge. A congestion of tables set with linen is surrounded by a welter of abstract-cum-absurd art.

★ **Inn of the Seventh Ray**   *455-1311*
11 mi. NE at 128 Old Topanga Canyon Rd. - Topanga
L-D. Sun. brunch.   *Expensive*
Salubrious ingredients are taken seriously in a California classic that lists foods by lightness and density (ranging from steamed vegies to hard-core red beef) "in order of their esoteric vibrational value." High wholesomeness and good vibes are further exalted by a tranquil setting where you have a choice of handcrafted wood-toned dining rooms or a charming multilevel heated patio in a creekside garden.

Moonshadows   *456-3010*
4 mi. E at 20356 Pacific Coast Hwy.
D only. Sun. brunch.   *Expensive*
Contemporary American fare is accompanied by a salad bar in this
large wood-and-plant-trimmed restaurant. The comfortable split-level
dining room or cozy corner lounge provide a splendid surf view.
★ **Saddle Peak Lodge**   *456-PEAK*
6.6 mi. N at 419 Cold Canyon Rd. - Calabasas
D only. Sat. & Sun. brunch. Closed Mon.-Tues.   *Very Expensive*
Venison, pheasant, buffalo, and other game entrees are prepared with
skill, and there are novel culinary flourishes. The five-level restaurant
has been a favorite mountain hideaway for more than fifty years. Each
room is a study in rustically elegant hunting-lodge decor. The firelit
lower level is perfect for a romantic dinner, while the top level with a
picture-window mountain view is best for brunch.
★ **Tra Di Noi Ristorante**   *456-0169*
downtown at 3835 Cross Creek Rd. #8A
L-D. No L Sun.   *Expensive*
Authentic Italian cuisine stars in dishes like boneless trout grilled
with sage and lemon, in a whole array of colorful antipastis displayed
near the entrance, and in several outstanding desserts made here.
This choice 1990s addition to the Malibu scene is housed in a posh
trattoria with an adjoining umbrella-shaded patio in a garden court.

LODGING

The few lodgings along the Malibu coast are all relatively small. None
is a bargain. Some reduce their midweek rates by as much as 20%.
Casa Malibu Inn on the Beach   *456-2219*
.9 mi. E at 22752 Pacific Coast Hwy. - 90265
This small older motel by the highway fronts on the ocean. Each nicely
furnished room has a refrigerator, phone and remote control color TV.
Toll-free: (800)831-0858.
   oceanfront—large, private deck,   K bed...$150
   regular room—garden view,   2 D or K bed...$105
★ **Malibu Beach Inn**   *456-6444*
.7 mi. E at 22878 Pacific Coast Hwy. - 90265
Malibu Beach Inn is the only luxury lodging on the famed beach. It is
within a stroll of the pier at the heart of the colony. Continental
breakfast buffet is complimentary. Each large, beautifully furnished
room has a stocked (honor) refrigerator/wet bar, gas fireplace, large
private balcony above the surf, phone, and remote control color TV
with movies. Toll-free: (800)4-MALIBU.
   "colony suite"—top floor, sitting room, french doors
     to big pvt. deck, shares grand beach view with   Q bed...$250
   #101,#102—big balcony with whirlpool by waves,   Q bed...$225
   "beachcomber rooms"—as above but no gas fireplace, Q bed...$215
   regular room—parking lot/pier and ocean view,   Q bed...$150
Malibu Country Inn   *457-9622*
8 mi. W at 6506 Westward Beach Rd. - 90265
Perched on a hill near a great beach is a motel with a little tropically
landscaped freeform pool and sundeck. Each compact, nicely furnished
room has a private patio with a mountain/ocean view, refrigerator,
phone, and color TV with movies. Toll-free: (800)899-9622.
   regular room—   Q or K bed...$155

Manhattan Beach

Manhattan Beach is a classic California beach town. The compact residential community spills down a gentle slope to two miles of clean sand and some of the finest surf anywhere. The village developed slowly early in the century as a seaside hideaway. That changed in the 1950s when a group of local kids called the Beach Boys started singing about surf, sand, sun and other delights of the area.

Manhattan Beach is still an upscale residential community with a deservedly popular beach enhanced by a pier and oceanfront walkway. In recent years, the compact downtown area above the pier has also become a desirable destination with an appealing array of specialty shops and some first-rate restaurants. Unfortunately, parking is a major hassle on weekends, and lodgings near the beach are very limited, although there are some attractive accommodations about a mile inland.

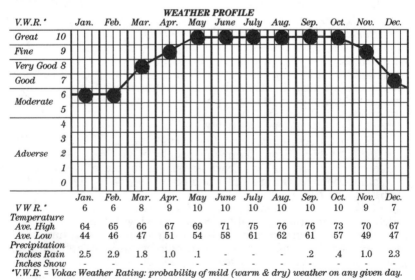

WEATHER PROFILE

V.W.R. *		Jan.	Feb.	Mar.	Apr.	May	June	July	Aug.	Sep.	Oct.	Nov.	Dec.
Great	10					●	●	●	●	●	●		
Fine	9				●							●	
Very Good	8			●									
Good	7												●
Moderate	6	●		●									
	5												
	4												
	3												
Adverse	2												
	1												
	0												

	Jan.	Feb.	Mar.	Apr.	May	June	July	Aug.	Sep.	Oct.	Nov.	Dec.
V.W.R. *	6	6	8	9	10	10	10	10	10	10	9	7
Temperature												
Ave. High	64	65	66	67	69	71	75	76	76	73	70	67
Ave. Low	44	46	47	51	54	58	61	62	61	57	49	47
Precipitation												
Inches Rain	2.5	2.9	1.8	1.0	.1	-	-	-	.2	.4	1.0	2.3
Inches Snow	-	-	-	-	-	-	-	-	-	-	-	-

*V.W.R. = Vokac Weather Rating: probability of mild (warm & dry) weather on any given day.

Population: 32,063   Area Code: 310
Elevation: 120 feet
Location: 19 mi. Southwest of Los Angeles
Manhattan Beach Chamber of Commerce   545-5313
   downtown at 425 15th St. - 90266

ATTRACTIONS

★ **Bicycling**
More than twenty miles of separated bikeways follow the strand through and beyond Manhattan Beach. You can rent cruisers, tandems, or skates by the hour or day to explore the coastline at:
Europa Bicycles   *1143 Manhattan Av.   545-8843*
Fun Bunns Beach Rentals   *1116 Manhattan Av.   372-8500*

★ **Manhattan State Beach**
downtown at W ends of 1st through 45th Sts.
A perfect embodiment of the California beach scene is the two miles of broad, sparkling sand that borders the entire western side of town. After all, the Beach Boys grew up here. Surfing and swimming are as popular as ever. So are a fishing pier and the Strand, a concrete beachfront pathway for strollers and bicyclists.

★ **Surfboard Rentals**
If you're finally overcome by an urge to "hang 10," but don't have a board, here is a place that rents surfboards and boogie boards by the hour or longer. They can tell you where surf's up, too.
Fun Bunns Beach Rentals *1116 Manhattan Av.   372-8500*

RESTAURANTS

Cafe Pierre   *545-5252*
downtown at 317 Manhattan Beach Blvd.
L-D. No L Sat. & Sun.   *Expensive*
Mediterranean cuisine is made from scratch including distinctive specialties like braised lamb shank over cous cous. Homemade desserts are displayed at the entrance. In the contemporary bistro-style dining room, closely spaced glass-topped tables are set with fresh flowers. A classy brassy little bar adjoins.

Koffee Kart   *372-6050*
downtown at 1104 Highland Av.
B-L.   *Low*
There are assorted pancakes and waffles; and omelets with a choice of hotcakes, muffins or biscuits in this plain little cafe.

★ **The Local Yolk**   *546-4407*
1 mi. N at 3414 Highland Av.
B-L.   *Moderate*
Omelets are featured, portions are generous, and there are some flavorful innovations. The light, bright dining areas are enhanced by vibrant wall photos, glass bricks, and other modish touches.

Mangiamo   *318-3434*
downtown at 128 Manhattan Beach Blvd.
D only.   *Very Expensive*
Updated Italian cuisine includes an appealing selection of seafoods like shrimp and lobster ravioli or swordfish poached in champagne with three-color peppercorn, plus homemade desserts. The intimate dining room is a neo-Art-Deco crowd-pleaser.

Manhattan Beach Brewing Company   *798-2744*
downtown at 124 Manhattan Beach Blvd.
L-D.   *Moderate*
Designer wood-fired pizzas and half-pound burgers are tops among
casual dishes served with handcrafted (and name brand) tap beers in
a comfortable wood-and-brick-trim pub backed by giant brew kettles.
Orville & Wilbur's Restaurant   *545-6639*
1.5 mi. N at 401 Rosecrans Blvd.
L-D. No L Sat. & Sun.   *Moderate*
Contemporary American fare is given careful attention. Downstairs
are handsome wood-toned dining rooms with an antique aircraft
theme. Abundant greenery and fresh flowers grace tables set with full
linen. A split-level upstairs lounge/dining room offers a town-and-
ocean view and music for dancing nightly.
★ **Pancho's**   *545-6670*
1.1 mi. N at 3615 Highland Av.
L-D. Only brunch on Sun.   *Moderate*
Pancho's classic and innovative Mexican dishes are among the best in
the Southland. For example, the budin azteca (a casserole of diced
chicken breast, roasted chiles, cilantro, corn and cheeses on a bed of
red sauce and covered with white sauce) is remarkable. Hardwood and
tile tables set with linen napkins are widely spaced throughout a
luxuriant tropical jungle in a covered courtyard, and on a surrounding
balcony. The adjoining wood-trimmed cantina, accented with stained
glass and trophy fish, has live music.
Reed's   *546-3299*
1.6 mi. NE at 2640 N. Sepulveda Blvd.
L-D. No L Sat. Closed Sun.   *Expensive*
The talented chef/owner of this young restaurant offers hits and
misses of New California cuisine. Hopefully he will have time to find
his niche and make this stylish dining room with its crisp, spare decor
and avant garde art and music a success.
★ **Sloopy's Beach Cafe**   *545-1373*
1 mi. N at 3416 Highland Av.
L-D.   *Moderate*
Several styles of fish baskets, assorted burgers with a choice of poppy
seed or whole wheat buns, Cobb and other salads, and drinks like
peanut butter and banana milkshakes are some reasons why this is an
excellent choice for lunch. The multilevel dining room is actually a
verdant conservatory full of flowers and exotic plants.
Sunsets   *545-2323*
downtown at 117 Manhattan Beach Blvd.
B-L-D. No B Mon.-Fri.   *Moderate*
The California and Mexican fare is generous. But, a peerless
panorama of the nearby pier, promenade and beach from the sun deck,
bars, and casual dining areas is the real draw.
★ **Uncle Bill's**   *545-5177*
downtown at 1305 Highland Av.
B-L.   *Low*
First-rate omelets, all kinds of pancakes (like buckwheat or banana-
nut) and waffles (like pecan or cheddar cheese and bacon) distinguish
this funky beach shack cafe. With food like this, no wonder there's
always a waiting list on weekends.

LODGING

Lodgings near the beach are scarce and plain, but there are good accommodations a mile inland. Summer is prime time. Some places reduce their rates by as much as 20% during the rest of the year.

Barnabey's Hotel   *545-8466*
    1.8 mi. NE at 3501 N. Sepulveda Blvd. (at Rosecrans) - 90266
South Bay's only English-style garden hotel is decorated with Old World art and antiques. A big tiled pool and whirlpool are showcased in a jungle of greenery in a room with a roll-back ceiling. Atmospheric rooms and a garden court provide romantic settings for Continental dining, and there is a plush pub, entertainment lounge, gift shop, and (fee) parking. Buffet breakfast is complimentary. Each comfortable, individualized room has antiques, a phone, and remote control color TV with (pay) movies. Toll-free: (800)552-5285.
    "Terrace"–private balcony over lush fountain court, K bed...$113
        regular room–   2 D or K bed...$98
Comfort Inn   *318-1020*
    1 mi. E at 850 N. Sepulveda Blvd. - 90266
This modern motel less than a mile from the beach opened in 1988 with a pool, whirlpool, and sauna. Each spacious, nicely furnished room has a phone and color TV with movies. Toll-free: (800)228-5150.
    "spa room" (4 of these)–refrigerator,
        big mirrored whirlpool in sight of   K bed...$95
        regular room–   Q or K bed...$65
★ **Radisson Plaza Hotel**   *546-7511*
    2.2 mi. NE at 1400 Parkview Av. - 90266
The area's largest (380 rooms) and best convention-oriented hotel opened in 1986. The seven-story post-modern complex includes a very large pool, whirlpool, exercise equipment and saunas, (pay) parking, and a (fee) executive 9-hole golf course, plus a dining room and entertainment lounge, and a gift shop. Each well-furnished room has a phone and color TV with movies. Toll-free: (800)333-3333.
    "golf course view side"–private balcony,   2 D or K bed...$109
        regular room–   2 D or K bed...$89
Residence Inn by Marriott   *546-7627*
    1 mi. NE at 1700 N. Sepulveda Blvd. - 90266
This all-suites motel has a landscaped outdoor pool and two whirlpools, a sport court, and complimentary breakfast and hospitality hour. Each spacious, well-decorated unit has a kitchen with microwave, living room, fireplace or balcony, phone and remote control color TV with movies. Toll-free: (800)331-3131.
    "penthouse suite" (many)–split-level,
        2 TVs, (request fireplace),   2 Q beds...$99
        regular room–studio, (request fireplace),   Q bed...$89

Newport Beach

Newport Beach is the heart of Southern California's gold coast. Six miles of broad sandy beach includes the narrow Balboa Peninsula, which shelters Newport Bay. The Southland's most glamorous recreation-oriented inlet has a dozen miles of gleaming waterways and nearly as many islands. With its unbeatable location and delightful year-round climate, Newport has been a major resort for a century.

Today, the beach is one of America's favorites, and the bay hosts one of the largest concentrations of pleasure boats in California. Every kind of saltwater sport and facility is now available in a setting that is inimitably attuned to serving multitudes of visitors in summer and on weekends year-round. Several urbane enclaves house outstanding arrays of smart shops, notable restaurants (many with splendid waterfront views), and plush lodgings.

WEATHER PROFILE

V.W.R.*		Jan.	Feb.	Mar.	Apr.	May	June	July	Aug.	Sep.	Oct.	Nov.	Dec.
Great	10						●	●	●		●	●	
Fine	9					●				●			
Very Good	8			●	●								
Good	7												● ●
Moderate	6 5	● ●											
	4												
	3												
Adverse	2												
	1												
	0												

	Jan.	Feb.	Mar.	Apr.	May	June	July	Aug.	Sep.	Oct.	Nov.	Dec.
V.W.R.*	6	6	8	9	10	10	10	10	10	10	9	7
Temperature												
Ave. High	63	64	65	67	69	71	74	75	74	71	68	64
Ave. Low	45	47	48	52	55	58	61	62	60	56	49	47
Precipitation												
Inches Rain	2.3	2.5	1.8	1.1	.2	.1	-	.1	.2	.5	1.0	2.3
Inches Snow	-	-	-	-	-	-	-	-	-	-	-	-

*V.W.R. = Vokac Weather Rating: probability of mild (warm & dry) weather on any given day.

Newport Beach

Population: 66,643   Area Code: 714
Elevation: 25 feet
Location: 39 miles Southeast of Los Angeles
Newport Beach Conference & Visitors Bureau   644-1190
4 mi. E at 366 San Miguel, Suite 200 - 92660   (800)94-COAST

ATTRACTIONS

★ Balboa Beach
.5 mi. S parallel to Balboa Blvd.

A wide sandy beach backed by palm-shaded parks and homes extends for three miles west from the mouth of Newport Bay. It is ideal for swimming and sunbathing. Midway is **Balboa Pier**, a century-old landmark that is still a favorite of fishermen and people-watchers. **West Jetty Park** is a perfect place to watch boats negotiate the entrance to Newport Bay. Nearby is "The Wedge"–a legendary shore break that challenges body surfers from all over the world.

★ Balboa Island
3 mi. E via CA 1 on Marine Av.

Balboa Island is actually three small islands in Newport Bay connected by bridges. It can be reached via the Marine Avenue bridge or by a delightful little three-car ferry from Balboa Peninsula. Walkways along the island's perimeter give strollers glimpses of a jaunty assortment of waterfront boats, and upscale homes amid luxuriant subtropical yards and gardens. The popular little business district along Marine Avenue is perfectly scaled for browsers. In addition to an enticing assortment of stores, dining possibilities range from fresh fruit juices to intimate Continental restaurants.

★ Balboa Peninsula
from downtown SE for 4 mi. via Balboa Blvd.

The city's most popular geographic feature is a long narrow peninsula between Newport Bay and the ocean. It is a delightful admixture of many of the elements that make Southern California appealing. At the west end is **Lido Marina Village** with classy bayfront shops amidst subtropical landscaping. Two miles east is the **Balboa Pavilion**, a picturesque Edwardian landmark next to the **Balboa Fun Zone**, a lively little amusement park with rides, arcades, trinket shops, and eateries. Nearby the tiny **Balboa Island Ferry** takes three cars and a bunch of pedestrians on a fast and cheap nautical excursion across the picturesque fifth-of-a-mile-wide main channel to Balboa Island. Piers, parks, marinas, a jetty, and the beach also attract visitors.

★ *Bicycling*
Scenic, relatively level terrain abounds in and around this water-oriented community. Bicycle paths and designated bikeways parallel the beaches and bay for miles. Bicycles, tandems, or three-wheelers can be rented by the hour or longer at:

  Ocean Front Wheel Works *105 Main St. at Balboa Pier* 723-6510

★ *Boat Rentals*
Sailboats and other rentals can be arranged by the hour or longer at:

  Balboa Boat Rentals   *Edgewater Av. & Palm St.*   673-7200

★ *Boat Rides*
2 mi. SE via Balboa Blvd. at 400 Main St.   673-5245

The Pavilion Queen offers narrated 45- and 90-minute sightseeing cruises around Newport Bay several times each afternoon.

Newport Beach

★ **The Bowers Museum of Cultural Art**   *567-3600*
11 mi. NE via CA 55 at 2002 N. Main St. - Santa Ana
A $12 million expansion in 1992 restored the original Spanish mission-style buildings (built in 1932) and created Orange County's largest museum. Dedicated to the fine arts and crafts of the Americas, Pacific Rim, and Africa, the complex includes permanent and revolving exhibits, **Topaz Cafe** (see listing), a big museum store, and **Kidseum** (nearby) with interactive fun for children of all ages. Closed Mon.

★ **Corona Del Mar State Beach**
5 mi. SE via CA 1 at W end of Jasmine Av. - Corona Del Mar
One of the West's best, and busiest, beaches is a broad half-mile-long crescent of fine sand backed by a palm-studded park and posh blufftop residences. The rocky East Jetty, topped by a walkway, is a popular fishing and boat-watching site at the scenic entrance to Newport Bay. Swimming, surfing, and skindiving also attract crowds. Picnic areas, ball courts, concessions, rentals, and lifeguards are available. A block to the east is **Little Corona City Beach**, a pretty little cove with tidepools and a sea arch.

★ **Gondola Company of Newport**   *675-1212*
downtown at 3404 Via Oporto, Suite 201
For a romantic change of pace, a one-hour cruise in a gondola rowed Venetian-style through the colorful canals of Newport can't be beat. A basket of fresh bread, cheese, salami, ice and glasses, and music are included. Wine can be purchased, or bring your own.

★ **Huntington Beach's Beaches**   *536-5281*
2 mi. NW from Santa Ana River - Huntington Beach
Nearly twelve miles of broad sandy beach extend between Sunset Beach, the best section to avoid crowds, and the Santa Ana River outlet. Midway is Huntington Pier (the place to watch legendary surfing action). Pacific Coast Highway (CA 1), a bike path, and vast parking lots parallel the entire strand. Gentle waves appeal to swimmers and families. Lifeguards, concessions, and restrooms are plentiful. **Bolsa Chica Ecological Reserve**, a protected wetland with a nature loop walk, is backed by a forest of big ugly oil pumpers.

★ **Newport Beach**   *644-3151*
.3 mi. W parallel to Seashore Dr.
A narrow beach of fine sand extends for more than two miles between the Santa Ana River mouth and Newport Pier. Easily accessed, it is popular for swimming, surfing and sunbathing. You can fish from the pier, or rent boogie boards for body surfing. The **Newport Dory Fishing Fleet** is beached nearby as it has been for a century. Local fishermen return here each day from trolling banks miles offshore to clean and display their catches until sold out in the afternoon.

★ **Newport Center Fashion Island**
3.7 mi. E via Coast Hwy. & Newport Center Dr.
Orange County's only open-air regional shopping complex is an architectural triumph enlivened by tropical landscaping and interactive water-design fountains throughout its interior plazas. In addition to more than 200 shops and over 40 dining opportunities, here is the premier **Irvine Farmers Market**, a cornucopia of first-rate grocery staples highlighted by an extensive salad bar with some novel selections. Adjoining is a vast atrium for gourmet fast-food dining open from 8 a.m. to 9 p.m. daily.

★ **Newport Dunes Aquatic Park**   *644-0510*
3 mi. E via Coast Hwy. & Jamboree Rd. at 1131 Backbay Dr.
A lagoon in Newport Bay is nearly surrounded by a half-mile-long broad sandy beach in a sheltered, private park oriented toward families and campers. Sail and paddle boats can be rented; swimmers and diving islands are overseen by lifeguards; and there are boat launching ramps, game courts, picnic areas, amusements, and campgrounds.

★ **Newport Harbor Art Museum**   *759-1122*
3.5 mi. E via Coast Hwy. & Jamboree Rd. at 850 San Clemente Dr.
Contemporary painting, sculpture, and photographs are featured, including a splendid permanent collection of post-World War II California art. The internationally famous museum also houses the **Sculpture Garden Cafe** serving light meals, and a gift shop.

★ **Orange County Performing Arts Center**   *556-2787*
6 mi. NE at 600 Town Center Dr. - Costa Mesa
Orange County's theatrical renaissance dates from 1986, with the opening of Segerstrom Hall, an avant-garde 3,000-seat auditorium which regularly features Broadway productions, ballet, opera and symphony. Two smaller stages comprise the adjoining South Coast Repertory Theatre, an increasingly renowned company offering a full range of live theater most of the year.

★ **Roger's Gardens**   *640-5800*
4.8 mi. E at 2301 San Joaquin Hills Rd. - Corona Del Mar
Southern California's quintessential nursery is a verdant showplace year-round. Pathways wind among a myriad of flowers artistically arranged in hanging baskets, planter boxes, and demonstration gardens. Exotic foliage is displayed in ornamental trees and shrubs. Roger's is an idyllic place to enjoy rare beauty and to study and purchase specimens of tropical and other premium-quality vegetation.

Sculpture Garden
6 mi. NE (near I-405) at Av. of the Arts & Anton Blvd. - Costa Mesa
Sequestered among the high tech towers of Town Center is a tranquil oasis. In this contemporary Japanese-style garden, sandstone structures, natural rocks, running water and plants symbolize various California scenarios. The lovely little park is free.

★ **Sherman Library & Gardens**   *673-2261*
4 mi. E at 2647 E. Coast Hwy. - Corona Del Mar
A historic estate has become a two-acre horticultural jewel and cultural center. Early California-style building house a research center and library specializing in the Pacific Southwest. Outside, fountains and sculpture accent exquisite gardens that include a desert section with rare cacti and succulents, luxuriant displays of tropical flora, flower-filled hanging baskets, and a touch-and-smell garden. There is also a tea garden for light dining, and a gift shop.

★ **South Coast Plaza**   *435-2000*
6 mi. NE (by I-405) at 3333 Bristol St. - Costa Mesa
You can shop 'til you drop in Southern California's biggest and best enclosed mall. Eight department stores, a vast selection of restaurants and specialty food outlets, and nearly three hundred quality shops are featured in the handsome mall and Crystal Court. The well-organized, artistically landscaped mega-complex is also one of the world's busiest.

★ *Sportfishing*

Sportfishing boats can be chartered daily year-round for deep sea fishing, and for whale watching in winter. Full or half-day trips aboard modern boats can be reserved near the Balboa Pavilion at:

Davey's Locker Sportfishing   *400 Main St.*   673-1434
Newport Landing Sportfishing   *503 E. Edgewater*   675-0550
Upper Newport Bay Ecological Reserve   640-6746
4 mi. NE via Coast Hwy. & Jamboree Rd. on Backbay Dr.
Southern California's largest estuary is a major stopover for avian users of the Pacific Flyway. Dozens of species, including some that are endangered, can be seen from the drive and pathways.

Warm Water Feature
★ **Wild Rivers**   768-9453
14 mi. E via CA 55 & I-405 at 8770 Irvine Center Dr. - Irvine
Water recreation is the theme at one of Southern California's two best water parks. Here are twenty acres of landscaped waterworks devoted to getting you in it, on it, and next to it in all kinds of exciting ways. A body-boarding wave pool, a gentle wave pool with sunbathing areas, assorted waterslides with gravity-defying curves, water flumes with speeds varying from fast to really fast, and a river with rapids for intrepid inner-tubers are among more than forty wet attractions. Closed mid-October to mid-May.

RESTAURANTS

Amelia's   673-6580
3 mi. E at 311 Marine Av. - Balboa Island
L-D. Sat. & Sun. brunch.   *Expensive*
Lasagna prepared several ways is a highlight among Southern Italian classics and seafoods. Abundant helpings are matched by warm decor in several cozy rooms of a decades-old island landmark.

★ **Antonello Ristorante**   751-7153
6.5 mi. NE at 1611 Sunflower Av.in S.Coast Plaza Village-Santa Ana
L-D. No L Sat. Closed Sun.   *Very Expensive*
Traditional Northern Italian cuisine is featured in a long-established local favorite. The pastry cart full of luscious desserts is especially notable. Both the informally elegant dining room and lounge are themed to a country inn in the Southern Alps.

The Arches   645-7077
.4 mi. N at 3334 W. Coast Hwy.
L-D. No L Sat. & Sun.   *Expensive*
Steak, veal and fresh fish are highlights among traditional Continental dishes. Newport's oldest restaurant has been a crowd-pleaser since 1922. It is dark, comfortable and delightfully unchanged with many colorful backlighted artworks.

★ **Baci**   965-1194
8 mi. NW at 18748 Beach Blvd. - Huntington Beach
D only. Closed Mon.   *Expensive*
Some of the finest Italian cuisine in the Southland has been served at Baci's since 1993. Classics range from pizzas and pastas through chicken and veal dishes to superb tiramisu. Lightness, freshness, and homemade quality reflect the skill and dedication of the chef/owner from Rome. Full linens enhance simply comfortable dining areas.

★ **Bistango**   752-5222
6.5 mi. NE at 19100 Von Karman Av. - Irvine
L-D. No L Sat. & Sun.   *Very Expensive*
The California-style Italian grazing fare (designer pizzas and a short
enticing list of entrees like wood-fired chicken with shitake
mushrooms) has the same light fresh appeal as the large modish
dining room. There is also a tony post-modern lounge and a dramatic
atrium garden court in this critically acclaimed restaurant.

★ **Bistro 201**   631-1551
.4 mi. N at 3333 W. Coast Hwy.
L-D. No L Sat. Closed Mon.   *Expensive*
A New California grazing menu is still featured after a move to this
location in 1994. The young gourmet haven is acclaimed for creative
finesse. A big tri-level dining room with an expo kitchen and fine bay
view provides a sophisticated backdrop for the cuisine.

The Cannery   675-5777
downtown at 3010 Lafayette Av. - Balboa Peninsula
L-D. Sun. brunch.   *Expensive*
Fresh fish and shellfish (including abalone) are featured. A historic
cannery now houses a big comfortable dining room, late-hour seafood
bar, and entertainment lounge amidst cannery paraphernalia. Picture
windows frame the waterfront, and there is an alfresco dining deck.

★ **Chanticlair**   752-8001
6 mi. NE at 18912 MacArthur Blvd. - Irvine
L-D. No L Sat. Sun. brunch.   *Very Expensive*
Traditional Continental cuisine and desserts are made here with the
kind of consistent professional skill that has made this one of Orange
County's primal award winners. Several dining areas and a lounge are
decorated in plush country charm with accents of yesteryear.

★ **Chinatown**   856-2211
7.5 mi. NE at 4139 Campus Dr. in Marketplace Mall - Irvine
L-D.   *Moderate*
Traditional dishes of various Chinese provinces share a menu with
tasty updates with names like firecracker lamb and camphor tea
smoked duck. Staff has a way with a wok. Tables are set with full
linen in several dining areas and a bar. Colorful wall art does justice
to the San Francisco Chinatown theme.

★ **Colima**   836-1254
9 mi. NE at 130 N. Fairview - Santa Ana
B-L-D.   *Moderate*
Whole fried perch or catfish with special house sauce, stuffed prawns,
shrimp soup, and lobster cooked half a dozen different ways are some
of the exciting seafood possibilities along with a wide range of Mexican
classics. The bright little dining rooms are a comfortable complement
to some of the best Mexican cuisine in the Southland.

★ **Crab Cooker**   673-0100
.4 mi. S at 2200 Newport Blvd. - Balboa Peninsula
L-D.   *Moderate*
For more than forty years, the Crab Cooker has been a popular source
of fresh (they have a little market up front), simply prepared (you can
watch them work in a glassed kitchen) seafood. Closely spaced tables
set with paper and plastic fill two capacious dining rooms awash with
nautical memorabilia overseen by a great white shark.

★ **Diva**   *754-0600*
  6.1 mi. NE at 600 Anton St., Suite 100 - Costa Mesa
  L-D. No L Sat. & Sun.   *Expensive*
New California cuisine is carefully prepared, and described on a grazing menu that also features desserts made here. A well-played grand piano and boffo view of the Performing Arts Center add elan to a chic post-modern dining room and lounge.

★ **Five Crowns**   *760-0331*
  5.2 mi. E at 3801 E. Coast Hwy. - Corona Del Mar
  D only. Sun. brunch.   *Expensive*
The best prime rib in the county highlights a menu of traditional Continental favorites. An English country inn has been artistically reproduced in several casually elegant dining rooms and a tavern where guests are attended by costumed serving wenches.

★ **Four Seasons Hotel**   *759-0808*
  3.5 mi. E at 690 Newport Center Dr. - by Fashion Island
  B-L-tea-D.   *Very Expensive*
The **Pavilion** offers meticulously prepared New California cuisine in dishes like sea bass broiled under fresh herb crust with chardonnay sauce. Housemade desserts are similarly light and lovely. The dining room offers quintessential contemporary opulence—California-style—with a picture-window view of tropical greenery. The **Conservatory Lounge** shares the luxuriant view and is a refined retreat for drinks, lunch or traditional afternoon tea. Grand piano stylings contribute to the ambiance each evening.

★ **Garduno's**   *645-5505*
  2 mi. NE at 298 E. 17th St. - Costa Mesa
  L-D. No L Sun.   *Moderate*
Assorted pasta made here daily are served with your choice of made-to-order sauces. The lasagna, cannelloni and specialties like stuffed chicken breast with veal and spinach in a creamy mushroom sauce are also terrific. Cannoli and other desserts are made here, including a tiramisu which is competition for the finest Italian dessert in the Southland. Ten tables and a tiny counter are wrapped around deli cases full of gourmet goodies backed by an exhibition kitchen.

George's Camelot Restaurant   *673-3233*
  downtown at 3420 Via Oporto, Lido Marina Village - Balboa Peninsula
  B-L-D.   *Expensive*
Their breakfast burrito may be the best breakfast on Newport Bay. The front dining room has both Old World ambiance (enhanced by wall art displaying arresting nudes) and an intimate waterfront view. There is also al fresco dining by the bay.

Giorgio La Trattoria Ristorante   *675-6193*
  3 mi. E at 305 Marine Av. - Balboa Island
  D only.   *Expensive*
Au courant pastas and Southern Italian specialties are attracting capacity crowds to the cozy congestion of this young trattoria.

★ **The Golden Truffle**   *645-9970*
  2 mi. N at 1767 Newport Blvd. - Costa Mesa
  L-D. No L Sat. Closed Sun.-Mon.   *Expensive*
Creative international cuisine is showcased in some of the region's most exciting dishes thanks to the renowned chef's adherence to freshness, innovation and details like sauces and condiments made

here from scratch. Extravagant housemade desserts are on display. The bistro's appealing little dining rooms and sidewalk patio are framed in greenery and flowers.

★ **Gustaf Anders**   *668-1737*
   6.5 mi. NE at 1651 Sunflower Av., S. Coast Plaza Village - Santa Ana
   L-D. No L Sun.   Very Expensive
Southern California's best Scandinavian cuisine is authentically rooted, yet given a New California topspin in dishes like wild rice pancakes with caviar and smoked salmon. The menu changes according to fresh seasonal ingredients. Everything from the breads to the desserts is made here. The big modish dining room/bar reflects the food's pristine elegance.

★ **Henry 'N Harry's Goat Hill Tavern**   *548-8428*
   2.1 mi. N at 1830 Newport Blvd. - Costa Mesa
   L-D.   Low
Beer drinkers rejoice! When you see the lineup, you won't doubt that this place holds the world's record for international and American premium brews on tap. Standard American pub grub is also served in funky rooms festooned with aging Americana, and outfitted with darts, pool tables, shuffleboard, and pinball games.

★ **Ho Sum Bistro**   *675-0896*
   downtown at 3112 Newport Blvd. - Balboa Peninsula
   L-D. Sun. brunch.   Low
East meets West in one of the best grazing menus in town. Assorted dim sum, soups, salads and hot and cold meat dishes are prepared with a uniformly light, healthy touch in an exhibition kitchen, and served in a tiny dining room with a counter and closely spaced tables.

John Dominis   *650-5112*
   .7 mi. E at 2901 W. Coast Hwy.
   D only.   Very Expensive
Contemporary American fare gets a Hawaiian topspin in macadamia sauce and in numerous wok-prepped dishes in the only branch of an island original. The vast dramatic dining room has a rock grotto waterfall and a wraparound window framing bay views. Upstairs, you can enjoy puupuus (appetizers) and an even better view from inside or on the sunny deck. Live entertainment happens nightly.

Kitayama   *725-0777*
   4.5 mi. NE at 101 Bayview Pl. (at Jamboree Rd.)
   L-D. No L Sat. & Sun.   Expensive
Fresh seafood is emphasized in customary Japanese fare served in this big modish restaurant. Diners can overlook a waterfall and garden, or a sushi counter, or you can opt for low tables in private rooms.

Ma Barker's   *646-4303*
   1.8 mi. N at 154 E. 17th St. - Costa Mesa
   B-L-D.   Low
Ma's is an easy winner for families. When they're fresh, humongous almond-laden cinnamon rolls made here highlight California country-style breakfasts. Similarly generous later meals are served in simply comfortable dining areas.

★ **Mandarin Gourmet**   *540-1937*
   4.5 mi. N at 1500 Adams Av. (at Harbor Blvd.) - Costa Mesa
   L-D. Sat. & Sun. brunch.   Moderate
Orange County's most renowned Chinese restaurant offers authentic

and masterful Szechwan, Hunan, and other regional dishes. Seasonally fresh ingredients like asparagus in the spring are worked into dishes ranging from hot and spicy to mild and smooth. Firecracker lamb or sizzling whole catfish are memorable possibilities served in stylish dining rooms that reflect the sophisticated cuisine.

Maxwell's by the Sea   *536-2555*
5.3 mi. NW at 317 Pacific Coast Hwy. at the Pier - Huntington Beach
B-L-D. Sun. brunch.   *Expensive*
Moderately priced breakfasts, including thick French toast stuffed with preserves and soaked in eggs and cream, are the best deal among American standards. Full linen and flowers enhance the big split-level dining room at all meals. Splendid beach and pier views are shared by a heated covered dining porch and entertainment lounge.

Mayur   *675-6622*
4.4 mi. E at 2931 E. Coast Hwy. - Corona Del Mar
L-D.   *Expensive*
Tandoor clay oven specialties and assorted fresh baked breads, plus a wealth of authentic chicken, lamb and seafood entrees are served in a posh, intimate dining room with Indian accents.

★ **The McCharles House**   *731-4063*
11 mi. NE at 335 S. C St. - Tustin
L-tea-D. Closed Sun.-Mon. No D Tues.-Thurs.   *Expensive*
Outstanding scones and raspberry preserves are featured during afternoon tea, and a short list of entrees highlight evening possibilities. All are carefully prepared from scratch, as are desserts displayed on an antique sideboard in one of several nostalgia-laden little dining rooms in a century-old house.

★ **Mother's Market & Kitchen**   *631-4741*
2 mi. NE at 225 E. 17th St. - Costa Mesa
B-L-D.   *Moderate*
Here is a landmark of lean cuisine amidst a giant emporium devoted to produce, pills, lotions and potions that are good for you. Fresh fruits and vegetables are blended with eggs, soy or tofu in American, Italian, and Mexican-style dishes. Diners surrounded by greenery overlook an exposition kitchen and wholesome produce displays in the comfortable remodeled coffee shop.

★ **Muldoon's Irish Pub**   *640-4110*
3.4 mi. E at 202 Newport Center Dr. - near Fashion Island
L-D. Sun. brunch.   *Moderate*
Southern California's finest Irish pub features classics like Irish stew and leg o' lamb, but it's the support dishes—Irish soda bread and mile-high Irish apple pie—that are remarkable. Both are made here and are as flavorful and unusual as any in the Southland. Tranquil padded booths or high-back wooden armchairs, fresh flowers, gas fireplace, garden and handsome wood-and-brick-trimmed dining areas and bar are just right for the great grub.

★ **Mutt Lynch's**   *675-1556*
.4 mi. S at 2300 W. Ocean Front - Balboa Peninsula
B-L-D.   *Moderate*
Basic California beach fare is background to more than a dozen draft beers in Newport's finest funky beachfront bar. Picture windows frame close-ups of the latest beachwear strutting by on the promenade.

Newport Beach Marriott Hotel & Tennis Club   640-4000
3.5 mi. E at 900 Newport Center Dr. - near Fashion Island
B-L-D.   *Expensive*
JW's California Grill features contemporary California cuisine in a
capacious, posh dining room with a distant ocean view. **The View
Lounge** with live entertainment and the best panorama of the city,
bay and ocean is a plush high-tech aerie.
Newport Landing   675-2373
2 mi. SE at 503 E. Edgewater Av. - Balboa Peninsula
L-D. Sat. & Sun. brunch.   *Expensive*
Fresh seafood is featured on a comprehensive menu of contemporary
California cuisine served in casually elegant, nautically themed dining
rooms. The waterfront view is even better upstairs on the heated deck,
and there is entertainment nightly.
★ **Oysters**   675-7411
4 mi. E at 2515 E. Coast Hwy. - Corona Del Mar
D only.   *Expensive*
Oak-grilled asparagus spears with whole shrimp sauce, or oak-grilled
beef and seafood, highlight contemporary California dishes in this
cosmopolitan restaurant. Intimate dining rooms, a popular oyster bar,
and a cozy garden patio are frequently full of knowledgeable natives.
★ **Pascal**   752-0107
4.5 mi. NE at 1000 Bristol St.
L-D. No L Sat. Closed Sun.   *Very Expensive*
French cuisine is authentically rendered in a well-thought-out short
list of classic and light updated dishes that can be topped off with
luscious desserts made here. The cozy split-level dining room has a
simple Gallic grace in spite of a nondescript shopping center location.
Next door is a handsome epicurie and wine shop with a tempting array
of light French entrees, support dishes, housemade desserts and wines
to go.
★ **The Pleasant Peasant**   955-2755
4.8 mi. NE at 4251 Martingale Way
L-D. No L Sat. Closed Sun.   *Moderate*
Robust French provincial country cuisine is skillfully prepared in
dishes like lamb shank, or meat loaf en croute with a splendid
mushroom sauce. A fine chicken liver pate starts each meal in cozy
dining areas with nostalgic appeal enhanced by luxuriant greenery
and art objects.
Renato at the Portofino Beach Hotel   673-8058
.4 mi. S at 2304 W. Oceanfront - Balboa Peninsula
D only.   *Very Expensive*
Italian classics have already won critical acclaim for this chic
congested trattoria with an exhibition kitchen.
★ **The Ritz**   720-1800
3.5 mi. NE at 880 Newport Center Dr. - near Fashion Island
L-D. No L Sat. Closed Sun.   *Very Expensive*
Continental haute cuisine is skillfully prepared in both classic and
updated renditions (like sauteed piccata-style abalone) and presented
by a formally attired staff in one of the region's most glamorous
culinary landmarks. Jackets are required for men in the evening. An
arresting array of paintings of nudes distinguishes the ultra-posh
adjoining dining lounge.

Newport Beach
★ Rothschild's Restaurant   *673-3750*
3.9 mi. E at 2407 E. Coast Hwy. - Corona Del Mar
L-D. No L Sat. & Sun.   *Expensive*
Pastas made fresh daily and half a dozen meat entrees are given
careful attention. For a really distinctive appetizer, try marinated
herb-baked artichokes. Several cozy dining rooms are embellished with
Victorian art in rococo-gilt frames, greenery, and stained glass.
Sapori Ristorante   *644-4220*
2.7 mi. E at 1080 Bayside Dr.
L-D. No L Sat. & Sun.   *Expensive*
Gourmet pizzas highlight a selection of light bright Italian dishes. So
do several desserts made here and displayed in a casually elegant
dining room adjoining an umbrella-shaded heated patio.
★ Sombrero Street   *547-0921*
11 mi. NE at 719 N. Main St. - Santa Ana
L-D. Closed Sat.-Sun.   *Low*
Traditional and California-style dishes are well represented in this
deservedly popular Mexican restaurant. For something offbeat, try the
German burrito, or the strawberry bunuelos for dessert. Generous,
zesty helpings are served amidst elaborate south-of-the-border decor
in a large restaurant/cantina with dining areas on two levels.
★ The Sutton Place Hotel   *476-2001*
5 mi. NE at 4500 MacArthur Blvd.
B-L-D. Sun. brunch.   *Expensive–Extremely Expensive*
One of the Southland's most acclaimed restaurants, **Antoine** (D only.
Closed Sun.-Mon.–Extremely Expensive) offers meticulously prepared
New California cuisine in seasonal specialties like venison with
huckleberry sauce and mussels with saffron soup in a setting of
contemporary opulence. **Cafe Fleuri** (B-L-D. Sun. brunch–Expensive)
serves contemporary California cuisine in a plush palm-garden atrium
enhanced by fountains. The posh lounge features grand piano stylings.
There is also a poolside cafe.
★ Tete-a-tete of Balboa Island   *673-0570*
3 mi. E at 217 Marine Av. - Balboa Island
D only. Sat. & Sun. brunch. Closed Mon.   *Expensive*
Distinctive contemporary California cuisine is evident in dishes like
roasted artichoke soup on a short appealing menu. The tiny romantic
dining room reflects the uncomplicated elegance of the exciting cuisine.
★ Topaz   *835-2002*
11 mi. NE via CA 55 at 2002 Main St. - Santa Ana
L only. Plus D Thurs. Closed Mon.   *Very Expensive*
The Southland's best dining-in-a-museum features New California
cuisine typified by delicious sweet corn tamales with shrimp. A snazzy
freeform dining room overlooks a lovely garden dining patio.
★ Trees   *673-0910*
4.2 mi. E at 440 Heliotrope - Corona Del Mar
D only.   *Expensive*
Trees can produce the best American standards and some of the finest
New American cuisine in Orange County, thanks to the uniform talent
and versatility of the chef/owner. An intimate refined dining room, and
a cozy bar with a menu of light fare, contribute to the ambiance of this
cosmopolitan dinner house.

★ **Tutto Mare**   *640-6333*
3.6 mi. E at 545 Newport Center Dr. - in Fashion Island
L-D. No L Sun.   *Expensive*
Pastas, rotisseried range chicken, or whole fish baked in a wood-burning oven are some gourmet grazing possibilities prepared in the exhibition kitchen. The pastry chef's luscious efforts are also on display. The classy contemporary cuisine is presented in a capacious bar and grill with the right kind of upscale informality.

★ **21 Oceanfront Restaurant**   *673-2100*
.4 mi. S at 2100 W. Ocean Front - Balboa Peninsula
D only.   *Very Expensive*
Fresh fish and crustaceans highlight an updated Continental menu. Victorian opulence prevails in split-level dining rooms and a saloon that shares a picture-window view of the pier. Waiters and waitresses in tuxedos, and pulchritudinous paintings of nudes contribute to the rich and romantic ambiance.

Villa Nova   *642-7880*
.4 mi. N at 3131 W. Coast Hwy.
D only.   *Expensive*
Traditional Italian cuisine has been the specialty of this Newport landmark since 1967. It hasn't changed. Neither has the picture-window view of the bay, the refined yesteryear decor of the front room, and the lounge which may feature grand piano stylings.

Warehouse Restaurant   *673-4700*
downtown at 3450 Via Oporto - Balboa Peninsula
L-D. Sun. brunch.   *Expensive*
Seafood is emphasized on a diverse menu of contemporary California dishes complemented by five distinctive sauces, and desserts made here. The vast comfortable dining room, mezzanine, entertainment lounge, and flower-decked patio share an enchanting bay view.

★ **Westin South Coast Plaza**   *540-2500*
6 mi. NE (near I-405) at 666 Anton Blvd. - Costa Mesa
B-L-D. Sun. brunch.   *Expensive*
The **Garden Court Cafe** (B-L-D. Sun. brunch—Expensive) serves contemporary California fare (typified by fresh fish prepared three ways with a choice of four sauces) in an upscale dining room and on a gracious garden/waterfall court. **Alfredo's Taverna** is a high-tech Italianate lounge, while the plush **Lobby Lounge** offers live entertainment.

★ **What's Cooking?**   *644-1820*
5.7 mi. E at 2632 San Miguel
L-D. No L Sat. & Sun.   *Expensive*
Delicious handmade pastas, pizzas from woodburning ovens, and a short list of updated Italian classics distinguish this young trattoria with a big cheerful bar and an umbrella-shaded patio tucked away in a neighborhood shopping center.

★ **Windows on the Bay**   *722-1400*
1 mi. E at 2241 W. Coast Hwy.
L-D. No L Sat. Sun. brunch.   *Expensive*
New California cuisine with an Italian topspin is skillfully prepared. So are desserts made here. In Newport's original extravaganza of contemporary decor, the elegant dining room and posh piano bar are unbeatable locales from which to enjoy breathtaking bay views.

★ **Zov's Bakery and Zov's Bistro**   *838-8855*
12 mi. NE at 17440 17th St. - Tustin
B-L-D. No D Mon. & Tues. Closed Sun.   *Expensive*
Sticky buns, Danish, brioche and muffins can accompany unusual
breakfast fare served in the handsome post-modern bakery cafe.
Mediterranean dishes ranging from Armenian pizza or lamb burgers
to poached salmon with citrus oil sauce are served later, along with
outstanding housemade desserts. The adjoining freeform bistro and
patio complement the appealing cuisine.

LODGING

Many luxurious hotels are within ten miles of Newport Bay, but there
are surprisingly few waterfront lodgings. Summer is prime time. Rates
are often at least 20% less at other times (apart from weekends near
the coast and weekdays inland).

Ana Mesa Inn   *662-3500*
6 mi. N at 3597 Harbor Blvd. - Costa Mesa 92626
This modern motel has a tiny outdoor pool. Each nicely furnished room
has a phone, refrigerator, and remote control color TV with movies.
Toll-free: (800)767-2519.

"Spa Room" (several)–big mirrored whirlpool near   K bed...$75
regular room–   Q bed...$50

Atrium Marquis Hotel   *833-2770*
6 mi. NE at 18700 MacArthur Blvd. - Irvine 92715
John Wayne Airport is across a highway from this 215-room business-
oriented hotel that was upgraded in 1992. The sprawling well-
landscaped complex (the area's first) has a large outdoor pool in a
garden court, plus a restaurant, coffee shop, entertainment lounge,
and a gift shop. Each attractively decorated room has a small private
patio or balcony, two phones, and remote control color TV with (pay
and free) movies. Toll-free in CA: (800)854-3012.

"The Pool Room"–spacious, champagne & breakfast,
refr./wet bar, tiny private mirrored pool in view of   K bed...$250
regular room–   2 Q or K bed...$89

★ **Costa Mesa Marriott Suites**   *957-1100*
6.2 mi. NE at 500 Anton Blvd. - Costa Mesa 92626
The Southland's best shopping center and the Performing Arts Center
are within walking distance of this 254-unit all-suites hotel. A
manicured park surrounds a small lake with a dramatic fountain next
to the eleven-story complex that combines California contemporary
architecture, earth tones, and luxuriant landscaping. Amenities
include a large palm-shaded pool and whirlpool by the lake, an
exercise room, restaurant and lounge. Each spacious, beautifully
furnished suite has a bedroom, living room, small standing balcony,
stocked (honor) refrigerator/wet bar, two phones and two remote
control color TVs. Toll-free: (800)228-9290.

#907,#909,#1007,#1009,#1107– facing lake,   2 D or K bed...$99
regular room–   2 D or K bed...$99

Country Side Inn   *549-0300*
4.5 mi. NE (near CA 55) at 325 Bristol St. - Costa Mesa 92626
This contemporary 290-unit motor hotel has two courtyard pools and
whirlpools, exercise room, restaurant, lounge, and gift shop. Breakfast
and afternoon appetizers and cocktails are complimentary. Each

attractively decorated unit in the four-story complex has a refrigerator/wet bar, phone, and color TV and VCR with (free and pay) movies. Toll-free: (800)322-9992.

suites—microwave, small in-bath whirlpool,	4-poster K bed...$99
regular room—	Q or K bed...$89

★ **Crown Sterling Suites**   *241-3800*
8 mi. NE (near CA 55) at 1325 E. Dyer Rd. - Santa Ana 92705
Santa Ana's largest (308 suites) and finest lodging is an all-suites hotel. The neo-Spanish-Colonial charmer is built around a ten-story atrium enclosing a tropical garden with ponds and a waterfall beside a restaurant and lounge. Other amenities are an indoor pool, whirlpool, sauna, steam room, and gift shop. Full breakfast is complimentary. Each spacious, beautifully furnished suite has a living room, refrigerator/wet bar, microwave, two phones, and two remote control color TVs with free and pay movies. Toll-free: (800)433-4600.

regular room—request 10th fl. with pvt. balc.,   2 D or K bed...$109

★ **Doryman's Inn Bed and Breakfast**   *675-7300*
.4 mi. S at 2102 W. Ocean Front - Balboa Peninsula 92663
The ocean, beach, pier and dory fleet are all within one hundred yards of this romantic retreat in the heart of the action. An elegant light breakfast is complimentary. Antiques, fern-filled skylights and floral-patterned decor are used throughout to evoke the building's Victorian origins. Each of ten rooms is beautifully and individually decorated with nostalgic pieces and furnishings, a gas fireplace, marble sunken tub in a skylit bathroom, phone and remote control color TV.

#8—spacious, corner room with multi-window	
ocean view, sunken whirlpool in bath,	K bed...$275
#7—fine ocean view from	K bed...$230
#1—corner, several ocean/pier view windows,	Q bed...$165
regular room—compact, ocean view,	Q bed...$135

★ **Embassy Suites Hotel**   *553-8332*
7.5 mi. NE (near I-405) at 2120 Main St. - Irvine 92714
This all-suites complex with 293 units is built around a luxuriant ten-story atrium. An indoor garden pool and whirlpool, sauna, atrium restaurant, lounge, and gift shop are available. Breakfast and afternoon cocktails are free. Each spacious, beautifully furnished suite has a refrigerator/wet bar, two phones, and two color TVs (one remote control) with movies. Toll-free: (800) EMBASSY.

regular room—   2 D or K bed...$159

★ **Four Seasons Hotel**   *759-0808*
3.5 mi. E at 690 Newport Center Dr. - near Fashion Island 92660
One of the Southland's most gracious lodgings is a twenty-story resort hotel with 285 newly renovated rooms amid palms and gardens. Amenities include an extra-large pool and whirlpool in a palm-shaded garden court, saunas, exercise room, bicycles; and (for a fee) two lighted tennis courts, massage and valet parking; plus a gourmet restaurant and a plush lounge (see listing), and a resort shop. Each luxuriously appointed room has a floor-to-ceiling window and standing balcony, an (honor) refrigerator/wet bar, two phones and two remote control color TVs with movies. Toll-free: (800)332-3442.

"Four Seasons Executive Suite" (many)—spacious	
LR/BR, large balcony with fine cityscapes,	K bed...$355
regular room—	2 T or K bed...$245

Newport Beach
Holiday Inn - Irvine/Orange County Airport   863-1999
7.3 mi. NE (by I-405) at 17941 Von Karman Av. - Irvine 92714
There are 340 rooms in this contemporary business-oriented thirteen-story hotel with an indoor pool, whirlpool, saunas, and an exercise room, plus restaurants, entertainment lounge and gift shop. Each well-furnished room has a stocked (honor) refrigerator/wet bar, phone, and color TV with (free and pay) movies. Toll-free: (800)HOLIDAY.

#802,#702,#602—corner, panoramic city/airport view,	K bed...$126	
"Executive Floor"—top floor, comp. food/drinks,	K bed...$133	
regular room—	2 D or K bed...$126	

★ Hyatt Newporter   729-1234
3 mi. E at 1107 Jamboree Rd. - 92660
An aquatic park on Newport Bay is across a road from this sprawling low-rise resort hotel. The recently upgraded 400-room complex is distinguished by palms and flowers surrounding three outdoor pools (one is enormous), three whirlpools, an exercise room; and (for a fee) parking, rental bikes, a tennis complex and par-3 golf; plus a dining room, entertainment lounge and gift shop. Each well-furnished room has an (honor) bar, a phone and remote control color TV with (free and pay) movies. Toll-free: (800)228-9000.

regular room—large, pvt. balc. with bay view,   2 D or K bed...$164
regular room—   2 D or K bed...$144

★ Hyatt Regency Irvine   975-1234
7.5 mi. NE (by I-405) at 17900 Jamboree Blvd. - Irvine 92714
Irvine's largest lodging is a 536-room convention-oriented hotel. The fourteen-story post-modern complex includes a large pool and whirlpool in a tropical garden court, saunas, exercise room and four lighted tennis courts, plus a gourmet restaurant, coffee shop, posh bar, nightclub, and gift shop. Each room has beautiful decor, a phone and remote control color TV with movies. Toll-free: (800)233-1234.

"Regency Club"—top floors, concierge, free Continental break-
     fast & afternoon drinks, fine city views,   2 D or K bed...$194
regular room—request corner balcony,
     11th to 8th floor for good city views,   2 D or K bed...$169

★ Irvine Marriott Hotel   553-0100
7 mi. NE (by I-405) at 18000 Von Karman Av. - Irvine 92715
One of the area's top convention-oriented hotels has 489 rooms in a sixteen-story contemporary skyscraper with a large indoor/outdoor pool and whirlpool in a sunken garden; plus (for a fee) four lighted tennis courts and a health club with exercise equipment, saunas, and massage; a restaurant, entertainment lounge and lobby piano bar; and specialty shops. Each well-furnished room has a phone and remote control color TV with (pay and free) movies. Toll-free: (800)228-9290.

"Concierge Level"—request 17th floor for best view,
     free Continental breakfast & evening appetizers,   K bed...$159
regular room—request private balcony on
     north side 14th floor for best city view,   2 D or K bed...$139

Key Inn   832-3220
11 mi. NE (by I-5) at 1611 El Camino Real - Tustin 92680
This big **bargain** motel has two outdoor pools. Each small, nicely furnished room has a phone and color TV with movies.
regular room—   Q bed...$28

Newport Beach
The Little Inn on the Bay   *673-8800*
downtown at 617 Lido Park Dr. - Balboa Peninsula 92663
The Old Cannery and Lido Marina Village shops are next to this small
bayside inn, and the ocean is a stroll away. Continental breakfast, a
social hour, and bicycles are complimentary, and there is a small
freeform pool by the picturesque waterfront. Each spacious unit is
attractively furnished to convey the warmth of a country inn, and has
a phone and remote control color TV. Toll-free: (800)438-4466.
  #44,#50—upstairs, picture windows on two sides with
    private panoramic view of harbor from   K bed...$200
    regular room—   K bed...$100
Marriott Residence Inn   *241-8800*
5.2 mi. NE (near CA 73) at 881 W. Baker St. - Costa Mesa 92626
Marriott's all-suites motel has a pool and whirlpool in a garden, and
a sports court. Breakfast and afternoon repast are complimentary.
Each spacious, well-furnished suite has a kitchen with microwave,
fireplace in the living room, two phones and a remote control color TV
and VCR with (free and pay) movies. Toll-free: (800)331-3131.
  "Two Bedroom Suite" (many)—2 TVs, loft with   Q bed...$119
    regular room—studio,   Q bed...$79
Motel 6   *957-3063*
5.5 mi. N (near I-405) at 1441 Gisler Av. - Costa Mesa 92626
A courtyard pool is a feature of this modern **bargain** motel. Each
compact, simply furnished room has a phone and color TV.
    regular room—   Q bed...$36
★ **Newport Beach Marriott Hotel**   *640-4000*
3.5 mi. E at 900 Newport Center Dr. near Fashion Island - 92660
The city's largest hotel (600 rooms) is a contemporary sixteen-story
resort complex amidst tropical gardens. A splendid shopping mall is
within an easy stroll and a lush golf course adjoins. Amenities include
two large tropically landscaped pools and whirlpools, exercise facilities,
sauna; and (for a fee) eight lighted tennis courts, bicycles, and
massage; plus a restaurant and lounge (see listing) and resort shop.
Each beautifully furnished room has a floor-to-ceiling window, tiny
balcony, phone, and remote control color TV with movies. Toll-free:
(800)228-9290.
  #916—superb harbor/ocean view,   K bed...$170
  "Concierge"—11,12, & 14 floors in North Tower, comp.
    light breakfast & appetizers, (request harbor side), K bed...$169
    regular room—request 10th to 7th floor
    North Tower,   2 T or K bed...$139
★ **Newport Beach Marriott Suites**   *854-4500*
4.5 mi. NE at 500 Bayview Circle by Jamboree Rd. - 92660
Overlooking the upper end of Newport Bay is a post-modern nine-story
hotel with 250 two-room suites. The handsome complex features a
large indoor/outdoor pool and whirlpool on a garden terrace, saunas,
exercise room, rental bicycles, comfortable bayview dining room, posh
lounge, and gift shop. Each beautifully decorated unit has a living
room with a stocked (honor) bar, bedroom, private balcony, two
phones, and two remote control color TVs with (free and pay) movies.
Toll-free: (800)228-9290.
  #646,#546,#446—fine corner view of bay,   K bed...$129
    regular room—request bay side,   K bed...$119

Newport Channel Inn   *642-3030*
1.5 mi. NW at 6030 W. Pacific Coast Hwy. - 92663
No amenities, but the beach is a short stroll across a busy highway.
Each nicely furnished room has a phone and color TV. Toll-free in CA:
(800)255-8614; elsewhere: (800)457-8614.

   regular room—   Q bed...$57

Portofino Beach Hotel   *673-7030*
.4 mi. S at 2306 W. Oceanfront - Balboa Peninsula 92663
The beach is beyond a parking lot in front of this twenty-room hotel.
Renato's (see listing) restaurant is downstairs. All rooms have a
private bath and some antiques, a phone and color TV.

   "Roma Suites"—in-bath whirlpool tub/shower,
     gas fireplace in view of   Q bed...$235
   "Portofino Suites"—in-bath whirlpool, ocean view,   Q bed...$210
   regular room—   Q bed...$100

Quality Inn   *536-7500*
5.6 mi. NW at 800 Pacific Coast Hwy. - Huntington Beach 92648
The beach is across a busy highway from this contemporary motel with
a rooftop whirlpool. Each well-furnished room has a floor-to-ceiling
window, small private balcony, refrigerator/wet bar, phone, and
remote control color TV with movies. Toll-free: (800)228-5151.

   #302,#301—spacious, gas fireplace, multi-window
     ocean view from raised whirlpool in view of   K bed...$199
   regular room—ocean view (request 3rd floor),   K bed...$99
   regular room—ground level,   K bed...$89

Quality Suites   *957-9200*
8 mi. NE (near CA 55) at 2701 Hotel Terrace Dr. - Santa Ana 92705
Quality's business-oriented all-suites hotel opened in 1986 with a
landscaped courtyard pool and whirlpool, and a gift shop. Breakfast
and afternoon beverages are complimentary. Each well-furnished two-
room suite has a wet bar and stocked (honor) refrigerator, microwave,
two phones, and two remote control color TVs with movies. Toll-free:
(800)228-5151.

   regular room—   2 D or K bed...$69

Radisson Plaza Hotel   *833-9999*
6 mi. NE at 18800 MacArthur Blvd. - Irvine 92715
John Wayne Airport is across a highway from this recently remodeled
300-room hotel. The ten-story convention-oriented complex has a large
freeform pool in a palm-shaded courtyard, whirlpool, one lighted
tennis court, exercise equipment, plus a restaurant, coffee shop, posh
lounge with a grand piano, and gift shop. Each well-furnished room
has a tiny balcony, phone, and remote control color TV with (pay)
movies. Toll-free: (800)333-3333.

   "plaza level"—top 2 floors, concierge, extras,   2 D or K bed...$119
   regular room—   2 D or K bed...$89

Ramada Limited   *840-2431*
11 mi. NW at 17205 Pacific Coast Hwy. (Box 1188) - Sunset Beach 90742
The area's best beach is across a parking lot from this contemporary
motel with a whirlpool. Each well-furnished room has a refrigerator,
phone and remote control color TV with movies. Toll-free: (800)2-
RAMADA.

   regular room—pvt. balcony with ocean view,   2 Q beds...$109
   regular room—by highway,   K bed...$79

★ **Red Lion Hotel**   *540-7000*
5.2 mi. NE at 3050 Bristol St. - Costa Mesa 92626
One of the area's best business-and-leisure hotels opened in 1987. The ultra-modern seven-story complex includes 484 rooms; an extra-large pool and whirlpool in a rooftop garden with a waterfall; sauna, steam room, and exercise room; gift shop; handsome restaurants and a plush entertainment lounge. Each attractively appointed room has a floor-to-ceiling window (most have a small private balcony), (honor) bar, phone and remote control color TV with free and pay movies. Toll-free: (800)547-8010.
"Executive Level"—top floor, extras, views,   2 Q or K bed...$139
regular room—request 6th or 5th fl. for best views,2 Q or K bed...$119
Regency Inn - Best Western   *962-4244*
7.4 mi. NW at 19360 Beach Blvd. - Huntington Beach 92648
A contemporary motel with an outdoor pool and whirlpool. Each well-furnished room has a phone and color TV. Toll-free: (800)524-1234.
#116—spacious, raised whirlpool in view of   plush K bed...$159
spa room (several)—in-room whirlpool,   K bed...$95
regular room—   2 Q beds...$79; K bed...$69
Rodeway Inn   *642-8252*
1.5 mi. NW at 6208 W. Pacific Coast Hwy. - 92663
This modern four-story motel, a block from the ocean across a busy noisy highway, has a small outdoor pool. Each nicely furnished room has a phone and color TV. Toll-free: (800)332-0011.
regular room—request 4th floor for ocean view,   Q bed...$62
★ **Sheraton Newport Beach Hotel**   *833-0570*
5 mi. NE at 4545 MacArthur Blvd. - 92660
John Wayne Airport is a block from Sheraton's contemporary California-style hotel. The ten-story, 350-room complex has a large freeform pool and whirlpool in a tropical garden court, gym, two lighted tennis courts, plus a dining room, coffee shop, entertainment lounge and gift shop. Breakfast and afternoon cocktails are complimentary. Each well-furnished room has a small private balcony, phone and color TV with (free and pay) movies. Toll-free: (800)325-3535.
regular room—10th floor for best cityscapes,   2 D or K bed...$139
Super 8 Motel   *545-9471*
3.5 mi. N at 2645 Harbor Blvd. - Costa Mesa 92626
Amenities in this modern motel include a landscaped pool, whirlpool and a sauna. Selected food and beverages are complimentary. Each nicely furnished room has a refrigerator, phone and remote control color TV with movies. Toll-free: (800)800-8000.
regular room—   2 Q or K bed...$49
★ **The Sutton Place Hotel**   *476-2001*
5 mi. NE at 4500 MacArthur Blvd. - 92660
This post-modern 435-room resort is one of Orange County's finest hotels. Fountains and tropical gardens surround a gleaming ten-story stair-step tower. Fine art is displayed throughout. Amenities include a large pool and whirlpool on a garden deck, two lighted tennis courts, saunas, exercise room; and (for a fee) massage, bicycling, plus lavish dining and drinking facilities (see listing) and fine shops. Each beautifully appointed room has a phone, (honor) bar, and remote control color TV with (free and pay) movies. Toll-free: (800)810-6888.
#1039,#1040,#1065,#1066—corner parlor
& large private balcony, fine cityscapes,   K bed...$250
regular room—   2 T or K bed...$155

The Waterfront Hilton Beach Resort   *960-7873*

5 mi. NW at 21100 Pacific Coast Hwy. - *Huntington Beach 92648*
A long popular beach is across a busy highway from Hilton's
contemporary 300-room resort hotel. Amenities of the twelve-story
complex include a large freeform pool, whirlpool, exercise room, and
two lighted tennis courts, plus a restaurant, lounge and gift shop.
Each of the well-furnished rooms has a small private balcony, stocked
(honor) bar, two phones and remote control color TV with free and pay
movies. Toll-free: (800)HILTONS.

#1026,#926,#826—spacious, wet bar/refr.,
fine beach views from   K bed...$300
regular room—   2 D or K bed...$125

★ **The Westin South Coast Plaza**   *540-2500*

6 mi. NE at 666 Anton Blvd. - *Costa Mesa 92626*
Southern inland Orange County's landmark hotel opened in 1975
across from the region's best shopping complex. It was completely
refurbished and upgraded in 1990. The Orange County Performing
Arts Center (see listing) is also within easy walking distance. The
sixteen-story convention-oriented facility has 390 rooms, a large
landscaped rooftop pool above a dramatic waterfall, exercise room, two
lighted tennis courts, gourmet restaurants and lounges (see listing),
a gift shop and garage. Each beautifully furnished room has a phone,
refrigerator (honor bar), and remote control color TV with free and pay
movies. Toll-free: (800)228-3000.

"Executive Floors"—15th & 16th floors, concierge,
comp. breakfast & cocktails, fine city/mtn. views,   K bed...$174
regular room—   2 D or K bed...$159

Woolley's Petite Suites   *540-1111*

8 mi. NE (near CA 55) at 2721 Hotel Terrace Rd. - *Santa Ana 92705*
Business travelers favor this neo-Spanish-Colonial all-suites motor inn
with a pool and whirlpool in a landscaped courtyard, and a gift shop.
Full breakfast and afternoon cocktails are complimentary. Each well-
furnished suite has a refrigerator/wet bar, microwave, two phones and
color TV with free and pay movies. Toll-free: (800)762-2597.

regular room—   K bed...$66

Wyndham Garden Hotel   *751-5100*

6.2 mi. NE at 3350 Av. of the Arts - *Costa Mesa 92626*
A lovely little lake with a fountain and the Performing Arts Center
adjoin this leisure-oriented hotel. The contemporary seven-story
complex has 238 rooms, a landscaped pool and whirlpool by the lake,
an exercise room, plus a restaurant and lounge. Each well-furnished
room has a private (standing only) balcony, three phones, and remote
control color TV with movies. Toll-free: (800)822-4200.

regular room—request lake side for fine view,   2 Q or K bed...$99

Ojai

Ojai is the West's Eden. When **Lost Horizons** was made into a movie, overview scenes of "Shangri-La" were filmed of this luxuriant little valley sheltered by towering Coast Range mountains. At the heart of the canyon lies Ojai, secluded among noble oaks and gardens surrounded by fruit and nut orchards. Since early in this century, the town has evolved as an artists' colony and a serene resort.

Among the fifty "great towns of the West" identified by the author in 1985, Ojai alone in Southern California has gotten even better. Today, the compact downtown is a charming combination of inspired Spanish-Colonial architecture, smart shops, and bountiful vegetation that lends itself to relaxing strolls and shopping. Sophisticated studios and galleries display local arts and crafts. Restaurants and lodgings are relatively scarce, but distinctive. Scenic golf courses, tennis complexes, and riding and hiking trails are enjoyed year-round.

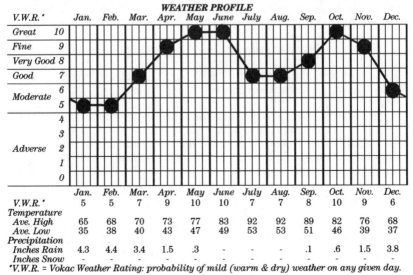

WEATHER PROFILE

V.W.R.*		Jan.	Feb.	Mar.	Apr.	May	June	July	Aug.	Sep.	Oct.	Nov.	Dec.
Great	10												
Fine	9												
Very Good	8												
Good	7												
Moderate	6												
	5												
	4												
	3												
Adverse	2												
	1												
	0												

	Jan.	Feb.	Mar.	Apr.	May	June	July	Aug.	Sep.	Oct.	Nov.	Dec.
V.W.R.*	5	5	7	9	10	10	7	7	8	10	9	6
Temperature												
Ave. High	65	68	70	73	77	83	92	92	89	82	76	68
Ave. Low	35	38	40	43	47	49	53	53	51	46	39	37
Precipitation												
Inches Rain	4.3	4.4	3.4	1.5	.3	-	-	-	.1	.6	1.5	3.8
Inches Snow	-	-	-	-	-	-	-	-	-	-	-	-

*V.W.R. = Vokac Weather Rating: probability of mild (warm & dry) weather on any given day.

Population: 7,613   Area Code: 805
Elevation: 746 feet
Location: 89 miles Northwest of Los Angeles
Ojai Valley Chamber of Commerce & Visitors Bureau   646-8126
   downtown at 338 E. Ojai Av. (Box 1134) - 93023

ATTRACTIONS

★ **Bart's Corner**   646-3755
   .3 mi. W at 302 W. Matilija St.
   Bart's Corner is the West's most remarkable outdoor bookstore. More than one hundred thousand used books are shelved in a labyrinth of rooms and courtyards under a giant oak tree that shades customers as they browse or read. After hours, visitors may select books from shelves that line the sidewalk and pay for them by putting coins in a slot in the gate. Closed Mon.

★ *Bicycling*
   A paved separated bikeway extends through Ojai and beyond to miles of flower-bordered paved byways throughout the relatively flat little Shangri-La valley. At every turn are citrus and avocado groves, lush gardens, and grand old California live oaks. Bicycles can be rented at:
   Bicycle Doctor *.3 mi. E at 212 Fox St. (Closed Mon.)* 646-7554
   Bicycles & *.3 mi. W at 108 Canada St. (Closed Wed.,Sun.)* 646-7736

★ **Friend's Ranch**   646-2871
   5 mi. NW on CA 33 at 15150 Maricopa Hwy.
   Fine local citrus, avocados, and nuts are sold at this roadside plant.

Golf
★   **Ojai Valley Inn Golf Course**   646-5511
   1 mi. SW via CA 150 on Country Club Dr.
   This challenging, spectacular 18-hole golf course is open to the public year-round, along with a pro shop, driving range, putting green, club and cart rentals, and a fine view restaurant and lounge.

★   **Soule Park Golf Course**   646-5633
   .8 mi. E at 1033 Ojai Av.
   Open to the public year-round, this lovely 18-hole championship course has rentals, driving range, pro shop, dining and drinking facilities.

Horseback Riding
   Ojai Valley Inn Riding Stables   646-5511
   2 mi. W via CA 150 on Hermosa Rd.
   Guided one and a half hour trail rides can be arranged year-round.

   Lake Casitas Recreation Area   649-2233
   6.4 mi. SW on CA 150
   The site of 1984 Olympic events is a many-armed reservoir surrounded by grass-and-oak-covered hills. It is also the source of state record bass and catfish. Scenic picnic sites and hundreds of campsites for tents and trailers overlook the lake. It is a domestic water supply, so swimming, waterskiing, and most boats are not allowed. Certain watercrafts can be launched or rented for fishing or sightseeing only.

★ **Libbey Park**
   downtown at Ojai Av. & Signal St.
   Noble oaks and giant old sycamores preside over lawns and gardens, a fountain court, picnic and play areas, eight tennis courts, and a famed music bowl in a lovely little park in the heart of town.

★ **Los Padres National Forest**   *646-4348*
starts 1 mi. N of town
A vast forest extending almost to the coast cloaks all of the mountains towering above town to the north. The highest peaks reach pine-covered elevations nearly 9,000 feet above sea level. The only giant California condors outside of zoos live in the Sespe Condor Sanctuary northeast of town. The rugged San Rafael Wilderness, Southern California's largest, is northwest of town. Horseback riding, hunting, backpacking, fishing, and camping are popular. Hikers especially enjoy scenic trails and natural swimming holes along Matilija Creek north of town and along Sespe Creek to the east.

Rancho Arnaz Country Store   *649-2776*
6.5 mi. SW on CA 33 at 9504 N. Ventura Av. - Ventura
The apple orchard and big red barn by the highway have drawn visitors since 1928. You can pick your own apples in fall. Several different kinds are grown. The family-run ranch market also sells them packaged to go, plus cold cider, and other seasonal produce.

★ *Scenic Drive*
for 10 mi. E of downtown
A ten-mile paved loop road (suitable for car or bicycle) showcases the lush valley. It is an especially memorable tour when citrus groves fill the valley with an intoxicating fragrance during spring blossom-time. Miles of rough stone walls that line part of the road were built by Chinese labor a century ago. Drive east on Ojai Avenue 3.2 miles, then left on Reeves Road, McAndrew Road, and Thacher Road.

Shopping
★ **Rains Department Store**   *646-1441*
downtown at 218 Ojai Av.
The centerpiece for the captivating "shopping arcade" downtown is Rains. Ojai's renowned department store is a delightfully fashionable link to a kinder, gentler past. Everyday merchandise and a wealth of unusual specialty items are displayed with a genuine flair and sold by a friendly, well-informed staff.

Valley of "Shangri-La"
3.5 mi. E on CA 150
The panorama representing Shangri-La seen by Ronald Coleman years ago in the movie "Lost Horizons" is still grand from this hilltop.

Warm Water Feature
★ **Wheeler Hot Springs**   *646-8131*
7.7 mi. NW on CA 33
In a luxuriant palm-shaded oasis at the base of a narrow canyon, a refurbished century-old spa is open to the public. Redwood tubs with both hot and cold mineral baths can be rented in private rooms with skylights. Massage is available by appointment, and spa guests can use a large (cold spring) outdoor pool. For toll-free reservations in Southern California, call: (800)9-WHEELER.

Winery
Old Creek Ranch Winery   *649-4132*
7.5 mi. SW at 10024 Old Creek Rd. - Oak View
The current winery, opened in 1981, is on the site of a winery established around 1900. Selected quality wines are being produced while the old winery is restored and vineyards replanted. Open Fri. & Sat. from 10-4 and Sun. from 12-4.

RESTAURANTS

★ **The Garden Terrace Restaurant**   *646-1133*
.7 mi. E at 1002 E. Ojai Av.
B-L-D.   *Moderate*
The emphasis is on fresh natural ingredients in New California dishes like shoofly buttermilk pancakes for breakfast or ginger shrimp stir fry for dinner. Luscious desserts made here are showcased by the cozy comfortable dining room.

★ **Gaslight**   *646-5990*
3.6 mi. SW on CA 33 at 11432 N. Ventura Av.
D only. Closed Mon.   *Moderate*
Several tasty veal dishes, Old World specialties, and al dente vegetables are highlights. The long-established dinner house also has a newly remodeled patio, and lounge with music for dancing.

Gerry's Busy Oak Cafe   *649-4712*
5.5 mi. SW on CA 33 at 490 Ventura Av. - Oak View
B-L.   *Moderate*
Heaping helpings of uncomplicated American fare, including fresh-from-the-fryer little donut balls, are served in a cheerful coffee shop distinguished by Indian artifacts and lush greenery decor, and on an umbrella-shaded patio.

★ **L'Auberge**   *646-2288*
.3 mi. W at 314 El Paseo Rd.
D only. Sat. & Sun. brunch. Closed Tues.   *Expensive*
French classics including sweetbreads and frog legs are served in a casually elegant dining room with a cozy fireplace and on a wonderfully tranquil garden porch of an artistically converted older home on a side street.

★ **Nora's Bistro**   *640-6672*
downtown at 423 E. Ojai Av.
L-D. Closed Tues.   *Expensive*
Ojai's newest dining venue stars with light, bright Italian delights like brick oven pizza (both traditional with pepperoni and bell pepper and designer with wild mushrooms). Desserts are homemade too, including tiramisu. The modish bistro is decorated with whimsical avant-garde art.

★ **Ojai Cafe Emporium**   *646-2723*
downtown at 108 S. Montgomery St.
B-L-D. No D Sun. & Mon.   *Moderate*
In 1991, Ojai's favorite coffee house/cafe relocated, expanded and got even better. Light and lovely New California cuisine ranges from an oven puffed egg blended with cheese and mild ortega for breakfast to sauteed chicken breast in herbs and fresh lemon juice for dinner. Premium coffees and other drinks including fresh local citrus juices are also served in cheerful indoor and outdoor dining rooms enlivened by warm wood tones, luxuriant greenery and flowers.

★ **Ojai Ice Cream & Candy Shoppe**   *646-6075*
downtown at 210 E. Ojai Av.
Many flavors of outstanding ice cream and sherbets are made here. So are several kinds of homemade fudge. All are on display in this tantalizing takeout shop.

★ **Ojai Valley Inn and Country Club**   *646-5511*
1 mi. W via CA 150 on Country Club Dr.
B-L-D. Sun. brunch.   *Expensive–Very Expensive*
The **Vista Dining Room** (B-D. Sun. brunch–Very Expensive) offers skillfully prepared fresh regional fare in a luxurious contemporary setting with a panoramic view of the golf course and mountains. The **Oak Grill Terrace** (L-D–Expensive) features seasonal New California cuisine in a cheerful wood-trimmed dining room and on an oak-shaded terrace overlooking the golf course. The **Club Bar** is a comfortable wood-paneled lounge.

★ **The Ranch House**   *646-2360*
3 mi. W via CA 33 on S. Lomita Av.
L-D. Sun. brunch. Closed Mon.-Tues.   *Very Expensive*
The valley's most illustrious restaurant is a progenitor of New California cuisine. Long before the regional style was widely known, unusual gourmet dishes were being created here with a light touch enhanced by locally grown herbs and vegetables, and distinctive homemade breads and desserts. The tradition of excellence is wonderfully intact. Picture windows in a refined dining room overlook flower and herb gardens. Outside, tables shaded by noble oaks are set under heat lamps for year-round enjoyment of gardens, pools, and fountains. Live chamber music frequently enhances the delightful setting.

★ **The Restaurant at Wheeler Hot Springs**   *646-8131*
7.7 mi. NW on CA 33
D only. Sat. & Sun. brunch. Closed Mon.-Wed.   *Expensive*
New California cuisine is acclaimed once more in this reborn romantic retreat. A medley of poached sea bass and salmon with sauvignon blanc sauce or oak-grilled New York steak with mushroom marsala sauce suggest creative possibilities. The large tasteful dining room has been exquisitely refurbished in a century-old lodge sporting a window wall by a stream and a dramatic river-rock fireplace. A firelit lounge has assorted premium wines and tap beers by the glass.

★ **Roger Keller's Restaurant**   *646-7266*
downtown at 331 E. Ojai Av.
L-D. In winter, no L Mon.-Fri.   *Expensive*
New California cuisine shows up on a regularly changing menu that reflects fresh seasonal produce. The dining room opened in 1989 with modish decor enhanced by vibrant art and greenery.

★ **Suzanne's Cuisine**   *640-1961*
.3 mi. W at 502 W. Ojai Av.
L-D. Closed Tues.   *Very Expensive*
In 1992, Suzanne's became an immediate superstar among Southern California's great dining destinations. No one makes better use of fresh regional produce and herbs and spices grown in their own garden. The result is nonpareil New California cuisine in dishes like home-smoked chicken, blue cheese and toasted walnuts on a bed of mixed greens with walnut vinaigrette; or fresh grilled fish with ginger sauce, and stellar desserts like ambrosial apricot and other homemade sorbets. The sophisticated dining room is enhanced by stylish wall hangings, but the decor tour-de-force is a heated covered flagstone patio that opens onto a lovely garden with a fountain and paths amidst some of the herbs and spices used in the kitchen.

LODGING

Accommodations in Ojai are notably scarce, and there are no bargains on weekends. Prices are often reduced by at least 15% midweek.

Capri Motel   646-4305
.8 mi. E at 1180 E. Ojai Av. - 93023
A large, scenic outdoor pool and whirlpool in a tranquil garden setting are features of this modern motel. Each spacious room has a private patio or balcony, a phone, and a color TV.
#210,#209—balcony with floor/ceiling view to mtns.,   K bed...$60
regular room—   2 D or K bed...$60

El Camino Lodge   646-4341
.3 mi. W at 406 W. Ojai Av. (Box 183) - 93023
This modern motel is the most convenient to downtown, and has an outdoor pool. Each comfortable room has a phone and color TV.
regular room—   2 Q or K bed...$50

★ **The Oaks at Ojai**   646-5573
downtown at 122 E. Ojai Av. - 93023
A historic hotel has become a popular health spa on luxuriant grounds. Prices include three flavorful low calorie meals daily; plus use of a large swimming pool, whirlpools, saunas and a gym. More than a dozen fitness and self-awareness programs are provided, plus (for a fee) massage, facials and other health and beauty services. There is a gift shop. Each comfortable room has a phone and color TV. Two-night minimum rate shown is per night for two people.
cottage—spacious,   2 D beds...$320
regular room—in lodge,   2 D beds...$250

★ **Ojai Valley Inn and Country Club**   646-5511
1 mi. SW via CA 150 on Country Club Dr. - 93023
Here is the premier resort of Ojai Valley. In 1988 it was expanded to 212 rooms and upgraded. Oak-shaded grounds of the renowned Spanish-Colonial-style hideaway include two extra-large outdoor pools; a whirlpool; a fitness center, steam rooms and saunas; ping pong; bicycles, plus (for a fee) a world-class 18-hole golf course, putting green, eight tennis courts (four lighted), horseback riding (see listing), as well as plush dining rooms (see listing) and a lounge, and shops. Each spacious, beautifully decorated room has a stocked (honor) bar/refrigerator, phone, and remote control color TV with (pay) movies. Most have a private patio or balcony. Toll-free: (800)422-6524.
#624,#613—1 BR suite, 2 fireplaces, in-bath whirlpool,
pvt. balc. with super fairway/mountain views,   2 Q beds...$395
#273,#253—top floor, large private balcony,
great fairways/mountain views,   2 Q beds...$260
regular room—   2 Q or K bed...$240

The Theodore Woolsey House   646-9779
1 mi. E at 1484 E. Ojai Av. - 93023
A century-old landmark is now the area's best bed-and-breakfast inn. Some period furnishings are used in each of six comfortable rooms. Mature trees shade a large outdoor pool. An elaborate Continental buffet breakfast, and finger foods each evening are complimentary.
#6—fireplace, private balcony, large clawfoot tub,   Q bed...$110
#1—overlooks pool, fireplace, clawfoot tub,   4-poster Q bed...$110
regular room—shared bath,   D bed...$50

Palm Desert

Palm Desert is California's new desert showplace. Stylish low-profile buildings amid luxuriant landscapes fill a cove of the broad Coachella Valley at the base of the towering San Jacinto Mountains. In spite of the choice location and warm, sunny climate, major development didn't begin here until the 1970s.

Today, sand dunes have been replaced by emerald-green golf courses, while the area's natural grandeur is displayed in the Living Desert, an expansive showcase for birds, animals, and plants indigenous to arid lands. The city boasts the desert's largest enclosed mall, and the burgeoning collection of shops and restaurants along El Paseo is now tonier than any in Palm Springs. In keeping with its 1990s status as the urbane alternative to its renowned rival, Palm Desert now has many of the region's finest restaurants and lodgings.

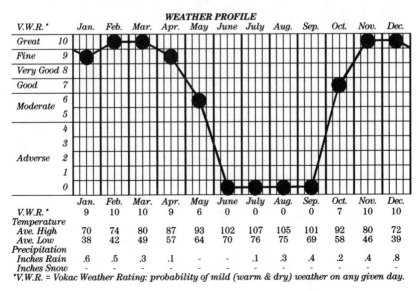

WEATHER PROFILE

V.W.R.*		Jan.	Feb.	Mar.	Apr.	May	June	July	Aug.	Sep.	Oct.	Nov.	Dec.
V.W.R.*		9	10	10	9	6	0	0	0	0	7	10	10
Temperature													
Ave. High		70	74	80	87	93	102	107	105	101	92	80	72
Ave. Low		38	42	49	57	64	70	76	75	69	58	46	39
Precipitation													
Inches Rain		.6	.5	.3	.1	-	-	.1	.3	.4	.2	.4	.8
Inches Snow		-	-	-	-	-	-	-	-	-	-	-	-

*V.W.R. = Vokac Weather Rating: probability of mild (warm & dry) weather on any given day.

179

Population: 23,252   *Area Code: 619*
Elevation: 183 feet
Location: 119 miles East of Los Angeles   (800)41-RELAX
Palm Springs Desert Resorts Convention & Visitors Bureau   770-9000
4.6 mi. NW at 69930 Hwy. 111, Rancho Mirage, Suite 201 - 92270

ATTRACTIONS

★ *Balloon Flights*

Scenic balloon flights offer an exciting new perspective on the desert and mountains. Passenger flights of approximately one hour can be arranged from October thru May at:

    American Balloon Charters   327-8544   *(800)FLY-OVER*
    Fantasy Balloon Flights   568-0997   *(800)GO-ABOVE*

Date Gardens

★ **Jensen's Date & Citrus Garden**   347-3897

2.4 mi. E at 80653 Hwy. 111 - Indio
This long-established roadside shop offers free samples, and low prices for assorted date products—including shakes. Fresh-squeezed orange, tangerine, and grapefruit juices are also featured in season. The desert's best free showcase garden of subtropical citrus and dates, all carefully labeled and described, is out back.

★ **Oasis Date Gardens**   399-5665

18 mi. SE at 59111 Hwy. 111 (Box 757) - Thermal
A mature date palm grove adjoins a contemporary cafe and gift shop where all locally grown date varieties are available for tasting (in season) and in gift packs. A palm-shaded grassy picnic area adjoins.

★ **Shields Date Gardens**   347-0996

2 mi. E at 80225 Hwy. 111 - Indio
For decades this has been a landmark oasis for travelers interested in enjoying dates in all kinds of configurations (don't miss the shakes), and learning about "the sex life of the date" in their free theater. Seasonal local grapefruit, oranges, etc. are also displayed for sale.

★ **Valerie Jean Date Gardens**

19 mi. SE on CA 86 at 66th Av. (Box 786) - Thermal
The nation's oldest commercial date oasis has been operating since 1928. The little landmark features date shakes reputedly invented here. For another unique treat, try the cactus shake made from prickly pear syrup—a refreshing winner. Date samples are generously offered and assorted dates and citrus are available in gift packs or to go.

★ **El Paseo**

downtown on El Paseo between Palms-to-Pines Hwy. & Portola Av.
This mile-long boulevard rivals Rodeo Drive in Beverly Hills as the best shopping street in Southern California. Chic boutiques with au courant names from around the world, and fine art galleries abound, interspersed with the greatest conflux of gourmet restaurants in the desert. The ambiance is enhanced by heraldic sculptures and gardenscapes. Among the tasteful shops, a personal favorite is:

★ **The Upper Crust**   568-1998

.5 mi. E at 73540 El Paseo
This culinary landmark was recently enlarged and made even better. Generous samples of preserves, cheese spreads and more are offered from a wealth of well-selected gourmet goodies showcased for sale here, along with premium kitchen wares.

★ **The Living Desert**   *346-5694*
2.3 mi. SE at 47900 Portola Av.
Almost two square miles have been set aside to depict deserts near
and far. Botanical gardens contain shady oases with tranquil pools,
and a myriad of unusual plants, many with vivid blossoms in spring.
Exhibits portray local geology, history and Indian culture. Eagle
Canyon is a state-of-the-art habitat for animals of the American
desert. Self-guided trails lead to African desert animals, and picnic
facilities. There is also a gift shop. Closed in summer.

★ **National Date Festival**   *863-8236*
10 mi. E on Hwy. 111 - Indio
The Arabian Nights (and days) atmosphere at the fairgrounds in
Indio—"the Date Capital of the World"—is the right setting for a unique
and popular ten-day celebration in mid-February that includes
parades, cultural exhibits, and live entertainment—even camel races!

RESTAURANTS

A Touch of Mama's   *568-1315*
1 mi. E at 74063 Hwy. 111
D only.   *Very Expensive*
Savory antipasto trays, a wealth of homemade pastas, and homemade
desserts including a superb tiramisu highlight classic Italian cuisine
served in a popular little trattoria.

Andreino's   *733-3365*
downtown at 73098 Hwy. 111
D only.   *Very Expensive*
A limited selection of Northern Italian classics includes a large
charbroiled T-bone veal chop with a mustard/mushroom white wine
sauce. The robust cuisine draws crowds to a cozy congested dining
room/bar and an enclosed sidewalk cafe.

★ **Beachside Cafe**   *564-4577*
5.5 mi. E at 78477 CA 111 - La Quinta
B-L-D.   *Moderate*
The most appealing coffee shop in the desert opened in late 1991.
Designer omelets and a wide assortment of well-prepared all-American
dishes, including a giant homemade cinnamon roll, are served in a
light and lively dining room with comfortably padded booths and
chairs and on an umbrella-shaded garden patio.

Cedar Creek Inn   *340-1236*
downtown at 73445 El Paseo
L-D.   *Expensive*
Contemporary American fare is offered in several comfortable plant-
filled dining rooms, an umbrella-shaded patio, and a cozy lounge. This
first of a small chain is one of the most popular family dining
destinations in the desert.

The Chart House   *324-5613*
4.2 mi. NW at 69934 Hwy. 111 - Rancho Mirage
D only.   *Expensive*
Fresh seafood, steaks, or prime rib and an impressive salad bar are
accompanied by a tour de force of freeform woodcraft architecture and
contemporary decor. All things considered, this is the best
representative of any national restaurant chain in the desert.

Club 74   *568-2782*
downtown at 73061 El Paseo
L-D. Closed Sun.   *Very Expensive*
Traditional French cuisine is presented by tuxedoed waiters in a
refined dining room with a grand piano, a natty bar, and a view.

★ **Cuistot**   *340-1000*
   downtown at 73111 El Paseo
   L-D. No D Sun. Closed Mon.   *Very Expensive*
Sauteed veal chop with wild mushrooms; grilled quail over golden
black chantrelles risotto or baked sturgeon with sea urchin sauce
typify the unusual New California cuisine that has made this one of
California's great dining experiences. The understated modern dining
areas and lounge accented with fresh flowers provide a suitable
backdrop for the sophisticated cuisine.

★ **Cunard's**   *564-4443*
   9 mi. SE at 78045 Calle Cadiz - La Quinta
   D only.   *Extremely Expensive*
One of the desert's most acclaimed restaurants went back to its roots
in 1995 for contemporary Continental cuisine. Fresh quality
ingredients are masterfully prepared from scratch daily including
baked goods and desserts. Piano entertainment accompanies meals
formally presented in several unique dining rooms in an elegant
country estate. A firelit back room and cozy piano bar lounge overlook
a tranquil garden with a waterfall.

★ **Hyatt Grand Champions Resort**   *341-1000*
   3.5 mi. E at 44600 Indian Wells Lane - Indian Wells
   B-L-D.   *Expensive–Very Expensive*
Charlie's (D only–Very Expensive) features distinctively updated
dishes from the American South and Southwest and from Latin
America by the tennis courts and swimming pool. **Trattoria
California** (B-L-D–Expensive) offers a New-California-via-Italy
grazing menu in a large handsome dining room and terrace that share
a tranquil fairway view with **Pianissimo's**, a modish lounge with live
entertainment.

★ **Jillian's**   *776-8242*
   1.2 mi. E at 74155 El Paseo
   D only.   *Very Expensive*
The newest darling of desert cognoscenti opened in 1994. The highly
regarded chef/owner features New California cuisine in specialties like
salmon in parchment and braised pork tenderloin with fresh plums
and figs. All of the pastas, breads and desserts like macadamia nut
cheesecake and raspberry creme brule are made here. Whitewashed
adobe rooms and a landscaped courtyard outfitted with full linen and
candles provide the look and feel of a posh hacienda.

★ **Kaiser Grille**   *779-1988*
   1.3 mi. E at 74225 Hwy. 111, Suite B
   D only.   *Expensive*
It's the extras—like first-rate oil-and-herb sauce for the foccaccio that
starts every meal, or the finger biscuit with coffee, or the three-draft
sampler enticement to try some of the world's great tap beers, or
frozen prickly pear margarita as the house special. New California
grazing fare is complemented by snazzy post-modern dining areas
surrounding an exhibition kitchen and island bar.

Keedy's Fountain Grill

Palm Desert

Keedy's Fountain Grill *346-6492*
.6 mi. E at 73633 Hwy. 111
B-L-D. No D Sun. Low
American short order standards have been served in this plain old-fashioned coffee shop for three decades. The "blast from the past" continues to attract a loyal following of budget-minded natives.

LG's Steakhouse *779-9799*
1.3 mi. E at 74225 Hwy. 111, Suite A
D only. Very Expensive
The hard-core beef (and it is prime) can't carry the uninspired accompaniments in this big neo-pueblo landmark, subdivided into several casually posh dining areas with dramatic Southwestern accents.

La Quinta Cliffhouse *360-5991*
5 mi. E at 78250 Hwy. 111 - La Quinta
L-D. Sun. brunch. Expensive
Contemporary American fare is served in dishes like baked sea bass with macadamia nuts or New York steak with Jack Daniels peppercorn sauce. A landmark built into a hill has been spectacularly converted into several casually elegant dining rooms and a lounge. All share fine picture window views of the desert and mountains.

★ **La Quinta Resort** *564-4111*
8 mi. SE at 49499 Eisenhower Dr. - La Quinta
B-L-D. Sun. brunch. Expensive
Montanas (D only. Sun. brunch only. Closed Mon.) presents masterfully prepared New California cuisine like roast maple chicken with date crust in an opulent dining room that is the desert's oldest. The **Adobe Grill** (L-D) skillfully combines New California and Mexican dishes in a display kitchen by a posh Southwestern dining room with fireplaces and a fountain patio. **Morgans** (B-L-D) serves traditional American dishes in a snazzy 1920s-style cafe. **La Cantina** features drinks and live music for dancing in a big border-themed bar with video and board games.

★ **Le Paon** *568-3651*
.5 mi. S at 45640 CA 74
D only. Extremely Expensive
Traditional and innovative French cuisine is expertly prepared and graciously served amid candlelit elegance or on a heated garden patio in one of the desert's most acclaimed dinner houses. Don't miss the award-winning souffles or flambes, for the final Gallic touch. Grand piano stylings contribute to the ambiance from a cozy lounge.

Lord Fletcher Inn *328-1161*
3.5 mi. NW at 70385 Hwy. 111 - Rancho Mirage
D only. Closed Sun. Expensive
Pot roast, loin of lamb, and other dishes are served by costumed staff in dining rooms with comfortable English country inn/pub decor.

★ **Marriott's Desert Springs Resort & Spa** *341-2211*
4 mi. NE at 74855 Country Club Dr.
B-L-D. Expensive–Very Expensive
Marriott's mega-resort has nearly a dozen eating and drinking places. **Tuscany's Ristorante** (D only–Very Expensive) features Northern Italian cuisine in a grandiose split-level room with a lake view. **Sea Grille** (D only–Very Expensive) serves fresh fish many ways in a large

and posh dining room. **Mikado** (D only–Expensive) serves teppan-yaki style Japanese dishes in a lovely garden setting. **LakeView Restaurant** (B-L-D–Expensive) offers contemporary American cuisine in a large stylish dining room or on a lakeview terrace, plus live entertainment for dancing. **Costas** is a big snazzy sports bar with live entertainment, and the **Atrium Lounge** offers plush seating and entertainment in the spectacularly waterscaped lobby.

Mayo's   *346-2284*
   downtown at 73990 El Paseo
   D only.   *Very Expensive*
Whitefish with caviar cream sauce and salmon in parchment suggest the creativity of the contemporary Continental cuisine featured in a classy little dining room enhanced by grand piano stylings.

★ **Palomino Euro Bistro**   *773-9091*
   downtown at 73101 Hwy. 111
   L-D. No L Sat. & Sun.   *Expensive*
Southern California's only link in an elite chain of mega-bistros opened to critical acclaim in 1993 with a seamless blend of Pacific Northwest and New California cuisines. Entrees like fresh oak-grilled salmon with wild greens and artichoke tartar, and desserts topped by wood-oven-roasted apple tart in puff pastry a la mode typify stellar possibilities. The fine fare is favored by smart dining and bistro areas embellished with an exhibition wood-burning spit roaster plus oversized avante garde lighting fixtures and wall art.

★ **Ristorante Mamma Gino**   *568-9898*
   .7 mi. E at 73705 El Paseo
   L-D. No L Sun.   *Very Expensive*
Authentic Florentine cuisine including an array of homemade pastries (plus gelato) is prepared by an acclaimed Italian chef. The classy, congested dining room and lounge provide an appropriate setting for one of the region's most sophisticated trattorias.

★ **The Ritz-Carlton Rancho Mirage**   *321-8282*
   5 mi. NW at 68900 Frank Sinatra Dr. - Rancho Mirage
   B-L-tea-D. Sun. brunch.   *Expensive–Very Expensive*
In **The Dining Room Restaurant** (D only. Closed Sun.-Mon.–Very Expensive), superb New California cuisine is formally presented in an opulent setting where jackets are appropriate for gentlemen. The **Mirada** (L-D. No D Sun.-Thurs.–Expensive) offers light and lively New California fare on a shady misted veranda overlooking the pool, mountains and desert. **The Cafe** (B-L-D. Sun. brunch–Expensive) features New American cuisine in a plush dining room overlooking an alfresco garden terrace and the valley. So does the luxurious **Lounge** where tea is served each afternoon, and a well-played grand piano contributes to the tranquility.

★ **Stouffer Esmeralda Resort**   *773-4444*
   3.5 mi. E at 44400 Indian Wells Lane - Indian Wells
   B-L-D. Sun. brunch.   *Expensive–Very Expensive*
Sirocco (D only–Very Expensive) presents highly regarded updated Mediterranean cuisine in an opulent tri-level dining room with a picture window view of a pond and fairways. **Charisma** (B-L-D. Sun. brunch–Expensive) features New California cuisine in a plush contemporary setting overlooking courtyard pools. **Las Estrellas** is a classy lounge with live entertainment and dancing, and a waterfall-and-mountains view from padded armchairs.

★ **Teresa's Cafe**   *347-7411*
10.2 mi. E at 45682 Towne St. - Indio
B-L-D.   *Low*
Most of the Mexican restaurants in the Coachella Valley are in Indio.
This is the best. The home cooking featured here since 1950 still
imparts the rich flavors and zesty bite of border Mexican fare with
uncompromising authenticity in two very plain dining rooms.

Vicky's of Santa Fe   *345-9770*
3.7 mi. E at 45100 Club Dr. - Indian Wells
D only.   *Expensive*
Beef, chicken, shrimp or fish are the uncomplicated choices. The
handsome room with an exhibition kitchen, island bar, and striking
lounge featuring a long well-played grand piano capture the Santa Fe
spirit with tile, wood and adobe decor, and folk art.

★ **Wally's Desert Turtle**   *568-9321*
2 mi. NW at 71775 Hwy. 111 - Rancho Mirage
D only, plus L on Fri. Closed in summer.   *Extremely Expensive*
Contemporary Continental cuisine receives the desert's quintessential
treatment in culinary masterpieces like wild mushroom soup,
limestone lettuce and bay shrimp salad, roast duck with Medjool date
sauce and ethereal Grand Marnier dessert souffles. The region's most
opulent dinner house is a split-level extravaganza of exotic floral
sprays, lush greenery, beveled mirrored ceilings, fine art and artifacts,
grand piano stylings, and candlelit tables formally set with linen,
crystal, china and silver.

★ **The Westin Mission Hills Resort**   *328-5955*
7 mi. N at Dinah Shore & Bob Hope Dr. - Rancho Mirage
B-L-D. Sun. brunch.   *Expensive*
La Concha - A Pacific Bistro (D only. Sun. brunch) features Pacific
Rim culinary styles smoothly blended and served in an elegant
multilevel setting with stylish contemporary decor and panoramic
views of the golf course and mountains. **Bella Vista** (B-L-D) features
New California fare like date French toast in a dramatic vaulted
atrium. There are also several plush bars and lounges.

LODGING

Palm Desert is surrounded by the largest concentration of luxury
resorts in Southern California. Most are encircled by emerald-green
golf courses, and offer a wealth of recreation and leisure facilities in
luxuriant subtropical settings. There are no bargains during the
prime winter and early spring season. Fall and late spring rates are
often reduced at least 20%, while summer rates are often reduced by
40% and more for bargain-seekers willing to endure the heat.

★ **Embassy Suites**   *340-6600*
1.7 mi. E at 74700 Hwy. 111 - 92260
Two-room suites in California-contemporary buildings surround a
landscaped courtyard with a large pool and whirlpool. Six lighted
tennis courts, a putting green, exercise room, a stylish restaurant and
lounge, and a gift shop, are also available. A full breakfast and two-
hour afternoon cocktail party are complimentary. Each well-furnished
suite has two phones, two color TVs (with free and pay movies and
remote control), and a refrigerator/wet bar. Toll-free in CA: (800)223-
1679; elsewhere: (800)633-2834.
    regular room—   2 D or K bed...$169

Palm Desert
Erawan Garden Resort   *346-8021*
3.5 mi. E at 76477 Hwy. 111 - Indian Wells 92210
Date palms tower over this tranquil, 220-room Oriental-inspired
garden hotel. Features include two large outdoor pools, a whirlpool,
saunas, a putting green, two posh restaurants, an entertainment
lounge and resort shop. Each nicely furnished room has a private
patio or balcony, refrigerator, phone and color TV, most with remote
control. Toll-free: (800)237-2926.

deluxe room—overlooks garden court, Q or K bed...$130
regular room—overlooks parking lot, 2 D or K bed...$100

★ **Hyatt Grand Champions Resort**   *341-1000*
3.5 mi. E at 44600 Indian Wells Lane - Indian Wells 92210
This post-modern pleasure palace opened in 1986 with a neo-Moorish
motif worthy of a sultan. Two 18-hole golf courses encircle the five-
level, 335-room complex. A palm and citrus-shaded courtyard is cooled
by waterfalls and four pools (two extra-large and freeform) and
whirlpools. For a fee there is golf; twelve tennis courts (eight lighted);
a complete beauty and health center (exercise equipment, steam room,
saunas, massage); and bicycles; plus fine dining and drinking places
(see listing), and resort shops. Each spacious, luxurious room has a
large private view balcony, stocked (honor) refrigerator/wet bar, phone,
and remote control color TV with free and pay movies. Toll-free:
(800)233-1234.

"Villa" (ten of these)—extra-large, 1 BR,
butler, gas fireplace, private yard & whirlpool, K bed...$725
#511,#515,#519, etc. thru #531—gas fireplace,
superb pools/mountains view from private balcony, K bed...$375
#405 & odd #s thru #431—superb view of
pools/mountain from large private balcony & K bed...$325
regular room—garden view, 2 D or K bed...$240

★ **La Quinta Resort**   *564-4111*
8 mi. SE at 49499 Eisenhower Dr. (Box 69) - La Quinta 92253
The most celebrated resort in the desert, built in 1926, retains all of
its timeless charm after a major expansion and renovation. Remote
and serene at the base of rugged desert peaks, the luxuriant 45-acre
oasis includes 25 outdoor pools and 35 whirlpools surrounded by
adobe-and-tile casitas and a myriad of flower gardens, citrus trees
and date palms, plus a putting green, 30 lighted tennis courts (with
all three surfaces—grass, hard and clay), and (for a fee) a top-rated
championship golf course and rental bicycles. Gracious public rooms
in the historic lodge are now complemented by new restaurants and
lounges (see listing) in a flower-filled plaza with specialty shops
surrounding fountains and waterfalls. Each beautifully furnished
adobe bungalow unit has a refrigerator, two phones, and remote
control color TV with movies. Toll-free in CA: (800)472-4316;
elsewhere: (800)854-1271.

#629,#626—"pueblo suites," extra large 1 BR, kitchenette,
fireplace, private garden court pool & whirlpool, K bed...$1800
#980,#735—"hacienda suites," as above, but larger, K bed...$2100
#665,#666,#669,#712—spacious room with
refr./wet bar, private garden with whirlpool, K bed...$600
regular room—deluxe contemporary, 2 Q or K bed...$265
regular room—charming 1926 remodel, 2 Q or K bed...$235

★ **Marriott's Desert Springs Resort & Spa**   *341-2211*
4 mi. NE at 74855 Country Club Dr. - 92260
One of America's most sensational convention-oriented resorts opened
in 1987 with 891 rooms in a lavish eight-story complex surrounded by
two 18-hole golf courses, colorful palm-shaded gardens, and the
desert's most spectacular "waterscaping." An awesome atrium lobby
encloses waterfalls and part of a lake, plus a dock for free boat rides
to far-flung restaurants. Ponds and water features are everywhere, including three garden court pools (one is huge), three
whirlpools, and a sandy beach. Other amenities (for a fee) include 20
tennis courts (7 lighted); lawn chess and other games; a world-class
state-of-the-art fitness center with saunas, steam rooms, inhalation
room, hot and cold plunge pools, and gym; beauty salon with massage;
plus bicycles. There are nearly a dozen eating and drinking places
(see listing) and resort shops. Each beautifully furnished room has a
large private balcony or patio; refrigerator/stocked (honor) bar; two
phones; and remote control color TV with pay and free movies. Toll-
free: (800)228-9290.
> #8039,#7039,#6039,#7035,#7027,#7025–magnificent
> lake/pool/mt. views from large private balcony &   K bed...$310
> #5253, #4253,#3253–lake & pool views,   K bed...$280
> regular room–   2 D or K bed...$250

★ **Marriott's Rancho Las Palmas**   *568-2727*
2.8 mi. NW at 41000 Bob Hope Dr. - Rancho Mirage 92270
The first of the current era of luxury desert resorts is a sprawling
Early California-style complex of 450 rooms. Amenities include two
big outdoor pools and whirlpools in palm-shaded gardens, an exercise
room; and (for a fee) a 27-hole golf course with small lakes and a
putting green, twenty-five tennis courts (eight lighted), a fitness
center, and bicycles. There are also resort shops. Diners can enjoy
elaborate Spanish-Colonial decor, a tropical courtyard, or a lake-view
patio. The lounge has live entertainment and dancing. Each well-
furnished guest room has a stocked (honor) bar, big private patio or
balcony, phone, and remote control color TV with free and pay movies.
Toll-free: (800)I-LUV-SUN.
> "Bldg. 28"–good lake views,   2 D or K bed...$235
> regular room–   2 D or K bed...$235

Radisson Resort - Indian Wells   *345-6466*
3.7 mi. E at 76661 Hwy. 111 - Indian Wells 92210
Palm trees and an adjoining golf course enhance this handsome post-
modern hotel. The low-rise, 151-room complex nearly encloses a big
landscaped courtyard pool and whirlpool. There are also two tennis
courts and an exercise room. A stylish dining room has a fine view of
the pool and gardens backed by a picturesque date palm orchard, and
an entertainment lounge adjoins. Each well-furnished unit has a patio
or balcony, phone, (honor) refrigerator, and remote control color TV
with free and pay movies. Toll-free: (800)248-3220.
> suite (25 of these)–spacious, posh,
> pool/greens view,   2 D or K bed...$329
> regular room–   2 D or K bed...$209

★ **The Ritz Carlton Rancho Mirage**   *321-8282*
5 mi. NW at 68900 Frank Sinatra Dr. - Rancho Mirage 92270
The desert's most luxurious conference resort crowns a spectacularly landscaped hill. The 240-room contemporary facility, embellished throughout with works of art, includes an extra-large pool and whirl-pool in a garden court overlooking the desert, a putting green, croquet lawn, fitness center and table tennis; and (for a fee) massage and ten lighted tennis courts; plus gourmet restaurants and a lounge (see list-ing), and boutiques. Each spacious, richly appointed room has a large private patio or balcony, stocked (honor) refrigerator, two phones, and remote control color TV with movies. Toll-free: (800)241-3333.

"Valley Suite" (four of these)—extra-large,
grand private desert view,   K bed...$650
"R.C. Club floor"—fine view, many deluxe extras,   K bed...$395
regular room—   2 D or K bed...$260

★ **Shadow Mountain Resort & Racquet Club**   *346-6123*
.4 mi. SE at 45750 San Luis Rey Av. - 92260
Lush vegetation surrounds 125 condos, four pools (one a giant in the figure "eight"), five whirlpools, saunas, 16 tennis courts (four lighted), gym; rental bicycles, and a cafe/bar. Each well-furnished apartment has a kitchenette, private patio or balcony, phone and color TV with remote control, pay and free movies. Toll-free: (800)472-3713.

regular room—1 BR, spacious,   Q or K bed...$215
regular room—studio,   Murphy Q bed...$160

★ **Stouffer Esmeralda Resort**   *773-4444*
3.5 mi. E at 44400 Indian Wells Lane - Indian Wells 92210
Two manicured 18-hole golf courses surround a 560-room resort hotel that opened in 1989. The spare post-modern eight-story complex includes a date-palm-shaded courtyard with three giant pools, two whirlpools, waterfalls and a sandy beach. Fee amenities include two 18-hole golf courses; seven tennis courts (two lighted); a fitness center with exercise equipment, saunas, steam room, massage; and bicycles. There are also plush restaurant and lounge facilities (see listing), and resort shops. Each luxuriously appointed room has a small private balcony, a stocked (honor) bar/refrigerator, three phones and two remote control color TVs with free and pay movies. Toll-free in CA: (800)552-4386; elsewhere: (800)HOTELS-1.

#G704,#G604,#G504—spacious, 2 small view balconies,
large mirrored whirlpool in view of   K bed...$600
regular room—   2 Q or K bed...$270

★ **The Westin Mission Hills Resort**   *328-5955*
7 mi. N at 71333 Dinah Shore Dr. - Rancho Mirage 92270
Surrounded by gardens and golf courses is a 512-unit neo-Moorish resort. The dramatic complex includes three landscaped pools (one extra-large with a 60-foot "S"-curve water slide), whirlpools; a one-mile paved track; outdoor games; complete beauty and fitness facili-ties; and (for a fee) two championship 18-hole golf courses, and seven lighted tennis courts. There are also fine dining and drinking places (see listing) and resort shops. Each of the spacious, attractively fur-nished rooms has a private patio or balcony, two phones, and remote control color TV with pay and free movies. Toll-free: (800)228-3000.

"Royal Oasis Club"—view, special extras,   2 Q or K bed...$310
regular room—   2 Q or K bed...$240

Palm Springs

Palm Springs was America's original desert showplace. A striking patchwork of low-profile buildings and lush landscapes is interspersed with barren sand and rocks along the base of the mountain with the greatest vertical rise above any American city. The precipitous bulk of towering Mt. San Jacinto (elevation: 10,804 feet) with its mantle of winter snow is a remarkable contrast to the broad valley floor where warm sunny days prevail even in winter. Here are America's most phenomenal oases. Desert canyons shelter thousands of giant native fan palms. Nearby, flatlands are sprinkled with luxuriant golf courses, tennis courts, swimming pools, parks, and gardens.

Today, boutiques, restaurants and hotels are mixed with fading businesses from earlier booms along beautifully landscaped Palm Canyon Drive. The city has been deposed as the ultimate desert showplace, but it remains a memorable potpourri of glitz and glamour.

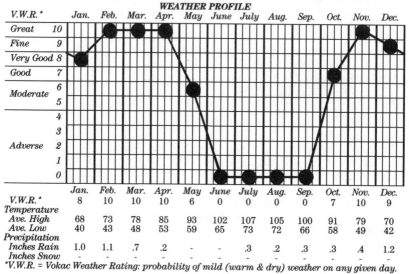

WEATHER PROFILE

V.W.R.*		Jan.	Feb.	Mar.	Apr.	May	June	July	Aug.	Sep.	Oct.	Nov.	Dec.
Great	10												
Fine	9												
Very Good	8												
Good	7												
Moderate	6												
	5												
	4												
	3												
Adverse	2												
	1												
	0												

	Jan.	Feb.	Mar.	Apr.	May	June	July	Aug.	Sep.	Oct.	Nov.	Dec.
V.W.R.*	8	10	10	10	6	0	0	0	0	7	10	9
Temperature												
Ave. High	68	73	78	85	93	102	107	105	100	91	79	70
Ave. Low	40	43	48	53	59	65	73	72	66	58	49	42
Precipitation												
Inches Rain	1.0	1.1	.7	.2	-	-	.3	.2	.3	.3	.4	1.2
Inches Snow	-	-	-	-	-	-	-	-	-	-	-	-

*V.W.R. = Vokac Weather Rating: probability of mild (warm & dry) weather on any given day.

Palm Springs

Population: 40,144 Area Code: 619
Elevation: 466 feet
Location: 107 miles East of Los Angeles
Palm Springs Desert Resorts Convention & Visitors Bureau 770-9000
8 mi. SE at 69930 Hwy. 111, Rancho Mirage, Suite 201 - 92270

ATTRACTIONS

★ **Aerial Tramway** *325-1391*
6 mi. NW via CA 111 & Tramway Rd.
One of the world's most spectacular aerial rides transports passengers almost 6,000 feet up from the desert (the Valley Station is 2,643 feet above sea level in Chino Canyon) to 8,516 feet above sea level on San Jacinto Mountain. Two eighty-passenger gondolas make the 2.5 mile trip in about fifteen minutes several times daily. Both stations have observation decks and picnic areas, plus a snack shop and lounge. The alpine restaurant (L-D–Expensive) features family-style fare with a grand view. In the Mt. San Jacinto Wilderness State Park at the top of the tramway, hiking, backpacking, and wilderness camping are popular in summer. In winter, cross-country skiing offers a startling contrast to warm weather in the desert below. Skiing and sledding equipment can be rented at the Nordic Ski Center on the mountain.

★ *Bicycling*
Bicycle trails are scenic, flat, and relatively safe (and occasionally separated) on more than thirty miles of streets in town. Bike rentals and maps are available at:
Canyon Bicycles *305 E. Arenas Rd. (closed Wed.)* *327-7688*
Dune Off Road Rentals *325-0376*
10 mi. NW at S side of CA 111
For quad runners, including instructions and one hour on your own on the dunes at Windy Point, call 567-2105 for reservations.

★ *Golf*
The Palm Springs-Palm Desert area is the "Winter Golfing Capital of the World." Nearly one hundred courses include many of championship quality. Several are open to the public, and others offer outside guest privileges. Collectively, they provide a remarkable variety of conditions and picturesque oases. Below are two championship 18-hole courses giving duffers a choice of naturalistic or oasis scenery.
Desert Dunes Golf Club *251-5366*
7 mi. NE at 19300 Palm Dr.
Palm Springs Golf Course *328-1005*
5 mi. SE at 1885 Golf Club Dr.
Horseback Riding
★ **Smoke Tree Stables** *327-1372*
3.5 mi. SE at 2500 Toledo Av.
Horses of all dispositions can be rented hourly with guides for rides on safe desert trails up into the scenic Palm Canyon areas.
Jeep Tours
Desert Adventures *864-6530*
.5 mi. S at 611 S. Palm Canyon Dr., Suite 7445
Jeep trips of one to four hours take visitors into the primitive high desert south of town. Drivers provide an ecotour, along with opportunities to view and photograph animal and plant life, distinctive geological formations, and archaeological sites.

Moorten Botanical Gardens   *327-6555*
1.4 mi. S at 1701 S. Palm Canyon Dr.
In this four acre arboretum, more than two thousand varieties of
desert plants from throughout the world have been arranged according
to geographic regions. The gardens have been a landmark since 1938,
and are also a sanctuary for birds and wildlife.
★ **Palm Canyon**   *325-5673*
6 mi. S on Palm Canyon Dr.
The nation's largest stand of native Washingtonia palms lines this
steep, narrow canyon for several miles. Hundreds of the giant fan
palms can be seen from the rim parking lot at the end of the road.
Hiking trails lead down to the canyon floor, where a stream meanders
among palms estimated to be up to 2,000 years old. Nearby Andreas
and Murray Canyons also have picturesque palm groves, spectacular
rock formations, and streams with deep pools and waterfalls that are
at their best in late winter and spring when they're filled with snow
runoff. All canyons are in somewhat natural condition as part of a
reservation belonging to a tiny group of Indians, who charge an entry
fee to hike or drive in. Closed July-Aug.
★ **Palm Springs Desert Museum**   *325-7186*
downtown at 101 Museum Dr.
This strikingly handsome two-story cultural arts center opened in
1976 on a twenty acre site against the San Jacinto Mountains. Fine
permanent collections and changing exhibits are displayed in several
galleries. A 450-seat theater is used for lectures and concerts. Dancing
fountains and sunken sculpture gardens embellish landscaped
grounds, and there is a large museum shop. Closed Mon.
★ **The Palm Springs Follies**   *327-0225*
downtown at 128 S. Palm Canyon Dr.
The historic (1936) Plaza Theatre has been skillfully restored to serve
as a showcase for delightfully lively performances filled with nostalgic
song, dance and comedy. Remarkably, every member of the big
talented cast is more than fifty years old! Adjoining are a museum of
Hollywood memorabilia, a Walk of Fame, and Pop's Back Stage Cafe.
★ **Palms-to-Pines Highway**
for 130 mi. W of town via CA's 111, 74 & 243 and I-10
A dramatically scenic highway climbs thousands of feet from desert
date palm groves to pine forests high in the San Jacinto Mountains.
Warm Water Features
★ **Oasis Waterpark**   *327-0499*
4 mi. SE at 1500 Gene Autry Trail
The desert's best waterpark, opened in 1986, has hydro-tubes and
speed slides, a lagoon with programmed waves, and hot spa. There is
also an elaborate health club. Food, drinks, and a gift shop are also
open daily mid-March thru Labor Day, and weekends thru Oct.
Palm Springs Swim Center   *323-8278*
1.2 mi. SE at Ramon Rd. / Cerritos Dr.
An Olympic-sized fifty meter swimming pool with high diving boards
is surrounded by spacious lawns, a deck, and good mountain views.
The Spa Hotel and Mineral Springs   *325-1461*
downtown at 100 N. Indian Av.
The public can (for steep fees) enjoy natural hot mineral waters at the
hotel's indoor and outdoor pools and whirlpool tubs.

Banducci's Bit of Italy   *325-2537*
1 mi. S at 1260 S. Palm Canyon Dr.
D only.   *Moderate*
Traditional Southern Italian fare is served in a thirty-year-old restaurant with a popular dining porch by the main thoroughfare.

Billy Reed's Restaurant   *325-1946*
1.6 mi. N at 1800 N. Palm Canyon Dr.
B-L-D.   *Moderate*
This huge coffee shop/restaurant/lounge complex is a local favorite for hearty American fare and their own baked goods served amid a profusion of old-time bric-a-brac and plants.

Bit Of Country   *325-5154*
downtown at 418 S. Indian Av.
B-L.   *Low*
Hearty helpings of American homestyle cooking are featured. The remodeled coffee shop remains popular and unpretentious. A "mister" cools the cozy sidewalk dining patio on hot days.

Bono   *322-6200*
1.7 mi. N at 1700 N. Indian Av.
D only.   *Expensive*
Traditional and updated Italian dishes can be good in a capacious restaurant with a trendy Southwestern theme shared by a glitzy downstairs nightclub.

Buddy's Deli   *325-6102*
downtown at 401 E. Tahquitz Way
B-L-D.   *Moderate*
All sorts of deli-cacies are served at booths or tables amidst greenery or on a sidewalk dining terrace.

★ **Cafe St. James**   *320-8041*
downtown at 254 N. Palm Canyon Dr.
D only. Closed Mon.   *Very Expensive*
Creative international cuisine like sea bass Castellina, chicken toscana, and shrimp curry are prepared with skill and flair, as are delicious housemade desserts. Balcony seating in the classy little upstairs cafe affords a great view of the main street below.

Eveleene's   *325-4766*
.4 mi. N at 664 N. Palm Canyon Dr.
L-D. No L Sat. & Sun.   *Very Expensive*
Traditional French cuisine is presented in old-fashioned refinement.

★ **Flower Drum**   *323-3020*
downtown at 424 S. Indian Canyon Dr.
L-D.   *Moderate*
Flower Drum, opened in 1985, is now the best Chinese restaurant in the desert. Delicacies from five major regions of China are prepared with the utmost respect for quality and authenticity. A circular aquarium is mounted in the middle of a mirrored stage backdrop flanked by dramatic gilt dragons. The large comfortable dining room also includes a pond with golden koi and a bridge over a stream.

Harley's Coffee & Beers Cafe   *778-5750*
downtown at 168 N. Palm Canyon Dr.
L-D.   *Moderate*
First-rate coffee drinks, a refreshing frozen cappuchino, and a dozen

premium beers on tap accompany light fare and desserts in a lively little sidewalk cafe overlooking the "action" in the heart of town.

Hyatt Regency Suites Palm Springs   *322-9000*
downtown at 285 N. Palm Canyon Dr.
B-L-D.   *Expensive*
The **Palm Court** (B-L-D–Expensive) offers contemporary California fare ranging from designer pizzas to roasted range chicken in lime-cilantro marinade in an urbane atrium amidst lush greenery, dramatic sculpture and polished marble surroundings.   The **Palm Court Lounge** adds occasional music to the airy ambiance of the atrium.

★ **Le Vallauris**   *325-5059*
downtown at 385 W. Tahquitz Way
L-D. Sun. brunch.   *Extremely Expensive*
Palm Springs' most renowned culinary landmark is Le Vallauris. Here, light French cuisine with an emphasis on fresh seafood is served amid congested, formal elegance.   The intimate, shady patio is a local favorite for lunch or brunch.   A posh piano lounge adjoins.

Louise's Pantry   *325-5124*
downtown at 124 S. Palm Canyon Dr.
B-L-D.   *Low*
Homemade pies and pastries have been featured here for many years. The authentically old-fashioned coffee shop remains popular, especially early in the day. A larger lesser clone is now in Palm Desert.

Lyons English Grille   *327-1551*
1.4 mi. S at 233 E. Palm Canyon Dr.
D only.   *Expensive*
Prime rib and steak, popovers and trifles have been popular for many years in this dining room and lounge with clubby Old English decor.

★ **Melvyn's Restaurant at the Ingleside Inn**   *325-2323*
.4 mi. S at 200 W. Ramon Rd.
L-D. Sat. & Sun. brunch.   *Expensive*
Continental cuisine and tableside cooking have been featured here for years.   The casually elegant dining room, glass-enclosed patio, and piano lounge of the romantic Ingleside Inn are popular paeans to Palm Springs' posh past.

★ **Otani**   *327-6700*
.6 mi. E at 1000 Tahquitz Way
L-D. No L Sat. Sun. brunch.   *Expensive*
The best Japanese cuisine in the desert includes an exciting selection of sashimi, teppan-yaki, traditional tempura and teriyaki dishes, and a sushi bar. The food is as good as it looks when it comes from the various exhibition kitchens, thanks to uniformly skilled chefs. The cavernous interior includes a cookhouse and display kitchens surrounded by comfortable dining areas from which guests can view both the action and a Japanese garden beyond picture windows.

★ **Riccio's**   *325-2369*
2 mi. N at 2155 N. Palm Canyon Dr.
L-D. No L Sat. & Sun.   *Very Expensive*
Riccio's is Palm Springs' best Italian restaurant. Classic specialties achieve gourmet distinction and are presented by tuxedoed waiters in an exuberant and congested dining room. A baby grand piano in the adjoining bar is played nightly.

Palm Springs

★ **The Wilde Goose**   *328-5775*
6 mi. SE at 67938 CA 111 - Cathedral City
D only.   *Expensive*
Continental cuisine is given a deft contemporary styling in this
consistent favorite among local dinner houses. Duck is a specialty
along with beef, lamb or pork Wellingtons in puff pastry. You can top
it all off with homemade ice cream or champagne sorbet.

LODGING

Resort hotels remain the city's most notable landmarks. Dozens of
smaller lodgings including three convenient bargain motels also dot
the area. From June through September, discounts of as much as 50%
are normally offered to desert heat-lovers.

★ **The Autry Resort Hotel & Tennis Club**   *328-1171*
4 mi. SE at 4200 E. Palm Canyon Dr. - 92264
One of the area's most venerable resort hotels has been skillfully
refurbished and upgraded. Beautifully landscaped grounds contain
three outdoor pools (including one that is Olympic-sized), two
whirlpools, sauna, exercise room and (for a fee) six lighted tennis
courts, plus fine dining, a genuine celebrity lounge with live
entertainment, and a gift shop. Each attractively furnished room has
a phone and color TV with movies. Toll-free: (800)443-6328.

"Celebrity Wing"—for adults only, spacious,
   refrigerator, some have private view patio,   2 D or K bed...$195
   regular room—   2 D or K bed...$135

★ **Desert Hot Springs Hotel & Spa**   *329-6495*
12.7 mi. NE at 10805 Palm Dr. - Desert Hot Springs 92240
One of the two most elaborate lodgings in laid-back "Spa Town" is a
modern motor hotel enclosing seven hot mineral pools (one extra-large)
and whirlpools on a palm-studded courtyard; plus saunas, ping pong,
and (for a fee) massage; a coffee shop/entertainment lounge; and a gift
shop. Each comfortable room has a big private view patio or balcony,
phone, and color TV. Toll-free in CA: (800)843-6053.

#202 thru #210—fine pools/mountains
   view from private balcony and from   2 Q or K bed...$89
   regular room—   K bed...$79

★ **Doubletree Resort Palm Springs**   *322-7000*
5.5 mi. NE at 67967 Vista Chino at Landau Blvd. (Box 1644) - 92263
Palm Springs' most complete resort opened in 1986. The isolated four-
story hotel with 289 rooms plus condos is on nearly half a square mile
of flatlands with a panoramic mountain view. Amenities include a
large swimming pool and whirlpools in a garden court; (for a fee) a 27-
hole championship golf course, ten tennis courts (five lighted), two
racquetball courts, and a fitness center with massage; plus a dining
room, coffee shop, lounge with live entertainment; and a gift shop.
Each spacious, well-furnished room has a refrigerator, private patio or
balcony, phone, and remote control color TV with free and pay movies.
Toll-free: (800)528-0444.

#482,#382,#282—windows on 2 sides with
   pool/golf course/mountain views, huge balcony,   K bed...$275
   condo (many)—1 BR, kitchen,   Q or K bed...$225
   regular room—desert view,   K bed...$160

Four Seasons Apartment Hotel   *325-6427*
.5 mi. SW at 290 San Jacinto Dr. - 92262
A mountain rises abruptly a block from this palm-shaded apartment
motel. The tranquil little complex has a pool and whirlpool in a
garden, and bicycles for guests. Each big, beautifully appointed unit
has a private patio, refrigerator, phone and remote control color TV.

    one-bedroom suite—extra-large, 2 phones, kitchen,   K bed...$130
    regular room—hotel room,   Q bed...$100

Holiday Inn Palm Mountain Resort   *325-1301*
downtown at 155 S. Belardo Rd. - 92262
The nearby mountain is a towering backdrop to this refurbished hotel
in a choice location downtown. Amenities include a palm court with a
pool and whirlpool, a restaurant and entertainment lounge. Each well-
furnished unit has a private balcony or patio, phone, and color TV with
remote control. Toll-free: (800)622-9451.

    #316,#314—top floor, mt. & pool view,   K bed...$159
    regular room—   2 D or K bed...$109

★ **Hyatt Regency Suites Palm Springs**   *322-9000*
downtown at 285 N. Palm Canyon Dr. - 92262
Palm Springs' most architecturally significant hotel opened in 1986.
The 194-room complex rises six stories above a prime location in the
heart of town. A long outdoor pool, indoor and outdoor whirlpools,
sauna, exercise room, and gift shop, plus a restaurant and lounge (see
listing) surround a striking marble-clad atrium lobby. Each spacious,
luxurious suite has a parlor, stocked (honor) mini-bar, private balcony,
three phones, and two remote control color TVs with free and pay
movies. Toll-free: (800)233-1234.

    #410,#310—large in-bath whirlpool,
      private balconies with fine mountain view,   K bed...$279
    regular room—request 6th floor mountain
      side for maximum privacy/view,   K bed...$219

★ **Ingleside Inn**   *325-0046*
.4 mi. S at 200 W. Ramon Rd. - 92264
The city's most historic small hotel is luxuriant with bougainvillea and
flowering trees. There is a small pool and whirlpool in a garden, plus
Melvyn's restaurant and lounge (see listing). Each comfortable room
is individually furnished including antiques, plus in-bath steam bath
and whirlpool, and has a stocked (complimentary) refrigerator, phone,
and remote control color TV with movies. Toll-free: (800)772-6655.

    #V1,#V2—fireplace, sitting area, pvt. terrace,   K bed...$235
    #143—(Lily Pons' Room), big, posh, pvt. patio,   K bed...$275
    Penthouse #4—end unit over lounge, mountain view,   Q bed...$75
    regular room—in main building,   D bed...$95

★ **The Inn at the Racquet Club**   *325-1281*
2 mi. N at 2743 N. Indian Canyon Dr. - 92262
A famed 1930s resort has been upgraded. The 150-unit complex of one-
story bungalows is on well-landscaped grounds with four big pools and
whirlpools, a fitness center with saunas; table tennis; and (for a fee)
twelve tennis courts (eight lighted), bicycles and massage. Each
spacious, well-furnished unit has a private patio, phone and color TV.
Toll-free: (800)367-0946.

    #66—1 BR, fireplace, kitchen, pvt. yard with pool,   K bed...$295
    regular room—(kitchen for extra $10),   K bed...$139

★ **La Mancha Private Villas & Court Club**   *323-1773*
1 mi. NE at 444 N. Avenida Caballeros (Box 340) - 92262
La Mancha is the desert's ultimate resort for playful adults. The Spanish-Colonial complex of condo-like villas has a tropically landscaped pool, cold plunge, and whirlpool, plus a sauna, gym, seven tennis courts (four lighted), two lighted paddle tennis courts, table tennis, croquet courts, and a dining room. Rental bicycles are available. Each spacious, luxuriously furnished suite has a phone, two color TVs (one with wide screen, remote control and VCR), fully equipped kitchen with microwave, living room, dining room, and a private patio. Best of all, each has a relatively large, very private outdoor pool or whirlpool, or both. Toll-free: (800)64-PRIVACY.

"pool/spa villa"—1 BR, (request gas fireplace),
    wet bar, gas BBQ, pvt. outdoor pool & whirlpool,   K bed...$350
"pool villa"—1 BR, (request gas fireplace),
    wet bar, private pool,   K bed...$325
"spa villa"—gas BBQ, walled yard with whirlpool,   K bed...$275
regular unit—no kitchen, request pvt. whirlpool,   K bed...$185

Mira Loma Hotel   *320-1178*
1.4 mi. N at 1420 N. Indian Canyon Dr. - 92262
This small, single-level older motel has a large outdoor pool. In February and March, citrus trees surrounding the pool and guest rooms have an intoxicating fragrance. Each nicely furnished room has a refrigerator, phone, and remote control color TV.

regular room—poolside,   K bed...$60; Q bed...$50

★ **Mirage Springs Hotel, Casino & Spa**   *251-3399*
12.8 mi. NE at 10625 Palm Dr. - Desert Hot Springs 92240
"Spa Town's" newest and most complete hotel planned to have a major casino open for 1995. But the main draw is warm mineral water showcased in a garden courtyard with a big freeform pool and six whirlpools—all with dramatic mountain views. Other features include (fee) health club, dining and drinking facilities, and a gift shop. Each comfortable room has a private balcony or patio, phone and color TV.

#215,#217,#219—fine pools/mountains view,   K bed...$119
regular room—   2 D or K bed...$119

Motel 6
7 mi. SE at 69570 CA 111 - Rancho Mirage 92270   324-8475
1.6 mi. SE at 595 E. Palm Canyon Dr. - 92262   325-6129
.6 mi. S at 660 S. Palm Canyon Dr. - 92262   327-4200
Motel 6's three large motels are **bargains**. All are conveniently located, and each has an outdoor pool. Each compact, simply furnished room has a phone and color TV with movies.

regular room—   D or Q bed...$36

★ **Oasis Water Resort Villa Hotel**   *328-1499*
3.9 mi. SE at 4190 E. Palm Canyon Dr. - 92264
Free passes to the major nearby water park (see listing) are included (in season) in this tropically landscaped condo resort. On-site amenities include eight garden court pools and nine whirlpools; and (for a fee) five lighted tennis courts, and bicycles. Each spacious, well-furnished two-bedroom unit has a kitchen with microwave, large private patio or balcony, two phones and two remote control color TVs. Toll-free: (800)247-4664.

regular unit—2-BR villa,   2 Q beds...$229

★ **Palm Springs Hilton**   *320-6868*
downtown at 400 E. Tahquitz Canyon Way - 92262
The first of several downtown resort hotels built during the 1980s
features contemporary California architecture and decor. The 260-
room complex encloses a courtyard with a large pool, two whirlpools,
and splendid mountain views. There is also a sauna; (a fee for) a
fitness spa with massage, six lighted tennis courts; dining rooms; an
entertainment lounge, and a gift shop. Each spacious, well-furnished
room has a stocked (honor) bar, balcony or patio, phone, and remote
control color TV with (pay) movies. Toll-free: (800)522-6900.
#340,#345,#366,#367—fine mt./courtyard pool view,   K bed...$215
#346,#365—1 BR suite, fine mt./pool views,   K bed...$310
regular room—   2 Q or K bed...$195

★ **Palm Springs Marquis Crown Plaza Resort & Suites**   *322-2121*
downtown at 150 S. Indian Canyon Dr. - 92262
This post-modern hotel with 260 rooms includes two courtyard pools
and two whirlpools on landscaped grounds; exercise room; and (for a
fee) two lighted tennis courts, massage and parking; plus a restaurant,
piano lounge, and a gift shop. Each spacious, well-furnished room has
a private balcony or patio, two phones, and a color TV with movies.
Toll-free: (800)HOLIDAY.
villa—1 BR, spacious, kitchen, fireplace, Roman tub,
private patio with pool/mountain view,   K bed...$259
regular room—   2 D or K bed...$149

Palm Springs Riviera Resort & Racquet Club   *327-8311*
1.5 mi. N at 1600 N. Indian Canyon Dr. - 92262
Palm Springs' largest resort hotel is a sprawling 480-room convention
facility. It has two pools (one Olympic-sized) and two whirlpools in a
palm-lined courtyard, an exercise room; and (for a fee) nine tennis
courts (three night-lighted); lighted 18-hole putting course, plus a restaurant, entertainment lounge, and gift shop. Most of the attractively
redecorated rooms have a patio or balcony, refrigerator, phone, and remote control color TV with free and pay movies. Toll-free: (800)444-8311.
suite—large, wet bar/refrigerator,   2 D or K bed...$375
regular room—   2 D or K bed...$210

Royal Fox Inn   *329-4481*
10.6 mi. NE at 14500 Palm Dr. - Desert Hot Springs 92240
A big mineral water pool and whirlpool in a courtyard are features of
this three-story motor hotel with a gym, saunas, steam room; and (for
a fee) massage; plus a coffee shop. Each spacious, comfortable room
has a phone and color TV. Toll-free in CA: (800)423-8109.
#120 thru #129—refrigerator, separate desert-view
room with warm mineral water whirlpool,   K bed...$125
regular room—request balcony,   K bed...$65; Q bed...$61

★ **Shilo Inn Suites**   *320-7676*
1.6 mi. N at 1875 N. Palm Canyon Dr. - 92262
One of the desert's best resort motels has two pools (one large) and two
whirlpools in a lovely garden court with a grand mountain backdrop,
plus a sauna, steam room, and an exercise room. Each well-furnished
room has a private patio or balcony overlooking a courtyard,
microwave oven, refrigerator, phone, and remote control color TV with
free and pay movies. Toll-free: (800)222-2244.
regular room—   2 Q or K bed...$110

Palm Springs
Spa Hotel Resort and Mineral Springs   *325-1461*
downtown at 100 N. Indian Canyon Dr. (Box 1787) - 92263
The city's only mineral springs are in a renovated five-story hotel in the heart of town. The conventional 230-room facility has a large outdoor pool, a hot mineral whirlpool, and still pools; (for a fee) three lighted tennis courts and a health spa with mineral springs whirlpools, steam baths, massage, and a co-ed gym; plus a restaurant, lounge and gift shop. Each nicely redecorated room has a refrigerator/(honor) bar, phone and remote control color TV with movies. Some have a private patio or balcony. Toll-free: (800)854-1279.

regular room—ask for 5th floor pool/mountain view,   K bed...$165
regular room—   2 Q or K bed...$125

★ Sundance Villas   *325-3888*
2.5 mi. NW at 303 Cabrillo Rd. - 92262
Here are nineteen of Palm Springs' most posh apartment villas. All units share well-landscaped grounds with a pool, whirlpool, sauna, and a lighted tennis court. Refreshments are provided on arrival. Each spacious two- or three-bedroom villa is glamorously, individually decorated, and has a small private outdoor pool and whirlpool in an enclosed patio, plus a gas fireplace, stocked (honor) bar, large sunken tub in the master bath, kitchen with microwave, private patio, phones, and remote control color TV with movies and VCR.

villa—3 BR, 3 baths,   2 Q & K beds...$450
regular suite—2 BR villa, 2 baths,   Q & K beds...$340

★ Villa Royale   *327-2314*
1.6 mi. SE at 1620 Indian Trail - 92264
One of Southern California's most romantic lodgings is a small single-level bed-and-breakfast inn that is ideal for adults. Lush tropical flower gardens and bubbling fountains, two courtyard pools and a whirlpool are linked by meandering brick paths, and there are bicycles for guests. Light breakfast is complimentary. **Europa** (L-D. Closed Mon.—Very Expensive) is open to both guests and the public and offers New California cuisine in a tranquil, casually elegant dining room. Each unit is individually decorated with distinctive international furnishings, and has a phone and color TV with remote control. Toll-free: (800)245-2314.

#305—spacious studio with kitchen, gas
  fireplace, private patio & whirlpool,   K bed...$250
#101—spacious 1 BR with kitchen, fireplace in LR,
  private patio with garden/mts. view,   oversized K bed...$250
#121—fireplace, private patio & whirlpool,   K bed...$165
"guest room with whirlpool in private patio"—   K bed...$135
regular room—   Q bed...$75

Wyndham Palm Springs   *322-6000*
.4 mi. E at 888 E. Tahquitz Canyon Way - 92262
The only lodging by the convention center is a 410-room luxury hotel that opened in 1988. The five-story post-modern complex has an extra-large pool and two whirlpools in a garden court, sauna, exercise room,and (for a fee) massage, plus restaurants, entertainment lounge, and specialty shops. Each attractively furnished room has a phone and remote control color TV with (pay) movies. Toll-free: (800)822-4200.

"Executive Suite"—spacious 1 BR, pvt. mt.-view balc.,K bed...$220
regular room—   2 D or K bed...$175

Pasadena

Pasadena is the paragon of gentility in the Los Angeles basin. Less than half an hour by car from the ocean, the compact city occupies a choice site at the base of the towering San Gabriel Mountains. Founded during the 1870s as a health refuge, it soon became a haven for the wealthy because of the normally warm, sunny winter weather. A unique cluster of cultural and scientific facilities followed.

Today, Pasadena is a beguiling blend of the gracious lifestyle of an earlier era and the dazzling promise of a high-tech future. Beautifully landscaped boulevards and streets lead to a wealth of museums, monumental public buildings, stylish shopping districts, stately mansions, and manicured gardens and parks. The area now has one of the Southland's preeminent concentrations of gourmet restaurants in "Old Town Pasadena," a born-again vibrant people pleaser. The 1990s also heralded the opening of two world-class hotels.

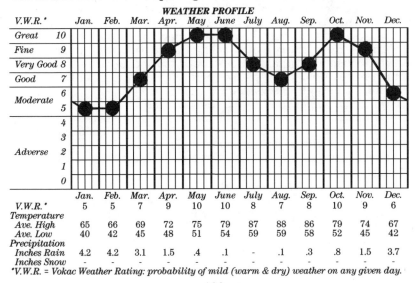

WEATHER PROFILE

V.W.R.*		Jan.	Feb.	Mar.	Apr.	May	June	July	Aug.	Sep.	Oct.	Nov.	Dec.
V.W.R.*		5	5	7	9	10	10	8	7	8	10	9	6
Temperature													
Ave. High		65	66	69	72	75	79	87	88	86	79	74	67
Ave. Low		40	42	45	48	51	54	59	59	58	52	45	42
Precipitation													
Inches Rain		4.2	4.2	3.1	1.5	.4	.1	-	.1	.3	.8	1.5	3.7
Inches Snow		-	-	-	-	-	-	-	-	-	-	-	-

V.W.R. = Vokac Weather Rating: probability of mild (warm & dry) weather on any given day.

Pasadena

Population: 131,591   Area Code: 818
Elevation: 865 feet
Location: 10 miles Northeast of Los Angeles
Pasadena Convention & Visitors Bureau   795-9311
.4 mi. E at 171 S. Los Robles Av. - 91101

ATTRACTIONS

★ **Ambassador College & Auditorium**   *304-6161*
   .8 mi. W at 300 W. Green St.
Beautiful gardens, fountains and handsome buildings have caused this complex to be honored as America's best landscaped and maintained campus. The Auditorium, one of the world's acoustically grand halls, hosts many prestigious concerts each season.

★ **California Institute of Technology**   *395-6327*
   1.7 mi. SE at 315 S. Hill Av.
Founded in 1891, this world famous center for scientific research and education—especially physics, geology, astronomy, aeronautics, and engineering—has produced almost two dozen Nobel Prize winners. The handsome campus of 124 acres was modeled after a medieval cloister.

★ **Civic Center**   *449-7360*
   downtown around intersection of Colorado Blvd. / Garfield Av.
The centerpiece of Pasadena's illustrious architectural heritage is a richly detailed complex completed more than sixty years ago. Mature trees and luxuriant landscaping enhance each building. Dominating the center is the baroque city hall with a splendid tiled dome, colonnade, and a fountain courtyard with gardens. To the north is the Renaissance-style public library. Nearby is a handsome 3,000-seat civic auditorium—home to television's Emmy awards.

★ **Descanso Gardens**   *952-4400*
   6 mi. NW via I-210 at 1418 Descanso Dr. - La Canada Flintridge
One of the largest camellia gardens in the world   displays 600 varieties each spring in a 165-acre preserve. Mature California live oaks also shade collections of azaleas, rhododendrons, lilacs, orchids, roses, and assorted annuals that collectively bloom year-round. There is an **Exhibition Complex** and an **Oriental Pavilion** with a teahouse amidst a lovely Japanese garden with a pool, stream, and waterfalls. **Hospitality House** sells gifts and books, and art and floral exhibits. Visitors can take a self-guided tour or conducted jeep train tours (except Mon.) along pathways throughout the arboretum.

El Molina Viejo   *449-5450*
   3 mi. SE at 1120 Old Mill Rd. - San Marino
The Old Mill, built about 1816 by Indians from Mission San Gabriel, was the region's first water-powered grist mill. Original millstones remain, along with a working model and free exhibits in a photogenic old adobe with a red tile roof and a tree-shaded courtyard. Closed Mon.

★ **Gamble House**   *793-3334*
   1.1 mi. W at 4 Westmoreland Pl.
California's finest Craftsman-style bungalow was built by renowned architects Charles and Henry Greene in 1908. The wood-shingled mansion is a masterful blend of American and Japanese influences with projecting rafters and sculptured woodwork. Complete original furnishings including Tiffany glass, lighting, and landscaping are displayed. One-hour tours are offered on Tues., Thurs., and Sun.

200

★ **Huntington Library, Art Collections, & Gardens**   *405-2141*
3 mi. SE at 1151 Oxford Rd. - San Marino
Here is the quintessential Southern California cultural experience.
Henry E. Huntington, a railroad tycoon, began developing gardens on
his 200-acre estate in the gentle hills southeast of Pasadena shortly
after the turn of the century. He also built a classically proportioned
mansion to house his extraordinary collection of art and books. Today,
the magnificent **Botanical Gardens** covering 150 acres are lush
green and in bloom year-round. The desert plant tract is the world's
largest outdoor collection of cacti and other succulents. An adjoining
luxuriant jungle features more than two hundred palm species.
Around the buildings, verdant lawns are bordered with Italian
statuary. Beyond are plots of roses, and nearly a thousand varieties of
camellias interconnected by a maze of pathways. A Shakespearean
garden features plants mentioned in the plays, and there is an
Australian garden full of species from "down under." An enchanting
Japanese garden fills a small canyon with a stream and koi pond,
arched bridges, a temple bell, and a teahouse amidst meticulously
tended ornamental trees, shrubs and flowers. The **Huntington
Library** houses one of the world's great collections of rare American
and British books and documents. Exhibits include a Gutenberg Bible,
a first folio of Shakespearean plays, and Benjamin Franklin's
handwritten autobiography. The **Huntington Gallery** was originally
the founder's home. It now houses a peerless collection of 18th and
19th century British paintings including Gainsborough's "Blue Boy"
and Lawrence's "Pinkie." Other permanent exhibits feature
Continental and English art, sculpture, porcelains, miniatures, and
period furniture. The **Virginia Steele Scott Gallery of American
Art** traces American art and furnishings from the 1730s to the 1930s.
An English tea with gourmet scones, finger sandwiches and assorted
desserts is delightfully presented in the lovely **Rose Garden Tea
Room** (early afternoons daily). More casual fare is available next door.
The entire complex including a gift/book shop is open every afternoon
except Monday and on holidays.

★ **Los Angeles State and County Arboretum**   *821-3222*
6 mi. E at 301 N. Baldwin Av. - Arcadia
Perhaps no other gardens in the world have been filmed as often as
this 127-acre botanical showcase where Tarzan swam; Humphrey
Bogart pulled the "African Queen;" and scenes from television's
"Fantasy Island" were taped. The grounds (in bloom year-round)
include a tropical lagoon, jungle trail, waterfalls, and lush plantings
(arranged by continent) from around the world. Peacocks and guinea
fowl roam freely since the arboretum is also a bird sanctuary. In 1875,
E.J. "Lucky" Baldwin (a silver magnate) bought part of a Spanish land
grant and began developing a working ranch and pioneer botanical
collections. His Queen Anne cottage remains as a splendid example of
Victorian craftsmanship with a fanciful turret; gingerbread trim; and
period hardwood, stained glass, crystal, and furnishings. Nearby is an
1890 railroad depot full of memorabilia, and a restored 1839 mud-
brick structure. Visitors can opt for a self-guided tour or a conducted
tram tour of the luxuriant labyrinth. There are also water
conservation gardens, tropical greenhouses, a horticultural research
center, and a gift/book shop.

Pasadena

★ **Mission San Gabriel**   *282-5191*
4 mi. SE at 537 W. Mission Dr. - San Gabriel
The fourth of twenty-one California missions was founded in 1771. Parts of the original stone and mortar remain in the renovated building, a splendid example of mission architecture next to a large cactus garden and ruins. The compound also includes the (closed) building where wine making began in California about 1770.

★ **Mount Wilson Observatory**   *793-3100*
24 mi. NE via I-210 & CA 2 on Mount Wilson Rd.
Near the top of 5,710-foot Mt. Wilson stands a landmark structure that surrounds a 100-inch reflecting telescope. The venerable instrument is credited with the discovery that the universe consists of more than a single galaxy. A visitors gallery and observatory museum are open to the public. Picnic sites are nearby, as are panoramic views across Los Angeles to the ocean—on clear days.

★ **Norton Simon Museum**   *449-6840*
.8 mi. W at 411 W. Colorado Blvd.
A contemporary building houses one of America's great displays of European and Asian art. Works in the capacious galleries span more than 2,000 years—from ancient Indian and Southeast Asian sculpture through masterpieces by Rembrandt and other Old Masters, to twentieth century paintings. The superb, idiosyncratic collections also include a landscaped sculpture garden with pieces by Rodin and Henry Moore, tours, and a first-rate museum shop. Closed Mon.-Wed.

★ **Pacific Asia Museum**   *449-2742*
downtown at 46 N. Los Robles Av.
A graceful Chinese palace-style building surrounding a garden courtyard features changing exhibits of traditional and contemporary art and culture of the Orient and Pacific Basin. There is a collector's gallery and gift shops. Closed Mon.-Tues.

★ **Rose Bowl and Rose Bowl Aquatics Center**   *564-0330*
2 mi. NW at 360 N. Arroyo Blvd.
Pasadena's renowned 104,000-seat stadium, built in 1902, is the site of the celebrated New Year's Day college football clash. The UCLA Bruins play their home games here, and other events are scheduled year-round. Nearby, the aquatics center, open to the public in 1990, is the only facility in the West with two fifty-meter pools.

★ **Santa Anita Park**   *574-7223*
6.5 mi. E at 285 W. Huntington Dr. - Arcadia
One of America's most beautiful racetracks has hosted thoroughbred horse races since 1934. The family-oriented complex includes a children's playground, picnic areas, gardens, landmark buildings and food purveyors. You can watch morning workouts during racing season for free on weekdays, and there are free tram tours on weekends. Closed Mon.-Tues., and late Nov. to late Dec. and May thru Sept.

★ **Tournament House & Wrigley Gardens**   *449-4100*
1 mi. SW at 391 S. Orange Grove Blvd.
The Tournament of Roses Association is headquartered in a splendid Edwardian mansion completed in 1914 by chewing gum magnate William Wrigley, Jr. Guided tours are offered on Wednesday afternoons from February through September, while the extensive formal gardens, highlighted by roses, are open free to the public daily.

Winter Sports

The San Gabriel Mountains that rise abruptly from the northern city limits extend in lofty ridges to popular ski areas nearer to Pasadena than to any other major city in the Los Angeles basin.

Mount Waterman   *790-2002*
40 mi. NE via I-210 on CA 2
The closest ski area to LA and Pasadena has a vertical rise of 1,200 feet and tops out at 8,000 feet. Three chairlifts serve the area. Basic ski rentals and food services are available at the area, but no lodgings. Skiing season is Thanksgiving thru April.

RESTAURANTS

★ **Aunt Gussye's Place**   *794-6024*
2.6 mi. N at 2057 N. Los Robles Av.
B-L-D. Closed Mon.   *Moderate*
New Orleans-style creole dishes are authentically rendered in specialties like creole omelets for breakfast with grits and biscuits, or file gumbo jambalaya or catfish fingers later—along with peach cobbler made and served in the bright, cheerful little coffee shop.

★ **Bistro 45**   *795-2478*
.8 mi. E at 45 S. Mentor Av.
L-D. No L Sat. & Sun. Closed Mon.   *Expensive*
Classy bistro fare like pan-roasted whitefish with shitake mushrooms or seared herb-crusted leg of lamb is featured along with a stylish array of appetizers and entrees that all reflect the chef's talent with New California cuisine. Crisp white linen and distinctive table settings balance polished hardwood floors and avant-garde wall hangings.

★ **Chez Sateau**   *446-8806*
6.5 mi. SE at 850 Baldwin Av. - Arcadia
L-D. Sun. brunch. No L Sat. Closed Mon.   *Expensive*
Here is one of Southern California's longest-established gourmet dining venues. Light and lovely presentations of Cal-Asian cuisine are the highlight in dishes like braised salmon and scallops on a bed of spinach with caviar cream sauce or crab-salmon cake with tomato coulis and grapefruit. The tranquil, casually elegant dining rooms allow guests to focus on the beauty and flavors of the exciting cuisine.

★ **The Chronicle**   *792-1179*
1.4 mi. SE at 897 Granite Dr.
L-D. No L Sat. & Sun.   *Expensive*
Chateaubriand, filet mignon, and saddle of lamb for two are among Continental classics that have been updated in this long-established local landmark. The constancy of the food preparation is matched by the gentility of the dining rooms and lounge.

★ **Cinnabar**   *551-1155*
8.5 mi. W at 933 S. Brand Blvd. - Glendale
L-D. No L Sat. Closed Sun.-Mon.   *Expensive*
Glendale's most creative cuisine is the result of a skilled combination of New California and Asian styles. A dish like medallions of pan-roasted veal served on a Hawaiian taro potato pancake really works. Desserts made here like baked apple with green peppercorn ice cream contribute to the allure of this 1993 dining room and bar in a converted Bekins warehouse. Half orders available on the grazing menu are another nice touch.

★ **Clearwater Cafe**   *356-0959*
.5 mi. W at 168 W. Colorado Blvd.
B-L-D. No B Mon.-Fri.   *Expensive*
Fresh seafood receives careful attention in an assortment of grilled,
sauteed, poached and pan-roasted treatments that highlight an
extensive grazing menu. The big stylish dining room provides a
picture-window view of Old Town and a lovely fountain court.

★ **Crown City Brewery**   *577-5548*
.3 mi. S at 300 S. Raymond Av.
L-D.   *Moderate*
Several beers drawn from gleaming copper kettles in Pasadena's first
exhibition brewery compete with more than a dozen super-premium
tap beers from around the world. An unusually varied selection of
updated American pub grub is also served in the split-level brew pub.

★ **Dragon Regency**   *282-1089*
6 mi. S at 120 S. Atlantic Blvd. - Monterey Park
L-D.   *Moderate*
Steamed or braised whole fish, and crustaceans many ways, are half
the pleasure of this excellent Chinese seafood restaurant. The other
half is the adventure in exotica—braised fish snout, suckling pig, or
pan-fried abalone with sea cucumber. Tables favoring groups of six or
more predominate in a big plebeian dining room.

★ **El Emperador Maya**   *288-7265*
8 mi. SE at 1823 S. San Gabriel Blvd. - San Gabriel
L-D. No L Sat. & Sun. Closed Mon.   *Moderate*
Rich moles and other sauces, specialty seafood dishes, and appetizers
like fried bananas are among authentic Yucatan specialties served in
a little roadhouse with tiny casual dining rooms.

★ **Far Niente Ristorante**   *242-3835*
8 mi. W at 204½ N. Brand Blvd. - Glendale
L-D. No L Sat. & Sun.   *Expensive*
The puffed-up pita loaf that starts each meal is a unique introduction
to the creative Italian cuisine to follow. Well-prepared dishes served
in cozy congested dining rooms with an expo rotisserie and bar have
made this restaurant a local favorite.

★ **Fresco**   *247-5541*
8 mi. W at 514 S. Brand Blvd. - Glendale
L-D. No L Sat. Closed Sun.   *Expensive*
In 1993 the original chef returned to restore Fresco to its lofty status
as one of Southern California's best Italian restaurants. Classic and
innovative dishes are prepared with consistent skill. Everything from
the bread through sausages to the ice cream is made here. The superb
cuisine is complemented by an urbane neo-art deco setting with a lot
of flowers. A well-played piano enhances the adjoining lounge.

★ **Gennaro's Ristorante**   *243-6231*
8.5 mi. W at 1109 N. Brand Blvd. - Glendale
L-D. No L Sat. Closed Sun.   *Very Expensive*
A limited but well-thought-out selection of Northern Italian cuisine is
served in this popular restaurant. Reached via an intimate lounge, the
handsome dining room has tables set with flowers and crisp linen, and
a cart displaying luscious homemade desserts.

★ **Goldstein's Bagel Bakery**   *792-7435*
.3 mi. W at 86 W. Colorado Blvd.
B-L-D.   *Moderate*
Goldstein's makes the best bagels in Southern California including all
of the great standards plus exotics like chile/cheddar bagels and
assorted "wraps" (barbecue, pastrami, turkey, etc.). All are excellent,
and can be enjoyed at a few tables in the always-busy shop or to go.

★ **Green Street Restaurant**   *577-7170*
.8 mi. E at 146 S. Shoppers Lane
B-L-D.   *Moderate*
Pasadena's best breakfasts involve seasonally fresh, quality ingredients skillfully converted into upscale California light fare like terrific
omelets, innovative chicken jalapeno sausage, and delicious zucchini
bread made here. You can opt for cheerful post-modern dining rooms,
a comfortable bar, or a heated and shaded sidewalk cafe.

★ **The Huntington Ritz-Carlton**   *568-3900*
2 mi. SE at 1401 S. Oak Knoll Av.
B-L-tea-D. Sun. brunch.   *Very Expensive–Extremely Expensive*
In **The Grill** (L-D. No L Sat.–Extremely Expensive), contemporary
Continental cuisine is served amidst wood-toned splendor at tables
lavishly furnished in linens, crystal, china, flowers and candles. **The
Cafe** (B-L-D. Sun. brunch–Very Expensive) has New California
cuisine in a light, lovely dining room and on an adjacent umbrella-
shaded terrace in a tropical court above the pool. **The Lounge**
(tea–Extremely Expensive) features classic afternoon tea service,
while **The Bar** offers drinks and light fare amidst similar opulence
and shares the delightful view of the valley beyond the terrace.

★ **Julienne**   *441-2299*
3 mi. SE at 2649 Mission St. - San Marino
B-L. Closed Sun.   *Expensive*
Breakfast pastries like apple-cinnamon coffee cake with walnuts
would easily justify a detour. Most of the breads and desserts made
here are delicious, as are the pastas, soups, salads and other light and
lovely dishes. Ignore the big painting of a chubby child while you're
carb-loading in the cozy dining room or sidewalk cafe.

★ **Les Arts**   *583-8275*
downtown at 70 S. Raymond Av.
L-D. No L Sat.-Wed.   *Very Expensive*
In 1994, the elan of Nouvelle French cuisine was reintroduced locally
in dishes like fresh lobster with basil, tomato, and truffle juice; broiled
whitefish with baby turnips and carrots; snails in a red wine sauce
with quail egg; or shrimp and wild mushroom ravioli. Grand piano
stylings are an appropriate accompaniment to the sophisticated
cuisine and smart decor of the dining room and bar.

★ **Market City Caffe**   *568-0203*
downtown at 33 S. Fair Oaks Av.
L-D. Sun. brunch.   *Expensive*
The excitingly diverse antipasto bar up front is well worth a visit. So
are the hand-thrown pizzas and charcoal-broiled fresh fish from an
exhibition kitchen. There is often a happy hubbub at the closely spaced
tables in the modish high-ceilinged room and fountain court in one of
Southern California's best trattorias.

★ **Merida**   *792-7371*
downtown at 20 E. Colorado Blvd.
B-L-D.   *Moderate*
Authentic Yucatan-style Mexican dishes include assorted seafood
soups. It's all cooked to order, and everything is fresh, flavorful and
distinctive. Guests have a choice between a skylit, brick-walled dining
room or an umbrella-shaded courtyard.

★ **Mi Piace**   *795-3131*
downtown at 25 E. Colorado Blvd.
L-D.   *Moderate*
California and New York-style pizzas in regular or thick crust
highlight a contemporary Italian menu. Best of all is an outstanding
display of breads and desserts made here and next door in the
Pasadena Baking Company (where breakfast is also served). The
cozy congested dining areas and on-the-sidewalk cafe are always busy.

★ **Noodles**   *500-8783*
8 mi. W at 215 N. Central Av. - Glendale
L-D. Sat. & Sun. brunch.   *Moderate*
Noodles is very popular for designer calzones and pizzas, mesquite-
grilled meats, pastas, and more served amidst tony art and decor.

★ **Old Town Bakery**   *792-7943*
.5 mi. W at 166 W. Colorado Blvd.
B-L-D.   *Expensive*
Pasadena's premier pastry parlor features the area's only homemade
English muffins. All sorts of luscious cakes and pies, cookies,
croissants and breads varying in quality are also served with light
meals and coffee next to the goodies, on a garden court, or to go.

★ **Parkway Grill**   *795-1001*
.5 mi. S at 510 S. Arroyo Pkwy.
L-D. No L Sat.   *Very Expensive*
The Parkway Grill is a tour de force of New California cuisine.
Everything is fresh and innovative. From a spectacular island kitchen
comes such treats as fried pecan-crusted red snapper with fennel and
orange sauce, whole catfish with ginger, and designer pizzas
handmade from scratch. Fine baked goods are made here, as are ice
creams and sorbets. The grandiose dining room and lounge with
artistic wood-toned decor enhanced by live greenery and spectacular
floral arrangements complement the delicious cuisine.

★ **The Raymond Restaurant**   *441-3136*
1.6 mi. S at 1250 S. Fair Oaks Av.
L-tea-D. Sun. brunch. Closed Mon.   *Very Expensive*
A well-thought-out, limited selection of contemporary American dishes
is expertly prepared and served in very complete four-course dinners
(or a la carte). A California-style bungalow has been artistically
converted into several intimate, elegant dining areas surrounded by
garden patios. Classical musicians perform at all meals.

Rose City Diner   *793-8282*
downtown at 45 S. Fair Oaks Av.
B-L-D.   *Moderate*
The 1950s are revisited—again—but with some concern for freshness.
All sorts of diner delights are accompanied by soda fountain treats,
golden oldies on the jukebox, snazzy rooms full of plastic, chrome,
stainless steel—and thousands of toothpicks stuck in the ceiling.

★ **Roxxi**   *449-4519*
1 mi. E at 1065 E. Green St.
L-D. No L Sat. & Sun.   *Expensive*
New California/Southwestern cuisine is showcased in designer pizzas
and pastas, plus appetizers and entrees with smoked, grilled and
roasted dishes. All are deftly prepared and served in several classy
congested little dining rooms.

★ **Saladang**   *793-8123*
.5 mi. SW at 363 S. Fair Oaks Av.
L-D.   *Moderate*
Whole catfish, crab curry, and sizzling beef with peanut sauce suggest
the range of specialties offered in Pasadena's best Thai restaurant.
Opened in 1993, the big dining room's very spare decor is usually
warmed by large crowds of fans of fine Thai food.

★ **Shiro**   *799-4774*
2.5 mi. S at 1505 Mission St. - South Pasadena
D only. Closed Mon.   *Expensive*
New California cuisine with Oriental overtones soars to new heights
in one of Southern California's great restaurants. Masterfully
prepared creations like Chinese ravioli stuffed with shrimp, salmon
mousse and shitake mushroom sauce, or Dungeness crabmeat
wrapped in crepe purses with a mustard sauce suggest the range of a
menu that changes nightly. Spare, chic decor of the intimate dining
room doesn't detract from the brilliant offerings.

★ **Twin Palms**   *577-2567*
.4 mi. W at 101 W. Green St.
L-D. Sun. brunch.   *Expensive*
The world's largest purveyor of New California cuisine opened in 1994.
Instant success attended a wealth of innovative dishes utilizing
rotisserie, special ovens, and a uniformly talented army of creators of
culinary delights. Two giant century-old date palms distinguish a vast
canopied open-air pavilion with heat lamps. An exhibition rotisserie
and two bars are part of the action and there are two big handsome
dining rooms open on one side to the happy tumult.

★ **Xiomara**   *796-2520*
downtown at 69 N. Raymond Av.
L-D. No L Sat. Closed Sun.   *Very Expensive*
Roast loin of venison with sour cherries and pan-fried chestnuts, or
oven-braised veal shank with black trumpet mushrooms suggest both
the French roots and New California spin on creations coming from
the highly regarded kitchen. Polished wood and stone accents enhance
the simply posh dining room.

★ **Yujean Kang's**   *585-0855*
downtown at 67 N. Raymond Av.
L-D.   *Expensive*
Yujean Kang's has the best "New Chinese" cuisine in the Southland.
Classic Oriental tradition and ingredients are seamlessly coupled with
top-quality seasonal American provisions. The resulting dishes are
complex, unique, and often wonderful. A perfect example is fresh sea
bass in sesame sauce with sauteed asparagus and enoki mushrooms.
A tranquil, stylish dining room and world-class wine cellar contribute
to the allure of this urbane young superstar.

LODGING

Pasadena began the 1990s with two new world-class hotels (one newly built downtown; the other a reborn landmark). Rates vary little year-round (except around New Year's Day when the sky's the limit). But, some places reduce rates by 10% or more on weekends.

Colorado Inn - Best Western   *793-9339*
2.3 mi. E at 2156 E. Colorado Blvd. - 91107
This modern motel has a small pool and whirlpool. Each comfortable room has a phone and color TV with movies. Toll-free: (800)528-1234.

regular room—(13 on 3rd & 2nd floor N side) above parade
route with sliding glass door to small private balcony,
3 nights minimum and must reserve before Jan. 15
for Rose Parade week when nightly rate is   2 Q or K bed...$250
regular room—   2 Q or K bed...$62

★ **Doubletree Hotel at Plaza Las Fuentes**   *792-2727*
downtown (near I-210) at 191 N. Los Robles Av. - 91101
Pasadena's largest (350 rooms) and finest convention-oriented hotel opened in late 1989. The post-modern twelve-story complex in a gracious courtyard complex overlooks City Hall in the heart of town. Amenities include a large outdoor pool and whirlpool, saunas, steam rooms, exercise room, gift shop, and (fee) parking, plus a tony dining room with an outdoor patio and a posh entertainment lounge. Each beautifully furnished room has a phone and remote control color TV with free and pay movies. Toll-free: (800)222-TREE.

#949,#849—splendid view of City Hall
& plaza from corner windows &   K bed...$150
"Concierge Level"—free light breakfast &
drinks/appetizers, good city/mountain views, 2 D or K bed...$175
regular room—   2 D, Q or K bed...$109

★ **Embassy Suites**   *445-8525*
7 mi. E (near I-210) at 211 E. Huntington Dr. - Arcadia 91006
One of the chain's best links is a seven-story complex of neo-Spanish-Colonial design with a tropically landscaped atrium with a stream and fountains, a restaurant and lounge, and a large pool and whirlpool in a plant-filled enclosure, plus a sauna, steam room, and gift shop. Breakfast and afternoon beverages are complimentary. Each of 194 attractively appointed suites has a kitchenette with microwave oven, two phones, and two color TVs (one remote control) with free and pay movies. Toll-free: (800)EMBASSY.

regular room—   2 D or K bed...$119

Holiday Inn   *449-4000*
downtown at 303 E. Cordova St. - 91101
One of the city's largest (320 rooms) hotels is a modern five-story complex in a park-like setting. Amenities of the convention-oriented facility (renovated in 1991) include an outdoor pool and (for a fee) two lighted tennis courts and covered parking, plus a restaurant, lounge, and gift shop. Each nicely furnished room has two phones and color TV with movies. Toll-free: (800)457-7940.

"King Leisure"—spacious, upgraded furnishings,   K bed...$125
regular room—   2 D beds...$98

★ **The Huntington Ritz-Carlton**   *568-3900*
2 mi. SE at 1401 S. Oak Knoll Av. - 91109
With completion of construction in 1991, Ritz-Carlton resurrected one
of the West's preeminent lodging landmarks dating from 1907. The
resort is once again Pasadena's largest, with 383 rooms, and its most
opulent. High on a verdant slope above a posh, tranquil neighborhood,
the gracious eight-story complex rises above spectacular Japanese and
waterscaped gardens. Other amenities include an extra-long pool in a
tropical courtyard, whirlpools, an exercise facility, and (for a fee) three
lighted tennis courts, rental bicycles, plus gourmet restaurants and
lounges (see listing), and resort shops. Each spacious, luxuriously
appointed room has a stocked (honor) refrigerator, phone and color TV
with free and pay movies. Toll-free: (800)241-3333.

Club Floor—top level, panoramic valley views,		
many food, beverage & other amenities,	K bed...$265	
"lanai"—large private balcony over pool,	K bed...$230	
regular room—overlooks a garden,	2 D or K bed...$165	

Motel 6   *446-2660*
6.5 mi. E at 225 Colorado Place - Arcadia 91006
Santa Anita Racetrack is by this modern **bargain** motel with a pool.
Each compact, plain room has a phone and color TV with movies.
    regular room—   D bed...$38

The Pasadena Hilton   *577-1000*
downtown at 150 S. Los Robles Av. - 91101
This thirteen-story 291-room hotel (renovated in 1991) is a modern
convention-oriented complex with a landscaped pool, exercise room,
restaurant and lounge, and shops. Each well-furnished room has a
phone, refrigerator, and remote control color TV with free and pay
movies. Toll-free: (800)HILTONS.
    regular room—request private balcony,   2 D or K bed...$99

Residence Inn by Marriott   *446-6500*
7 mi. E (near I-210) at 321 E. Huntington Dr. - Arcadia 91006
Renovated in 1994, Marriott's all-suites hotel has a landscaped pool
and whirlpool, and a game court. Afternoon appetizers and beverages
are complimentary on weekdays. Each spacious, well-decorated suite
has either one or two bedrooms, plus a kitchen with a microwave oven,
a living room with a duralog fireplace, phone and remote control color
TV with movies. Toll-free: (800)331-3131.
    regular room—2 bedrooms,   2 Q beds...$142
    regular room—1 bedroom,   Q bed...$112

Siesta Inn   *795-2017*
3.3 mi. E at 2855 E. Colorado Blvd. - 91107
This small motel is a no-frills **bargain**. Each simply furnished room
has a phone and color TV.
    regular room—   Q bed...$33

Travelodge - Pasadena Central   *796-3121*
2.2 mi. E at 2131 E. Colorado Blvd. - 91107
This modern **bargain** motel has a small pool and whirlpool. Each
nicely furnished room has a phone and remote control color TV with
movies. Toll-free: (800)255-3050.
    "Jacuzzi room" (3 of these)—in-bath whirlpool,   K bed...$60
    regular room—   K bed...$39

Rancho Santa Fe

Rancho Santa Fe is the wealthiest planned residential community in California. Stately mansions and posh horse ranches surrounded by lush gardens and orchards of citrus and avocado cover gentle slopes above San Dieguito River several miles inland from the ocean. Eucalyptus trees are abundant. When the Santa Fe Railroad's attempt to use the wood for railway ties failed, the site was subdivided into large estates. Bing Crosby and Douglas Fairbanks, Sr. were among early denizens. It has been home to the rich and famous ever since. Residents and visitors alike enjoy scenic countryside, manicured golf courses, a picturesque village center and tranquil resorts amidst a profusion of flowers.

Population: 4,720   *Area Code:* 619
Elevation: 246 feet
Location: 27 miles North of San Diego

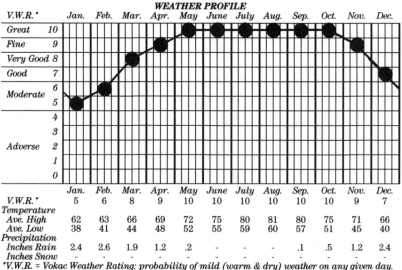

WEATHER PROFILE

V.W.R. *		Jan.	Feb.	Mar.	Apr.	May	June	July	Aug.	Sep.	Oct.	Nov.	Dec.
Great	10					●	●	●	●	●	●		
Fine	9				●							●	
Very Good	8			●									
Good	7												●
Moderate	6		●										
	5	●											
	4												
	3												
Adverse	2												
	1												
	0												

	Jan.	Feb.	Mar.	Apr.	May	June	July	Aug.	Sep.	Oct.	Nov.	Dec.
V.W.R. *	5	6	8	9	10	10	10	10	10	10	9	7
Temperature												
Ave. High	62	63	66	69	72	75	80	81	80	75	71	66
Ave. Low	38	41	44	48	52	55	59	60	57	51	45	40
Precipitation												
Inches Rain	2.4	2.6	1.9	1.2	.2	-	-	-	.1	.5	1.2	2.4
Inches Snow	-	-	-	-	-	-	-	-	-	-	-	-

*V.W.R. = Vokac Weather Rating: probability of mild (warm & dry) weather on any given day.

ATTRACTIONS

★ **Chino's Vegetable Shop**   *756-3184*
1.2 mi. S at Calzada del Bosque / Via de Santa Fe
Here is the quintessential California roadside produce shop. By a
dusty little parking lot often full of Mercedeses, local cognoscenti
queue up to buy incomparable white corn and other vegies (including
many exotics) picked daily. The peerless produce is the result of years
of hard work, great soil, and a mild climate. The shop is open daily
10-3, Sun. 10-1. Closed Mon.

Golf
★ **Morgan Run Resort and Club**   *756-2471*
2.8 mi. S at 5690 Concha de Golf
One of the Southland's loveliest 27-hole golf courses (redesigned in
1995) encircles a handsome residential enclave on the gentle floor of
the San Dieguito River Valley. The public can make reservations in
advance. Facilities include clubs and cart rentals, driving range and
practice area, lodgings (see listing), a restaurant and lounge.

★ *Scenic Drives*
downtown and all roads for several miles
Paved roads respect the contours of gentle hills and meandering
arroyos throughout the carefully planned enclave. Grand mansions
crown the ridgetops above immaculate horse ranches. Mature
eucalyptus, orchards, and gardens border every building and roadway.

RESTAURANTS

★ **Delicias**   *756-8000*
downtown at 6106 Paseo Delicias
L-D. Closed Mon.   *Very Expensive*
Delicias is one of the Southland's most sophisticated feasts for the
senses. New California cuisine is masterfully prepared, and showcased
in dishes like grilled filet mignon with green peppercorn sauce or
sauteed escolar in mustard sauce. Diners have a choice of
contemporary elegance in a romantic firelit dining room, or the
intimacy of a heated canopied patio beyond a cozy lounge.

★ **The Inn at Rancho Santa Fe**   *756-1131*
downtown at Linea del Cielo & La Gracia
B-L-D.   *Expensive*
The **Garden Room** offers traditional American and Continental fare
in a gracious setting enhanced by hand-painted murals, fresh flowers,
and a window-wall view of the pool and gardens. Nearby in the posh
Vintage Room, guests may dine and dance in a garden patio.

★ **Mille Fleurs**   *756-3085*
downtown at 6009 Paseo Delicias
L-D. No L Sat. & Sun.   *Extremely Expensive*
Creative New California cuisine is presented from a short changing
list of dishes like grilled sea bass with pineapple and cilantro sauce or
Sonoma duck with chestnuts and tangerine sauce. A talented staff,
innovative use of the best seasonal ingredients, and meticulous
attention to detail have made this one of San Diego County's best
restaurants. Haute cuisine is complemented by intimate, elegant
dining areas, and a handsome lounge featuring grand piano stylings
nightly. A flower-filled fountain courtyard in also used for lunch.

★ **Rancho Valencia Resort**   *756-1123*
3.4 mi. S at 5921 Valencia Circle
B-L-D. Sun. brunch.   *Very Expensive*
The Restaurant is the resort's signature showcase for New California
cuisine, featuring Chino's fresh vegetables. Luscious desserts are made
here, too. The dining room and lounge exude contemporary California
elegance, and share a view of the luxuriant surroundings with a tiered
dining terrace.

LODGING

There are three appealing accommodations on the Ranch. Summer is
busiest, but the rates stay the same year-round.

★ **The Inn at Rancho Santa Fe**   *756-1131*
downtown at Linea del Cielo & La Gracia (Box 869) - 92067
The epitome of Ranch style is an elegant small hotel that has topped
a rise in the heart of the village since the 1920s. The low-profile
charmer is surrounded by eucalyptus and citrus groves. Amenities
include an extra-long pool in a garden, three tennis courts, a
manicured croquet court, a beach cottage in Del Mar, and fine dining
(see listing). Each recently upgraded, beautifully appointed unit has
a phone and remote control color TV. Toll-free: (800)654-2928.

#175—"deluxe" (12 similar), spacious, refrigerator/
　　wet bar, glass door to big private deck, in-bath
　　whirlpool, fireplace in view of   K bed...$185
#18 "Acacia"—large room with kitchen, fine
　　overviews from hillside deck, fireplace in view of   K bed...$155
　　regular room—smaller, well-furnished,   2 T or Q bed...$105

★ **Morgan Run Resort & Club**   *756-2471*
2.8 mi. S at 5690 Concha de Golf (Box 3209) - 92067
In 1995, this small resort was completely upgraded. Amenities now
include a big outdoor lap pool and whirlpool, plus (for a fee) a palm-
studded 27-hole championship golf course and eleven (four lighted)
tennis courts. The clubhouse has a comfortable fairway-view dining
room and lounge, and a pro shop. Each spacious, well-furnished unit
has a sliding glass door to a small private patio or balcony, phone, and
remote control color TV. Toll-free: (800)378-4653.

"One Bedroom Suite"—refr., gas fireplace in parlor,   K bed...$179
regular room—request Buildings 200 or 400,   2 Q or K bed...$109

★ **Rancho Valencia Resort**   *756-1123*
3.4 mi. S at 5921 Valencia Circle (Box 9126) - 92067
Secluded in luxuriant rolling hills is a tranquil young resort that
captures the grandeur of early California's elegant haciendas.
Amenities include two large garden court pools and three whirlpools,
eighteen tennis courts, beauty and exercise facilities, saunas, rental
bicycles, gourmet restaurant (see listing) and lounge, and resort shops.
Each of 43 spacious, luxurious suites has a fireplace, big private patio,
wet bar/refrigerator, oversized tub, phone and two remote control color
TVs with movies and a VCR. Toll-free: (800)548-3664.

#117 (one of "Rancho Santa Fe Suites")—extra-large
　　1BR, fireplace in LR, big garden view deck,   K bed...$395
#120 (one of "Del Mar Suites")—garden view terrace,
　　sitting room with fireplace in view of   raised K bed...$375
　　regular room—"Del Mar Suite" (request #116 for view), K bed...$315

Redondo Beach

Redondo Beach is the hub of one of California's most complete seaside playgrounds. A handsome manmade harbor and marina, piers, a boardwalk, and a superb beach share the city's waterfront which extends almost to the hills of the Palos Verdes Peninsula. Redondo was already a major seaside resort when it was incorporated more than a century ago. It was here in 1907 that George Freeth introduced surfing to America, and later served as the country's first lifeguard. He became a legend, surfing became the epitome of "the California lifestyle," and Redondo Beach flourished.

Today, the city is the water recreation center of South Bay. Surfing, swimming, snorkeling, sportfishing, sailing, windsurfing, and jet skiing are all popular. Many waterfront shops, sea-view eateries and amusement arcades line the piers and boardwalk. Nearby, two first-class hotels offer fine marine views.

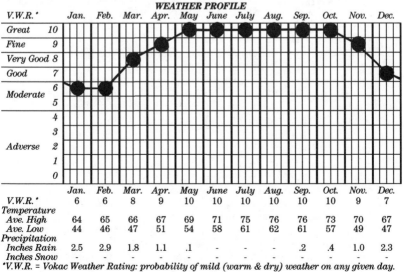

WEATHER PROFILE

V.W.R. *		Jan.	Feb.	Mar.	Apr.	May	June	July	Aug.	Sep.	Oct.	Nov.	Dec.
Great	10												
Fine	9												
Very Good	8												
Good	7												
Moderate	6												
	5												
	4												
	3												
Adverse	2												
	1												
	0												

	Jan.	Feb.	Mar.	Apr.	May	June	July	Aug.	Sep.	Oct.	Nov.	Dec.
V.W.R. *	6	6	8	9	10	10	10	10	10	10	9	7
Temperature												
Ave. High	64	65	66	67	69	71	75	76	76	73	70	67
Ave. Low	44	46	47	51	54	58	61	62	61	57	49	47
Precipitation												
Inches Rain	2.5	2.9	1.8	1.1	.1	-	-	-	.2	.4	1.0	2.3
Inches Snow	-	-	-	-	-	-	-	-	-	-	-	-

*V.W.R. = Vokac Weather Rating: probability of mild (warm & dry) weather on any given day.

Population: *60,167*   *Area Code: 310*
Elevation: *50 feet*
Location: *21 miles Southwest of Los Angeles*
Redondo Beach Chamber of Commerce and Visitors Bureau   376-6911
.5 mi. N at 200 N. Pacific Coast Hwy. - 90277 (800)282-0333

ATTRACTIONS

Abalone Cove Beach   377-1222
9 mi. S on Palos Verdes Dr. South - Rancho Palos Verdes
About a mile of sheltered sandy beach highlights a park with restrooms, picnic areas, and pay parking nearby. Fishing, swimming and tidepooling are popular. Headlands at Portuguese and Inspiration Points bound a half-mile-long secluded beach near the east end of the park. It is a favorite of nude sunbathers.

★ *Bicycling*
All South Bay towns are connected by pathways, separated from streets and highways, along the beach. Bicyclists can pedal more than a dozen miles along one of the most exhilarating shorelines anywhere, before skirting Marina Del Rey, and then continue along the coast to Santa Monica. Bicyclers (as well as skates) can be rented at:

Hermosa Cyclery   *20 13th St. - Hermosa Beach   374-7816*
Jeffers   *39 14th St. - Hermosa Beach   372-9492*
Marina Bike Rental   *505 N. Harbor Dr.*   *318-BIKE*

★ **Hermosa Beach**   376-0951
1.5 mi. NW at W ends of 3rd thru 35th Sts. - Hermosa Beach
Nearly two miles of fine sand borders Hermosa Beach. Surfers and swimmers enjoy the waves, while the Municipal Pier attracts fishermen. Strollers, joggers and bicyclists are well served by a paved pathway that parallels the entire beach (and continues for miles to the north and south). Note: limited-time parking meters are everywhere.

Malaga Cove Plaza
3 mi. S on Palos Verdes Dr. West - Palos Verdes Estates
Of four community centers envisioned for the peninsula in the 1920s, only this one was constructed (circa 1924). The picturesque complex includes two levels of shops and restaurants in a Spanish-revival arcade, enhanced by an arresting fountain and lush vegetation.

Point Vicente Interpretive Center   377-5370
7.5 mi. S on Palos Verdes Dr. South - Rancho Palos Verdes
This small museum features exhibits on the dramatic evidences of uplift and landslides that continue to shape the peninsula, and on gray whales. Each winter, an observation deck (admission fee) and surrounding viewpoints attract visitors intent on spotting migrating gray whales as they round Point Vicente near shore.

★ **Redondo Beach Pier**
.3 mi. W at W end of Torrance Blvd.
A delightful complex of piers and walkways newly reconstructed and expanded in the mid-1990s extends over the waves, with views of King Harbor to the north and silver sand extending southward to the Palos Verdes Peninsula. Angers come here to try their luck. But, the real attraction is the nautical scenery, shops with trinkets and treasures, food stalls, entertainment lounges, and seafood restaurants with surf views. The adjacent **International Boardwalk** also bristles with souvenirs and seafoods, while the **Redondo Fun Factory** on the

lower level offers a labyrinth of arcade games and minor amusement rides. Nearby, inexpensive twenty-minute boat rides take people a mile out for scenic views on weekends.

★ **Redondo State Beach** *372-2166*

.3 mi. SW along Esplanade

One of Southern California's most popular beaches extends for more than two miles south of the Pier through Torrance Beach to the precipitous Palos Verdes Peninsula. A bicycle path and jogging trail parallel the fine sand. The surf is usually up. Lifeguards look after hordes of swimmers, surfers, skin divers, and sunbathers in summer.

South Coast Botanic Gardens *544-6815*

6 mi. SE at 26300 Crenshaw Blvd. - Palos Verdes Peninsula

A one-time landfill has been transformed since 1960. The rolling terrain now contains an 87-acre garden (fee) with hundreds of plant species from nearly every continent. In addition to horticultural and botanical displays, there is a gift shop.

★ *Sportfishing*

Deep sea and coastal sportfishing boats with all necessary equipment leave year-round from King Harbor. In winter, whale watching expeditions are regularly scheduled. Contact:

Redondo Sport Fishing *.5 mi. NW at 233 N. Harbor Dr. 372-2111*

★ *Surfboard Rentals*

If you're finally overcome by an urge to "hang 10," but don't have a board, Hermosa Beach has places that rent surfboards and accessories by the hour or longer. They can tell you where the "surf's up," too.

Bay Surf Rentals *2 mi. NW at 117 Greenwich Village Dr. 376-2503*

Jeffers *2.5 mi. NW at 39 14th St. 372-9492*

★ **Wayfarers Chapel** *377-1650*

9 mi. S at 5755 Palos Verdes Dr. South - Rancho Palos Verdes

A remarkable "glass church" occupies a dramatic hillside location overlooking the ocean. Built entirely of glass framed by redwood, the structure was designed by Frank Lloyd Wright's son in 1946. Details like the native stonework in the simple altar and graceful campanile, and a surrounding redwood grove and garden, are further evidence of the inspired interplay of art and nature. The church, built as a memorial to Emanuel Swedenborg (a Swedish theologian and mystic) is a haven of tranquility for all people, regardless of faith.

RESTAURANTS

Admiral Risty *377-0050*

7 mi. S at 31250 Palos Verdes Dr. West - Rancho Palos Verdes

D only. Sun. brunch. *Expensive*

They broil, poach, grill or saute any of the fish that are available each evening, and there is an extensive selection of standard American fare. Many of the fully linened tables in the large, split-level dining room have a distant ocean view.

Ajeti's Restaurant *379-9012*

2 mi. N at 425 Pier Av. - Hermosa Beach

D only. Closed Mon. *Moderate*

Lamb is featured in various spicy or mild Albanian specialties in keeping with the owner's Balkan roots. All entrees come with robust portions of soup, slaw, vegies, and whole wheat pita bread in a cozy candlelit dining room with a fireplace and Old World art.

Alpine Village Inn   *323-6520*
6 mi. E at 833 W. Torrance Blvd. - Torrance
L-D.   *Moderate*
German specialties and traditional American fare are served in a
comfortable dining room and in a barn-like dine/dance hall. They also
feature beer made here along with live entertainment for dancing. The
adjoining **Alpine Market** has many German sausages, baked goods,
beers and wines. The complex also includes related specialty shops.
★ **Back Burner Cafe**   *372-6973*
2.5 mi. NW at 87 14th St. - Hermosa Beach
B-L.   *Low*
The Back Burner serves some of the best breakfasts in Southern
California. Imaginative omelets, biscuits with country gravy, and
superb homemade cinnamon rolls stand out among all-American
specialties. The coffee shop decor in the two rooms is as casual as the
location (on a side street a block from the beach).
Buona Vita   *379-7626*
2 mi. N at 439 Pier Av. - Hermosa Beach
L-D. No L Tues., Sat. & Sun.   *Moderate*
A short list of chicken, pizzas and pastas captures the full flavor and
spirit of contemporary Italian fare in this popular tiny trattoria.
CJ's Pantry   *318-2411*
downtown at 324 S. Catalina Av.
B-L.   *Moderate*
Hearty helpings of all-American fare are served in an appealing funky
coffee shop. Wood-trimmed dining areas are embellished with
humorous wall murals of local scenery.
Casablanca   *379-4177*
2.4 mi. NW at 53 Pier Av. - Hermosa Beach
L-D. No L Sat. & Sun.   *Expensive*
Continental dining is enhanced by homemade pastas and desserts.
Many plants and intimate nooks and several draped booths contribute
to the romantic candlelit ambiance of this cozy upstairs restaurant.
Cheesecake Factory   *376-0466*
.7 mi. NW at 605 N. Harbor Dr.
L-D. Sun. brunch.   *Expensive*
Display counters, brimming with all kinds of cheesecakes and other
desserts, grace the entrance to cavernous dining rooms with a harbor
view shared by a sunny garden patio and a lounge. This is the best of
several representatives of chains that line the harbor.
★ **Chez Melange**   *540-1222*
1.5 mi. SE at 1716 S. Pacific Coast Hwy.
B-L-D. Sat. & Sun. brunch.   *Expensive*
New American cuisine is skillfully prepared from scratch for exciting
presentations that change nightly. Possibilities include herb-crusted
swordfish over steamed greens with Mediterranean salsa, or turkey
jalapeno sausage with roasted tomato salsa and jack cheese, or
popcorn shrimp with ranch dipping sauce. Booths and banquettes line
a refined dining room with brass lamps, greenery and floral accents.
Cuisine from around the world is featured in frequent special culinary
events. A beautiful blondwood wine bar near the entrance showcases
selections from the restaurant's excellent wine cellar.

★ **Country Touch Cafe**   *323-5614*
4 mi. NE at 3717 W. 190th St. - Torrance
B-L.   *Low*
Homemade apple dumplings and other pastries complement carefully
prepared all-American dishes. The fine home cooking is served in a
cheerful cafe with a lot of greenery and country touches.

★ **Depot**   *787-7501*
4 mi. E at 1250 Cabrillo Av. - Torrance
L-D. No L Sat. & Sun. No D Mon.   *Expensive*
New California cuisine stars in one of Southern California's best young
restaurants. Creative delights like three-flavor Thai dumplings
steamed in ale for starters, or fig-and-pecan-crusted lamb loin with
roasted mushrooms and barley, receive ideal treatment thanks to the
talent of master chef Michael Shafer. The fresh flavorful cuisine is
complemented by crisp white linens and polished hardwood accents in
a handsomely restored depot. While all of the desserts are delightful,
the chocolate bento box with its wondrous array of chocolate flavors
and textures is worth a long pilgrimage for all chocoholics.

★ **Descanso**   *379-7997*
2.2 mi. N at 705 Pier Av. - Hermosa Beach
L-D. Sun. brunch.   *Expensive*
A wealth of Pacific Rim cuisine is featured in dishes like rock shrimp
and fish cakes with a tropical fruit salsa, or beef satay with green
papaya slaw and sauteed sweet plantains. Distinctive desserts are
made here too. A big trilevel dining room and lounge are outfitted in
padded booths and chairs amid faux tropical foliage. The adjoining
Pier Avenue Bakery also opened in 1994 with some well-displayed
pastries and many breads. They are available with coffee at a few
indoor and outdoor tables, or to go.

Fat Face Fenner's Falloon   *376-0996*
2 mi. NW at 837 Hermosa Av. - Hermosa Beach
B-L-D. No B Mon.-Fri.   *Moderate*
When you're looking for a really big, tasty burger, the fully loaded
half-pounder is a good choice. It can be enjoyed with several kinds of
premium tap beers in a wood-trimmed plant-filled saloon or on an
adjoining patio.

★ **Fino**   *373-1952*
4 mi. SE at 24530 Hawthorne Blvd. - Torrance
D only.   *Expensive*
Hot and cold tapas star on an international grazing menu that ranges
from lamb stew or grilled venison medallions to decadent desserts. A
handsome lounge and expo kitchen accent multilevel dining areas
outfitted in crisp white linens.

★ **The Golden Lotus**   *377-5892*
7 mi. S at 31176 Hawthorne Blvd. - Rancho Palos Verdes
L-D.   *Moderate*
Far from the maddening crowds, the Golden Lotus offers some of the
most extraordinary Chinese cuisine in California. Stellar presentations
of Szechwan, Hunan, and Mandarin classics include Chinese filet
mignon, bubbling seafood casserole, tea-smoked duck, whole fish in hot
bean sauce, and spicy sea cucumber. Wondrous food is matched by the
refinement and serenity of two capacious dining areas.

Redondo Beach
Good Stuff on the Strand   *374-2334*
2.5 mi. NW at 1286 Strand at 13th St. - Hermosa Beach
B-L-D.   *Moderate*
Contemporary light American fare is served in a casual little cafe and
open-air patio by the action on the adjoining promenade and beach.
★ **Il Boccaccio**   *376-0211*
2.4 mi. NW at 39 Pier Av. - Hermosa Beach
D only.   *Expensive*
Tuscan and Florentine-style veal, poultry, seafood and homemade
pastas and desserts are all given careful attention. The casually
elegant, intimate dining room has become a popular destination for
authentic Italian cuisine.
★ **J'Adore**   *541-3316*
5.5 mi. SW at 724 Yarmouth Rd. - Palos Verdes Estates
D only. Closed Sun.-Mon.   *Very Expensive*
Fresh contemporary California cuisine stars in J'Adore's forte—seven-
course dinners that provide an opportunity to fully explore exciting,
personalized cuisine. An intimate dining room complements the spare
elegance of the meals.
Joe's   *376-9570*
.7 mi. N at 400 N. Pacific Coast Hwy.
B-L-D. No D Sun.   *Low*
Hearty helpings of cheap all-American grub have attracted crowds for
years to shared tables in a genuine old-time Western diner.
King's Hawaiian Bakery Restaurant   *530-0050*
3 mi. SE at 2808 Sepulveda Blvd. - Torrance
B-L-D.   *Moderate*
Hawaiian baked goods and foods hit the mainland in 1988 with the
opening of this monumental restaurant/bakery. Up front, cases brim
with all sorts of carb-laden goodies. Beyond, American standards and
some island specialties are served in big dining areas that include a
spectacular aquarium.
★ **La Playita Cafe**   *376-2148*
2.5 mi. NW at 37 14th St. - Hermosa Beach
B-L-D. Closed Mon.   *Low*
South Bay's best California-style Mexican breakfasts include morning
delights like breakfast burritos or machaca scrambles. You can dine
in either a little cafe/cantina or on a sunny patio with a view of the
nearby promenade and adjoining beach.
★ **Le Beaujolais**   *543-5100*
.7 mi. N at 522 S. Pacific Coast Hwy.
L-D. Sat. & Sun. brunch.   *Very Expensive*
Classic French cuisine like salmon with dill sauce or rack of venison
has been skillfully updated with fresh regional embellishments. In
addition to a well-rounded selection of entrees, fine French pastries
and desserts are made on the premises. Posh table settings enhance
the intimate dining room of a converted bungalow.
Martha's Twenty-second Street Grill   *376-7786*
3 mi. N at 25 22nd St. - Hermosa Beach
B-L.   *Moderate*
Contemporary American fare (steel-cut oatmeal, etc.) is served in a
cheerful coffee shop, or on a pleasant sidewalk patio.

Millie Riera's Seafood Grotto   *375-0531*
1.5 mi. S at 1700 Esplanade St.
L-D. No L Sat. & Sun.   *Expensive*
Traditional Fisherman's wharf style dishes like cioppino compete with
a fine window-wall view of the coast across a street from the big casual
split-level dining room of this long-established restaurant.
★ **Misto**   *375-3608*
4 mi. SE at 24558 Hawthorne Blvd. - Torrance
L-D. Sat. & Sun. brunch. No D Mon.   *Expensive*
One of South Bay's most delightful bakeries displays a mind-boggling
assortment of pastries, muffins, breads, cookies and cakes. In the
adjoining cafe and garden court, classic California grazing fare ranging
from tomato-basil bisque through potstickers to pastas and pizzas are
given skilled attention.
★ **Rive Gauche**   *378-0267*
3 mi. S at 320 Tejon Pl. - Palos Verdes Estates
L-D. No L Mon. Sun. brunch.   *Very Expensive*
Traditional and updated French entrees are served with soup, salad,
and five vegetables. The dining room, inspired by a French country
inn, has been a tranquil hideaway for many years.
Scotty's on the Strand   *318-7152*
2.4 mi. NW at 1100 Strand at 11th St. - Hermosa Beach
B-L-D.   *Low*
Standard American fare is served in a big coffee shop with picture
windows providing good views of the promenade, pier and beach.
★ **Thai Thani**   *316-1580*
.8 mi. S at 1109 S. Pacific Coast Hwy.
L-D.   *Moderate*
Here is some of the finest Thai cuisine in Southern California. All of
the traditional and innovative dishes are meticulously prepared using
fresh—and often exotic—ingredients. The flavorful culinary delights are
served in a handsome dining room with stylish glass etchings and wall
hangings, abundant greenery, and live anthuriums on each candlelit
table.
Zack's   *316-1081*
.7 mi. S at 800 S. Pacific Coast Hwy.
L-D. Sun. brunch. Closed Mon.   *Expensive*
Contemporary American cuisine shows up in dishes like beer and
buttermilk dipped onion rings with chile barbeque sauce. Post-modern
decor and wall art distinguish a small dining room/bar outfitted with
padded booths and blondwood tables and chairs.

LODGING

Accommodations are numerous, ranging from deluxe hotels by the
coast to bargain motels inland. Summer is the busiest season, but
rates are seldom reduced more than 10% during the rest of the year.
East-West Inn   *540-5998*
downtown at 435 S. Pacific Coast Hwy. - 90277
A modern **bargain** motel only a few hundred yards from a superb
beach. Each simply refurbished room has a phone and color TV.
   "spa room" (3 of these)—big mirrored whirlpool near   K bed...$65
   regular room—   2 D beds...$40; Q bed...$35

Galleria Inn - Best Western   *370-4353*
3 mi. NE at 2740 Artesia Blvd. - 90278
A contemporary motel with an outdoor whirlpool and a sauna. Each spacious, nicely furnished room has a refrigerator, phone and color TV with movies. Toll-free: (800)528-1234.

spa room (several)—two-person raised tiled mirrored whirlpool in view of	K bed...$85
regular room—	K bed...$61

★ **Holiday Inn Crowne Plaza**   *318-8888*
.6 mi. NW at 300 N. Harbor Dr. - 90277
Redondo's largest lodging is a five-story, 339-room luxury hotel that opened in 1987 across a street form the harbor. Refurbished in 1994, amenities include a big outdoor view pool and whirlpool, a lighted tennis court, exercise room, sauna, game room, rental bicycles, restaurant, lounge, and piano bar. Each spacious, beautifully furnished room has a refrigerator/wet bar, two phones, and color TV with (pay and free) movies. Toll-free: (800)368-9760.

#4000 to #4004—small private balcony & picture window with superb coast view,		K bed...$185
regular room—small pvt. balc., harbor view,	2 D or	K bed...$155
regular room—city view,		K bed...$145

Motel 6   *549-9560*
6 mi. SE (by I-110) at 820 W. Sepulveda Blvd. - Harbor City 90710
The chain offers a modern **bargain** motel with an outdoor pool. Each simply furnished room has a phone and color TV with movies.

regular room—	Q bed...$40

★ **Palos Verdes Inn**   *316-4211*
1.5 mi. SE at 1700 S. Pacific Coast Hwy. - 90277
The ocean is a half mile from this fine small hotel with a large landscaped indoor pool and whirlpool, tropical sun deck, bicycles (free for guests), an award-winning restaurant (see **Chez Melange**) and wine bar. Each beautifully refurbished room has a phone and remote control color TV with pay movies. Toll-free: (800)421-9241.

ocean view deluxe king—(request 4th floor), spacious, wet bar/refr., distant ocean view from big pvt. balc. &		K bed...$140
regular room—distant ocean view from pvt. balc. &		K bed...$120
regular room—city view,	2 D or	K bed...$110

★ **The Portofino Hotel & Yacht Club**   *379-8481*
.8 mi. NW at 260 Portofino Way - 90277
The area's only waterfront lodging reopened for the 1990s after a complete remodeling on a peninsula between the ocean and harbor. Enlarged to 176 rooms, the three-story motor hotel amidst palms and flowers has a landscaped pool and whirlpool, free bicycles for guests, exercise room, marina-view cafe, dining room sharing a nautical panorama with a plush lounge, a gift shop, and pay parking. Each beautifully appointed room has a sliding-glass door to a large private patio or balcony, stocked (honor) refrigerator, two phones, and remote control color TV with (pay) movies. Toll-free: (800)468-4292.

"Jacuzzi Room" (8 of these)—on first floor, patio with breakwater view, raised tiled whirlpool,		K bed...$245
"Ocean View Deluxe" (several)—request third floor for best ocean/channel view from		K bed...$153
regular room—marina view,	2 D or	K bed...$143

Redondo Beach Inn - Best Western   *540-3700*
1.7 mi. SE at 1850 S. Pacific Coast Hwy. - 90277
This California-contemporary motel has a small outdoor pool,
whirlpool, sauna, exercise room, cafe and bar. Each spacious, well-
furnished room has a phone and color TV with movies. Toll-free:
(800)528-1234.
"Bridal Suite"—wet bar/refr., pressed-wood fireplace,
   big, tiled in-bath whirlpool, tiny balcony,   K bed...$160
   regular room—request private balcony,   2 D or K bed...$89
Redondo Beach Pier Travelodge   *318-1811*
downtown at 206 S. Pacific Coast Hwy. - 90277
The beach and pier are half a mile from this modern motel with a
small outdoor pool and whirlpool. Each comfortable room has a
refrigerator, phone and remote control color TV with movies. Toll-free:
(800)255-3050.
   #216—parlor, 2 TVs, large whirlpool in alcove,   K bed...$85
   regular room—   2 D beds...$63; K bed...$59
Sea Sprite Motel-Apartments   *376-6933*
1.9 mi. NW at 1016 Strand at 10th St. - Hermosa Beach 90254
The beach adjoins the small complex with an outdoor pool by the prom.
Each comfortable unit has a refrigerator, phone and color TV.
   #28,#27—1 BR, LR, kitchen, large private balcony
     above prom with great beach/pier view,   2 D or Q bed...$105
   "deluxe unit" (several)—LR & kit. above beach, 2 D or Q bed...$105
   regular room—small, no view,   D bed...$82
Sunrise Hotel - Best Western   *376-0746*
.7 mi. NW at 400 N. Harbor Dr. - 90277
King Harbor is across a highway from this contemporary three-story
motel with a pool and whirlpool, coffee shop and rental bicycles for
guests. Each well-furnished room has a phone and remote control color
TV with (pay) movies. Toll-free: (800)334-7384.
   "third floor harborside" (several)—marina view beyond
     highway, request refrigerator/wet bar,   2 Q or K bed...$100
   regular room—no view,   2 Q or K bed...$90
★ **Torrance Marriott**   *316-3636*
2.4 mi. E at 3635 Fashion Way - Torrance 90503
The area's largest lodging is a handsome seventeen-story convention
hotel with 487 rooms by Del Amo Fashion Center, one of California's
biggest shopping malls. Amenities include an extra-large indoor/
outdoor landscaped pool, whirlpool, sauna, exercise facilities,
restaurants, lounge with dancing, piano bar, and gift shop. Each well-
furnished room has a phone and remote control color TV with (free and
pay) movies. Toll-free: (800)228-9290.
   "Concierge Level"—extra amenities,   2 D or K bed...$119
   regular room—   2 D or K bed...$89
Travelodge Hermosa Beach   *374-2666*
2 mi. N at 901 Aviation Blvd. - Hermosa Beach 90254
The beach is less than a mile from this modern motel with a whirlpool.
Each spacious, comfortable room has a refrigerator, phone, and remote
control color TV with movies and a VCR. Toll-free: (800)553-1145.
   "Spa Suite" (9 of these)—raised large
     mirrored whirlpool in view of   K bed...$89
   regular room—(request kit. or small pvt. balc.), 2 Q or K bed...$59

Riverside

Riverside is the center of Southern California's inland empire. It is situated in the broad Santa Ana River valley less than an hour by car from the Pacific Ocean. The region's highest peaks crown the surrounding skyline. Thanks to a mild climate year-round and a mutant orange from Brazil planted here in 1873, a few years after the town was founded, Riverside is the birthplace of the navel orange.

That parent navel orange tree still bears fruit, and the city remains an important citrus-producing center. It is also the region's largest inland metropolis, and a home of the University of California. Some of the finest historic and contemporary public buildings in the Southland are concentrated near a landscaped outdoor mall downtown. The heart of town is once again the grandiose Mission Inn, recently meticulously restored after years of decline. The best shops, restaurants, and lodgings are scattered throughout the metropolis.

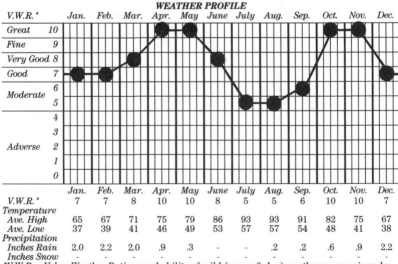

WEATHER PROFILE

V.W.R. *		Jan.	Feb.	Mar.	Apr.	May	June	July	Aug.	Sep.	Oct.	Nov.	Dec.
Great	10												
Fine	9												
Very Good	8												
Good	7												
Moderate	6												
	5												
	4												
	3												
Adverse	2												
	1												
	0												

	Jan.	Feb.	Mar.	Apr.	May	June	July	Aug.	Sep.	Oct.	Nov.	Dec.
V.W.R. *	7	7	8	10	10	8	5	5	6	10	10	7
Temperature												
Ave. High	65	67	71	75	79	86	93	93	91	82	75	67
Ave. Low	37	39	41	46	49	53	57	57	54	48	41	38
Precipitation												
Inches Rain	2.0	2.2	2.0	.9	.3	-	-	.2	.2	.6	.9	2.2
Inches Snow	-	-	-	-	-	-	-	-	-	-	-	-

*V.W.R. = Vokac Weather Rating: probability of mild (warm & dry) weather on any given day.

Population: 226,546   Area Code: 909
Elevation: 852 feet
Location: 58 miles East of Los Angeles
Riverside Visitors Center   715-4636
downtown at 3720 Main St. - 92501

ATTRACTIONS

Asistencia Mission de San Gabriel   793-5402
13 mi. NE at 26930 Barton Rd. - Redlands
This adobe branch of Mission San Gabriel, built about 1830, was the
last of the California missions. The restored chapel captures some of
the spirit of those early times. There is a small museum devoted to
pioneers, padres, and Indians. Closed Mon.-Tues.

★ **Castle Amusement Park**   785-4140
7.3 mi. SW at 3500 Polk St.
Riverside's big well-landscaped amusement center is a fun place to
stroll, experience a few lively thrill rides, and play on four elaborate
18-hole miniature golf courses. "The Castle" has more than 400
electronic and mechanical games including pool and hand-hockey.
Days open vary seasonally. Parking and admission fee.

★ **Civic Center**   782-5312
downtown at 3900 Main St. at 10th St.
The Riverside County Court House (closed in the mid-1990s for
earthquake-proofing) is a spectacular 1903 beaux-arts edifice with
imperial Roman-style statuary along the facade and a grandiose
vaulted central chamber. Nearby, the contemporary city hall is a
seven-story tribute to the essence of the Spanish arch.

Fairmont Park   782-5301
1 mi. N on Market St.
Towering clumps of fan palms distinguish little Evans Reservoir, a
tranquil oasis for migratory waterfowl, hikers, bikers, picnickers, and
fishermen. Roadways, bikeways, and sidewalks connect a rose garden,
palm groves, picnic and play areas, lighted tennis courts, a 9-hole golf
course, and restrooms throughout the park.

★ **Heritage House**   689-1333
4.2 mi. SW at 8193 Magnolia Av.
An 1891 Queen Anne-style mansion has been painstakingly restored.
The lavish interior is a treasury of milled and carved oak woodwork,
sculpture and tile fireplaces, lace curtains, and antiques. Tours and a
gift shop are open Tues., Thurs., and Sun. afternoons.

Horseback Riding
★   **Dave's Stables**   371-9640
17.7 mi. SW at 18000 Paseo Grande - Corona
The Old West lives on. For decades this stable has backed up against
Cleveland National Forest. Good riders (no guides are available) are
invited to enjoy trails up oak-shrouded creeks to high chaparral in the
mountains above on rides of one hour or more.

★ **Lake Perris State Recreation Area**   657-9000
17 mi. SE via CA 60 at 17801 Lake Perris Dr. - Moreno Valley
Fishing (bass, trout, catfish) is good, as is boating (rentals are
available) in this popular, four-square-mile reservoir. Swimming and
scuba diving are enjoyed off designated beaches. There is also a
waterslide area, and a complete campground. Toll-free: (800)444-7275.

★ **Mission Inn**   *784-0300*
   downtown at 3649 7th St.
Riverside's most famous landmark is one of America's extraordinary
hotels (see listing). The complex evolved from humble origins in the
1880s into a city-block labyrinth of alcoves and courtyards, terraces,
towers, and balconies of Spanish, Moorish, and Oriental design.

★ **Mount Rubidoux**   *782-5301*
   1.5 mi. W via University Av. on Mt. Rubidoux Dr.
Riverside's dominant landmark (1,339 feet above sea level) rises 500
feet above the city. A narrow paved road (which may be closed for
repairs) winds among towering cactus forests to the summit, topped
by a cross dedicated to Father Serra and the World Peace Tower. A
well-marked hiking trail through exotic vegetation is a popular
alternative route. Panoramic views reward both drivers and hikers.
The (free) road is closed to vehicles Thurs.-Sat.

★ **Oak Glen**
   approx. 30 mi. E via CA 60 & Beaumont Av. on Oak Glen Rd.
Southern California's most bountiful apple orchards blanket foothills
above orange groves east of Redlands. A paved highway winds past
apple orchards and quaint roadside stands, craft and gift shops, cafes
and cider mills in and around the village of Oak Glen. The landscape
is especially appealing during the autumn harvest when you can enjoy
apple treats ranging from ice-cold cider-sicles to warm apple pie. You
can pick your own apples in the fall at **Riley's Farm and Orchard**.
They also offer assorted apples for tasting, and for sale in boxes and in
cider, preserves, syrup—even soap. The other notable sources are **Los
Rios Rancho**; **Snowline Ranch**; **Wilshire's**; **Parrish Pioneer
Ranch** and **Hi Country Orchards**. For fine apple pie and related
baked goodies, try the **Creekside Kitchen** and **Apple Dumplin's**.

★ **Orange Empire Railway Museum**   *657-2605*
   17 mi. SE via CA 215 at 2201 S. A St. - Perris
Over two hundred steam engines, freight and passenger cars,
cabooses, trolleys, depots and buildings have been assembled into a
free display at a sprawling railyard. The gift shop has many related
books. Trolley and train rides are offered most weekends.

★ **Parent Washington Navel Orange Tree**
   3 mi. SW at SW corner of Magnolia / Arlington Avs.
Navel orange trees from Brazil that Mrs. Elizabeth Tibbetts planted
in 1873 may be the most historically important fruit stock in America.
The California orange industry began with the propagation of this
thick-trunked specimen that continues to flourish.

★ **Redlands**   *793-2546*
   15 mi. NE via I-215 & I-10
Downtown Redlands has a distinctive civic center and park complex.
Highlights include the **Lincoln Memorial Shrine** at 125 W. Vine St.,
an octagonal polished stone building housing a free museum dedicated
to Abraham Lincoln (Closed Sun.-Mon.). Next door, the **A.K.Smiley
Public Library** (Closed Sun.) is listed on the National Register. Built
in 1898 and artistically expanded in 1990, it includes some original
furnishings and sculptures. Across the street is **Redlands Bowl**, a
handsome amphitheater with scheduled concerts in summer. These
public facilities and nearby tree-lined streets of Victorian homes
suggest the grandeur of the town's early years.

★ **Riverside Municipal Museum**   *782-5273*
downtown at 3720 Orange St. (at 7th)
A handsome old post office is now a free museum that traces the development of the Inland Empire through the citrus boom near the turn of the century when Riverside was the wealthiest town per capita in America. Natural history is highlighted by a saber-toothed tiger found locally. There is a well-stocked gift shop. Closed Mon.

★ **San Bernardino County Museum**   *798-8570*
14 mi. NE at 2024 Orange Tree Lane - Redlands
Three floors of exhibits include extensive collections of birds, mammals, and reptiles of Southern California; regional history and geology; art; and a gift shop. The grounds feature railroad and mining relics amidst orange groves and cacti gardens. Closed Mon.

★ **University of California at Riverside**   *787-1012*
3 mi. E at 900 University Av.
About 9,000 full-time students are enrolled on a park-like campus founded in 1954 on 1,200 acres near the foothills east of downtown. The **Carillon Tower** is a 161-foot-high landmark. On a hillside near Parking Lot #13 are free **Botanical Gardens** featuring dry-climate flora from all parts of the world. Peak bloom is March through May.

RESTAURANTS

Bit O Country   *790-1953*
18 mi. E at 32971 Yucaipa Blvd. - Yucaipa
B-L-D.   *Low*
All-American fare served in abundance at all meals contributes to the popularity of this big, comfortable coffee shop. So do the baked goods and desserts made here.

★ **Bobby Ray's Bar-B-Que**   *885-9177*
13 mi. N at 1657 W. Base Line St. - San Bernardino
L-D. Closed Sun.-Tues.   *Low*
Bobby Ray's is one of the best sources of barbecue-and-soul-food in Southern California. Imported Texas hot sausage is featured. But, the meaty, messy, tender ribs, beef and chicken smothered in smooth, spicy Q-sauce are unbeatable. So is the homemade sweet potato pie. You can get it to go or at a few tables in a tiny roadside cafe.

★ **Gerard's French Restaurant**   *687-4882*
6.4 mi. SW at 9814 Magnolia Av.
D only. Closed Mon.   *Expensive*
Gerard's has been a major culinary outpost for years. French and Cajun antecedents provide the discipline behind a distinctive California cuisine with light bright treatments of fresh quality ingredients in dishes ranging from alligator filet with shitake mushrooms to filet mignon flambe. The sophisticated fare is perfectly matched by the romantic, casually elegant little dining room.

★ **Joe Greensleeves**   *792-6969*
15 mi. NE at 222 N. Orange St. - Redlands
D only. Plus L on Fri. Closed Sun.-Mon.   *Expensive*
Joe Greensleeves is a classic showcase for New California cuisine. The award-winning chef uses fresh seasonal ingredients for creative dishes like the "green sleeve" of roasted green chile filled with venison and cheese. Exciting treatments of pheasant, antelope, rabbit and other

game are usually among specialties grilled over orangewood. Polished wood booths overlook a copper-hooded fireplace in a sophisticated little dining room with hardwoods, flagstone and elegant accents.

Magnone   781-0886
1.5 mi. NE at 1630 Spruce St.
D only. Closed Sun.-Mon.   *Expensive*
Flavorful traditional and innovative Northern Italian cuisine including homemade desserts is served amidst neo-art deco decor with floral and art accents in a multi-angled dining room and lounge.

★ **Mission Inn**   784-0300
downtown at 3649 7th St.
B-L-D. Sun. brunch.   *Expensive*
Duane's (D only. Closed Sun.-Mon.–Very Expensive) is downtown Riverside's most elegant restaurant. Prime steaks and chops star in two dining rooms lavishly outfitted in hardwoods, luxuriant table settings, and wall art including a heraldic Civil War painting. In the **Spanish Dining Room** (B-L-D. Sun. brunch–Expensive) sauteed sea bass with lobster sauce or seared filet mignon with merlot pepper sauce typify New California cuisine served in a dining hall worthy of a castle in Spain, and on an enchanting fountain court. Piano stylings enliven the **Presidential Lounge** on weekends.

★ **Oscar's Mexican Restaurant**   792-8211
15 mi. NE at 19 N. Fifth St. - Redlands
B-L-D.   *Low*
Authentic Mexican breakfasts include a wide assortment of flavorful burritos, omelets, and scrambles–and they're featured all day in a long-established little coffee shop hidden away in downtown Redlands.

★ **Palazzo D'Italia**   785-1105
7 mi. SW at 10461 Magnolia Av.
L-D.   *Moderate*
Pizza should be made from just-raised dough, hand-thrown, and covered with rich sauce, pure mozzarella, and fresh quality ingredients. Here, it is. Pastas, veal, chicken, and seafood dishes are also prepared with the same dedication, as are the homemade ice creams and cannoli. The decor is pizza-parlor-pleasant.

★ **Riverside Brewing Company**   784-2739
downtown at 3397 7th St.
L-D.   *Moderate*
Southern California's best source of handcrafted brews opened in 1993 with beers ranging from pilsners to stouts created in kettles on display behind a picture-window backbar. All are available from samples to pitchers. As impressive are wood-fired beer-battered designer pizzas and pub fare like buffalo chili or turkey potless pie with beer dough. The vast pub, dining room and covered patio are often full.

★ **Su Casa**   883-4640
21 mi. NE at 1566 E. Highland Av. - San Bernardino
L-D. Closed Sun.   *Low*
Su Casa has the West's most memorable Mexican cuisine. The Yucatan region is highlighted in meat empanadas, assorted shrimp and fish specialties (don't miss the burrito marinero–shrimp and fish with a white wine cream sauce), and unusual dishes like spicy pork baked in banana leaves. Every selection is authentic and superb in this homespun cafe tucked away in a nondescript shopping center.

★ **Templo Del Sol**   *682-6562*
2 mi. E at 1365 University Av.
L-D.   *Low*
Diced cactus and pork cubes in a piquant sauce or spiced seafood
stuffed into a baked green pepper star among flavorful Mexican fare
offered in a casual colorful dining room.

LODGING

While many prosaic motels are along University Avenue, the best and
the bargain lodgings are scattered. Rates are often reduced at least
10% apart from summer.
Days Inn   *358-2808*
7.1 mi. SW at 10545 Magnolia Av. - 92505
One of the area's notable motels opened in 1992 with an outdoor pool.
Each nicely furnished room has a phone and remote control color TV
with movies. Toll-free: (800)325-2525.
     "Jacuzzi Suite" (6 of these)—large whirlpool in view of K bed...$75
     regular room—   Q bed...$42
Dynasty Suites   *369-8200*
2 mi. E at 3735 Iowa Av. (at University) - 92507
This 1990s motel has a tiny outdoor pool, and both **bargain** rooms and
fantasy rooms. Each comfortably furnished, spacious unit has a refrigerator, phone and remote control color TV with movies. Toll-free:
(800)842-7899.
     #215, #115—green (upstairs), red (downstairs), heart-shaped
          mirrored whirlpool in view of raised round mirrored K bed...$80
     regular room—   K bed...$35
Good Nite Inn   *793-3723*
11 mi. NE (by I-10/Alabama St.) 1675 Ind. Park Av.-Redlands 92374
This contemporary **bargain** motel has an outdoor pool and whirlpool.
Each clean, plain room has a TV with movies and phone.
     regular room—   Q bed...$32
Holiday Inn   *784-8000*
downtown at 3400 Market St. - 92501
The Inland Empire's prime convention-oriented hotel opened in 1986
by the Convention Center in the heart of town. Amenities of the 285-
room, twelve-story complex include a big landscaped pool and
whirlpool, restaurant, coffee shop, lounge, and gift shop. Each well-
furnished room has a phone and remote control color TV with (pay)
movies. Toll-free: (800)HOLIDAY.
     "Roman Tub" room—big bathtub, good town views,   K bed...$141
     regular room—   K bed...$88
★ **Mission Inn**   *784-0300*
downtown at 3649 7th St. - 92501
Southern California's most extraordinary hotel occupies an entire
block in the heart of town. Constructed from 1902 to 1935 in the
Mission Revival style, it grew into a unique five-story assemblage of
catacombs and catwalks, spiraling staircases, arcades, secret
courtyards and gardens, turrets, domes and carillon towers. Following
years of decline as Riverside lost its cache as a travel destination, the
property closed in 1985. After elaborate renovation, the hotel, now a
National Historic Landmark, reopened in 1993 with a wealth of fully
restored elegant decor touches and art objects, 240 rooms, a large pool

and whirlpool in a tropical courtyard, exercise room, grandiose restaurants and a romantic lounge (see listing). Each room has unique decor and attractive furnishings, including a stocked (honor) bar, phone and remote control color TV with free and pay movies. Toll-free: (800)843-7755.

#431 ("Presidential Suite")–top floor by hideaway
 garden court, vast chamber under towering rotunda
 with (nonworking) fireplace visible from   K bed...$430
#342–pvt. balcony with superb courtyard/parapet/
 clock tower view, unique bathroom accouterments
 and tile treatment,   K bed...$115
#344–as above, plus parlor,   Q bed...$180
 regular room–   Q, 2 Q or K bed...$100

★ **Morey Mansion Bed and Breakfast Inn** 793-7970
14 mi. NE at 190 Terracina Blvd. - Redlands 92373
The Morey Mansion is Southern California's most spectacular Victorian home now serving as a bed-and-breakfast. The 1882 landmark lies in isolated splendor amid gardens, towering palms and citrus on a side street near Redlands. It is an extravaganza of Victorian architecture with an onion dome and French mansard roof, arched windows, ornate balustrades and a traceried veranda. Inside is a treasury of skill-crafted hardwood, inlaid tile, Persian carpets, stained and beveled glass, and ornate metal fixtures. Each public room has a distinctive alcove and quality antiques. Complimentary Continental breakfast is served in the grandiose dining room. Public (fee) guided tours of the building occur on Sunday afternoons. Five upstairs bedrooms are individually embellished with rare appointments and period furniture. All have a view of the valley or mountains, and a remote control color TV and phone.

"Sarah's Chamber"–spacious, sitting room with turret
 alcove has mountain view and fireplace, carved Q bed...$185
"Blue Room"–multi-window alcove, fireplace, brass Q bed...$145
"Tower Room"–intimate view alcove, secluded,
 pvt. bath, dramatic wood-framed   Q bed...$145
 regular room–compact hideaway room with pvt. bath, D bed...$125

Motel 6
2.1 mi. E at 1260 University Av. - 92507 784-2131
.3 mi. W at 4045 University Av. - 92501 686-6666
7.8 mi. SW at 3663 La Sierra Av. - 92505 351-0764
The **bargain** chain is represented in Riverside by three motels with outdoor pools. Each has compact, simply furnished rooms with phone and color TV with movies. Prices vary slightly.
 regular room–   D bed...$30

★ **Travelodge Riverside La Sierra** 688-5000
7.3 mi. SW at 11043 Magnolia Av. - 92505
The area's most sybaritic lodging, opened in 1988, is a four-story neo-art deco motel with an outdoor pool and some **bargain** rooms. Each well-decorated room has a phone and color TV with movies. Toll-free: (800)578-7878.

#416,#415,#414,#316,#315,#314–spacious,
 kitchenette, big private patio with mountain view,
 large raised mirrored whirlpool in sight of K bed...$149
 king room (14 of these)–in-room whirlpool, K bed...$79
 regular room–   2 D beds...$39

228

San Clemente

San Clemente is the quiet corner of Orange County's coastal communities. Homes and businesses cover gentle hills above four miles of sandy beach. The only fanfare in a century of steady growth occurred when this was Richard Nixon's "Western White House." Since then, population has surged in response to coastal attributes and mild climate. Today, a municipal pier is the center of popular beach parks backed by palm-shaded lawns. Downtown is a well-landscaped little enclave of shops and restaurants. Lodgings are similarly unassuming and relatively scarce.

Population: 41,100   *Area Code:* 714
Elevation: 208 feet
Location: 61 miles Southeast of Los Angeles
Chamber of Commerce 492-1131
.7 mi. NW at 1100 N. El Camino Real (Box 338) - 92672

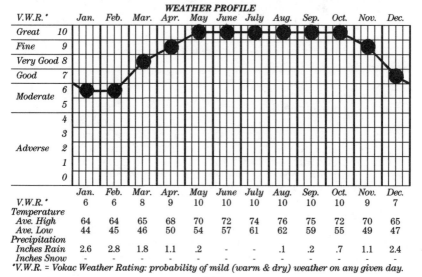

WEATHER PROFILE

V.W.R.*		Jan.	Feb.	Mar.	Apr.	May	June	July	Aug.	Sep.	Oct.	Nov.	Dec.
Great	10												
Fine	9												
Very Good	8												
Good	7												
Moderate	6												
	5												
	4												
	3												
Adverse	2												
	1												
	0												

	Jan.	Feb.	Mar.	Apr.	May	June	July	Aug.	Sep.	Oct.	Nov.	Dec.
V.W.R.*	6	6	8	9	10	10	10	10	10	10	9	7
Temperature												
Ave. High	64	64	65	68	70	72	74	76	75	72	70	65
Ave. Low	44	45	46	50	54	57	61	62	59	55	49	47
Precipitation												
Inches Rain	2.6	2.8	1.8	1.1	.2	-	-	.1	.2	.7	1.1	2.4
Inches Snow	-	-	-	-	-	-	-	-	-	-	-	-

*V.W.R. = Vokac Weather Rating: probability of mild (warm & dry) weather on any given day.

ATTRACTIONS

★ **San Clemente City and State Beaches**   *492-3156*
.5 mi. W at W end of Avenida del Mar
A fine sand beach extends for more than four miles along the city's western boundary at the base of sandstone bluffs. So do railroad tracks. A municipal pier attracts anglers and strollers. On either side lifeguards look after swimmers and surfers by a lovely palm-shaded beachfront park with picnic areas and restrooms. To the south is a sandy beach at the base of a towering bluff. The state has provided lifeguards, restrooms, picnic areas, and a complete campground.

★ **San Onofre State Beach**
7 mi. SE on I-5 frontage road
Huge twin domes of San Onofre Nuclear Generating Station dominate the north, a U.S. Border Patrol checkpoint on I-5 is on the bluff to the east, and America's largest Marine base, Camp Pendleton, borders the south. Nevertheless, the state's narrow four-mile strand along the base of a cliff is a popular destination. Campers are drawn to informal sites along the blufftop, surfers seek out remote breaks, and nude sunbathers congregate along the isolated south end.

RESTAURANTS

Beach Garden Cafe   *498-8145*
.5 mi. W at 618½ Av. Victoria
B-L-D. No D Mon. & Tues.   *Moderate*
Tasty Belgian waffles and assorted wheat cakes are featured on a contemporary American menu. The coffee shop across a road from an oceanside park has served beach-goers for decades.

Carbonara Trattoria Italiana   *366-1040*
downtown at 111 Del Mar
L-D. No L Sat. & Sun.   *Moderate*
Veal (prepared nine ways) highlights generous contemporary Italian dishes offered in this moderne trattoria.

Casa Tropicana Grill   *498-TROP*
.5 mi. W at 610 Av. Victoria
L-D. Sat. & Sun. brunch.   *Moderate*
A wide selection of California and Mexican fare is served amid cozy congestion in a dining room and bar with a pier view.

★ **Etienne's**   *492-7263*
downtown at 215 S. El Camino Real
D only. Closed Sun.   *Very Expensive*
Etienne's is one of the Southland's best French restaurants. Updated Gaelic classics (sauteed frog legs, escargot, rack of lamb, filet mignon with cognac sauce, etc.) are carefully prepared from scratch, along with elegant desserts like Grand Marnier souffle. Colorful floral bouquets accent candlelit tables set with full linen in graceful dining rooms. A fountain court and ocean view deck are also enjoyed.

The Fisherman's Restaurant & Lounge   *498-6390*
.5 mi. W at 611 Av. Victoria
B-L-D. Sun. brunch.   *Expensive*
Fish and shellfish are featured in a comfortable dining room with a heated shaded deck and an adjoining lounge that share a bird's-eye view of the beach from a choice location on the pier.

Sea Breeze Cafe   *498-4771*
1.4 mi. NW at 1640 N. El Camino Real
B-L.   *Moderate*
Contemporary California fare is simply prepared and served in
abundance in a bright and cheerful coffee shop which has been a local
favorite for years.

LODGING

There are no beachfront lodgings, but a few places are near the coast.
Summer weekends are prime time. Rates may be reduced by 30% or
more on weekdays during the rest of the year.
Best Western Casablanca Inn   *361-1644*
1.4 mi. NW at 1601 N. El Camino Real - 92672
The beach is a few blocks from this 1988 Mediterranean-style motel.
Each of the large, attractively decorated rooms has a refrigerator,
phone and remote control color TV with movies and VCR. Toll-free:
(800)752-9726.

"king whirlpool"(4 of these)–in-bath
  whirlpool, private courtyard-view balcony,   K bed...$79
  regular room–   2 Q beds...$69
★ **Casa Tropicana Bed & Breakfast Inn**   *492-1234*
.5 mi. W at 610 Avenida Victoria - 92672
San Clemente's most distinctive lodging is a getaway for adults. The
1990 bed and breakfast has nine rooms across a street from a park and
pier that extends beyond a lovely broad sandy beach. Light breakfast
during the week and full breakfast on weekends is complimentary. A
popular restaurant (see listing) is downstairs. Each room is
comfortably outfitted in fantasy decor. Most have whirlpools and gas
fireplaces. All have a phone and color TV.

"penthouse"–extra large 1 BR, big private deck
  with large whirlpool, 3-sided gas fireplace, raised
  whirlpool in bath, great ocean views,   K bed...$350
"Out of Africa"–kitchenette, big in-bath whirlpool,
  tropical decor, raised gas fireplace, ocean view from Q bed...$240
  regular room–refr., gas fireplace,   waterbed Q bed...$120
Holiday Inn   *361-3000*
downtown (by I-5) at 111 S. Av. de Estrella - 92672
Built in the 1990s, this small hotel has a little outdoor pool and
whirlpool plus a dining room and lounge. Each well-furnished room
has a refrigerator, phone and remote control color TV with movies.
Toll-free: (800)HOLIDAY.

#337,#338,#237,#238–spacious, private balcony,
  refr./wet bar, small raised whirlpool in view of   K bed...$135
  regular room–   Q bed...$70
Oceanview Inn & Suites   *361-0636*
1.2 mi. NW at 1301 N. El Camino Real - 92672
This contemporary four-story motel is a few blocks from the beach.
Each nicely furnished room has a refrigerator, phone and remote
control color TV with movies. Toll-free: (800)346-6441.

#405–spacious, private balcony, in-room whirlpool, Q bed...$125
"spa room" (several)–refr., in-bath whirlpool,   K bed...$88
  regular room–   2 Q beds...$68

San Diego

San Diego is one of America's leading year-round vacationlands. The West's second largest city sprawls for miles along Pacific Ocean beaches and Southern California's biggest natural harbor. It also extends inland for miles across valleys and mesas, and south to the Mexican border. The appealing setting is complemented by the best year-round climate in the United States.

California's first town was established in 1769 by a Spanish soldier, Portola, and Franciscan friars led by Father Junipero Serra. Growth was slow—only 3,000 people lived here a century later, and there were only 17,700 residents by 1900. Real growth began after the United States Navy adopted the harbor as a fleet base and training center. An additional boost came during World War II with the aircraft industry. Aerospace powered a post-war boom that recently ended. Electronics, biomedical and travel industries will fuel the next boom.

Today, San Diego is one of the most popular vacation destinations in the West—at all times of year. Two of the world's finest city parks are here. Balboa Park features an abundance of recreation and cultural facilities including landmarks from two world fairs that now serve as museums, galleries, theaters and restaurants. It also is the beautifully landscaped setting of America's finest zoo. Mission Bay Park is a saltwater labyrinth of palm-shaded lawns, bikeways, swimming beaches, boating facilities, fishing charters, resort hotels and a splendid marine-life park. Several business districts take advantage of waterfront locales, like La Jolla and Seaport Village, while Old Town and the Gaslamp Quarter reflect local history. Restaurants are abundant. Many offer pleasing marine views. A substantial number serve gourmet cuisine. Lodgings are similarly plentiful, and range from bargains to luxury resorts. Many are conveniently situated near the beaches, bay, or harbor.

Population: 1,110,623   Area Code: 619
Elevation: 40 feet
Location: 121 miles Southeast of Los Angeles
San Diego Convention & Visitor's Bureau   236-1212
   downtown at 401 B St., #1400 - 92101

San Diego

WEATHER PROFILE

V.W.R. *		Jan.	Feb.	Mar.	Apr.	May	June	July	Aug.	Sep.	Oct.	Nov.	Dec.
Great	10												
Fine	9												
Very Good	8												
Good	7												
Moderate	6 / 5												
	4												
	3												
Adverse	2												
	1												
	0												

	Jan.	Feb.	Mar.	Apr.	May	June	July	Aug.	Sep.	Oct.	Nov.	Dec.
V.W.R. *	7	8	8	9	10	10	10	10	10	10	10	8
Temperature												
Ave. High	65	66	67	68	69	71	75	77	76	74	71	67
Ave. Low	46	48	50	54	57	60	64	65	63	58	52	47
Precipitation												
Inches Rain	2.1	1.7	1.6	.8	.2	-	-	.1	.1	.5	1.0	1.9
Inches Snow	-	-	-	-	-	-	-	-	-	-	-	-

*V.W.R. = Vokac Weather Rating: probability of mild (warm & dry) weather on any given day.

ATTRACTIONS

★ **Aerospace Historical Center**   234-8291
   2 mi. NE at 2001 Pan American Plaza - Balboa Park
The museum is located in the remodeled Ford Building—an art deco classic that was the most impressive contribution of the 1935 Exposition. Highlights include a full-scale replica of Lindbergh's "Spirit of St. Louis" (the original was built in San Diego) and an original space capsule. In addition to aircraft, spacecraft, and related exhibits, there is a well-stocked gift shop. The Hall of Fame honors individuals who have contributed to aerospace progress.

★ **Balboa Park**   239-0512
   1 mi. NE along Sixth Av.
Here is one of the world's largest and liveliest urban parks. The 1,100 acre showcase of recreational and cultural attractions was established in 1870. Today, hills and canyons are covered with subtropical gardens, emerald lawns, exotic woods, and natural brush areas interconnected by miles of walkways and trails. The park's most popular attraction, the **San Diego Zoo** (see listing) is both a horticultural wonderland and the world's largest animal collection. Nearby, legacies of two international expositions—the Panama Pacific in 1915 and the California Pacific in 1935—have been faithfully preserved or restored to house an extraordinary array of museums, art galleries, theaters, restaurants and recreation facilities. The **California Building** (1915) at the west end of El Prado (the Laurel Street extension that was the main promenade for the first exposition) may be the city's most photographed building. The tower is a classic of Spanish Renaissance design. Below is The **Museum of Man**, with exhibits about early cultures of American Indians. The **Simon Edison Centre for the Performing Arts** adjoins with the **Old Globe Theater**, a classic Elizabethan-style centerpiece for a Tony-award-winning complex of three theaters. Further east on the south side

of El Prado, the **Hall of Champions** and **Hall of Fame** have a display and film related to San Diego's past sports stars. The **San Diego Model Railroad Museum** features the world's largest collection of mini-gauge trains. All layouts simulate the landscapes and history of railroading in Southern California. The **Museum of Photographic Arts** displays film, video, and color and black-and-white works of well-known photographers. The San Diego Historical Society's documents and photographs are also here. Across El Prado, the **Botanical Building** by a lily basin is a latticework model of a depot. Exotic tropical plants fill the vaulted space. Next door on El Prado Plaza are the **Timken Art Gallery**, a free collection of Old Masters, Early American paintings and Russian icons, and the **San Diego Museum of Art** with a diverse collection of European, American and Asian art and sculpture. At the east end of El Prado is a dramatic fountain flanked by the **Reuben H. Fleet Space Theater and Science Center** and the **Natural History Museum** (see listings). Structures from the 1935 exposition extend south from El Prado Plaza. The **Spreckels Organ Pavilion** contains an outdoor pipe organ said to be the world's largest. Just beyond is the **House of Pacific Relations** in a cluster of adobe-style cottages with free cultural exhibits of nearly thirty nations. They hold open house and stage a lawn party each Sunday with native foods and entertainment. The **Starlight Bowl**, which fills a natural amphitheater nearby, offers a wide range of musical events. At the south end is an art deco delight, now fully restored to serve as the **Aerospace Historical Center** (see listing). South of the zoo is the **Spanish Village Art Center**, a cluster of studios where artists and craftsmen create, display, and sell their works. Nearby is a spectacular Moreton Bay Fig tree.

★ *Beaches*

More miles of sandy beaches line San Diego's shoreline than any city in California. Nature's bounty includes miles of sandy coastline, while an even lengthier beach now borders manmade islands and inlets of Mission Bay. Thanks to the mild climate, sunbathing and beach-combing can be enjoyed year-round. However, the water is only warm enough from July to October to attract hordes of swimmers. **Torrey Pines Beach** (15 mi. N) extends southward along the base of towering sandstone bluffs to **Black's Beach** (13 mi. N). California's renowned nude beach can only be reached via a precipitous trail down a bluff or long hikes along Torrey Pines or La Jolla Beaches. To the south is a palm-lined park at lovely **La Jolla Shores Beach** (11 mi. NW). Beyond is **La Jolla Cove**, the Southland's most photogenic beach. Nearby "Children's Pool" (see front cover) recently became America's first and only animal-initiated interactive habitat. Sunbathing harbor seals and frolicking people peacefully share the warm beach and clear water of an idyllic cove. Two miles more of scenic coves and stately mansions along the base of low bluffs in La Jolla give way to **Pacific & Mission Beaches** (7 mi. NW). The city's most popular strand is bisected by a pier and paralleled by a concrete promenade with real appeal to strollers, skaters, and bicyclists. Across the entrance channel to Mission Bay is broad and funky **Ocean Beach** (7 mi. NW) with another popular pier. For Mission Bay beaches (5 mi. NW), see the park listing. For more information, contact:

San Diego City Lifeguard Service   *224-2708*
6 mi. NW at 2581 Quivira Ct. - Mission Bay Park

★ Bicycling

Separated bikeways and designated bike routes provide opportunities year-round to explore along the bays and coastline for miles in and beyond the city. Terrain is gentle and the scenery is sensational. Assorted bikes can be rented by the hour or longer at:

Bicycle Barn *8 mi. NW at 746 Emerald St. 581-3665*
Hamel's Action Sports Center *6.4 mi. NW at 704 Ventura Pl. 488-5050*
Mike's Bikes *6.4 mi. NW at 756 Ventura Pl. 488-1444*

★ Boat Rentals

Navigate the picturesque shoreline of Mission Bay Park in a sailboat or other boats that can be rented by the hour or day on Mission Bay at:

Mission Bay Sports Center *1010 Santa Clara Pl. 488-1004*
San Diego Princess Boat Rentals *1404 W. Vacation Rd. 274-4630*
Seaforth Boat Rentals *1641 Quivira Rd. 223-1681*

★ Boat Rides

Sightseeing cruises, whale watching trips in winter, day sails, overnights to nearby islands, and sportfishing trips can be arranged any day year-round. For information and reservations, call:

Bahia Belle *(sternwheeler cruise, meals / music / dancing) 488-0551*
Fisherman's Landing *(sportfishing & whale watching) 222-0391*
H & M Landing *(sportfishing & whale watching) 222-1144*
Invader Cruises *(cruises, dinner / dance, whale watching) 234-8687*
Islandia Sportfishing *(sportfishing & whale watching) 222-1164*
San Diego Harbor Excursion *(harbor tours, dinner / dance) 234-4111*

★ Cabrillo National Monument   557-5450

10 mi. SW at S end of Cabrillo Memorial Dr.

The first white men to set foot in California, led by Juan Rodriguez Cabrillo, sailed past this promontory into San Diego Bay in 1542. A visitor center offers films and exhibits about his voyage. Outside, the panoramic view of the harbor and city from the lofty ridgetop is one of the most dramatic anywhere. A nearby overlook 400 feet above the sea is a popular vantage point for observing the annual winter migration of gray whales. An 1855 lighthouse has been refurbished. More than two miles of trails wind along chaparral-covered slopes, and provide access to tidepools filled with colorful marine life.

★ Golf

Several dozen golf courses are sprinkled around San Diego County. Many are of championship quality. Most are public. Collectively, they provide a remarkable diversity of challenges and scenery ranging from coastal to desert. Almost all can be played year-round, thanks to the area's mild climate. Additional information can be obtained from the Convention and Visitors Bureau, or at two of America's most renowned championship 18-hole courses, the beautiful public

Torrey Pines Golf Course   *570-1234*
15.7 mi. NW at 11480 N. Torrey Pines Rd. - La Jolla

★ Maritime Museum of San Diego   234-9153

.7 mi. W at 1306 N. Harbor Dr.

Three restored historic shops include the tall ship "Star of India" (1863), the nation's oldest iron-hulled merchant vessel still seaworthy. Visitors can also go aboard the steam ferry "Berkeley" (1898) which helped evacuate San Francisco during the 1906 earthquake, and luxury steam yacht "Medea" (1904). All have nautical exhibits.

★ **Mexico**

16 mi. SE at S end of I-5

Tijuana, with about one million residents, has the West Coast's second largest Mexican population (after Los Angeles). U.S. citizens can visit for up to 72 hours without a visa or passport. U.S. auto insurance is not valid, so Mexican insurance should be obtained before driving across the border, which is open 24 hours daily. Shoppers are lured by the deflated peso and the city's status as an international port of entry. Authentic Mexican culture (so near and yet so different) fuels tourism that is helping transform tawdry areas into skyscrapers and shopping centers, and contributing to ever-longer waits at the two border crossings. For information, call:

Tijuana Chamber of Commerce *(1-706-6-)858414*
Mission Basilica San Diego de Alcala *281-8449*

9 mi. NE at 10818 San Diego Mission Rd.

California's first mission, founded by Junipero Serra in 1769 on Presidio Hill, was superseded by one at this location in 1774. The restored building is still used for services. A visitor center displays relics from the early days. Taped tours are available.

★ **Mission Bay Park** *276-8200*

5 mi. NW on Mission Bay Dr.

The world's largest aquatic city park is a 4,600-acre playground dredged from tidal flats near the mouth of the San Diego River. It is a fabulous labyrinth of channels and coves, islands, twenty-seven miles of shoreline and sandy beach backed by settings that range from tropical palm-shaded lagoons to barren desert strands. Sunbathing is enjoyed year-round, along with fishing, sailing, waterskiing and windsurfing. Several marinas offer boat rentals, sportfishing charters, and sightseeing cruises. Landscaped parks encompass a model yacht basin, golf course, miniature golf, tennis courts, ballfields, playgrounds, and picnic areas. Miles of scenic walkways follow the shorelines. So does the city's best system of separated bikeways and jogging paths. Every summer for two zany weeks, Fiesta Island is the site of San Diego's unique contribution to the world of sports—the "Over-the-Line Tournament." This laid-back variation of baseball features teams sporting (barely) creative costumery and (extremely) inventive team names. **Campland on the Bay** offers a marina, beach, and complete tree-shaded camping facilities for everyone from tenters to RVers. **Sea World** (see listing) is the park's most popular attraction. Several resort hotels and restaurants also share the aquatic bonanza.

Natural History Museum *232-3821*

1.8 mi. NE at 1788 El Prado - Balboa Park

Whale skulls highlight permanent displays devoted to plants, animals and geology of the San Diego environs. Special exhibits, lectures, and outings occur frequently, and there is a museum store.

★ **Old Town** *237-6770*

4 mi. NW around San Diego Av. & Twiggs St.

Permanent settlement in California began here in 1769. The compact area, best explored on foot, includes preserved, restored, and reconstructed buildings dating back to the first mission and presidio. Old Town San Diego State Historic Park is a six-block area with landmark adobes around the original plaza. Several are outfitted with period furnishings. Other historic structures in the well-landscaped district and nearby Heritage Park house restaurants and shops that contribute to the flavor of yesteryear.

★ **Palomar Observatory**   *742-2119*
62 mi. NE via County Hwy S-6
More than 6,000 feet high near the top of Mount Palomar is the 200-inch Hale telescope, for many years the world's largest. It and several lesser telescopes are used by astronomers from Cal Tech for ongoing celestial research. There is a visitors gallery inside the giant silver dome. The Greenway Museum (also free) contains photographs from observatory sightings and related exhibits.

★ **Presidio Park and Junipero Serra Museum**   *297-3258*
4.3 mi. NW at 2727 Presidio Dr.
The city's most luxuriant small park covers a slope above Old Town where the original mission and presidio stood. Nothing remains. Ongoing archaeological digs are open to public viewing. The mission site is now the Serra Museum, a landmark of Spanish-Colonial architecture. The tile-roofed, whitewashed adobe structure (circa 1929) houses exhibits and relics showcasing local history. Closed Mon.

★ **Reuben H. Fleet Space Theater and Science Center**   *238-1168*
1.8 mi. NE at 1875 El Prado - Balboa Park
Balboa Park's most popular museum features America's first theater and planetarium with a tilted hemisphere screen. Omnimax seventy-minute films and other special equipment give the comfortably seated audience a "you-are-there" sensation enhanced by wraparound images, color, and sound. The Science Center features hands-on exhibits of contemporary phenomena. There is also a well-stocked gift shop.

★ **San Diego Wild Animal Park**   *234-6541*
29 mi. NE via CA 163 at 15500 San Pasqual Valley Rd.
The nation's largest zoo sprawls across 2,100 acres of gentle valley floor and rocky hills near Escondido. More than 2,500 animals from around the world roam freely in expansive enclosures landscaped to simulate their native habitats. Several endangered species not found in other zoos are on display here. Visitors can view the animals along miles of hiking trails. Most opt for a nearly hour-long monorail tour across five miles of grassy veldts, rocky hills, and lush jungles. Photographers (and others), by reservation, can enjoy a unique safari (one to three hours) to get close (via park truck) to animals in fields. In the Africa-themed Nairobi Village, animal and bird shows are scheduled daily, and there are snack bars, dining rooms, and gift shops. Beyond, walkways wind through gardens and jungles with waterfalls to small mammal enclosures, aviaries, and a petting corral.

★ **San Diego Zoo**   *234-3153*
2.1 mi. NE at 2920 Zoo Dr. - Balboa Park
The world's foremost zoo sprawls across more than 100 acres of beautifully landscaped plateaus and canyons. More than 3,200 animals representing over 800 species are displayed. Most live in cageless, moated enclosures that simulate natural environments. Highlights include the 1995 arrival of the only pair of giant pandas in America; a large collection of cuddly koalas from Australia; a remarkable assemblage of rare primates; "Tiger River"—an enchanting display of flora and fauna of a tropical jungle; "Hippo Beach"—including underwater views; huge walk-through aviaries where exotic birds fly in a tropical rain forest; and an unsurpassed collection of reptiles. The entire zoo is resplendent with exotic greenery and

flowering plants from tropical and subtropical areas around the world. In addition to miles of walkways from canyon depths to mesa tops, visitors can opt for a bird's-eye view from the "Skyfari" aerial tramway, take a narrated three-mile bus tour, or board moving sidewalks. The delightful "Children's Zoo" gives children (and adults) a chance to pet gentle creatures; see inside a wild animal nursery; check out a hatchery; and get close to a colorful collection of hummingbirds. To view the animals in a novel mood, be there when the zoo is open on summer nights. Picnic areas, fast-food stands, dining rooms, and an excellent gift shop are also available.

★ **Sea World of California**   *226-3901*
   4.8 mi. NE at 1720 South Shores Rd. - Mission Bay Park
One of the world's largest oceanariums occupies an idyllic waterfront site in Mission Bay Park. Subtropical trees and gardens enliven the entire complex of aquariums, exhibits, shows and rides, plus a marina and research and medical labs. Highlights include the Penguin Encounter—a simulated Antarctic habitat with nearly 400 penguins; Rocky Point Preserve—the world's largest interactive marine mammal habitat; Shark Encounter where you get eerily close via an underwater walkway; a huge stadium where Shamu, the "killer whale," performs; watery stage shows starring dolphins, sea lions and walruses; a dolphin petting pool and a superb morey eel and bat ray exhibit. Shamu's Happy Harbor is a new tropically themed interactive water play area for children of all ages. Other attractions include an aerial tram and a Sky Tower with an elevator that winds up to the 320-foot summit for memorable panoramas. There are also guided tours, snack bars, restaurants, and well-stocked gift shops.

★ **Seaport Village**   *235-4014*
   .8 mi. SW at W. Harbor Dr. & Kettner Blvd.
Early California-themed adobes and clapboard buildings share a splendid locale by San Diego Bay in this popular re-creation of a yesteryear village center. Dozens of specialty shops and galleries are intermixed with numerous restaurants and a spectacular Gay 90s carousel. Gardens and walkways link to a bayside promenade which extends to Embarcadero Marina Park—where visitors view the busy harbor and skyline from a tranquil palm-shaded greensward.

★ **Steven Birch Aquarium - Museum**   *534-FISH*
   11 mi. NW at 2300 Expedition Way off La Jolla Shores Dr. - La Jolla
Southern California's best aquarium was tripled in size for the 1990s. Featuring over 150 species of fish, it is the largest oceanographic exhibit in the U.S. There are also spectacular views of the La Jolla coastline, an outdoor tidepool display, a bookstore, and a gift shop.

Wineries
   30 mi. NE around Escondido
The Escondido area has nurtured vineyards for more than a century. Four wineries are open daily for tasting and sales. All have inviting picnic areas. **Bernardo Winery** (13330 Paseo del Verano Norte, 487-1866), the oldest (1889), is in a rustic complex of art and gift shops. **Deer Creek Escondido** (29013 Champagne Blvd., 746-1666) also includes a deli, gift/wine boutique, and a car museum. **Ferrara Winery** (1120 W. 15th Av., 745-7632) is a small family winery dating from the 1930s. High on a picturesque hillside, **Orfila Vineyards and Winery** (13455 San Pasqual Rd., 738-6500) is the newest and biggest winery and has a handsome gift shop.

RESTAURANTS

★ **Alfonso's of La Jolla**   *454-2232*
  11.5 mi. NW at 1251 Prospect St. - La Jolla
  L-D.   *Moderate*
Carne asada or shrimp in several specialties star among California-
style Mexican dishes served in a comfortable firelit cantina with
stained-glass and tile accents. A heated patio by La Jolla's main street
is a long-time favorite for people-watching.

★ **Alize**   *234-0411*
  downtown at 777 Front St. (atop the Paladion)
  L-D. No L Sun.   *Expensive*
Caribbean cuisine was recently added to San Diego's fine dining
options. Delightfully light, bright four-course meals (appetizer, soup
or salad, entree, dessert) involve distinctive herbs, spices and tropical
ingredients to capture the flavors of the French West Indies. Apropos
music, decor, and live greenery complement the cuisine.

★ **Anthony's Star of the Sea Room**   *232-7408*
  .7 mi. W at 1360 N. Harbor Dr.
  D only.   *Very Expensive*
Anthony's Star of the Sea is the oldest outstanding restaurant in San
Diego. As flagship of a fleet of local seafood houses, the Star gets the
pick of the catch from the owner's fishing boats. A well-rounded menu
of (exclusively) seafood includes hard-to-find seasonal specialties like
sculpin and abalone. The dining room is as sumptuous as the cuisine,
and takes fullest advantage of an over-the-waterfront location with a
bay view that is nonpareil. In keeping with the venerable landmark's
refinement, jackets are required for gentlemen.

★ **Bayou Bar & Grill**   *696-8747*
  .3 mi. S at 329 Market St. - Gaslamp Quarter
  L-D. No L Mon.-Tues. Sun. brunch.   *Expensive*
San Diego's best Cajun/creole cuisine arrived with the Bayou in the
1990s. Authenticity is assured because the chef/owner gets crayfish
and other key ingredients from New Orleans, his earlier home. Spicy
dishes can be topped off with housemade desserts like ethereal peanut
butter mousse pie in a snazzy dining room/bar or on an umbrella-
shaded glassed-in sidewalk cafe.

★ **Bella Luna**   *239-3222*
  downtown at 748 Fifth Av. - Gaslamp Quarter
  L-D.   *Expensive*
Bella Luna's thick, tender grilled veal chop is extraordinary in this
haven of Southern Italian cuisine. Quality, freshness and in-house
preparation are apparent in everything from the breads to tiramisu,
gelatos, and seasonal citrus sorbets. A historic building now sports an
urbane dining room and bar with dozens of whimsical wall hangings
that reflect the restaurant's name.

Brothers Family Restaurant   *287-0880*
  10 mi. NE at 5150 Waring Rd. (.8 mi. N of I-8)
  B-L-D. No D Sun.   *Low*
Hearty American breakfasts include specialties like homemade
biscuits and gravy, cinnamon rolls, or pancakes with apple filling.
Later, country-fried steak and other California comfort foods prevail
in this unaffected new coffee shop.

Cafe Beignet   *483-5500*
8.2 mi. NW at 4535 Mission Blvd. - Pacific Beach
B-L-D.   *Moderate*
Puffy egg-rich Old-Country-style beignets star at breakfast. Cajun popcorn, gator chili, or catfish nuggets are also authentically rendered in this rustic outpost of a New Orleans coffee house.

★ **Cafe Pacifica**   *291-6666*
4 mi. NW at 2414 San Diego Av. - Old Town
L-D. No L Sat. & Sun.   *Expensive*
Seafood is featured among New California dishes like petrale sole stuffed with crab and shrimp in Old Town's favorite restaurant. For dessert, the housemade lemon key lime pie is terrific. Full linen enhances tables in congested dining rooms.

★ **Cajun Connection**   *741-5680*
31 mi. N at 740 Nordahl Rd.(at Hwy. 78) - San Marcos
L-D. No L Sat. & Sun. Closed Mon.   *Moderate*
Cajun country cookin' is here in popcorn shrimp, fried catfish, 'gator, and other dishes from the bayous. Homemade rolls and bread pudding with whiskey sauce are great ways to begin and end meals in a big comfortable dining hall enhanced by colorful bon temps wall art.

★ **California Cuisine**   *543-0790*
3 mi. N at 1027 University Av. - Hillcrest
L-D. No L Sat. & Sun. Closed Mon.   *Expensive*
Some of the best New California cuisine in the Southland is produced by a chef with a genuine creative flair and a dedication to the best seasonal ingredients. Everything (except the bread) is made here from scratch. Dishes like grilled venison with molasses mashed parsnips and wild mushroom glaze, and desserts like lemon-spearmint sorbet typify exciting possibilities served in a tony dining room with colorful wall art or on a romantic heated garden deck.

★ **Calliope's Greek Cuisine**   *291-5588*
2.2 mi. N at 3958 Fifth Av. - Hillcrest
L-D. No L Sat. & Sun.   *Moderate*
Classic Greek dishes like fresh feta salad, a lovely light moussaka, and extraordinary baklava are the best of their kind in town. The whitewashed high-ceilinged dining room with its cozy congestion of flower-set tables captures the spirit of the isles.

Casa de Bandini & Casa de Pico   *297-8211 & 296-3267*
4 mi. NW at 2660 & 2754 Calhoun St. - Old Town
L-D.   *Moderate*
Hearty helpings of California-style Mexican fare and gigantic margaritas are served in enchanting settings that make these two of the busiest restaurants in town. Patrons have a choice of folk-art-filled dining rooms in restored adobes, or large umbrella-shaded courtyards with a flamboyant melange of mariachis, fountains and gardens.

★ **Catamaran Resort Hotel**   *488-1091*
7.7 mi. NW at 3999 Mission Blvd. - Mission Bay Park
B-L-D. Sun. brunch.   *Expensive*
The **Atoll** features tasteful renditions of New California cuisine, coupled with upscale contemporary decor in a dining room with a delightful bay view. The capacious **Cannibal Bar** has the view, plus dancing and live entertainment nightly. **Moray's** is a posh cozy lounge with a well-played grand piano and a show-stopping aquarium.

★ **Cecil's Cafe & Qwiggs Bar & Grill**   *222-1101*
   6.1 mi. W at 5083 Santa Monica Av. - Ocean Beach
   B-L-D.   *Moderate*
Cecil's has the finest view-breakfast in the city with American
specialties like macadamia nut pancakes. Later, fresh fish stars in
both Cecil's and Qwiggs (upstairs). Both pleasant dining rooms have
a window wall view of waves breaking against the beach and pier
beyond a park across the street.

★ **Chart House**   *459-8201*
   11.5 mi. NW at 1270 Prospect St. - La Jolla
   D only.   *Expensive*
Steak, seafood, and an upscale salad bar are offered in the national
chain's tour de force of contemporary California architecture perched
on a bluff overlooking La Jolla Cove. Dramatic wood-trim, regional art,
luxuriant greenery and panoramic windows maximize a superb
seascape from the dining room and lounge.

Cindy Black's   *456-6299*
   10 mi. NW at 5721 La Jolla Blvd. - La Jolla
   D only. Closed Mon.   *Very Expensive*
The touted chef/owner's eclectic selection of American and provincial
fare is served in a simply sophisticated dining room.

★ **The Cottage**   *454-8409*
   11.4 mi. NW at 7702 Fay Av. - La Jolla
   B-L-D. No D Mon.   *Moderate*
Fine pastries like big raspberry millet muffins are displayed and
served with light fresh California fare all day in a cheerful little coffee
shop amid lush greenery. Adjoining is a popular umbrella-shaded
garden patio that is quintessential La Jolla.

★ **D. Z. Akin's Restaurant/Bakery**   *265-0218*
   9.5 mi. NE (near I-8) at 6930 Alvarado Rd.
   B-L-D.   *Moderate*
San Diego's best Jewish deli restaurant features generous portions,
and a tempting selection of bagels, rugalehs, and many other baked
goods made and displayed on the premises. There are several dining
areas with padded booths. A specialty foods and gift shop adjoins.

★ **Dobson's Bar & Restaurant**   *231-6771*
   downtown at 956 Broadway Circle
   L-D. No L Sat. Closed Sun.   *Very Expensive*
Mussel bisque in puff pastry is superb on a distinctive menu of
contemporary American cuisine that changes daily in downtown's
original power lunch spot. Small tables fill a simply elegant little
dining room on a mezzanine above a handsome old-fashioned bar.

★ **The Donut Corner**   *745-7774*
   28 N at 903 S. Escondido Blvd. (at 9th Av. 1 mi. E of I-15) - Escondido
Humongous Vienna creams, flavorful fruit logs, and cream-filled
French donuts are among delectable delights that have propelled this
tiny 24-hour takeout to the top of the county's donut purveyors. There
is usually a line at the takeout window by the tempting displays.

El Tecolote   *295-2087*
   5 mi. N at 6110 Friars Rd. - Mission Valley
   L-D. No L Sun.   *Moderate*
Mole poblano, chile verde and carne asada are among specialties that
have made "the owl" deservedly popular. The colorful dining room is
worth discovering for authentic Mexican dishes.

★ **Emerald Chinese Seafood Restaurant**   *565-6888*
7 mi. N at 3709 Convoy St., Suite 101
L-D.   *Moderate*
The Emerald is San Diego's best Chinese restaurant. Szechwan,
Mandarin, and other culinary styles are well represented on a wide
ranging menu. The highlight is seafood and especially live fish and
shellfish from their tank. The remarkably talented staff assure that
every dish has both eye appeal and a wealth of authentic flavors. The
large dining room has a cosmopolitan air enhanced by full linen table
settings, fresh flowers on each table, jade accents and aquariums.

Filippi's Pizza Grotto   *232-5094*
.9 mi. NW at 1747 India St.
L-D.   *Moderate*
Pizza and old-fashioned Southern Italian fare have been served in
abundance here for more than forty years. The pizza grotto dining
areas beyond a storefront deli have an assuredly big-city ambiance.

★ **Fio's Cucina Italiana**   *234-3467*
downtown at 801 Fifth Av. - Gaslamp Quarter
L-D. No L Sat. & Sun.   *Expensive*
Fio's has downtown's premier grazing menu of exciting antipasti,
pastas, pizzas, calzones, and meat entrees, plus delicious breads and
desserts made here. Diners in armchair comfort can watch meals being
prepared in an exhibition kitchen or at a pizza island with a wood-
fired oven. Flamboyant murals and floral sprays accent both the
modish dining room and handsome bar.

★ **The French Pastry Shop**   *454-9094*
9.9 mi. NW at 5550 La Jolla Blvd. - La Jolla
B-L-D. No D Mon.   *Moderate*
One of San Diego's long-established breakfast places has display cases
brimming with classic French breads, pastries, desserts, quiches, and
pates. The cheerful coffee shop is accented by an abundance of healthy
greenery and an umbrella-shaded dining patio is on La Jolla Blvd.

★ **George's at the Cove**   *454-4244*
11.5 mi. NW at 1250 Prospect St. - La Jolla
L-D.   *Expensive*
New California cuisine is masterfully correlated to choice seasonally
available fresh produce. Consistent quality and a delightful shoreline
panorama have made the chic post-modern dining room a well-
deserved favorite. Upstairs, **George's Cafe & Ocean Terrace** serves
creative light fare and the same delicious housemade desserts in a
stylish dining room/bar, on a covered balcony, and alfresco on a
heated, umbrella-shaded terrace with an even better view.

★ **Girard Gourmet**   *454-3321*
11.6 mi. NW at 7837 Girard Av. - La Jolla
B-L-D.   *Moderate*
First-rate French pastries, desserts and flavorful deli fare can be
enjoyed to go, in a plain little dining room, or at sidewalk tables.

★ **Great Harvest Bread Company**   *272-3521*
8.2 mi. NW at 1808 Garnet Av. - Pacific Beach
Here are the best whole wheat baked goods in San Diego County.
Delectable breads (traditional, sprouted, with honey, cranberries, nuts,
sunflowers, etc.) are abundantly available, along with rolls, muffins,
cookies, and cinnamon rolls. Samples are generously offered.

★ **Harry's Coffee Shop**   *454-7381*
11.6 mi. NW at 7545 Girard Av. - La Jolla
B-L.   *Moderate*
In La Jolla's premier coffee shop, carefully prepared American fare includes distinctive dishes like flavorful hash, or terrific oatmeal pancakes or nutty banana waffles with a variety of fruit syrups. Diners have a choice of overstuffed booths or counter stools in rooms accented by a gallery of Americana prints.

★ **Hob Nob Hill**   *239-8176*
1.1 mi. N at 2271 First Av.
B-L-D.   *Moderate*
Since 1946, venerable American dishes have been carefully prepared and accompanied by first-rate housemade breads, pastries, desserts, and extras like the complimentary (ask for it) piccalilli. San Diego's favorite uptown coffee shop offers a choice of overstuffed booths or a comfortably old-fashioned dining room. It is one of the few places that is deservedly busy at both breakfast and dinner.

★ **Hyatt Regency San Diego**   *687-6080*
.8 mi. S at One Market Place
B-L-tea-D. Sun. brunch.   *Expensive*
Sally's (L-D) offers Continental updates in hip, airy rooms by an expo kitchen. **Laels** (B-L-D. Sun. brunch) has healthy California cuisine and features assorted buffets. **Worthington's** is a posh lounge overlooking the bay. The star, however, goes to the **Top of the Hyatt** (light lunch-tea). Windows on three sides of the 40th floor give the refined club-like lounge San Diego's most breathtaking views.

★ **JR's Family Restaurant**   *276-0808*
6.4 mi. NW at 2565 Clairemont Dr.
B-L-D.   *Low*
JR's stars as the top spot for breakfast in San Diego. Here are American standards at their uncomplicated best. Careful preparation and freshness are apparent in everything from omelets to the chicken pot pie or beef stew. Homemade biscuits and gravy and pies, cheerful waitresses and casual comfortable surroundings illustrate why this modern coffee shop is (deservedly) the city's most popular.

Kaiserhof Restaurant   *224-0606*
5.9 mi. W at 2253 Sunset Cliffs Blvd. - Ocean Beach
L-D. Closed Mon.   *Expensive*
Old-style German dishes are taken seriously here including wild boar, venison and other game served along with fine German beer on tap in a pleasant dining room, bar, and biergarten.

Kansas City Barbeque   *231-9680*
downtown at 610 W. Market St.
L-D.   *Low*
For a Midwestern Q-experience, the barbequed beef, pork ribs, and chicken are first-rate, as are the giant onion rings. Paper and plastic are everywhere, but the tap beer is served in cold glasses in the funky little dining rooms, bar and sunny patio.

Karl Strauss Old Columbia Brewery & Grill & Bakery *234-2739*
.5 mi. W at 1157 Columbia St.
L-D.   *Moderate*
Housemade breads, wood-fired pizzas, and California grill fare are featured along with San Diego's best handcrafted beers. An expansive historic brick building now includes several comfortable dining areas.

The Kruze Galley   *222-3317*
5.6 mi. NW at 1729 Quivira Rd. - Mission Bay Park
B-L.   *Moderate*
The big breakfast burrito with sausage, ham, bacon, cheese and eggs
is a winner—if lathered with a side of warm Spanish sauce. So is the
machaca. They start serving at 5 a.m. in this little coffee shop by the
sportfishing fleet.

★ **Kung Food**   *298-7302*
1.7 mi. N at 2949 Fifth Av. - Hillcrest
B-L-D. No B Mon.-Fri.   *Moderate*
Fresh ingredients are prepared from scratch in San Diego's oldest and
most esteemed temple of lean cuisine. Militantly meatless and
rennetless entrees are specialties served at padded booths amid
greenery and "New Age" music. Garden patios and a store full of
salubrious products adjoins.

★ **La Valencia Hotel**   *454-0771*
11.3 mi. NW at 1132 Prospect St. - La Jolla
B-L-D. Sun. brunch.   *Expensive—Very Expensive*
The **Sky Room** (D only. Closed Sun.—Very Expensive) features
contemporary Continental cuisine in fixe prix dinners, but it is the
panoramic view of La Jolla Cove and the ocean that is unbeatable from
this romantic and luxurious little aerie. The **Cafe La Rue & Whaling
Bar** (L-D—Very Expensive) serves classic Continental cuisine with
some creative updates amid posh wood-trimmed ambiance. The
Mediterranean Room & Patio (B-L-D. Sun. brunch—Expensive)
offers American fare like thick crunchy french toast with real maple
syrup for breakfast in a stylish dining room with an ocean view and in
a tropical garden. **La Sala**, the hotel's genteel lounge, features floral
sprays, an enchanting cove view, and a well-played grand piano.

★ **Lamont Street Grill**   *270-3060*
8 mi. NW at 4445 Lamont St. - Pacific Beach
D only.   *Moderate*
Robust treatments of New California cuisine are served in several cozy
dining areas overlooking a lovely firelit garden court.

★ **Manhattan Restaurant**   *554-1444*
11.5 mi. NW at 7766 Fay Av. - La Jolla
L-D. No L Sat. & Sun.   *Expensive*
New York City-style Italian cuisine is represented with robust and
flavorful authenticity in everything from colorful antipasti trays to
cannoli made here. Even the formally attired staff has a decidedly
midtown-Manhattan look. Elaborate aquariums accent simply posh
dining areas and a bar tucked away in the Empress Hotel.

★ **Marine Room**   *459-7222*
11 mi. NW at 2000 Spindrift Dr. - La Jolla
L-D. Sun. brunch.   *Very Expensive*
The Marine Room is the Southland's most remarkable restaurant.
New California cuisine with Continental and Pacific Rim overtones is
uniformly excellent in dishes ranging from mock turtle soup with a
splash of sherry to baked sea bass with a macadamia crust on bok
choy with lemon grass essence. The acclaimed chef arrived in 1994,
when the dining room and lounge were upgraded to contemporary
romantic elegance. Now, both cuisine and decor contribute to the
enchantment of a unique view of night-lighted surf breaking against
the window wall by your table.

★ **Milligan's** *459-7311*
10 mi. NW at 5786 La Jolla Blvd.
L-D. Sun. brunch.   *Moderate*
Steaks star among tasteful, generous American fare served at
banquettes in a wood-trim-and-etched glass dining room or upstairs
with a distant ocean view. A cozy popular lounge adjoins.

★ **Mister A's** *239-1377*
1.1 mi. N at 2550 Fifth Av.
L-D. No L Sat. & Sun.   *Very Expensive*
Traditional Continental fare has been formally presented for more
than a quarter century in dining rooms with a rococo Victorian
elegance. But, the real reason for dining in this penthouse aerie is the
grand view of the park, downtown, and the bay—especially from the
raised circular room. An adjoining piano lounge offers an even more
spectacular panorama. Jackets are required for gentlemen.

★ **Old Trieste Restaurant** *276-1841*
6 mi. NW at 2335 Morena Blvd.
L-D. No L Sat. Closed Sun.-Mon.   *Very Expensive*
Traditional Northern Italian cuisine has been showcased for more
than thirty years in one of the city's most venerable gourmet havens.
The tranquil little wood-paneled dining room and lounge similarly
convey an old-fashioned gentility enhanced by crisp white linens,
waiters in tuxes, and a jackets-for-gentlemen rule.

★ **150 Grand Cafe** *738-6869*
29 mi. N at 150 W. Grand Av. - Escondido
L-D.   *Expensive*
Escondido's finest restaurant opened downtown in 1993. Fresh light
New California cuisine stars on a grazing menu ranging from grilled
cheese-stuffed chilis or sweet potato pancakes to braised lamb loin.
Housemade desserts might include luscious multilayer chocolate
espresso cake. A basket of superb breads (like marbled pumpernickel
and rosemary French) heralds each dining experience. Full linen and
fresh flowers (even for lunch) enrich the tony firelit dining room and
lounge. Out back is a trellis-shaded palm garden patio.

★ **The Original Pancake House** *565-1740*
7.4 mi. N at 3906 Convoy St.
B-L.   *Moderate*
In spite of the fact that the restaurant is now only a link in a
burgeoning chain, their humongous oven-baked apple pancake with
cinnamon glaze is the superstar among San Diego's best pancakes.
The two family-oriented dining areas are noisy when they're
busy—which is most of the time.

★ **The Pan Pacific Hotel** *338-3640*
.4 mi. W at 400 W. Broadway
B-L-D.   *Expensive*
The Grill is a fine source for "fusion" cuisine, where light fresh fare
receives deft combinations of California, Italian, Oriental and Southwestern accents. Consider, for example, roasted lamb loin with
macadamia nut satay sauce. The casually posh dining room and patio
overlook a downtown street scene. Nearby, the **Atrium Lounge**
provides a cushy setting for relaxing with a view of the landmark's
lofty post-modern interior.

Pannikin Brockton Villa   *454-7393*
11.6 mi. NW at 1235 Coast Blvd. - La Jolla
B-L. D in summer.   *Expensive*
Assorted pastries, a few egg dishes, french toast and hotcakes for
breakfast, plus light fare and desserts later are background to all
kinds of coffees and teas. A transformed Victorian cottage with a rare
abalone fireplace has a porch above famed La Jolla Cove.

★ **Papa Teddy's**   *483-2600*
8.4 mi. NW at 1762 Garnet Av. - Pacific Beach
L-D.   *Low*
In 1994 Papa Teddy's got off to a fine start with generous portions of
fresh and flavorful pizzas, pastas and calzones. Several premium tap
beers by the half-yard or yard flagon contribute to the fun. The plain
dining room is by an exhibition kitchen. An umbrella-shaded garden
patio adjoins, shared by **Lotsa Pasta** (581-6777) where all kinds of
low-priced homemade noodle dishes can be topped with an appealing
selection of tomato or cream-based sauces.

Point Loma Sea Foods   *223-1109*
4.6 mi. W at 2805 Emerson St. - Point Loma
L-D.   *Low*
San Diego's most elaborate fresh and smoked seafood market includes
a blackboard listing a wide selection of seafood plates and sandwiches
that you can take, with premium tap beer or wine, next door to picnic
tables in a dining area with a good marina view.

★ **Rainwater's on Kettner**   *233-1514*
.6 mi. W at 1202 Kettner Blvd.
L-D. No L Sat. & Sun.   *Very Expensive*
Aged prime corn-fed beef is featured in some of the finest steaks in the
Southland. Chops, fowl, and seafood are also skillfully prepared.
Housemade desserts like chocolate lasagne (really different) or apple
or pecan pie are delightful. Armchairs surround tables set with fresh
flowers, candles, and white linen in urbane dining areas and a lounge
by an atrium and an exhibition kitchen.

★ **Rancho Bernardo Inn**   *487-1611*
24 mi. N at 17550 Bernardo Oaks Dr. - Rancho Bernardo
B-L-D. Sun. brunch.   *Expensive–Very Expensive*
In **El Bizcocho** (D only. Sun. brunch–Very Expensive), traditional
and updated Continental cuisine has been acclaimed for many years.
The dining room recalls the spirit of a plush California rancho. Tables
set with candles, crystal, silver, and flowers overlook lush fairways.
Grand piano music accompanies each meal. **Veranda** (B-L-D–
Expensive) offers creative California cuisine in a comfortable setting
with a lovely fairway view shared by a shaded dining terrace. **La
Bodega Bar** features live music for dancing in a darkly handsome
lounge.

★ **San Diego Chicken Pie Shop**   *295-0156*
3.8 mi. NE at 2633 El Cajon Blvd.
L-D.   *Low*
Chicken pie has been featured for nearly half a century in this
(relocated) restaurant. The unaffectly tasty treats with homestyle
American accompaniments coupled with fast and friendly service and
remarkably cheap prices continue to draw crowds to the bright and
bustling coffee shop with chicken-themed accents.

★ **San Diego Marriott Hotel & Marina**   *234-1500*
8 mi. S at 333 W. Harbor Dr.
B-L-D. Sun. brunch.   *Expensive–Very Expensive*
Molly's (D only–Very Expensive) features fine updated Continental cuisine amidst contemporary elegance enhanced by a well-played grand piano. **Marina Sea Grill** (B-L-D. Sun. brunch–Expensive) showcases daily buffets in a big handsome dining room with a bay view shared by **The Yacht Club** (light L-D) with live entertainment for dancing. **Las Cascadas** has casual American breakfasts. **DW's Pub** is a snazzy piano lounge.

★ **Sheraton Grande Torrey Pines**   *558-1500*
15.6 mi. NW at 10950 N. Torrey Pines Rd. - La Jolla
B-L-D. Sun. brunch.   *Expensive*
The resort's **Torryana Grill** is a showcase for New California cuisine like housemade deep dish pecan pie with Jack Daniels sauce. The capacious split-level dining room is a gracious post-modern triumph backed by grand piano stylings, a sleek exposition kitchen, and views of gardens and the distant ocean.

★ **Souplantation**   *222-7404*
4.8 mi. NW at 3960 W. Point Loma Blvd.
L-D.   *Low*
The Southland's best salad bars are in a small chain of salad buffet restaurants. Each features cafeteria-style displays of a remarkable number of fresh vegies; several fine soups, muffins and pizza; plus a soft ice cream dessert bar in dining areas enhanced by live greenery.

★ **Summer House Inn**   *459-0541*
10.5 mi. NW at 7955 La Jolla Shores Dr. - La Jolla
B-L-D. Sun. brunch.   *Very Expensive*
Elario's recently became one of San Diego's finest sources of New California cuisine, thanks to the skill and dedication of the young chef. Sherried cream of wild mushroom soup baked under a puff pastry cap, or roast venison loin with raspberry peppercorn sauce, typify the outstanding possibilities. There is also a remarkably diverse wine collection. As a sublime bonus, the plush firelit dining room offers a romantic seagull's-eye view of La Jolla and the coast. A big modern lounge has occasional entertainment—and the view.

★ **Sweetlips**   *587-4600*
12 mi. N (near I-5) at 8980 University Center Lane - La Jolla
L-D. No L Sat. Closed Sun.   *Expensive*
Sweet Lips, opened in 1994, is already San Diego's leading source of fusion cuisine. Pacific Rim and regional American cuisines are masterfully blended using prime seasonal ingredients to create exciting new dishes. Everything from breads to extraordinary desserts are made fresh from scratch daily. Whimsical fish art and tropical flowers contribute to the pleasure of the smart, post-modern dining room and lounge.

Thee Bungalow   *224-2884*
5.8 mi. W at 4996 W. Point Loma Blvd. - Ocean Beach
D only.   *Expensive*
Crisp roast duck and swiss chicken highlight traditional and updated Continental fare. Intimate dining rooms in a converted cottage are outfitted with candlelit tables set with full linen and bud vases, wall hangings, stained glass and art objects.

★ **Top O' The Cove**   *454-7779*
11.5 mi. NW at 1216 Prospect St. - La Jolla
L-D. Sun. brunch.   *Extremely Expensive*
In 1994, a new chef assured the Cove's continuing status as a premier
source of classic and contemporary Continental favorites, accompanied
by a selection of delicious desserts made here. One of La Jolla's historic
cottages has been artfully transformed into romantic, opulent dining
areas and a posh skylit lounge. Giant fig trees shade a luxuriant
garden court by the entrance. Guests adjacent to the picture windows
have an enchanting view of La Jolla Cove and the ocean.

★ **Trattoria La Strada**   *239-3400*
downtown at 702 Fifth Av. - Gaslamp Quarter
L-D. No L Sun.   *Expensive*
Delicious housemade breads of several kinds herald good things to
come. In one of San Diego's best sources of Northern Italian cuisine,
quality is apparent in dishes like the fish chowder or homemade
ravioli cheese pockets. The sophisticated trattoria with a lively expo
kitchen, lounge, and sidewalk cafe occupies a historic building.

★ **U.S. Grant Hotel**   *239-6806*
downtown at 326 Broadway
B-L-tea-D. Sat. & Sun. brunch.   *Very Expensive*
In the **Grant Grill**, roast game hen with ricotta and blueberry
stuffing, and famed mock turtle soup typify New American cuisine
prepared in a sophisticated exhibition kitchen. The large dining room
is distinguished by polished wood-paneled walls, deeply padded chairs
and banquettes, gleaming brass, and luscious pastries on display. A
darkly handsome **Grant Grill Lounge** adjoins the grand lobby.

★ **The Westgate Hotel**   *238-1818*
downtown at 1055 Second Av.
B-L-D. Sun. brunch.   *Expensive–Very Expensive*
Le Fontainebleau (L-D. No L Sat. Sun. brunch–Very Expensive)
presents traditional French specialties amidst formal elegance. Tables
set with flowers, candles, silver, china, crystal and linen are
surrounded by museum-quality art. Grand piano entertainment
accompanies all meals.   Jackets are appropriate for men. The
Westgate Room (B-L-D–Expensive) serves contemporary American
fare in a casually posh setting. The **Lobby Lounge** is a resplendent
piano salon.

★ **The Wine Sellar & Brasserie**   *450-9557*
14 mi. N at 9550 Waples St., Suite 115
D only. Closed Mon. Only prix-fixe on Sun.   *Very Expensive*
New California cuisine is skillfully prepared in dishes utilizing the
best available fresh produce. The tony upstairs brasserie offers closely
spaced tables in a room centered around an exhibition bar and kitchen
and tres courant politically correct art.

★ **Woodstock's Pizza**   *265-0999*
8.9 mi. NE at 6548 El Cajon Blvd.
L-D.   *Moderate*
Some of the best pizza in San Diego is hand-thrown at Woodstock's.
You get a choice of either white or whole wheat dough, robust sauce,
and all kinds of meat and vegie toppings. Several premium tap beers
are also available in a little parlor outfitted with plastic and paper
place settings, wood booths, and (usually) a college crowd din.

LODGING

San Diego has a greater number of fine lodgings with ocean or bay views than anyplace else in Southern California. In addition, lodgings ranging from world-class resorts to bargain motels are plentiful. Rates are usually reduced about 10% from fall through spring.

★ **Bahia Resort Hotel**   *488-0551*
6 mi. NW at 998 W. Mission Bay Dr. - Mission Bay Park 92109
Seals cavort in a tropical pond in front of one of Mission Bay Park's largest (325 rooms) and oldest (1960) resorts. The five-story complex sprawls along a choice peninsula amidst gardens a block from the ocean. Amenities include bayfront beaches; boat rentals and stern-wheeler bay cruises; a large pool and whirlpool; two lighted tennis courts and a game room; bay-view dining room, entertainment lounge, coffee shop, and gift shop. Each comfortable unit has a phone and remote control color TV with (pay) movies. Toll-free: (800)288-0770.
#483 & odd #s to #497—spacious, kitchenette, extra-
large balcony shares fine bay/La Jolla view with   K bed...$155
regular room—request water view,   Q bed...$125

The Bay Club Hotel & Marina   *224-8888*
5.5 mi. W at 2131 Shelter Island Dr. - Shelter Island 92106
This contemporary motor hotel sprawls along a marina, across a street from San Diego Bay. Amenities include a pool and whirlpool that share a marina view with a restaurant and plush lounge, exercise room, bicycle rentals, and a gift shop. Each spacious, attractive room has a private view balcony, refrigerator, phone and remote control color TV. Toll-free in CA: (800)833-6565; elsewhere: (800)672-0800.
#255—extra large, fine panorama of bay,   Q bed...$185
#268,#270—tranquil view of pool/marina/Pt. Loma,   K bed...$150
regular room—some bay or marina view,   2 Q or K bed...$110

Blue Sea Lodge - Best Western   *488-4700*
7.7 mi. NW at 707 Pacific Beach Dr. - Pacific Beach 92109
Only a promenade lies between this modern motel and a popular ocean beach. Other amenities include a sea-view pool and whirlpool. Each compact, comfortable room has a private balcony, phone and remote control color TV with movies. Toll-free: (800)BLUE-SEA.
#362—big private balcony, great ocean view from   K bed...$141
regular room—compact, no view,   2 Q beds...$136; K bed...$126

Budget Motels of America
7.5 mi. NE (by I-8) at 4370 Alvarado Canyon Rd. - 92120   281-2222
3.5 mi. N (by I-8) at 641 Camino del Rio South - 92108   295-6886
These modern **bargain** motels have no frills, but each compact, simply furnished room has a phone and color TV with movies.
regular room—   Q bed...$40

Carmel Highland Doubletree Resort   *672-9100*
18 mi. N (near I-15) at 14455 Penasquitos Dr. - 92129
An 18-hole golf course provides a beguiling backdrop to a 172-room conference resort that opened in 1989. The post-modern complex has two landscaped extra-large pools and a whirlpool; saunas; steam rooms; and (for a fee) golf and six lighted tennis courts. A dining room, coffee shop, and entertainment lounge share fairway views, and there is a gift shop. Each spacious, well-furnished room has a private patio or balcony, stocked (honor) bar, phone and remote control color TV

San Diego
with (pay) movies. Toll-free: (800)622-9223.
#312,#314—parlor, 2 TVs, big pvt. view balcony,   loft K bed...$179
regular room—(add $20 for fairway view),   2 D or K bed...$119
★ **Catamaran Resort Hotel**   *488-1081*
7.7 mi. NW at 3999 Mission Blvd. - Mission Bay Park 92109
Palms in abundance shade luxuriant tropical gardens and waterfalls
in San Diego's best-situated hotel. On Mission Bay, the thirteen-story,
315-room resort is a short block from a superb ocean beach. Amenities
include a big freeform pool and whirlpool in a jungle courtyard; wide
sandy beach; dock with (fee) boat rentals and bay cruises; bike rentals;
and fine dining, drinking, and entertainment facilities (see listing).
Each attractive unit has a large private balcony or patio, phone, and
remote control color TV with (pay) movies. Toll-free: (800)288-0770.
#1261,#1061,#961—floor-to-ceiling window & big pvt.
balc. offer peerless tranquil bay/ocean view from   K bed...$170
#1259,#1257,#1255,#1253,#1251—spacious, kitchenette, win-
dows & big pvt. balc. with great bay/ocean view, 2 D beds...$195
#601—spacious, refr., intimate beach/bay
close-ups from large private end balcony,   K bed...$195
regular room—garden view,   2 D or K bed...$140
★ **Colonial Inn**   *454-2181*
11.5 mi. NW at 910 Prospect St. - La Jolla 92037
La Jolla's oldest continuously operating hotel has been artistically
restored to capture the charm of the 1920s. Crystal chandeliers, fires
in fireplaces, dramatic floral sprays, and lots of greenery, cushy
furniture and a grand piano help capture the mood, along with a
circular pool in a garden, and a plush dining room and lounge. Each
spacious guest room has a blend of period and contemporary
furnishings, a refrigerator, phone, and remote control color TV with
movies. Toll-free in CA: (800)826-1278; elsewhere: (800)832-5525.
#474—top, corner, fine ocean/cove/village views,   Q bed...$180
regular room—village view,   Q bed...$140
★ **Crystal Pier Motel**   *483-6983*
8.2 mi. NW at 4500 Ocean Blvd. - Pacific Beach 92109
The West's only over-the-water lodging is a little cottage colony that
has been on the Crystal Pier above a splendid beach since 1936. Six
larger upscale cottages were added in the 1990s. At high tide, waves
wash under your bed. Each cottage has a living room, kitchen,
bedroom and patio, plus phone and color TV. Toll-free: (800)748-5894.
"Cottage A"—contemporary, well-furnished,
big private deck with view of beach to Pt. Loma,   Q bed...$180
"Cottage B"—as above, but view to La Jolla,   Q bed...$180
regular room—old, shared patio,   2 T or D bed...$140
Doubletree Hotel at Horton Plaza   *239-2200*
downtown at 910 Broadway Circle - 92101
San Diego's most garish public art, an egregious obelisk of blue plastic
taller than an oil derrick, lamentably fronts Doubletree's post-modern
fifteen-story hotel. The convention-oriented 450-room complex, circa
1987, has a long pool, whirlpool and sauna; and (for a fee) two lighted
tennis courts, exercise equipment, and pay parking; plus a restaurant,
coffee shop, lounge and lobby bar. Each well-furnished room has a
stocked (honor) refrigerator, phone and remote control color TV with
(pay) movies. Toll-free: (800)222-TREE.
regular room—request 14th fl. W side for view, 2 D or K bed...$185

E-Z 8 Motel
4.3 mi. N (by I-8) at 2484 Hotel Circle Pl. - 92108   291-8252
4.3 mi. NW (near I-5) at 4747 Pacific Hwy. - 92110   294-2512
4.5 mi. NW (by I-8) at 3333 Channel Way - 92110   223-9500
San Diego's **bargain** chain of three- or four-level contemporary motels
each has a landscaped pool or whirlpool and compact, nicely furnished
rooms with a phone and color TV with movies.
    regular room—   Q bed...$39

★ **Embassy Suites - San Diego Bay**   *239-2400*
.7 mi. SW at 601 Pacific Hwy. - 92101
The convention center, Seaport Village and harbor are within a block
of Embassy's 337-suite hotel. The pink neo-Spanish-Colonial complex
surrounds a thirteen-story atrium with tropical foliage and ponds.
Other amenities include an indoor pool and whirlpool amidst jungle
greenery, sauna, exercise room, atrium-view restaurant, lounge, gift
shop, and pay parking. Full breakfast and afternoon beverages are
complimentary. Each spacious, beautifully furnished two-room suite
has a wet bar and refrigerator, microwave, phone and two remote
control color TVs with movies. Toll-free: (800)EMBASSY.
    regular room—request bay-view 12th floor,   2 D or K bed...$160

★ **Hacienda Hotel - Best Western**   *298-4707*
4 mi. NW at 4041 Harney St. - Old Town 92110
Old Town's most distinctive lodging is a modern Spanish-Colonial-
style hotel on a hillside with panoramic views of Old Town. Amenities
include a garden view pool and whirlpool, an exercise room, restaurant
and lounge. Free beverages are served most nights. Each unit has
attractive Santa Fe-style furnishings, a refrigerator, microwave oven,
phone, and color TV with (pay) movies. Toll-free: (800)888-1991.
    #527—private balcony, fine historic area view,   Q bed...$119
    #526 thru #521—private balcony, good panorama,   2 Q beds...$119
    regular room—   Q bed...$119

★ **Hanalei Hotel - Best Western**   *297-1101*
4.4 mi. N (by I-8) at 2270 Hotel Circle North - Mission Valley 92108
San Diego's only Polynesian-themed lodging was recently fully
renovated and upgraded. The eight-story 412-room hotel is near Old
Town. Amidst water features, palms and exotic vegetation are a big
pool and whirlpool in a garden court used in summer for authentic
luaus with live entertainment; a beguiling Polynesian restaurant with
tropical woods, a stream and aquariums shared by a lounge, plus a gift
shop. Each attractive room has a private balcony or patio, phone and
remote control color TV with (pay) movies. Toll-free: (800)882-0858.
    #1809,#1709—floor-to-ceiling windows & wraparound
      private balcony, fine golf course/valley/mts. view,   K bed...$98
    regular room—some have partially blocked views,   Q bed...$88

Holiday Inn on the Bay   *232-3861*
.7 mi. W at 1355 N. Harbor Dr. - 92101
Holiday's 600-room convention hotel is across a highway from the
harbor. The well-worn thirteen-story complex has a large outdoor pool,
exercise room, restaurant, coffee shop, entertainment lounge, shops,
and pay parking. Each comfortable room has a private balcony, phone,
and remote control color TV with movies. Toll-free: (800)HOLIDAY.
    #1463,#1460—grand waterfront/bay view,   K bed...$165
    regular room—no view,   2 D or K bed...$129

Humphrey's Half Moon Inn & Suites   *224-3411*
5.5 mi. W at 2303 Shelter Island Dr. - Shelter Island 92106
Tropical landscaping surrounds this low-rise motor hotel by a marina with a big garden court pool and whirlpool, putting green, rental bicycles, marina-view restaurant and entertainment lounge, and a gift shop. Each well-furnished room has a refrigerator, phone and remote control color TV with movies. Toll-free: (800)345-9995.

#430—spacious, parlor, kitchen, big private
   balcony shares marina view with   K bed...$209
   regular room—overlooking courtyard & pool,   2 Q or K bed...$119

★ **Hyatt Islandia**   *224-1234*
5.6 mi. NW at 1441 Quivira Rd. - Mission Bay Park 92109
Mission Bay surrounds one of the world's great resort hotel sites, and the ocean is a stroll through the park. Tropical gardens further distinguish the 421-room, eighteen-story complex by a marina. Amenities include a huge pool and whirlpool in a luxuriant courtyard with a waterfall and pond, a bay-view dining room and entertainment lounge, a garden-view coffee shop, and a resort shop. Each beautifully furnished room has a private view balcony, phone, and remote control color TV with free and pay movies. Toll-free: (800)233-1234.

#1720,#1620,#1702,#1602—windows on 2 sides, con-
   cierge, light breakfast & afternoon appetizers, refr.,
   awesome private ocean/bay entrance view from   K bed...$190
#1520,#1420,#1220,#1120—windows on 2 sides,
   refr., awesome private bay/ocean view from   K bed...$165
#1502,#1402,#1202,#1102,#1002—as above, but
   grand private view of bay/ocean/La Jolla from   K bed...$165
   regular room—overlooking gardens,   2 Q or K bed...$119

Hyatt Regency La Jolla   *552-1234*
12 mi. N (near I-5) at 3777 La Jolla Village Dr. - 92122
Hyatt's controversial post-modern convention hotel (circa 1990) features a monumental mausoleum-moderne facade for a fourteen-story 400-room complex with a vast pool and whirlpool in a stark courtyard; and (for a fee) two tennis courts and an elaborate sports club; plus an airy dining room, lobby piano bar, and plush entertainment lounge; gift shop; and pay parking. Each well-furnished room has a stocked (honor) bar, phone and remote control color TV with free and pay movies. Toll-free: (800)233-1234.

"Regency Club"—concierge, extra amenities,   2 D or K bed...$190
   regular room—   2 D or K bed...$149

★ **Hyatt Regency San Diego**   *232-1234*
.8 mi. S at One Market Place - 92101
The tallest waterfront hotel on the West Coast is Hyatt's slender forty-story building next to the bay. The 875-room landmark opened in 1992 with a large palm-lined pool and whirlpool, four tennis courts, exercise room, specialty shops, and (for a fee) complete fitness and beauty center, rental boats, and parking. Restaurants and lounges (see listing) include a phantasmagoric aerie nearly 500 feet above the bay. Each beautifully furnished room has a bay view window, (honor) refrigerator/bar, two phones and remote control color TV with free and pay movies. Toll-free: (800)233-1234.

"Regency Club"—many extras, grand views,   2 D or K bed...$265
#2640,#2540,#2440—splendid bay panoramas,   K bed...$230
   regular room—   2 D or K bed...$195

★ **Kona Kai Plaza Los Glorias Resort & Marina**   *222-1191*
5.8 mi. W at 1551 Shelter Island Dr. - Shelter Island 92106
A sandy beach and marina are features of Shelter Island's most luxurious lodging. Completed in 1995, the 205-room low-rise resort offers two pools and whirlpools amidst tropical landscaping, two lighted tennis courts, putting green, fitness center with sauna, guest dock, bicycle and boat rentals, waterfront restaurant and lounge with live entertainment, and a gift shop. Each beautifully furnished room has a private balcony or patio, phone and remote control color TV with free and pay movies. Toll-free: (800)KONA-KAI.

"deluxe Junior Suite"–kitchenette,	
marina or bay view,	2 Q beds...$195
regular room–marina or bay view,	2 Q or K bed...$165
regular room–garden view,	2 Q or K bed...$145

★ **La Jolla Beach & Tennis Club**   *454-7126*
11 mi. NW at 2000 Spindrift Dr. - La Jolla 92037
Hundreds of fan palms tower over a low-rise apartment resort on renowned La Jolla Shores Beach. The Spanish-Colonial-style landmark includes a magnificent sandy beach, an extra-large pool, fitness center, and (for a fee) twelve tennis courts (eight lighted), a luxuriant 9-hole par-3 golf course, plus massage and beauty services. There is also a plush beachfront dining room and lounge, and the famed Marine Room (see listing). Each nicely refurbished unit has a refrigerator, phone, and color TV with movies. Toll-free: (800)624-2582.

#237,#130–2 BR, kitchen, windows on 3 sides	
of LR overlook beach, grand surf view from	2 T & Q beds...$315
#114,#113,#109–corner, beach beyond walkway,	Q bed...$169
"oceanfront one-bedroom"–kitchen, beach view,	D or Q bed...$279
regular room–courtyard view,	T & D, or K bed...$130

★ **La Jolla Cove Motel**   *459-2621*
11.5 mi. NW at 1155 Coast Blvd. - La Jolla 92037
The only lodging by La Jolla Cove and Scripps Park is a large four-story apartment motel with an outdoor pool, whirlpool, putting green, and a sundeck with a terrific ocean view. Each nicely furnished unit in the main building or simply comfortable annex has a phone and color TV with movies. Toll-free: (800)248-COVE.

#150,#140,#130–kitchen, corner windows and large	
private balcony with awesome cove/park view,	2 Q beds...$190
#401,#423–kitchenette, corner windows & large	
private balcony with super park/ocean view,	Q bed...$175
studio–kitchenette, large private balcony	
with fine park/ocean view from	Q bed...$125
regular room–hillside view,	2 T or Q bed...$95

★ **La Jolla Marriott**   *587-1414*
12 mi. N at 4240 La Jolla Village Dr. - 92037
The premier convention hotel in the "Golden Triangle" opened in 1985 near one of the city's largest malls. It is a 360-room, fifteen-story tower with an indoor and an outdoor pool, whirlpool, saunas, and exercise equipment; plus a restaurant, coffee shop, lounge, and lobby bar; a gift shop, and pay parking. Each beautifully furnished room has a private landscaped balcony, phone, and remote control color TV with free and pay movies. Toll-free: (800)228-9290.

#1505,#1403,#1201–corner windows, fine view,	K bed...$135
regular room–	2 D or K bed...$135

★ La Valencia Hotel   454-0771

11.3 mi. NW at 1132 Prospect St. - La Jolla 92037
La Jolla's landmark lodging is a lovely Spanish-Colonial-style hotel on
a bluff in the heart of town above a lush park and ocean beaches. The
exquisitely decorated 100-unit complex has a pool and whirlpool in
luxuriant gardens, and there is a sauna, ping pong table, exercise
equipment, and pay parking. Romantic restaurants and lounges (see
listing) overlook the sea or tropical patios. Each beautifully appointed
room has an ocean or city view, phone and remote control color TV
with movies. Toll-free: (800)451-0772.

#906,#806—parlor, in-bath whirlpool, small balcony, enchanting view of park/ocean,	K bed...$475
#908,#904,#808—in-bath whirlpool, superb park/ocean view,	K bed...$325
regular room—overlooks La Jolla,	2 T or Q bed...$160

Motel 6

4.3 mi. N (by I-8) at 2424 Hotel Circle North - 92108   296-1612
10 mi. NE (near I-8) at 7621 Alvarado Rd. - La Mesa 92041 464-7151
The **bargain** chain's local motels have an unlandscaped pool. Each
compact, no-frills room has a phone and color TV with movies.

regular room—   Hotel Circle D bed...$42; La Mesa Q bed...$34

★ Pacific Terrace Inn   581-3500

8.4 mi. NW at 610 Diamond St. - Pacific Beach 92109
Pacific Terrace Inn is San Diego's best motel. It crowns a bluff next to
a park above a long, popular beach. Amenities include an ocean-view
pool and whirlpool. Each beautifully appointed unit has a big private
balcony, refrigerator, phone and remote control color TV with movies.
Toll-free: (800)344-3370.

"Kingston Suite","Trinidad Suite"—2 TVs, parlor, kitchen, big in-bath raised whirlpool, 2 large balconies share glorious private seascapes with	K bed...$380
#303,#325—kitchenette, large raised in-bath whirlpool, grand sea view from big pvt. balc.,	2 Q or K bed...$300
#305—fine pier/ocean view,	K bed...$195
regular room—some ocean view,	K bed...$165

★ The Pan Pacific Hotel   239-4500

.4 mi. W at 400 W. Broadway - 92101
One of San Diego's most dramatic landmarks is also downtown's most
complete hotel. The twenty-five-story, 436-room complex has a lap pool
and whirlpool on a terrace sundeck; and (fee) fitness center with
sauna, steam, massage, and exercise rooms; valet parking; restaurant
(see listing) and lounge; and gift shop. Each beautifully appointed
room has a stocked (honor) refrigerator, three phones, and remote
control color TV with (pay) movies. Toll-free: (800)327-8585.

#2401,#2301,#1806,#1706—great city/bay view,	K bed...$180
regular room—city view,	2 D or K bed...$170

★ Rancho Bernardo Inn   487-1611

24 mi. N at 17550 Bernardo Oaks Dr. - Rancho Bernardo 92128
The city's finest inland resort has 287 rooms in a handsome Spanish-
Colonial-style complex by a scenic 18-hole golf course. Amenities
include two garden court pools and whirlpools; and (for a fee) twelve
tennis courts (four lighted) and a fitness center with steam bath,
sauna, exercise equipment and massage, plus bicycle rentals. A superb

restaurant and entertainment lounge (see listing) and a resort shop are also available. Each beautifully furnished room has a patio or balcony, refrigerator/stocked (honor) bar, phone, and remote control color TV with movies. Toll-free: (800)542-6096.

"VIP Suite" (2 of these)—extra-large, in-bath
whirlpool, fireplace, fine golf course view,   K bed...$255
regular room—   2 Q or K bed...$165

Red Lion Hotel - San Diego   *297-5466*
4.4 mi. NE (near I-8) at 7450 Hazard Center Dr. - 92108
This eleven-story, 300-room business-oriented hotel has indoor and outdoor pools, whirlpool, two lighted tennis courts, sauna, exercise room, restaurant, lobby bar, night club, and gift shop. Each well-furnished room has a stocked (honor) bar, two phones, and remote control color TV with (pay) movies. Toll-free: (800)547-8010.

regular room—   2 Q or K bed...$155

★ **San Diego Hilton Beach & Tennis Resort**   *276-4010*
6 mi. NW (near I-5) at 1775 E. Mission Bay Dr. - Mission Bay 92109
One of Southern California's most complete resort hotels was thoroughly upgraded in 1995. The eight-story, 357-room complex of handsome Spanish-Colonial-style buildings is sequestered among palms and tropical gardens by a long sandy beach on the east side of Mission Bay Park. Amenities include an extra-large pool and three whirlpools in tropical courtyards, three putting greens, jogging and bicycle paths, saunas, table tennis, and an exercise room. For a fee there are five lighted tennis courts, rental bicycles and boats, and sternwheeler boat rides. Other features include a bay-view dining room and an entertainment lounge, Italianate dinner house, coffee shop, and specialty shops. Each spacious, well-furnished room has a sliding glass door to a big private patio or balcony, refrigerator/(honor) bar, two phones, and remote control color TV with free and pay movies. Toll-free: (800)HILTONS.

#327—large corner suite, in-bath whirlpool,
fine private bay view,   K bed...$375
#544,#548,#552—private patio by beach,   2 Q or K bed...$225
#539,#543,#547—private balcony by beach,   2 Q or K bed...$225
regular room—overlooks freeway and city,   2 Q or K bed...$136

★ **San Diego Marriott Hotel & Marina**   *234-1500*
.8 mi. S at 333 W. Harbor Dr. - 92101
San Diego's biggest hotel (1,355 rooms) is also the most complete near downtown. Dramatic twin twenty-five-story towers loom over a marina by San Diego Bay and the convention center. Amenities include two garden court pools (one is a freeform giant by a waterfall), two whirlpools, a sauna; and (for a fee) six lighted tennis courts, a fitness center with massage, seasonal bicycle rentals, a marina with rental boats, sailing and deep sea fishing; and pay parking. Fine dining and drinking places (see listing) round out the facilities. Each beautifully furnished room has a bay or city view, refrigerator, phone and remote control color TV with free and pay movies. Toll-free: (800)228-9290.

"Manchester Suite"—top floor, 2 BR on 2 levels, in-room
whirlpool, awesome harbor/city panorama, 2 T & K bed...$2200
#2471,#2371,#2271,#2171,#2071—spacious,
parlor, private balcony, terrific bay view,   K bed...$325
#2507,#2509—superb waterfront & bay view,   K bed...$225
regular room—city view,   2 D or K bed...$200

San Diego Marriott Mission Valley   *692-3800*
5 mi. NE (near I-8) at 8757 Rio San Diego Dr.-Mission Valley 92108
This contemporary 350-room, sixteen-story hotel has a big pool and whirlpool in a delightful tropical garden court with a waterfall. The convention-oriented complex also has a sauna, exercise room, tennis court, restaurant, coffee shop, plush lounge with live entertainment, and a gift shop. Each well-furnished room has a phone and remote control color TV with free and pay movies. Toll-free: (800)842-5329.

    regular room—   2 D or K bed...$125

San Diego Marriott Suites - Downtown   *696-9800*
downtown at 701 A St. - 92101
The top fifteen floors of an office tower opened in 1989 as an executive hotel with 264 suites, an indoor pool, whirlpool, saunas, and exercise equipment, plus pay parking, a restaurant and lounge. Each spacious, beautifully decorated suite has a parlor, refrigerator/wet bar, two phones, and two remote control color TVs. Toll-free: (800)962-1367.

    regular room—request N side for park view,   2 D or K bed...$129

★ **San Diego Princess Resort**   *274-4630*
6 mi. NW at 1404 W. Vacation Rd. - Mission Bay Park 92109
The loveliest corner of an island in the middle of Mission Bay is a 462-room single-level resort amidst a dazzling array of tropical flowers and greenery. A sandy beach surrounds the forty acre complex with five pools and a whirlpool in gardens backed by lagoons, fish ponds, waterfalls, a wonderfully whimsical observation tower, sauna, exercise room, game room, parcourse, resort shop; and (for a fee) six lighted tennis courts, an 18-hole putting golf course in a banana orchard, bike rentals, and a small boat marina with sailboat rentals. A posh bay-view restaurant, a dining room and patio featuring island specialties in a tropical setting, a freeform greenhouse coffee shop, and an entertainment lounge are also popular. Each beautifully furnished unit has a large private patio, refrigerator, phone, and remote control color TV with pay movies. Toll-free: (800)344-2626.

    #119,#121,#123,#125,#127—spacious, kitchenette,
      private tranquil view of beachfront/bay/La Jolla,   K bed...$285
    "studio suite" (many)—kitchenette, garden views,   K bed...$225
    regular room—request bayside,   2 Q or K bed...$150

★ **Sea Lodge on La Jolla Shores Beach**   *459-8271*
11 mi. NW at 8110 Camino Del Oro - La Jolla 92037
Magnificent mile-long La Jolla Shores Beach and palm-lined Scripps Park adjoin this 128-room motor hotel with a courtyard pool, two tennis courts, exercise room, and sauna. The Spanish-Colonial-style complex also has a recently upgraded split-level dining room that shares a beachfront view with a handsome lounge. Each spacious, well-furnished unit has a private balcony or patio, refrigerator, phone and remote control color TV with movies. Toll-free: (800)237-5211.

    #334,#234,#134—extra large, corner windows,
      huge private balcony with the ultimate
      La Jolla oceanfront & park view,   D & Q bed...$329
    #333,#233,#133—kitchenette, grand park/ocean view, K bed...$199
    #332,#232,#132—grand park/ocean view,   D & Q bed...$189
    oceanfront room—   2 Q or K bed...$239
    regular room—request park side for view,   Q & D, or K bed...$155

★ **Sheraton Grande Torrey Pines** *558-1500*
15.6 mi. NW at 10950 N. Torrey Pines Rd. - La Jolla 92037
A world-class view across renowned Torrey Pines Golf Course to the
ocean has been matched by Sheraton's 400-room tour-de-force resort
opened in 1990 and fully refurbished in 1995. Legendary Black's
Beach and a forest of rare trees are within strolling distance. Exquisite
art objects, floral sprays, polished stone and burnished copper
distinguish public areas with window walls overlooking a large garden
court pool and whirlpool. Other amenities include exercise facilities
and saunas, and (for a fee) golf, plus a resort shop, a fine restaurant
(see listing) and view lounge. Each spacious, luxuriously appointed
room has a stocked (honor) bar/refrigerator, private balcony or patio
with a fairway/ocean view, two phones and remote control color TV
with pay movies. Toll-free: (800)762-6160.

 #4048,#4117,#4014–top floor, parlor, 2 TVs,
  huge private balcony & extra windows, peerless
  panorama of lush fairways & distant ocean,   K bed...$475
 #4046,#4078,#4074,#4114,#4012–great view
  across golf course to La Jolla/ocean from   K bed...$205
 #4115,#4079,#4047–as above, but pines/ocean from   K bed...$220
 regular room–some fairways/ocean view,   2 D or K bed...$180

★ **Sheraton Harbor Island Resort** *291-2900*
3.3 mi. W at 1380 Harbor Island Dr. - Harbor Island 92101
The nearest lodging to the airport is this 1,050-room convention hotel
by a marina on Harbor Island in San Diego Bay. The contemporary
twelve-story complex was recently lavishly upgraded and expanded.
Amenities include a tiny sandy beach, three big tropical pools including
one with hydraulic features unique for the Southland, two whirlpools,
sauna, and (for a fee) four lighted tennis courts, a health club, marina
with rental boats, and parking. There are also two smart restaurants
including one that shares a marina view with an entertainment
lounge, and specialty shops. Each beautifully furnished room has a
private balcony, stocked (honor) bar/refrigerator, phone and remote
control color TV with free and pay movies. Toll-free: (800)325-3535.

 #1220 & even #s to #1200–fine bay view from 2 D or K bed...$200
 regular room–no view,   2 D or K bed...$160

★ **Summer House Inn** *459-0261*
10.5 mi. NW at 7955 La Jolla Shores Dr. - La Jolla 92037
La Jolla's finest beach is a stroll from this modern eleven-story hotel
with a landscaped pool and whirlpool, sauna, and fine ocean-view
restaurant and lounge (see listing). Each well-furnished room has a
floor-to-ceiling window and private see-through balcony, refrigerator,
phone, and color TV with movies. Toll-free: (800)666-0261.

 #910,#810,#710,#901–LR/kitchenette, in-room whirlpool,
  corner windows, grand La Jolla/shore view from   K bed...$209
 regular room–some have ocean view,   2 D or K bed...$129

Torrey Pines Inn *453-4420*
15.7 mi. NW at 11480 N. Torrey Pines Rd. - La Jolla 92037
Renowned Torrey Pines Golf Course adjoins this older 74-room motor
hotel with an extra-large courtyard pool overlooking fairways. Each
recently refurbished comfortable room has a semi-private patio or balcony, phone and color TV with (pay) movies. Toll-free: (800)777-1700.

 #120 thru #133–big patio, fairway/ocean view, 2 D or Q bed...$90
 regular room–no view,   2 D or Q bed...$80

Town and Country Hotel   *291-7131*
4 mi. N (by I-8) at 500 Hotel Circle North - Mission Valley 92108
Mission Valley's biggest (nearly 1,000 rooms) lodging is an older convention-oriented hotel on palm-shaded grounds by Fashion Valley, the city's premier mall. Amenities include four large garden court pools, a whirlpool, sauna, shops, and the valley's biggest convention center. A restaurant, coffee shops, and lounges offer a diversity of food and entertainment. Room quality ranges from plain to well-furnished. All rooms have a phone and color TV with (pay) movies. Toll-free: (800)77-ATLAS.

"West high rise"–spacious, pvt. view balc.,	2 Q or K bed...$105
regular room–compact, older,	2 Q or K bed...$75

★ **Travelodge Hotel - Harbor Island**   *291-6700*
3.6 mi. W at 1960 Harbor Island Dr. - Harbor Island 92101
Travelodge's best area lodging was upgraded for the 1990s. The nine-story 207-room hotel on Harbor Island by a marina on San Diego Bay has a garden pool and whirlpool, a fitness room, marina-view restaurant and lounge, and gift shop. Each beautifully upgraded room has a floor-to-ceiling window, large private view balcony, phone and remote control color TV with movies. Toll-free: (800)578-7878.

#811,#711,#611,#511–terrific bay/city view,	2 Q or K bed...$119
regular room–some marina view,	2 Q or K bed...$119

★ **U.S. Grant Hotel**   *232-3121*
downtown at 326 Broadway - 92101
Downtown San Diego's first landmark hotel opened in 1910 across from Horton Plaza. Restored to its former elegance, the eleven-story, 280-room complex has convention facilities, an exercise room, a gourmet restaurant and lounge (see listing), gift shop, and pay parking. Each beautifully refurbished room has a phone and remote control color TV with movies. Toll-free: (800)334-6957.

one-bedroom suite (several)–11th & 10th floor, extras,	
parlor, in-bath whirlpool, fine city views,	K bed...$375
regular room–	2 D or K bed...$135

★ **Welk Resort Center**   *749-3000*
37 mi. N (by I-15) at 8860 Lawrence Welk Dr. - 92026
Lawrence Welk's legacy is a vast self-contained resort and conference center tucked into a secluded valley. Facilities include an 18-hole championship golf course, executive course, and par-3 course; two outdoor view pools and three whirlpools; three lighted tennis courts; fine dining room and lounge; live dinner theater; and specialty shops. Each of 132 large well-furnished rooms has a semi-private patio or balcony, phone, and color TV. Toll-free: (800)932-9355.

#423,#413,#520,#510–quiet, corner window view,	K bed...$110
regular room–	2 Q or K bed...$110

★ **The Westgate Hotel**   *238-1818*
downtown at 1055 Second Av. - 92101
Opulent decor and furnishings distinguish the most elegant downtown hotel. The modern nineteen-story tower has 223 rooms, gourmet restaurants (see listing) and lounges, specialty shops, and pay parking. Each luxuriously appointed room has a floor-to-ceiling window, standing-room balcony, stocked (honor) bar/refrigerator, phone and remote control color TV with movies. Toll-free: (800)221-3802.

regular room–top floors west for bay view,	2 D or K bed...$194
regular room–	2 D or K bed...$164

Santa Barbara

Santa Barbara is Southern California's loveliest collaboration between man and nature. It is a unique seaside city of intense beauty in a natural amphitheater between a rare south-facing coastline and the towering Santa Ynez Mountains. Palm-shaded lawns and walkways border miles of fine sandy beaches that extend into some of the gentlest surf on the Pacific coast. "Santa Barbara style" architecture is everywhere. Red-tile roofs and whitewashed adobe distinguish buildings embellished with graceful curves and dramatic arches, passageways and secret courtyards, sculpture and fountains in harmony with luxuriant vegetation and vibrant gardens. The subtropical climate is as idyllic as the setting.

Santa Barbara was established in 1782 as one of four presidios (military fortresses) to protect the coastline of California for Spain. Four years later, Father Junipero Serra founded a mission in the hills above the new village. The present church, a building of classic grace called the "Queen of California Missions," was built in 1821. The Spanish legacy was reinforced through beautification movements that began well over a century ago. In 1925, much of downtown was destroyed by a devastating earthquake. The tragedy fostered an Architectural Review Board that established redevelopment guidelines reflecting the city's heritage.

Today, the city has more Spanish-Colonial adobes, arched facades, enclosed garden courtyards, and wrought-iron embellishments than anyplace in the United States. Some of America's loveliest public buildings glorify the spectacularly landscaped downtown area. The flourishing district, with its diverse and growing assortment of specialty stores, is alive with shoppers and strollers both day and night. A recently completed freeway overpass and other improvements have renewed the link between downtown and the beach, pier, and harbor where a wealth of water-oriented recreation is available year-round. Gourmet restaurants, including some of California's finest, contribute to the vitality of picturesque business districts throughout the city. Lodgings are similarly abundant and appealing, ranging from modern motels or romantic bed-and-breakfast inns to world-class resorts by the sea.

Population: 85,571   Area Code: 805
Elevation: 37 feet
Location: 100 miles West of Los Angeles
Santa Barbara Conference & Visitors Bureau   966-9222
   downtown at 510 State St., Suite A - 93101   (800)927-4688

WEATHER PROFILE

V.W.R.*		Jan.	Feb.	Mar.	Apr.	May	June	July	Aug.	Sep.	Oct.	Nov.	Dec.
Great	10												
Fine	9												
Very Good	8												
Good	7												
Moderate	6 / 5												
	4												
	3												
Adverse	2												
	1												
	0												

	Jan.	Feb.	Mar.	Apr.	May	June	July	Aug.	Sep.	Oct.	Nov.	Dec.
V.W.R.*	5	6	7	9	10	10	10	10	10	10	9	6
Temperature												
Ave. High	65	65	67	69	71	73	77	78	78	75	72	67
Ave. Low	41	43	44	48	50	52	56	56	55	51	44	42
Precipitation												
Inches Rain	3.7	3.6	3.0	1.3	.3	.1	-	-	.2	.7	1.3	3.5
Inches Snow	-	-	-	-	-	-	-	-	-	-	-	-

*V.W.R. = Vokac Weather Rating: probability of mild (warm & dry) weather on any given day.

ATTRACTIONS

★ **Alameda Plaza and Alice Keck Park Memorial Garden**
  .5 mi. NW along Santa Barbara St.
A delightful collection of wood-form play equipment (slides, tunnels, passages, bridges and swings) is at "Kid's World" in the shade of a giant Moreton Bay fig. Picnic areas, playgrounds, and pathways are shaded by the luxuriant foliage of more than seventy species of mature trees. Nearby is a lovely botanical garden with a pond and flowers amidst year-round lush greenery. Both parks are free.

★ **Arroyo Burro Beach County Park**   *687-3714*
  3.5 mi. SW via Carrillo St. & Meigs Rd. at 2981 Cliff Dr.
Palm-shaded lawns and picnic tables overlook a small stream by a lovely sandy corridor backed by picturesque bluffs. The surf is usually up, and swimming and shore fishing are good. Lifeguards, restrooms, and food concessions have been provided.

★ ***Banana Plantation***   *643-4061*
  15 mi. SE (on US 101 - La Conchita exit) - La Conchita
Richardson's Seaside Banana Garden is the West's only commercial source of the finicky fruit. Since 1985, the owners have proved that they're not just monkeying around. Their twelve acre plantation now includes thousands of plants and nearly sixty varieties, including enough exotic specialties to make any banana-lover go ape. (The author thinks the Brazilian has the most appeal.) They are expanding to include other tropical edibles like guavas and papayas.

★ ***Bicycling***
Terrain is relatively gentle and the scenery is terrific along many miles of separated bikeways and designated bike routes throughout

the city. Beyond, paved byways beckon bicyclists to explore lush orchards, foothills, and the shore. Cycle surreys (for up to six riders), tandems, mountain and touring bikes can be rented at:

Beach Rentals   *1 mi. SE at 8 W. Cabrillo Blvd.*   *963-2524*
Ocean Wear Sports   *1 mi. SE at 22 State St.*   *966-6733*

★ *Boat Rentals*
Santa Barbara Sailing Center   *962-2826*
1.4 mi. S at Breakwater
Sailboats and other boats (with or without motors) can be rented by the hour or day at this convenient harborside location.

★ *Boat Rides*
1.4 mi. S via Cabrillo Blvd. at Santa Barbara Harbor
Sightseeing cruises, whale watching excursions in winter, day sails and overnights to the Channel Islands can be arranged almost any day year-round. For information and reservations, call:
Captain Don's Harbor Cruises   *969-5217*
Santa Barbara Sailing Center   *962-2826*
Sea Landing   *963-3564*
Sunset Kidd's Sailing Charters   *962-8222*

★ *Botanical Garden*   *682-4726*
2.6 mi. N via State St. at 1212 Mission Canyon Rd.
High in the foothills is a 60-acre garden devoted to native California trees, shrubs, cacti, and wildflowers. Five miles of nature trails wind through desert, forest, and meadow sections of the preserve.

★ **Carpinteria State Beach**   *684-2811*
12 mi. E at W end of Palm Av. - Carpinteria
"The world's safest beach" is the immodest claim of local boosters about this mile-long crescent of fine sand. The slogan has merit. Thanks to an offshore reef, swimming and skin diving are excellent. Surfing and tidepooling are popular. The Santa Ynez Mountains offer a dramatic backdrop for beachcombers and sunbathers. Lifeguards, restrooms, showers, and picnic areas have been provided. Lining the beach behind dunes is a large, well-landscaped campground with all facilities. For toll-free reservations, call (800)444-PARK.

★ **County Courthouse**   *962-6464*
downtown at 1100 Anacapa St.
The most beautiful public building in America is of Spanish-Colonial architecture masterfully evolved into a peerless California design. The palatial U-shaped structure extends along three sides of an exquisitely landscaped block. Emerald lawns and subtropical greenery complement brilliant white walls and red-tiled roofs. Sunken flower gardens, fountains, and sculptures enhance the grounds. The interior is a tour de force of tile floors, rounded corridors, archways, beamed ceilings, regional art objects, and historical exhibits. Walls in the Assembly Room are decorated with dramatic murals depicting California history. From the balconied clock tower (reached by a free elevator), visitors have a stunning panoramic view of palms and red-tiled rooftops from the mountains to the sea.

★ **East Beach & West Beach & Santa Barbara Harbor**   *564-5418*
1 mi. SE at E end of State St. along Cabrillo Blvd.
Here are quintessential California beaches. Palm-shaded lawns back most of East Beach, a broad sandy strand extending for two miles between a lovely freshwater lagoon and Stearns Wharf. Beyond is the

rare east-facing coastline of West Beach, which ends at Santa Barbara Harbor, a marina (sheltered by a half-mile-long seawall promenade) with boat rentals and sportfishing charters. Nearby is a public fifty-meter outdoor pool heated year-round. Calm waters off the beaches attract swimmers—not surfers. Hordes of sunbathers, picnickers, volleyball players, and beachcombers also enjoy the site. A palm-lined park and the lofty Santa Ynez Mountains provide a backdrop, while the placid Pacific accented by sailboats (plus a few oil drilling platforms) and the Channel Islands complete the scene.

★ **El Presidio de Santa Barbara State Historical Park**   *966-9719*
downtown at 123 E. Canon Perdido St.
The last Spanish presidio in America was founded here in 1782. It protected settlers and missionaries, and was the governmental and cultural heart of the region. Surviving structures include El Cuartel (1782) (soldiers' barracks), the oldest building in the state park system, and the Caneda Adobe—a restored military residence. Authentically reconstructed buildings include the Padres Quarters and a surprisingly colorful Chapel. The free complex includes historic displays, a slide show, and a gift shop.

★ **Goleta Beach County Park**   *967-1300*
9.5 mi. W via US 101 & CA 217 on Sandspit Rd. - Goleta
This lovely half-mile sandy crescent extends to UCSB. A popular fishing pier, bar/cafe, and a palm-lined linear park with restrooms, picnic tables, and bike paths are other amenities.

★ *Golf*
Numerous manicured courses operate year-round in the area. Both well-landscaped 18-hole courses listed below are open to the public, and have club and cart rentals, food, and beverage services.
Sandpiper Golf Course (near the ocean)   *968-1541*
12 mi. W via US 101 at 7925 Hollister Av. - Goleta
Santa Barbara Community Golf Course   *687-7087*
2 mi. NW via State St. & Las Positas Rd. at 3500 McCaw Av.
Horseback Riding
Circle Bar B Stables   *968-3901*
26 mi. NW via US 101 at 1800 Refugio Rd. - Goleta
Waterfalls and swimming holes up nearby oak-shaded canyons provide idyllic destinations. You can view the ocean and islands from horseback en route. Guided rides only. Reservations required.

★ **Leadbetter Beach and Park**
2 mi. S via State St. along Shoreline Dr.
A beautiful park along headlands southwest of Santa Barbara Harbor provides picnic sites and scenic overlooks of the city and ocean. Below is a popular mile-long beach. Stairs access secluded sandy coves.

★ **Mission Santa Barbara**   *682-4713*
1.6 mi. NW via State St. at Los Olivos & Laguna Sts.
The "Queen of the Missions" is the loveliest of California's historic Catholic churches. Founded in 1786 on a rise overlooking the city, the twin-towered building was completed in 1820 and is still in use as a parish church. Spanish and Roman styles are apparent in the beautifully proportioned church, monastery, and colonnaded courtyard. Self-guided tours begin at the gift shop, and include stops at a multicolored altar in the chapel, rooms filled with Chumash Indian and missionary artifacts, tranquil flower gardens, and a cemetery by a huge fig tree.

Santa Barbara

★ **Moreton Bay Fig Tree**
1 mi. SE at Chapala & Montecito Sts.
Here is the author's favorite tree. Planted in 1877, it is now an awe-inspiring green landmark with branches that spread 160 feet and a labyrinthine system of surface roots. As many as 10,000 people could stand in the shade of this tree, the largest of its kind in America.

★ **Nude Beach**
7 mi. W via State St. at S end of Mockingbird Lane
The area's best nude beach is a remote spot with fine sand backed by relatively undisturbed hills. There are no facilities. But, on hot days, swarms of suitless sunseekers share the silver strand. Surfers, swimmers, frisbee throwers, volleyball players, and horseback riders all contribute to the conviviality.

Santa Barbara Historical Society Museum   *966-1601*
downtown at 136 E. De La Guerra St.
A big classic adobe houses free exhibits depicting the Spanish, Mexican and American eras of local history. The U-shaped structure encloses a pepper-tree-shaded courtyard with a fountain. Closed Mon.

★ **Santa Barbara Museum of Art**   *963-4364*
downtown at 1130 State St.
A handsome 1914 post office has been converted into a three-level showcase of American and European paintings, Oriental art, Greek and Roman sculpture, and a photographic collection. Closed Mon.

★ **Santa Barbara Museum of Natural History**   *682-4711*
1.8 mi. NW via State St. at 2559 Puesta Del Sol Rd.
Uphill from the mission is a beautifully landscaped complex of exhibit halls displaying extensive collections of animals, birds, plants and minerals related to both prehistoric and historic life in the area. There is also a planetarium; auditorium with music, theater, and art events; and a fine gift shop. You can walk through an authentic 72-foot-long blue whale skeleton out front.

★ **Santa Barbara Zoological Gardens**   *962-6310*
2.5 mi. E via US 101 at 500 Ninos Dr.
An expanding collection of animals and exotic birds is exhibited in a garden setting. Winding pathways lead to displays that reflect the animals' natural environments like a walk-through tropical aviary and a squirrel monkey island. Other features include a miniature railroad, picnic areas and a snack bar, gift shop, and panoramic hilltop views of the ocean, mountains, and bird refuge.

★ **Solvang**   *688-3317*
33 mi. NW via CA 154 on CA 246
Solvang is the Danish capital of America. All the sights, sounds, and delicious aromas of an authentic Danish village are present. Descendants of Danish-Americans who founded the town still preside in Scandinavian import shops, gourmet food stores, bakeries and restaurants. Hordes of visitors, especially on weekends year-round, savor the flavors of fudge made in exhibition kitchens, pretzels and cheese, European beers and Danish pastries. Restaurants are plentiful. Many serve the town's specialty—"aebleskiver" (a Danish pancake ball). At **The Little Mermaid** (1546 Mission Dr., B-L-D—Low), try them with homemade raspberry jam and Danish sausage. **Mollekron** (435 Alisal Rd., L-D—Low) offers well-prepared Danish specialties and a bountiful smorgasbord. The most celebrated local

smorgasbord is featured at the **Danish Inn Restaurant** (1547 Mission Dr., L-D—Expensive). **The Ballard Store** (3.8 mi. NE via Alamo Rd. at 2449 Baseline Av., L-D. Sun. brunch. Closed Mon.-Tues.—Expensive) is the Santa Ynez Valley's premier gourmet outpost in a long-ago country general store.

★ *Sportfishing*

Full or part-day fishing trips including all gear can be chartered year-round. For information and reservations, contact:

Captain Don's Sportfishing   *969-5217*
Sea Landing Sportfishing   *963-3564*

★ **Stearns Wharf**   *564-5518*
1.2 mi. SE at SE end of State St.
California's oldest walking pier has been a local landmark since 1872. Passenger ships no longer dock here as they did through the 1930s. Today, the pier (free to pedestrians) sports an appealing array of specialty shops, seafood and ice cream carryouts, view restaurants and lounges. The **Sea Center** (962-0885), a maritime museum with an aquarium, touch tank, and exhibits including a huge gray whale replica, is at the end of a Wharf extension. Fishing remains a popular pastime. Strollers are rewarded with nifty nautical close-ups of the harbor and a picturesque panorama of the city and mountains.

★ **University of California Santa Barbara**   *893-2485*
10 mi. W via US 101 at W end of CA 217
The only university in the West where the entire campus borders the ocean is UCSB. Founded in 1944, it now sprawls across more than 800 acres of headlands above a beach at Goleta Point. About 18,000 full-time students use a campus distinguished by ocean views, tropical and subtropical landscaping, and an eclectic mix of modern buildings. Maps and schedules of events are available at the Student Union.

Wineries (in town)

★   **Santa Barbara Winery**   *963-3633*   ★
.9 mi. SE at 202 Anacapa St.
The county's oldest winery, established in 1962, includes an expansive tasting area and a gift shop overlooking a wine barrel storage area. Tasting, sales, and tours 10-5 daily. Toll-free: (800)225-3633.

★   **Stearns Wharf Vintners**   *966-6624*
1.2 mi. SE at 217-G Stearns Wharf
Several cellars' wines may be sampled in an upstairs tasting room and gift shop with a picture-window view of the harbor. Tasting and sales 9-6 daily, until 8 on Fri. & Sat.

Wineries (in Santa Ynez Valley)

The Santa Ynez Mountains provide a convenient northern boundary for "Southern California." However, one of America's great wine-producing districts lies just beyond—and it is a delightful day trip from Santa Barbara. As a result, the following premium wineries are included as a helpful bonus for adventurous oenophiles.

★   **Copenhagen Cellars**   *688-4218*
33 mi. NW via CA's 154 & 246 at 448 Alisal Rd. - Solvang
Santa Ynez and Copenhagen Cellars wines are featured in an appealing underground wine cellar. The room also showcases a variety of regional specialty food products and gifts. Tasting and sales 11-5 daily, 10-5 Sat. & Sun.

★ **Fess Parker Winery & Vineyard** *688-1545*
40 mi. NW via CA 154 at 6200 Foxen Canyon Rd. - *Los Olivos*
The newest major Santa Ynez Valley winery is dramatically situated on the lush floor of Foxen Canyon. A baronial tasting center/barrel aging facility (circa 1992) makes excellent use of stone in walkways, columns, and a monumental fireplace. Group picnic tables occupy a sunny lawn area. Selected estate-grown premium wines are offered for a fee in the dramatic tasting room. Tasting and sales 10-4 daily. Toll-free: (800)841-1104.

★ **The Firestone Vineyard** *688-3940*
39 mi. NW via CA 154 & Zaca Station Rd. - *Los Olivos*
A dramatically contemporary structure on a blufftop promontory is the heart of the winery, established in 1972. The wood-toned interior includes unique views of both flourishing vineyards and barrels aging wine from different sets of windows in the tasting room. Numerous estate-bottled wines are poured for tastes. Picnic tables line a fountain court. Tasting, tours and sales 10-4 daily.

★ **The Gainey Vineyard** *688-0558*
30 mi. NW via CA 154 at 3950 E. CA 246 - *Santa Ynez*
This 1984 winery is houses in a large Spanish-Colonial-style building. A handsome tasting room overlooks vineyard-covered hills. Nearby are oak-shaded picnic tables. Fee tastings of premium wines are regularly scheduled. Tasting, tours and sales 10-5 daily.

★ **Rancho Sisquoc Winery** *934-4332*
54 mi. NW via CA 154 & Foxen Canyon Rd. - *Santa Maria*
The picturesque headquarters of a large, diversified ranch in the pastoral Sisquoc River valley houses a small redwood and stone winery bonded in 1977. Premium wines from grapes grown on ranch lands are sold at a tasting room where the entire line is offered. Large trees shade picnic tables on lawns amidst gardens. Tasting and sales 10-4 daily.

★ **Sanford Winery** *688-3300*
42 mi. NW at 7250 Santa Rosa Rd. - *Buellton*
Tucked away in gentle foothills of the Santa Ynez Mountains is an atmospheric little winery founded in 1981. A short list of estate-grown premium wines is offered in a comfortably rustic tasting room. Nearby, picnic tables adjoin a picturesque creek. While this is the only listed winery west of CA 154, the setting and wines are well worth the drive. Tasting and sales 11-4 daily. Toll-free in CA: (800)426-9463.

★ **Santa Ynez Winery** *688-8381*
30 mi. NW via CA's 154 & 246 at 343 N. Refugio Rd. - *Santa Ynez*
Opened in 1975, Santa Ynez is one of the valley's best-known wineries, with white wines the specialty. A trellis-shaded deck with picnic tables overlooking the surrounding vineyards adjoins a tasting room where most of the premium wines are offered. Tasting, tours and sales 10-5 daily. Toll-free: (800)864-3443.

★ **Zaca Mesa Winery** *688-3310*
42 mi. NW via CA 154 on Foxen Canyon Rd. - *Los Olivos*
A large barnlike building houses a 1978 cellar where several premium wines are produced. Picnic tables are arrayed under an overhang. Tours and tastings of all premium varietals are available. Tasting, tours and sales 10-4 daily.

★ **Acacia**   *969-8500*
3.5 mi. E at 1212 Coast Village Rd. - Montecito
D only, plus brunch Sat.-Sun.   *Expensive*
Since it opened in 1992, Acacia has become a popular source of contemporary California cuisine. How about lemon pepper onion rings with sun-dried ketchup, or buttermilk fried chicken? Light flavorful dishes are served in intimate dining areas amid simply stylish decor.

Andria's Harborside Restaurant   *966-3000*
1.3 mi. S at 336 W. Cabrillo Blvd.
D only.   *Moderate*
Seafood stars in dishes charbroiled, grilled, sauteed, steamed or fried. Specialties like beer-and-coconut batter shrimp, potato souffles and housemade desserts distinguish the comfortable wood-and-greenery-trimmed dining room and lounge with a harbor view.

★ **The Bakery & Cafe**   *962-2089*
downtown at 129 E. Anapamu St.
B-L-D. Sun. brunch.   *Expensive*
Wraparound cases display a wealth of pastries, breads, cakes and pies that are served with light fare in one of the city's most popular coffee shops or on a patio with a courthouse view, or to go.

Beachside Bar/Cafe   *964-7881*
10 mi. W at 5905 Sandspit Rd. in Goleta Beach Park - Goleta
L-D.   *Moderate*
Contemporary California seafood is featured in dishes like shrimp soup served in a big comfortable split-level dining room/bar festooned with greenery and flowers, and on an adjoining heated patio. Both offer a superb view of a palm-lined beach and adjoining fishing pier.

★ **Brigitte's**   *966-9676*
downtown at 1325 State St.
L-D. No L Sun.   *Expensive*
Brigitte's is a landmark for New California cuisine. The well-rounded grazing menu ranges from venison tenderloin with red currant-peppercorn sauce and sage popovers, through designer pizzas or filet mignon with cheese-filled chile peppers to extraordinary desserts. It's all creative and delicious. The modish dining room of this first-rate bistro is built around an exhibition kitchen. A deli/bakery next door also displays assorted goodies to eat here, or to go.

Brophy Brothers Clam Bar & Restaurant   *966-4418*
1.7 mi. S at 119 Harbor Way
L-D.   *Moderate*
Fresh fish, listed on a menu that changes daily, are served broiled, sauteed, or deep-fried with traditional accompaniments. Diners in the upstairs restaurant are seated at a cozy congestion of casual tables behind a bar with an intimate view of boats in the inner harbor. A sunny heated view deck adjoins.

The Brown Pelican   *687-4550*
3.5 mi. SW at 2981½ Cliff Dr. at Arroyo Burro County Park Beach
B-L-D.   *Expensive*
Contemporary California fare is generously served. But the feature of this beachside restaurant/lounge is a window-wall view of surf splashing a few yards away. A sunny terrace shares the view.

★ **Cajun Kitchen**   *687-2062*
1.2 mi. NW at 1924 De La Vina
B-L.   *Moderate*
Santa Barbara's best source of Cajun specialties offers the popular
regional fare for all meals, even breakfasts. Bourbon Street chili
omelets, wheat germ pancakes, egg scrambles, and cornbread or
biscuits can be fabulous. The congested little storefront cafe trimmed
with greenery and an adjoining sidewalk patio are often packed.

★ **Casa de Sevilla**   *966-4370*
.5 mi. SE at 428 Chapala St.
L-D. Closed Sun.-Mon.   *Expensive*
The longest-established major restaurant in Santa Barbara offers
Continental cuisine with Spanish-Colonial overtones. Informally
elegant table settings enhance several clubby dining rooms and a
lounge enlivened with bold red-toned walls and decor.

★ **Chad's**   *568-1876*
.4 mi. SE at 625 Chapala St.
L-D. No L Sun.   *Expensive*
One of Santa Barbara's best dining adventures opened in 1992.
Contemporary California dishes enhanced by some robust Cajun/creole
adaptations follow a basket of memorable muffins that might include
jalapeno-cheddar or rosemary buttermilk. The sophisticated cuisine is
served in a beautifully restored Victorian house with several intimate
dining rooms and a popular piano bar.

★ **Citronelle**   *963-0111*
1.8 mi. E at 901 E. Cabrillo Blvd.
B-L-D.   *Very Expensive*
This young spin-off by an LA celebrity chef won instant critical
acclaim for New California cuisine. Dinner can still be special in the
pleasant upstairs bistro. Other meals may disappoint.

★ **Clementine's Steak House**   *684-5119*
12 mi. E (near US 101) at 4631 Carpinteria Av. - Carpinteria
D only. Closed Mon.   *Moderate*
Steak is featured among old-fashioned all-American dishes.
Homemade bread and pie accompany every meal. Carpinteria's only
culinary outpost is a big, very popular dinner house.

★ **Cold Spring Tavern**   *967-0066*
13 mi. NW via CA 154 at 5995 Stagecoach Rd.
L-D.   *Expensive*
Wild game stars among American classics like sauteed medallions of
rabbit or grilled filet of venison with wild lingonberries. Everything is
skillfully prepared and accompanied by delicious homemade bread. All
of the charm of a bygone era is present in this historic stagecoach stop.
Buildings have a ramshackle authenticity unmatched in Southern
California. The tiny firelit bar is particularly romantic, while the
rustic saloon next door is often loud and lively late at night.

★ **Crossroads**   *969-6705*
3 mi. E at 50 Los Patos Way
L-D. No L Sat. Sun. brunch.   *Expensive*
In this newcomer, New California cuisine is displayed in dishes like
bisque of wild mushroom, or grilled venison chops, and desserts made
here. Fresh flowers, candles, full linen and padded booths or armchairs
enhance dining areas. A tony greenhouse lounge adjoins.

★ **Downey's**   *966-5006*
downtown at 1305 State St.
L-D. No L Sat. & Sun. Closed Mon.   Very Expensive
Downey's is one of Southern California's best restaurants. The menu changes daily to assure a continuous meld between the best seasonal provisions and the novel notions of the chef/owner. Grilled duck with huckleberries or boneless veal chop with artichokes exemplify the soul-stirring New California cuisine. An intimate, elegant dining room is accented by vivid wall art, floral displays, and a pastry cart showcasing ambrosial desserts made here.

★ **El Encanto Hotel & Garden Villas**   *687-5000*
2 mi. N at 1900 Lasuen Rd.
B-L-D. Sun. brunch.   Very Expensive
New American cuisine with a French accent is typified by papillote of striped bass with white wine sauce. In the hotel's romantic restaurant, meals are matched by a polished dining room with an incomparable window-wall view of the city and ocean far below. A sunny split-level terrace and plush firelit lounge share the enchanting site.

★ **El Paseo Mexican Restaurant**   *962-6050*
downtown in El Paseo at 813 Anacapa St.
L-D. Sun. brunch   Expensive
The most enchanting Santa Barbara-style dining venue recently reopened. First-rate contemporary California and Mexican dishes are enhanced by peerless tortillas prepared in an expo kitchen in a corner of the spectacular courtyard dining room. A profusion of flowers, full-sized magnolia trees, a multilevel flower-strewn fountain, and bougainvillea-draped balconies extend high up to a retractable roof. Through dramatic arches at one side is a lounge outfitted with classic Spanish-Colonial decor.

★ **Emilio's**   *966-4426*
1.3 mi. S at 324 W. Cabrillo Blvd.
D only.   Expensive
The California/Italian grazing cuisine featured in this young restaurant reflects a notable preoccupation with purity, quality and freshness of meats and produce. Pastas, pizzas, antipasti, entrees, housemade breads and desserts also suggest real creativity. The casual comfortable dining room has an exposition kitchen and windows overlooking the marina.

Esau's Coffee Shop   *965-4416*
.5 mi. SE at 403 State St.
B-L.   Moderate
Breakfasts have been served here longer than anywhere in town. Scrambles, omelets, pancakes and other morning delights are fresh and homemade. The California-casual cafe decor gives Esau's the honest look and feel of a place unspoiled by creeping croissantism.

★ **Farmer Boy**   *687-7011*
2.6 mi. NW at 3427 State St.
B-L.   Moderate
All-American homestyle cooking has been pleasing natives for over a third of a century in one of Santa Barbara's best coffee shops. Homemade biscuits and cinnamon rolls complement a choice of nearly one hundred omelets featured among breakfasts served at padded booths in comfortable dining rooms.

★ **Four Seasons Biltmore**   *969-2261*
3.5 mi. E at 1260 Channel Dr.
B-L-tea-D. Sun. brunch.   *Expensive–Very Expensive*
The resort's **La Marina** (D only. Sun. brunch–Very Expensive)
presents creative American cuisine amidst formal grandeur. Floral
bouquets, crystal, china, and fine linen at widely spaced tables
complement magnificent ocean views. **The Patio** (B-L-D–Expensive)
features updated California fare and casual elegance in an enclosed
tropical courtyard overlooking the sea. **La Sala** is the most gracious
lounge in the city. A wealth of polished stonework, luxuriant greenery,
and overstuffed sofas and armchairs outfit a romantic ocean-view room
with a fireplace, where high tea is presented in the afternoon.
The Harbor   *963-3311*
1.2 mi. SE at 210 Stearns Wharf
L-D. Sun. brunch.   *Expensive*
Fresh seafood is a lure in the city's best over-the-waves restaurant.
Thrilling close-ups of surf and sand also draw crowds to the big
contemporary dining room. Upstairs in **Longboards Bar & Grill** you
can enjoy the same view with lighter fare and tap beers or local wines
in a casual lounge, or on a sunny deck.
J.K. Frimple's   *569-1671*
.8 mi. NW at 1701 State St.
B-L-D.   *Moderate*
Ordinary American fare is not the reason why this long-established big
coffee shop/lounge is a local landmark. It is the gigantic Moreton Bay
fig tree in the middle of the building, surrounded by floor-to-ceiling
glass windows, that is remarkable.
★ **Jeannine's Cookies & Muffins**   *962-8868*
downtown at 5 W. Carrillo St.   *Expensive*
Scones (buttermilk, blueberry, orange, and whole wheat), sticky buns,
muffins, and soda bread are delicious specialties served with coffee or
to go. The deservedly popular little pastry parlor is closed Sunday.
Joe's Cafe   *966-4638*
.4 mi. SE at 536 State St.
L-D. No L Sun.   *Moderate*
Old-time American fare like T-bone steak with onion rings, broiled
pork chop with apple sauce, or liver and onions are generously served
with spaghetti in a big dining room and saloon with a stamped-tin
ceiling, a lot of nostalgic photos, and a handsome backbar.
La Capannina Ristorante   *962-6366*
.9 mi. S at 302 W. Montecito St.
D only. Closed Mon.   *Expensive*
A new source for authentic Italian cuisine opened in 1992 in a
handsome cottage awash in crisp white linen. The cuisine (including
desserts made here), staff, decor and even the music honestly reflect
the restaurant's Old Country origins.
★ **La Super Rica**   *963-4940*
1.2 mi. NE at 622 N. Milpas St.
L-D.   *Low*
Homemade soft corn tortillas filled with chicken breast, mushroom,
and red chile sauce topped with cheese and avocado is just one of the
extraordinarily creative specialties described on blackboard menus.
You queue up to place your order in a (frequently long) line into the

Santa Barbara

casual converted fast-foodery. Then, help yourself to as much as you want of the fine red or green salsa or tomato/onion salsa, and dine at picnic tables in an enclosed patio framed by greenery.

Moby Dick   *965-0549*
1.2 mi. SE at 220 Stearns Wharf
B-L-D. Sun. brunch.   *Moderate*
Standard American fare is offered in a very large fishhouse overhanging the side of Stearns Wharf with a fine view of the inner harbor from the dining rooms, lounge and sunny deck.

★ **Montecito Inn**   *969-3392*
4 mi. E at 1295 Coast Village Rd. - Montecito
L-D.   *Moderate*
The hotel's **Montecito Cafe** is a deservedly popular source for an appealing selection of New California cuisine. Note expecially the grilled chicken breast with roasted chile, and unusual seafoods. The cheerful, posh dining room/bar is accented by a fountain.

★ **Mousse Odile**   *962-5393*
.4 mi. SE at 18 E. Cota
B-L-D. Closed Sun.   *Moderate*
Santa Barbara's uncompromising French restaurant reflects the skill and attitude of its Gaelic progenitor. Dishes are authentic and austere. So is the ambiance of polished wood floors, bentwood chairs, greenery, and objets d'art.

★ **Old Towne Cafe**   *962-3574*
downtown in El Paseo at 813 Anacapa St.
L-D.   *Expensive*
An inviting selection of contemporary California dishes is carefully prepared including a scrumptious white chocolate macadamia nut pie in a graham cracker crust with cognac. The light, bright cuisine is matched by a handsome Santa Fe-style dining room with a corner fireplace and lounge. A lovely garden court adjoins.

★ **Our Daily Bread**   *966-3894*
downtown at 831 Santa Barbara St.
B-L. Closed Sun.   *Moderate*
This post-hippie paragon among bakeries features a limited selection of first-rate pastries, cookies, breads and (until they're sold out, which is usually early) bodacious bear claws. Baked goods and light fare can be enjoyed at a few tables or to go.

★ **Oysters**   *962-9888*
downtown at 9 W. Victoria St.
L-D. Sun. brunch. Closed Mon.   *Expensive*
Updated American cuisine with a shellfish emphasis is served in the refined cozy congestion of a dining room by an exposition kitchen or in a pleasant little fountain court patio.

★ **The Palace Cafe**   *966-3133*
.4 mi. SE at 8 E. Cota St.
D only.   *Expensive*
Cajun-creole-Caribbean cuisine ranging from cajun popcorn to Caribbean coconut shrimp is enriched by assorted unusual muffins and delightfully decadent desserts like key lime pie. Authentic preparations and exotic ingredients (flown in) are skillfully combined in an exhibition kitchen by multilevel dining rooms with an easygoing sophistication enhanced by colorful artwork.

★ **Palazzio**   *969-8565*
3.4 mi. E at 1151 Coast Village Rd. - Montecito
L-D. No L Sun.   *Moderate*
This new hot spot among local pasta parlors has some notable touches.
Abundant Southern Italian fare is accompanied by garlic yeast rolls
(made fresh all day) and courtesy house wine (honor system). The
trendy trattoria is usually crammed and noisy.

Papagallo's   *963-8374*
downtown at 731 De La Guerra Plaza
D only, plus L on Fri.   *Moderate*
If you would guess that Peruvian cuisine is about as exciting as that
country's major culinary contribution—the potato—try Papagallo's.
Dishes won't appeal to everyone, but they are flavorful. The cozy
congested dining room with an exposed kitchen is as atmospheric as
the food. The fountain courtyard is a quiet alternative.

★ **Paradise Cafe**   *962-4416*
downtown at 702 Anacapa St.
L-D. Sun. brunch.   *Moderate*
An oakwood broiler is used for 22-oz. T-bone steak, pork or lamb chops.
Seafoods range from grilled mussels to cioppino; and there are other
specialties like sirloin-chunk chili; plus luscious chocolate-paradise pie
made here. The ever-popular complex has a cozy cottage-style dining
room, a stylish bar, and a flowery patio.

Rio Bravo   *966-1561*
.9 mi. SE at 202 S. State St.
L-D. Closed Mon.   *Moderate*
Some of the flavors of the northern Rio Grande have arrived locally in
dishes like honey-roasted cilantro-crusted chicken breast and
adaptations like fire-roasted artichoke with chile mayo. Diners can opt
for full linen tables, a bar (they brew their own), or a beer garden.

Rose Cafe   *965-5513*
2 mi. W at 1816 Cliff Dr.
B-L-D. No D Sun. Closed Mon.   *Moderate*
Chile verde omelets and other zesty, carefully prepared Mexican
breakfasts distinguish three colorful, comfortable dining rooms.

★ **San Ysidro Ranch**   *969-4100*
5.6 mi. NE at 900 San Ysidro Lane - Montecito
B-L-D. Sun. brunch.   *Very Expensive*
Here is one of the few resorts in the West that produces many of their
own herbs, spices and vegetables. The **Stonehouse Restaurant**
highlights New California cuisine in a pleasing selection of creations
that maximize seasonally fresh ingredients. Breakfast possibilities
might include raspberry vanilla bean pancakes, while pan-roasted
pork T-bone with sweet potato enchilada might be served for dinner.
Several cultivated dining rooms in a historic stone building evoke the
ranch's gracious spirit. Downstairs, the elegant rusticity of the **Plow
and Angel Bar** is just right for a romantic nightcap.

Sea Cove Cafe   *965-2917*
2 mi. S at 801 Shoreline Dr. (on the sand at Leadbetter Beach)
B-L-D.   *Moderate*
Contemporary American fare is listed on menu boards. The real draw,
though, is an umbrella-shaded patio built right out onto a popular
scenic beach.

★ **Sojourner Coffeehouse**   *965-7922*
downtown at 134 E. Canon Perdido
L-D. No L Sun.   *Moderate*
The city's most venerable vegetarian-oriented restaurant also offers
some chicken dishes. Most notable are the outstanding desserts (like
chocolate peanut butter cake or apple streudel pie) enhanced by a
wealth of plain and fancy coffees, teas, and fruit drinks. Warm wood
tones, candles and wall art contribute to the conviviality.

★ **Tutti's**   *969-5809*
3.5 mi. E at 1209 Coast Village Rd. - Montecito
B-L-D.   *Expensive*
Creative Italian cuisine includes offerings like spit-roasted Cornish
game hen stuffed with dried apricots and almonds, plus decadent pies
and cakes. Exciting dishes are matched by post-modern charcuterie
decor in a dining room built around an exhibition kitchen and lavish
displays of pastas, desserts, wines and cheeses.

★ **21 Victoria**   *962-5222*
downtown at 21 W. Victoria
D only. Closed Mon.   *Expensive*
New California cuisine receives adventurous international topspin in
dishes like seafood potstickers with spicy citrus sauce. Stylish tables
fill several small dining areas decorated with live plants and avant-
garde art objects around an exhibition kitchen. Live jazz happens late
on Wed. through Sun. evenings.

★ **The Upham**   *963-7003*
.7 mi. W at 1404 De La Vina St.
L-D. No L Sun.   *Expensive*
Watercress and pear salad; designer pizzas; New York steak with
shitakes and pineapple potato pancakes; or sauteed pork with port,
green chiles, pine nuts, red onion marmalade and spinach typify New
California cuisine served in **Louie's**, a dining room that reflects the
historic hotel's gentility. The garden patio is a charmer, too.

★ **Wine Cask**   *966-9463*
downtown in El Paseo at 813 Anacapa St.
L-D. Sat. & Sun. brunch.   *Expensive*
Classic New California cuisine is represented by dishes like roasted
duck breast or braised rabbit in this sophisticated paragon of Santa
Barbara style. Bentwood armchairs, full linen table settings, and floral
sprays grace a room surrounded by heraldic contemporary art, a
baronial fireplace and a chic bar. A heated cobblestone fountain court
adjoins, backed by the area's most complete wine store.

★ **Woody's BBQ**   *963-9326*
.9 mi. S at 229 W. Montecito St.
L-D.   *Moderate*
Woody's is Santa Barbara's best Q-parlor, thanks to their tender and
tasty oak-smoked beef, pork ribs and chicken. Dining room and bar
decor includes a salad bar, a jukebox, sawdust on the floor, barnwood,
farm relics, patios— and a bathtub.

★ **Xanadu French Bakery**   *969-3550*
3.3 mi. E at 1028 Coast Village Rd. - Montecito   *Moderate*
Xanadu is Santa Barbara's finest source of croissants. Other baked
goods (ranging from extraordinary to overcooked) can also be enjoyed
with fresh juices and light fare at a few tables, or to go.

★ **Your Place Restaurant**   *966-5151*
1.9 mi. E at 22-A N. Milpas St.
L-D. Closed Mon.   *Moderate*
This place should be your place for Thai food in Santa Barbara. Among many possibilities are a dozen soups, including ginger chicken soup and a spicy baby clam soup (a house special made with hot/sour baby clams, coconut milk, and mushrooms). Special touches are plentiful, too, in exotic treats like pineapple fried rice served in a scooped-out pineapple shell at glass-topped tables in a casual dining room.

LODGING

Accommodations are plentiful and diverse—including superb luxury resorts, urbane small hotels, sybaritic bed-and-breakfast inns, and bargain motels. Nearly all are full throughout summer and on weekends year-round. Rates are often reduced at least 20% on weekdays from fall through spring.

Beachside Inn - Best Western   *965-6556*
1.3 mi. S at 336 W. Cabrillo Blvd. - 93101
This modern three-story motor hotel is on a corner across from a park and the marina. Amenities include a small courtyard pool and a harbor-view restaurant. Each nicely furnished room has a phone and remote control color TV with movies. Toll-free: (800)528-1234.

    #318-#322–big pvt. balcony with fine marina view, K bed...$131
    regular room–   D bed...$85

★ **The Cheshire Cat Bed & Breakfast**   *569-1610*
.9 mi. W at 36 W. Valerio St. - 93101
Two of Santa Barbara's oldest homes have been restored to elegance and now serve as one of the city's best bed-and-breakfast inns. Lovely gardens surround a whirlpool in a gazebo. Breakfast buffet and afternoon regional wines are complimentary, as are bicycles. Each room is beautifully furnished with quality antiques enhanced by gracious decor. All have private baths and phones.

    "Tweedledum Suite"–spacious, LR with gas
      fireplace & wet bar, whirlpool,   K bed...$249
    "Eberle Suite"–gas fireplace, big in-room whirlpool, Q bed...$195
    "Cheshire Cat Suite"–spacious,
      built-in TV & VCR, in-room whirlpool,   Q bed...$189
    "Dormouse"–sloping ceilings, cozy, gas fireplace, Q bed...$139
    regular room–bay-window seating area,   Q bed...$119

★ **El Encanto Hotel & Garden Villas**   *687-5000*
2 mi. N at 1900 Lasuen Rd. - 93103
One of the West Coast's time-honored hideaways occupies a luxuriant hillside overlooking Santa Barbara and the sea. The 84-unit complex, sequestered amidst flamboyant gardens, has a large pool backed by a jungle of banana plants, a tennis court, and a plush restaurant and entertainment lounge with an enchanting view (see listing). Each room is comfortably furnished, and has a phone and remote control color TV with movies. Toll-free in CA: (800)346-7039.

    #402,#404,#406 (best of 20 contemporary "courtside
      suites with fireplaces")–living room with fireplace
      and private balcony with tennis/town/ocean view, Q bed...$160
    #314–big, private patio, fireplace, city/ocean view, K bed...$280
    regular room–compact, garden views,   Q or K bed...$140

Santa Barbara

★ **Fess Parker's Red Lion Resort**   *564-4333*
1.6 mi. E at 633 E. Cabrillo Blvd. - *93103*
Santa Barbara's newest and largest luxury resort is a Spanish-Colonial-inspired extravaganza on a choice site across a highway from a prime beach. The 360-room low-rise hotel features an extra-large garden court pool and whirlpool, a putting green, exercise room, saunas, and (for a fee) three lighted tennis courts, bicycles, plush restaurant, coffee shop, entertainment lounge, and a gift shop. Each spacious, beautifully furnished room includes a private patio or balcony, mini-bar with stocked (honor) refrigerator, phone, and remote control color TV with free and pay movies. Toll-free: (800)879-2929.

#316—separate bedroom, gas fireplace, in-bath whirlpool, shared ocean-view balcony,	K bed...	$630
#312,#314,#315—as above, but no in-bath whirlpool,	K bed...	$395
Bldg. H #303,#306; Bldg. E #727,#729—extra large, private balcony with fine beach/ocean view,	K bed...	$289
Bldg. B #468,#469—pvt. balc., fine beach/ocean view,	K bed...	$269
regular room—mountain view,	2 Q or K bed...	$189

★ **Four Seasons Biltmore**   *969-2261*
3.5 mi. E at 1260 Channel Dr. - *93108*
Santa Barbara's peerless resort hotel since the Roaring 20s retains all of its traditional grandeur. Emerald lawns extend from the Spanish-Colonial landmark to a roadway above the sea. The 234-room complex includes a low-profile lodge and cottages surrounded by gardens. There are two large tropically landscaped pools, whirlpools, saunas, exercise facilities; an 18-hole putting green, and other lawn game courts; and (for a fee) bicycles, and three lighted tennis courts; gracious dining and drinking facilities with superb ocean views (see listing); and resort shops. Each luxurious guest room has a stocked (honor) mini-bar, phone, and remote control color TV with movies and VCR. Toll-free: (800)332-3442.

"Anacapa Suite"—1 BR, parlor with gas fireplace, large private patio with grand ocean view,	K bed...	$795
#216,#623—gas fireplace, large private balcony, fine ocean view,	K bed...	$370
#448—spacious, gas fireplace, tiny private balcony,	K bed...	$370
"deluxe" (many)—spacious, patio or balcony, intimate garden view,	2 D or K bed...	$320
regular room—compact, garden view,	2 D or K bed...	$280

★ **Harbor View Inn**   *963-0780*
1 mi. SE at 28 W. Cabrillo Blvd. - *93101*
Santa Barbara's best all-around motor lodge is a charmer that was expanded and completely upgraded in 1995. The wharf and beach are across a street from the graceful Spanish-Colonial-style complex. Palms shade colorful gardens on grounds that include a big pool and whirlpool, and a harbor-view restaurant. Light breakfast and afternoon wine and cheese are complimentary. Each attractively furnished room has a phone and remote control color TV with movies. Toll-free: (800)755-0222.

#301,#201—refr., sunken tub, 2 private balconies, corner windows with superb wharf/ocean/mountain view,	K bed...	$240
"deluxe east wing"—spacious, refr., pvt. balc. or patio,	K bed...	$150
regular room—garden patio,	2 D or K bed...	$150

(King's) Country Inn by the Sea   963-4471
1.2 mi. S at 128 Castillo St. - 93101
This newly upgraded lodging is a block from the ocean with a small outdoor pool and whirlpool, and saunas. Light breakfast is complimentary. Each well-furnished room has a phone and remote control color TV with movies. Toll-free: (800)455-4647.

"Spa Suite"—spacious, in-room whirlpool,   canopy K bed...$179
#351—big, private balcony, pool/mountain view,   K bed...$149
regular room—   Q bed...$99

Miramar Resort Hotel   969-2203
4.2 mi. E (by US 101) at San Ysidro Rd. exit (Box 429) - 93102
Santa Barbara's only lodging directly on the beach is a sprawling older hotel. Unfortunately, it is hard by the freeway, and split by main line railroad tracks. In addition to some rooms on the beach, amenities include two courtyard pools (one large and tropically landscaped) and a whirlpool; ping pong table; and (for a fee) four tennis courts, exercise rooms and saunas, massage, and bicycles; plus a restaurant, coffee shop and gift shop. Each simply furnished unit has a phone and color TV with movies. Toll-free in CA: (800)322-6983.

#621,#618,#615,#611,#607—top (2nd) floor, sliding
glass doors to big pvt. balc., beachfront view from   K bed...$145
regular room—request away from freeway,   D, Q or K bed...$75

★ **Montecito Inn**   969-7854
4 mi. E (by US 101) at 1295 Coast Village Rd. - Montecito 93108
A small hotel circa 1928, the landmark of an exclusive area, has been fully restored to the spirit of the Roaring 20s when it was popular with the Hollywood crowd. The handsome Spanish-Colonial complex (now adjoining a freeway) has a palm-shaded pool and whirlpool; sauna; exercise equipment; complimentary bicycles; and a stylish restaurant (see listing). Each attractive unit includes a phone, and remote control color TV with movies. Toll-free in CA: (800)843-2017.

#302,#301—fine mt./town view from 2 sides,   Q bed...$150
regular room—with VCR & refrigerator,   K bed...$165
regular room—compact,   Q bed...$150

Motel 6
2 mi. E at 443 Corona Del Mar - 93103   564-1392
13 mi. E (by 101) at 5550 Carpinteria Av. - Carpinteria 93013   684-8602
8 mi. W (by US 101) at 5897 Calle Real - Goleta 93117   964-3596
2.7 mi. NW at 3505 State St. - 93105   687-5400
The **bargain** chain has several local motels including one (on Corona Del Mar) a block from the beach. All have an outdoor pool and compact, plain rooms with a phone and color TV with movies.

regular room—in Santa Barbara,   D bed...$48
regular room—in Goleta, D bed...$43; in Carpinteria,   Q bed...$38

Old Yacht Club Inn   962-1277
2 mi. E at 431 Corona Del Mar Dr. - 93103
A large 1912 home a block from the beach was converted into Santa Barbara's first bed-and-breakfast inn in 1980. A full breakfast and evening wine are complimentary. So are bicycles. Each of the nine individually appointed rooms in the main building and in an adjoining house has period furnishings, a private bath and a phone. Toll-free in CA: (800)549-1676; elsewhere: (800)676-1676.

"Castellammare Room"—balc., in-room whirlpool,   Q bed...$140
regular room—private bath,   Q bed...$90

Radisson Hotel Santa Barbara   *963-0744*
2.1 mi. E at 1111 E. Cabrillo Blvd. - 93103
A historic lodging across a highway from the beach and ocean has been
modernized to serve as a well-situated convention hotel. Amenities of
the 174-room, three-story Spanish-Colonial complex include a large
courtyard pool, whirlpool, saunas, and exercise equipment; plus a
restaurant, entertainment lounge and gift shop. Each well-furnished
room has a stocked (honor) refrigerator, phone and remote control
color TV with movies. Toll-free: (800)333-3333.

> #375,#377,#379,#381,#363,#359,—spacious,
> private balcony with fine beach/ocean view,   2 Q or K bed...$219
> regular room—mountain view,   2 Q or K bed...$179

★ **San Ysidro Ranch**   *969-5046*
5.6 mi. NE at 900 San Ysidro Lane - Montecito 93108
Nestled in the lush foothills of the Santa Ynez Mountains is Southern
California's most enchanting hideaway. First opened as a guest ranch
in 1893, it is situated amidst ancient oaks; lovely gardens of flowers,
herbs, and vegetables; and Victorian Box trees whose intoxicating
fragrance make February and March unforgettable. Amenities include
a large well-landscaped pool, two tennis courts, a game room with ping
pong, and (for a fee) guided horseback rides, plus a gourmet restaurant
(see listing) and cozy firelit lounge. Each spacious, luxuriously
appointed cottage or room has a fireplace, refrigerator, phone and
remote control color TV with VCR and movies. Toll-free: (800)368-6788.

> "Lilac One"—most private, separate 1-room cottage,
> whirlpool on deck near creek, fireplace in view of   K bed...$650
> "Creek"—separate 2-room cottage, wet bar & fireplace
> in living room, deck with whirlpool & creek view,   K bed...$550
> "Jasmine"—separate 1-room cottage, whirlpool on
> oak-shaded deck above creek, fireplace in view of   K bed...$475
> "Forest"—separate 2-room cottage, kitchen, whirlpool
> on deck near creek, fireplace in living room,   K bed...$650
> regular room—in multiroom cottage,   K bed...$225

★ **Simpson House Inn**   *963-7067*
.6 mi. NW at 121 E. Arrellaga St. - 93101
One of the West's most sybaritic lodgings is in a quiet neighborhood,
surrounded by lovely gardens and shade trees. A large 1874 Eastlake-
style home has been faithfully restored and transformed, along with
cottages and a barn, into an elegant fourteen-room bed-and-breakfast
inn. Full breakfast featuring fresh local fruits and juices, and
afternoon beverages (especially area wines) and appetizers, are
complimentary. So are bicycles and beach gear. Each spacious room
has a private bathroom, and sumptuous antiques and furnishings that
romanticize Victorian opulence. Toll-free: (800)676-1280.

> "Greenwich"—elegant cottage, concealed TV
> and VCR, whirlpool and fireplace in view of   Q bed...$235
> "Abbeywood"—as above,   Q bed...$225
> "Hayloft"—upstairs in barn, hidden color TV & VCR,
> loveseat by the fireplace, pvt. balc. amid trees,   K bed...$220
> "Weathervane"—similar to above,   K bed...$215
> "Robert & Julia Simpson Room"—clawfoot
> tub & showers, pvt. deck above gardens,   brass K bed...$155
> regular room—detached pvt. bath,   antique D bed...$105

★ **Tiffany Inn**   *963-2283*
.6 mi. W at 1323 De La Vina St. - 93101
A stately Victorian home has been skillfully restored to its former elegance and now serves as one of the region's great bed-and-breakfast inns. A sumptuous breakfast and afternoon wine and cheese are complimentary. Each of seven rooms is beautifully furnished with classic antiques and period furnishings.
   "Honeymoon Suite"—pvt. entrance, refr., pvt. large sunken
      whirlpool tub, fireplace in view of brass canopied   Q bed...$175
   "Sommerset Room"—private bath, fine mountain view
      & fireplace visible from   Q bed...$145
   "Victoria's Room"—private bath, garden
      view & fireplace visible from   Q bed...$145
      regular room—shared bath, ask for "Nichole" room,   Q bed...$75

★ **The Upham**   *962-0058*
.7 mi. W at 1404 De La Vina St. - 93101
The Southland's oldest continually-operated lodging is an 1871 hotel that has been refurbished to continue as a bed-and-breakfast inn. The handsome 49-room complex includes several cottages amidst gardens and the skillfully restored hotel with an urbane dining room (see listing). A light breakfast and afternoon wine and appetizers are complimentary. Each well-furnished room includes some period furnishings blended with contemporary decor and full baths, a phone and color TV with movies. Toll-free: (800)727-0876.
   "Master Suite"—spacious, pvt. yard with swing,
      big whirlpool, gas fireplace & refr./wet bar in LR,   K bed...$325
   #38—private garden area, gas fireplace in view of   Q bed...$175
      regular room—   Q bed...$105

★ **Villa Rosa**   *966-0851*
1.1 mi. SE at 15 Chapala St. - 93101
One of Santa Barbara's finest bed-and-breakfast inns is tucked away in a tranquil setting only half a block from the main beach. The eighteen-room replica of a Spanish-Colonial villa was built during the 1930s. It is the epitome of "Santa Barbara architecture" with pink-toned stucco, red tile, graceful arches, and wood and wrought-iron accents. A tiny courtyard sequesters a pool and whirlpool in the shade of a banana palm. Light breakfast and wine and cheese in the afternoon are complimentary. Each individually decorated spacious room captures a romantic spirit with soft pastel hues and beautiful furnishings, and has a private bath and phone.
   #13—corner with multi-window view of mtns./ocean,   Q bed...$145
   "deluxe garden view room" (several)—gas fireplace,   K bed...$190
      regular room—   Q bed...$90

West Beach Inn   *963-4277*
1.2 mi. S at 306 W. Cabrillo Blvd. - 93101
A palm-shaded pool and whirlpool in a garden are features of this tile-and-stucco motel across a street from Santa Barbara's main beach. Light breakfast and afternoon wine and cheese are complimentary. Each spacious, well-furnished unit has a refrigerator, phone, and remote control color TV with movies. Toll-free: (800)423-5991.
   #315,#215—3rd & 2nd floors, corner windows & big
      patio have superb view of marina & waterfront,   K bed...$165
   #316-#320—big private balcony, fine marina views,   K bed...$165
      regular room—   Q bed...$115

Santa Monica

Santa Monica is one of California's busiest coastal cities. An interstate freeway ends by a big municipal pier centered on two miles of broad sandy beach. Nearby bluffs are topped by a mile-long strip of palm-shaded lawns and walkways overlooking the Pacific. The city was founded during the 1870s, and grew rapidly as a favorite seaside destination with an appealing coastline and a mild climate.

Today, the compact city is surrounded on three sides by Los Angeles. But the allure lingers on, for hordes of both vacationers and "street people." Wide beaches and a rejuvenated pier still attract sunbathers, sightseers, and saltwater aficionados. Shoppers and diners are drawn to the upgraded open-air mall along Third Street, as well as strollable sections of Main Street and Montana Av. The city's four memorable hotels are all near the beach and offer panoramic ocean views.

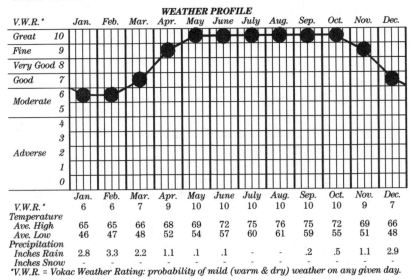

WEATHER PROFILE

V.W.R.*		Jan.	Feb.	Mar.	Apr.	May	June	July	Aug.	Sep.	Oct.	Nov.	Dec.
V.W.R.*		6	6	7	9	10	10	10	10	10	10	9	7
Temperature													
Ave. High		65	65	66	68	69	72	75	76	75	72	69	66
Ave. Low		46	47	48	52	54	57	60	61	59	55	51	48
Precipitation													
Inches Rain		2.8	3.3	2.2	1.1	.1	.1	-	-	.2	.5	1.1	2.9
Inches Snow		-	-	-	-	-	-	-	-	-	-	-	-

*V.W.R. = Vokac Weather Rating: probability of mild (warm & dry) weather on any given day.

Santa Monica

Population: 86,905   *Area Code: 310*
Elevation: 101 feet
Location: 15 miles West of Los Angeles
Santa Monica Convention & Visitors Bureau   392-9631
  1 mi. SE at 2219 Main St. - 90405

ATTRACTIONS

★ **Bicycling**

Santa Monica is connected by an on-the-beach bike/stroll way with Venice and other neighborhoods to the south. Bicyclists can pedal for many miles along the flat scenic shoreline. Bicycles as well as skates and assorted beach gear can be rented at:

   Perry's Sport Shop .5 mi. W at 1200 Pacific Hwy. 458-3975
   Spokes & Stuff   .6 mi. S by Loew's beachfront 395-4748

★ **La Mesa Drive**

   2.3 mi. N at N end of 19th St.

Moreton Bay figs are Southern California's most magnificent trees. Half-mile-long La Mesa Drive is the only street in the West where you can drive under a continuous canopy of their verdant foliage. The exotic trees with their surprisingly well-behaved massive surface roots distinguish a collection of estates.

★ **Palisades Park**

   .3 mi. W along Ocean Av.

Topping steep cliffs above the beach is the city's oldest park. Towering palms and subtropical landscaping are being rehabilitated along the narrow greensward that extends for well over a mile. Strollers, joggers and "street people" share walkways, and everyone gets a bird's-eye view of sunsets, surf and sand from picnic sites and overlooks. Upstairs in the Senior Recreation Center is a "Camera Obscura," with a unique 360° perspective on the surroundings.

★ **Santa Monica Pier**

   .4 mi. S at foot of Colorado Av.

People-watchers, pier fishermen, and fun-seekers love this restored landmark. Along the over-the-water boardwalk are carnival games and rides, junk food takeouts, gift shops, surf-view restaurants, and a splendiferous antique carousel with hand-carved wooden horses.

★ **Santa Monica State Beach**

   .3 mi. W along Pacific Coast Hwy.

One of California's favorite beaches extends for three miles in a broad sandy strand backed by bluffs. A popular paved promenade along the reach gives strollers, skaters and bicyclists close-up views of surf and sand. Volleyball courts, picnic areas, snack bars, restrooms, and lifeguards are available. Santa Monica Pier (see listing) is at the historic heart of the action.

★ **Third Street Promenade and Santa Monica Place**

   downtown on 3rd St. between Broadway & Wilshire Blvd.

In the 1950s, a principal shopping street was converted into a pedestrians-only mall. The three-block-long experiment didn't work. Multimillion dollar remodeling in 1989 made it a semi-pedestrian promenade with whimsical sculptures and an ever-improving array of shops. Across Broadway is fashionable Santa Monica Place—a vast skylit galleria mall with au courant shops on three levels.

RESTAURANTS

★ **Abiquiu**   *395-8611*
downtown at 1413 5th St.
L-D. No L Sat. & Sun.   *Expensive*
After the 1994 earthquake, one of the Southland's stellar chefs, John
Sedlar, launched a new culinary adventure. The restaurant, related to
his roots, is named after a remote village in the northern Rio Grande
valley of New Mexico. Exciting dishes blend the owner's origins, classic
training and California locale into an exciting dining experience
affirmed by a simply sophisticated setting.

★ **Border Grill**   *451-1655*
downtown at 1445 Fourth St.
D only.   *Expensive*
Designer Mexican cuisine (classic stuff with a lot of creative California
topspin) is fresh and flavorful in dishes like chilled seafood tacos,
grilled cactus salad, or sauteed rock shrimp with roasted chiles.
Housemade desserts are on display at one side of a big bustling room
that captures the colorful spirit of the "Nuevo Mexican" cuisine.

★ **Camelions**   *395-0746*
3 mi. N at 246 26th St.
L-D. Sun. brunch. Closed Mon.   *Very Expensive*
New American cuisine is presented in regional dishes like Lake
Superior whitefish and Louisiana crabcakes complemented by
seasonally fresh vegetables and fruits. Firelit little dining rooms with
elegant table settings and a romantic garden court for alfresco dining
contribute to the restaurant's continuing appeal.

★ **Chinois on Main**   *392-9025*
1.5 mi. SE at 2709 Main St.
L-D. No L Sat.-Tues.   *Extremely Expensive*
Oriental cuisine with New California topspin stars in one of Southern
California's most renowned dining experiences. Celebrity chef
Wolfgang Puck created an extraordinarily appealing style that
combines subtle flavors and textures of the Orient with light,
innovative treatments of the peerless diversity of seasonal fresh
ingredients found in California. The exciting results are served in a
chic dining room that is usually crowded and noisy. Trend-setting
post-modern decor includes an open kitchen, a freeform bar, dramatic
art objects, and a staff dressed to fit the Pan-Pacific milieu.

★ **Drago**   *828-1585*
1.7 mi. NE at 2628 Wilshire Blvd.
L-D. No L Sat. & Sun.   *Very Expensive*
Drago is one of the newest among Italian superstar restaurants in the
Southland. Skill and dedication are apparent, as are the freshness and
quality of unusual Sicilian specialties. Waiters in starched white
aprons swirl among tables surrounding a flamboyant floral centerpiece
and array of the evening's luscious housemade desserts.

★ **Fama**   *451-8633*
downtown at 1416 4th St.
L-D. No L Sat. & Sun. Closed Mon.   *Expensive*
New California cuisine is showcased in a short list of homemade
pastas and pizzas, fresh innovative salads, and light creative entrees.
Post-modern blond wood decor softens an airy dining room/bar.

★ **Giorgio Ristorante**   *459-8988*
2 mi. NW at 114 W. Channel Rd.
D only.   *Very Expensive*
Authentic Italian classics and homemade desserts have attracted a
major following to this tony little trattoria.
★ **I. Cugini Trattoria**   *451-4595*
downtown at 1501 Ocean Av.
L-D.   *Expensive*
A wealth of California-style wood-fired pizzas, pastas and Northern
Italian specialties is enhanced by breads and desserts made here. The
big cheerful complex includes a bakery display area, lounge, exhibition
kitchen, casual dining rooms and umbrella-shaded patio.
★ **Il Forno**   *450-1241*
1.7 mi. SE at 2901 Ocean Park Blvd.
L-D. No L Sat. Closed Sun.   *Expensive*
Pizzas, pastas and bread dough are made fresh daily on the premises.
An unusual selection of spa cuisine is also prepared in an exhibition
kitchen surrounded by a cozy congestion of glass-topped tables. The
trendy trattoria has earned its place as a local favorite.
Ivy at the Shore   *393-3113*
downtown at 1541 Ocean Av.
L-D.   *Extremely Expensive*
New American cuisine ranges from Louisiana crabcakes and assorted
designer pizzas to homemade ice cream. Fun food with an attitude, a
frenetic dining room/lounge, and a covered patio can't individually
explain this clone's apparent appeal to grazing glitterati.
Joe's Main Street Diner   *396-8804*
1.7 mi. SE at 2917 Main St.
B-L-D.   *Moderate*
Good bets for breakfast are the contemporary California diner delights
like blue cornmeal pancakes served in this prosaic retro-1950s diner.
★ **Knoll's Black Forest Inn**   *395-2212*
1.6 mi. NE at 2454 Wilshire Blvd.
L-D. No L Sat. & Sun. Closed Mon.   *Expensive*
Knoll's serves the best German cuisine in Southern California. The
menu changes seasonally to feature delights like asparagus in spring.
There are also superb standbys like meat-and-spinach-filled pastry
pillows, and golden caviar on potato pancakes with sour cream. A
polished dark-toned dining room/lounge is decorated with German art
objects, while a plant-filled garden room has banquettes overlooking
a luxuriant patio with tables set amidst fountains and flowers.
L. A. Farm   *829-0600*
2.3 mi. NE at 3000 W. Olympic Blvd.
L-D. No L Sat. Closed Sun.   *Expensive*
Au courant Angeleno cuisine can be rewarding in dishes like limestone
salad or braised lamb shank with cabbage. Abundant greenery and an
exhibition kitchen lend hip appeal to a heated covered courtyard and
adjoining dining room with uncomfortable little wicker chairs.
★ **Loews Santa Monica Beach Hotel**   *458-6700*
.6 mi. S at 1700 Ocean Av.
B-L-D. Sun. brunch.   *Expensive*
In **Riva** (D only. Only brunch on Sun.), New California cuisine is
showcased in masterful productions like parmesan-crusted sea bass

in champagne citrus sauce and (seasonal) artichoke heart and spinach salad with lemon pesto vinaigrette. The lavish little dining room has an enchanting window-wall view of the beach and pier. Grand piano stylings contribute to the ambiance each evening and to the adjoining posh **Lobby Bar**. **Coast Cafe** (B-L-D) offers New California cuisine amid tony decor and vibrant color in wall hangings and sculpture in a big bilevel room with a surf view.

★ **Michael's**   *451-0843*
.3 mi. N at 1147 3rd St.
L-D. No L Sat. Closed Sun.-Mon.   *Extremely Expensive*
Michael McCarty, one of the earliest progenitors of New California cuisine, oversees a stunning showcase. The finest and freshest available ingredients from regional sources are masterfully prepared to maximize exciting combinations of flavors, textures, and colors in innovative dishes. Glitterati in fashionably casual attire dine at formally elegant tables set with floral bouquets, linen, crystal, silver and china surrounded by au courant art objects. Beyond a display of exquisite desserts is a plush bar and a heated tropical garden patio accented by fountains and sculpture. Michael's remains (thankfully) the only Southland restaurant with a 15% mandatory "service charge."

★ **Ocean Avenue Seafood**   *394-5669*
downtown at 1401 Ocean Av.
L-D. Sun. brunch.   *Expensive*
An elaborate menu posted daily identifies fresh seafood and describes how it is presented in soups, stews, pan roasts, and specialties ranging from petrale sole with asparagus, shitakes, tomatoes and herbs to whole catfish in peanut oil. Desserts made here are similarly appealing. The multilevel extravaganza has plush high-tech dining areas, a classy oyster bar and lounge, and a sidewalk garden patio.

★ **Remi**   *393-6545*
downtown at 1451 3rd St. Promenade
L-D.   *Very Expensive*
A short, well-thought-out selection of Northern Italian dishes receives skilled New California topspin in entrees like mesquite-grilled game hen with sauteed eggplant and peppers. The snazzy dining room has a picture-window view and several tables on the downtown mall.

★ **Rockenwagner**   *399-6504*
1.4 mi. SE at 2435 Main St.
L-D.   *Very Expensive*
The namesake showcase of one of the Southland's great chefs turns out delicious New California cuisine like smoked salmon canneloni with cucumber and jicama salad or herb-crusted tuna cooked in rice paper. The airy post-modern dining room (sort of wooden-rafter quansat-hut-style) is outfitted with neo-art deco chairs at tables set with full linen, flowers, and candles.

Schatzi on Main   *399-4800*
2 mi. SE at 3110 Main St.
L-D. Sat. & Sun. brunch.   *Expensive*
Several Austrian specialties and a few body-builder items like Arnold's dry pan seared swordfish with vegies enhance the contemporary California grazing menu in Arnold Schwartzenegger's hideaway restaurant. Blond wood, brass and brick distinguish the casual multiangled dining room and shaded heated patio.

★ **Shutters on the Beach** *458-0030*
.8 mi. S at 1 Pico Blvd.
B-L-D. *Expensive–Very Expensive*
One Pico (L-D–Very Expensive) is the hotel's showcase for New California cuisine amidst contemporary elegance. Diners enjoy picture-window views on three sides of the adjoining promenade and beach. **Pedals Cafe** (B-L-D–Expensive) serves light, bright New California cuisine including rotisserie and wood grill entrees and notable baked goods made here. The big cheerful bistro has an exhibition kitchen, a heated umbrella-shaded patio and a fine beach view shared by the cleverly named **Handle Bar**. (It's right by the bike path.) Upstairs, the **Lobby Lounge** is outfitted with overstuffed chairs, big gas fireplaces, a grand piano, and a picture-window panorama of the beach.

★ **Valentino** *829-4313*
2.6 mi. E at 3115 Pico Blvd.
D only, plus L on Fri. Closed Sun. *Very Expensive*
Valentino is one of the West's preeminent sources for Northern Italian haute cuisine. Piero Selvaggio has been doing nearly everything right for a quarter of a century. Consistent, masterful preparation of top-quality ingredients results in some of the most delightful traditional and innovative Italian dishes anywhere, and there is a world-class wine cellar. The cosmopolitan dining rooms and lounge couple striking contemporary decor with sophisticated formality in both table settings and staff.

★ **Warszawa** *393-8831*
.3 mi. E at 1414 Lincoln Blvd.
D only. *Expensive*
Warszawa may well be Southern California's best Polish restaurant. Pierogi (pasta shells stuffed with meat, cheese, or vegies lightly fried or steamed), hunter's stew, stuffed cabbage, and other traditional dishes are as hearty and flavorful as they are authentic. Several gracious little dining rooms contribute to the warm feeling of an Old-Country inn.

★ **Ye Olde King's Head** *451-1402*
downtown at 116 Santa Monica Blvd.
L-D. *Moderate*
Authentic English dishes like Cornish pasties, shepherd's pie and terrific fish and chips can be topped off with a sherried trifle or bread pudding with brandy sauce. Wash it down with warm beer among a choice of nearly a dozen premium international beers on tap. Stirring memorabilia from back home lines walls throughout the genuine pub. There are usually a bunch of Brits throwing darts.

★ **Zenzero** *451-4455*
downtown at 1535 Ocean Av.
L-D. No L Sat. & Sun. *Very Expensive*
One of the region's most exciting dining experiences opened in 1993. New California cuisine is given an Oriental topspin in dishes like cilantro-cured salmon accompanied by warm potato and salmon roe salad, and steamed sea bass with spicy parsnip/chile sauce. Crisp post-modern decor in the simply elegant dining room is enhanced by high-tech art objects.

LODGING

Lodgings near (but not by) the beach are fairly common, ranging from landmark hotels to frayed old motels. Summer is the busiest season. Some places reduce rates at least 15% at other times.

The Georgian   *395-9945*
downtown at 1415 Ocean Av. - 90401
The Georgian was fully renovated sixty years after it opened in 1933 across from Santa Monica's blufftop park. The eight-story, 84-room hotel captures the spirit of a Depression-era ocean view escape. Free Continental breakfast is delivered to your room which includes some period decor, a phone, and a remote control color TV with movies. Toll-free: (800)538-8147.

#801,#802—good park & ocean view,	Q bed...$200
regular room—	2 Q or K bed...$145

Guest Quarters Suite Hotel   *395-3332*
.5 mi. SE (near I-10) at 1707 4th St. - 90401
The city's newest all-suites hotel opened in the 1990s. The 253-unit complex (built around an eight-story atrium) has a view pool, whirlpool, sauna, exercise room, restaurant/lounge, gift shop, and (pay) parking. Each nicely furnished one-bedroom suite has a phone, (honor) bar/refrigerator, and remote control color TV with (pay and free) movies. Toll-free: (800)424-2900.

regular room—distant ocean view,	2 D or K bed...$205
regular room—city view,	2 D or K bed...$155

Holiday Inn - Bay View Plaza   *399-9344*
.7 mi. E at 530 Pico Blvd. - 90405
The area's best Holiday Inn is a contemporary ten-story 309-room hotel with two small outdoor pools, whirlpool, exercise room, and entertainment lounge. Each nicely decorated room has a sliding glass door to a small private balcony, an (honor) bar, phone, and remote control color TV with movies. Toll-free: (800)HOLIDAY.

#924,#824,#724,#624—spacious, refrigerator, big private balcony with downtown/ocean panorama & raised tiled whirlpool,	K bed...$250
#840 & odd #s to #832—fine view of ocean beyond city from private balcony,	2 D or K bed...$133
regular room—city view,	2 D or K bed..$113

★ **Loews Santa Monica Beach Hotel**   *458-6700*
.6 mi. S at 1700 Ocean Av. - 90401
One of the LA area's best lodgings near the beach opened in 1989 with 350 rooms a block from the pier on a low bluff. The neo-Victorian sendup is built around an airy five-story atrium with lavish decor. Amenities include an Olympic-length indoor/outdoor lap pool with a sea-view sundeck; whirlpool; and (for a fee) health spa with salon, sauna, steam room and exercise equipment; two fine dining rooms (see listing); plush lobby lounge; pay parking; and a gift shop. Each spacious, beautifully decorated room has a tiny private balcony, refrigerator/(honor) bar, three phones, and remote control color TV with (pay and free) movies. Toll-free: (800)223-0888.

#744,#644,#544—parlor, 3 private mini-balconies, picture window, beach/pier/ocean panorama from	K bed...$455
#751,#701,#601—grand pier/beach/ocean view from	K bed...$295
regular room—	2 D or K bed...$215

★ **Miramar Sheraton Hotel**   *576-7777*
.4 mi. W at 101 Wilshire Blvd. - 90401
A magnificent Moreton Bay fig tree distinguishes this landmark hotel across a street from a blufftop park above the beach. Lavishly upgraded in the mid-1990s, the ten-story complex now includes 302 units, a large pool in a lush tropical garden, (fee) health spa, two restaurants, entertainment lounge, (pay) parking, and specialty shops. Each beautifully decorated room has an (honor) bar, phone and remote control color TV with (pay and free) movies. Toll-free: (800)325-3535.
"Bungalow"—large, private patio, in-bath whirlpool, K bed...$275
#1039, & odd #s to #1021—private balcony with
   outstanding tree/park/ocean/pier view,   2 D or K bed...$205
   regular room—   2 D or K bed...$205

Radisson Huntley Hotel   *394-5454*
.3 mi. NW at 1111 2nd St. - 90403
This eighteen-story 213-room hotel has a rooftop dining room and lounge with superb coastal and city views, a gift shop, and (pay) parking. Each refurbished attractive room has a phone and remote control color TV with (pay) movies. Toll-free: (800)333-3333.
   regular room—request N side 16th fl. for fine view,   K bed...$125

★ **Shangri-La Hotel**   *394-2791*
downtown at 1301 Ocean Av. - 90401
The classic art deco facade of this seven-story apartment hotel across from a blufftop park has been artistically enhanced by landscaping, as has the interior with a wealth of glass bricks, beveled mirrors and polished chrome. Continental breakfast and afternoon tea and appetizers are complimentary. Each unit conveys the essence of the deco style and includes a refrigerator, phone, and remote control color TV with free movies. Toll-free: (800)345-STAY.
#700—2 BR, windows on 2 sides, 2 baths, kitchen,
   big pvt. deck with fine ocean/pier/park view, 2 T & K bed...$450
#500,#400,#300—as above, but no balcony,   2 T & K bed...$230
#600,#604—1 BR, superb park/beach/ocean view,   K bed...$205
   regular room—studio,   K bed...$110

★ **Shutters on the Beach**   *458-0030*
.8 mi. S at 1 Pico Blvd. - 90405
Santa Monica's premier lodging opened in 1993. The 198-room seven-story luxury hotel is the only one on the sand—separated only by a boardwalk from miles of broad sandy beaches. Amenities include a large pool, whirlpool and terrace with a beach/ocean view, spa with exercise equipment, steam, sauna and (for a fee) massage, bicycles, and garage. There is also a gift shop, fine dining and a lounge (see listing). Each luxuriously appointed room features the namesake shutters and a large in-bath whirlpool tub, plus three phones, an (honor) bar/refrigerator, standing balcony and remote control color TV with (pay and free) movies and VCR. Toll-free: (800)334-9000.
#645—extra spacious, 2 balconies,
   great ocean view from   K bed...$750
#306—woodburning fireplace, 2 balconies
   on promenade, great beach/ocean view,   K bed...$350
#720—great pool/beach/ocean view,   K bed...$350
#620—2 balconies with great beach/ocean views,   K bed...$350
#747,#647—small pvt. balc. with pool & beach view, K bed...$350
   regular room—request balcony,   K bed...$250

Temecula

Temecula is the heart of Southern California's premium wine country. The historic community, which finally incorporated in 1989 with burgeoning surrounding developments, borders the Santa Margarita River about an hour by car from the ocean. The broad valley, nearly surrounded by mountains, benefits from moderating sea breezes flowing through Rainbow Gap. Agriculture has been important here since the beginning during the 1880s, yet vineyards were introduced only twenty-five years ago.

Today, premium wineries are the valley's major attraction. A few century-old buildings and many replicas lend character to an Old West style downtown where gift shops, galleries, and family restaurants may soon be joined by an opera house and other entertainment centers in a major western-theme complex. A first-rate golf resort and a wine country bed-and-breakfast top a growing number of lodgings.

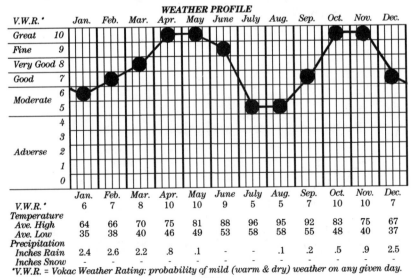

WEATHER PROFILE

V.W.R. *		Jan.	Feb.	Mar.	Apr.	May	June	July	Aug.	Sep.	Oct.	Nov.	Dec.
Great	10												
Fine	9												
Very Good	8												
Good	7												
Moderate	6												
	5												
	4												
	3												
Adverse	2												
	1												
	0												

	Jan.	Feb.	Mar.	Apr.	May	June	July	Aug.	Sep.	Oct.	Nov.	Dec.
V.W.R. *	6	7	8	10	10	9	5	5	7	10	10	7
Temperature												
Ave. High	64	66	70	75	81	88	96	95	92	83	75	67
Ave. Low	35	38	40	46	49	53	58	58	55	48	40	37
Precipitation												
Inches Rain	2.4	2.6	2.2	.8	.1	-	-	.1	.2	.5	.9	2.5
Inches Snow	-	-	-	-	-	-	-	-	-	-	-	-

*V.W.R. = Vokac Weather Rating: probability of mild (warm & dry) weather on any given day.

Temecula

Population: 27,099   Area Code: 909
Elevation: 1,010 feet
Location: 79 miles Southeast of Los Angeles
Temecula Valley Chamber of Commerce   676-5090
  1.2 mi. N at 27450 Ynez Rd.

ATTRACTIONS

Ballooning

Sunrise champagne balloon flights over vineyards and orchards are a popular local attraction. For trips of one hour or longer, call:
A Rainbow at Dawn   676-2709 or (800)446-6222
A Skysurfer Balloon Co. Inc.   (800)660-6809
Fantasy Balloon Flights   (800)GO-ABOVE
Sunrise Balloons   (800)548-9912

Fallbrook

14 mi. SW via I-15 & Mission Rd.
Sequestered into the most luxuriant hills in north San Diego County is a burgeoning community that may be "The Avocado Capital of the World." An idyllic subtropical climate also supports bountiful orchards of citrus trees, and exotic crops ranging from kiwis to macadamia nuts (grown and sold at **Cooper's Nut House**, 1378 Willow Glen Rd.–look for signs 3.5 mi. NE of town). The compact town center has some appealing collectibles shops and restaurants (see listing).

Lake Elsinore

16 mi. NW via I-15 on CA 74
There is less than meets the eye in the two-by-five-mile water body. This is partly due to a shore choked with weeds. Boating, waterskiing and fishing are available in only a few designated areas. Lake Elsinore State Recreation Area on the north shore has a complete campground and (for a fee) the only designated swimming beach. Humble historic Lake Elsinore Village on the east shore still meets basic needs of visitors.

Lake Skinner County Park   926-1541

9 mi. NE via Rancho California Rd. at end of Warren Rd.
The small reservoir nestled in gentle brush-covered hills is popular for fishing, with numerous boat rental and launching sites. Swimming is not permitted in the lake (water supply), but there is a large swimming pool (summer only). A full-service campground and picnic areas are some distance from the lake.

Vail Lake   676-5695

11 mi. E on CA 79
Picturesque live oaks dot gentle hills around a square-mile reservoir that is a major source of bass, catfish, trout, and panfish. Boat rentals are available (swimming and waterskiing are not allowed) and there is an RV campground nearby.

Warm Water Features

★ **Glen Ivy Hot Springs**   277-3529
25 mi. NW via I-15 at 25000 Glen Ivy Rd. - Corona
"Club Mud" (as it is affectionately known) is an ultimate experience for anyone who ever wondered what wallowing would be like. The resort's chief claim to fame is a warm wet wallow of caramel-colored clay. The idea is to sink into the ooze, cover your body with it, climb out and sunbathe until you harden into a human mud pie. It is stimulating

and refreshing. (Be sure to bring an old extra swimsuit.) Nearby are large warm mineral pools and numerous whirlpools on terraces surrounded by lush subtropical gardens. Other features include hot mineral baths; sauna; beauty treatments and massage; food, beer and wine service; and a gift shop. Open daily 10-6.

Murrieta Hot Springs Resort   677-7451
5 mi. N via I-15 at 39405 Murrieta Hot Springs Rd. - Murrieta
Warm mineral waters have drawn city dwellers since the turn of the century. Refurbished facilities include mineral pools, whirlpools and tennis courts on palm-shaded grounds with fountains and ponds. Saunas, massage, and fitness programs are also available, along with meals and lodgings (see listing).

★ *Wineries*
Premium-quality wine grapes are juxtaposed with flourishing citrus orchards in the Temecula Valley. Nevertheless, a wine industry is burgeoning just beyond the city's exploding suburbs. A dozen facilities offer tours, tasting, and sales.

Baily Tasting Room   695-1895
5 mi. E at 33833 Rancho California Rd.
In 1986, the tasting room for this young winery opened at the top of a ridge overlooking wine country. (Fee) tasting and sales are offered in a handsome shop from 10-5 daily.

Callaway Vineyard & Winery   676-4001
4 mi. E at 32720 Rancho California Rd.
The longest-established winery in Temecula Valley began with premium quality grapevines planted in 1969. Facilities now include a large handsome ridgetop visitor center surrounded by vineyards, citrus trees and gardens, with a well-stocked gift shop. Grape arbors cover group-oriented picnic facilities adjoining the winery. Structured (fee) tasting, hourly tours, and sales 10:30-4:45 daily.

Cilurzo Vineyard & Winery   676-5250
5.5 mi. E via Rancho California Rd. at 41220 Calle Contento
Trellis-shaded picnic tables overlook a tree-lined pond on a ridgetop adjoining this small family-operated winery's appealingly homespun tasting room/gift shop. (Fee) tasting, tours, and sales 9:30-4:45 daily.

Hart Winery   676-6300
4 mi. E at 32580 Rancho California Rd.
Some of the district's best wines are produced in a small family-operated winery built in 1980. (Fee) tasting and sales 9-4:30 daily.

Maurice Carrie Vineyard & Winery   676-1711
5.5 mi. E at 34225 Rancho California Rd.
Nestled in a little valley amidst rolling hills is a tasting room/gift shop that captures the area's country charm in a large neo-Victorian structure with hardwood and brass trim. Picnic tables are scattered around bucolic grounds. Their sourdough hot out of the oven (weekends only) is a perfect complement to some of the valley's best wines. Tasting and sales 10-5 daily.

Mount Palomar Winery   676-5047
5 mi. E at 33820 Rancho California Rd.
A first-rate gift shop and deli adjoin the handsome, well-organized tasting room of Mt. Palomar Winery, which opened in 1975. Tree-shaded picnic tables next to atmospheric wine barrels overlook the winery. (Fee) tasting, tours and sales 9-5 daily.

Thornton Winery   *699-0099*
4 mi. E at 32575 Rancho California Rd.
Baronial splendor arrived in the Temecula wine district in 1988 with
the opening of a massive rock-trimmed complex reminiscent of a
French chateau. Southern California's best sparkling wines are served
at tables in a handsome tasting room by a well-appointed shop with a
view of the cellar and bottling areas. Next door is **Cafe Champagne**
(see listing). (Fee) tasting and sales daily; tours on weekends only.
Open 12-6 Mon.-Wed. and 12-7 Thurs.-Sun.

RESTAURANTS

★ **Baily Wine Country Cafe**   676-9567
   1.1 mi. N at 27644 Ynez Rd.
   L-D.   *Expensive*
One of the area's best restaurants opened in 1992. New California
cuisine receives light and lively attention in a well-thought-out
selection of entrees, pastas, and desserts made here. Full linen,
candles and fresh flowers, greenery and a nouveau grapevine wall
hanging complement the cuisine. There is also a covered patio.

★ **Cafe Champagne**   *699-0088*
   4 mi. E at 32575 Rancho California Rd.
   L-D.   *Expensive*
Creative New California cuisine is featured in dishes like roasted
Poblano chiles stuffed with Muenster topped with rellano sauce, and
in decadent dessert. Sparkling wines made here along with many of
the district's still wines are served in the light modish dining room and
trellis-covered heated patio sharing the area's best vineyard view.

★ **The Captain's Table**   *676-9334*
   .8 mi. NW at 28551 Rancho California Rd.
   L-D. No L Sat. Closed Sun.   *Moderate*
Generous portions of fresh fish on a changing menu and prime rib or
steaks cut from Angus Midwestern beef are skillfully prepared.
Comfortable dining areas are decorated with greenery, wall hangings,
and hardwood. A stone passageway leads to a cozy firelit cellar
featuring sixteen wines by the glass.

Fallbrook Restaurants
   14 mi. SW via I-15 & Mission Rd.   *Low–Expensive*
Four of the area's five best restaurants are downtown. In **The Lace
Apron** (118 N. Main St., B-L. Closed Sun.–Moderate) desserts and
morning delights fill display cases in a bright cheerful bakery with a
few tables. At the **Packing House** (125 S. Main St., L-D–Moderate),
contemporary American standards continue to make the comfortable
book-trimmed dining room and lounge a local favorite. In **Le Bistro**
(119 N. Main St.) updated Continental cuisine is featured in the (L-D–
Moderate) cafe in a garden patio and in the (D only–Expensive)
upstairs dining room. **La Caseta** (111 N. Vine St., L-D. Closed
Sun.–Low) gives California-style Mexican fare careful attention in a
greenery-trimmed dining room/cantina and heated patio. Best of all is
Garden Center Cafe (1.3 miles south of downtown at 1625 S.
Mission Rd., B-L–Moderate). Big luscious sticky buns, muffins and
other baked goods made here complement light fresh fare. In the
area's prettiest restaurant, lovely gardens and fresh flowers enhance
a heated covered patio next to a handsome contemporary dining room.

★ **The Fish Exchange**   *677-9449*
4 mi. NW at 24910 Washington Av. - Murrieta
L-D.   *Moderate*
Mahi-mahi basted with macadamia nut butter and hot or mild Cajun
catfish typify first-rate seafood served in all sorts of interesting ways
with accompaniments like black bean chili, a choice of premium tap
beers, and super sourdough bread. Luxuriant greenery and blondwood
accents, plus a choice of booths or chairs, further distinguish the best
dining room in the boondocks.

Penfold's   *676-6411*
.5 mi. N at 28250 Front St.
B-L-D.   *Moderate*
The giant cinnamon rolls and sticky buns displayed out front are made
here to enjoy with a wealth of all-American standards in Temecula's
most popular coffee shop.

★ **Temecula Creek Inn**   *694-1000*
2.5 mi. S (near I-15) at 44501 Rainbow Canyon Rd.
B-L-D. Sun. brunch.   *Expensive*
The **Temet Grill** offers carefully prepared New California cuisine
including housemade desserts in a capacious dining room with artistic
Southwestern decor. A window-wall view of fairways beyond a pond is
shared by a plush firelit lounge with glove-leather sofas.

★ **Tom's Farms**   *(714) 277-9992*
26 mi. NW via I-15 at 23900 Temescal Canyon Rd. - Corona
B-L-D.   *Moderate*
Tom's is a triple treat for food-lovers. The big amiable complex has a
major produce market, a gourmet food and wine shop with a (fee)
tasting bar and an emphasis on regional products, and a good cafe.
Terraced dining and picnic areas adjoin a tranquil pond in a garden.

LODGING

From resorts to bargain motels, rates remain about the same year-
round. But, weekdays may be 10% less than weekends.

Country Inn - Best Western   *676-7378*
.8 mi. N (by I-15) at 27706 Jefferson Av. - 92590
A freeway adjoins this contemporary motel with an outdoor pool and
whirlpool and a sauna. Each nicely furnished room has a phone and
color TV with movies. Toll-free: (800)528-1234.

> #225,#125—spacious, refr./wet bar, raised in-room mirrored
>   whirlpool and (presto-log) fireplace in view of   K bed...$115
> #119 (and 3 others)—in-room mirrored whirlpool,   K bed...$85
> regular room—   K bed...$48

★ **Embassy Suites**   *676-5656*
.9 mi. NE (by I-15) at 29345 Rancho California Rd. - 92591
The best lodgings in town are in a California-style four-story complex
with a garden court pool, whirlpool, fitness center, restaurant and
lounge, and gift shop. Full breakfast and afternoon beverages are
complimentary. Each beautifully furnished unit has a private patio or
balcony, living room and bedroom, refrigerator/wet bar and microwave,
two phones, two cable color TV (one remote) and VCR with free and
pay movies. Toll-free: (800)EMBASSY.

> #429,#427—top floor, view across pool to mtns.,   K bed...$129
> regular room—request pool/courtyard view,   K bed...$119

★ **Loma Vista Bed and Breakfast**   676-7047
4.5 mi. E at 33350 La Serena Way - 92591
A delightful bed-and-breakfast inn with six guest rooms opened in
1988 on a hilltop overlooking vineyards, a luxuriant grapefruit orchard, and the Palomar Mountains. A hot tub in a gazebo in a garden
shares the view. A full breakfast and afternoon wine and cheese are
complimentary. Each spacious room is beautifully, individually decorated and has a private bath and expansive views.
   "Chardonnay"—furnished in oak with pull-chain toilet,
     small private patio with fine vineyard view,   Q bed...$105
   "Sauvignon Blanc"—Southwestern pastel colors &
     furnishings, large private patio with valley view, Q bed...$125
   "Champagne"—snazzy red/black toned art deco look, K bed...$95
   regular room—   Q bed...$95
Motel 6   676-7199
.5 mi. N (by I-15) at 41900 Moreno Dr. - 92590
The chain's modern **bargain** motel by the freeway has a small pool.
Each compact, plain room has a phone and color TV with movies.
   regular room—   D bed...$33
Murrieta Hot Springs Resort   677-7451
5 mi. N at 39405 Murrieta Hot Springs Rd. - Murrieta 92563
Here is one of California's oldest health spa resorts. Towering palms
shade turn-of-the-century buildings, the big warm springs, an extra-
large outdoor pool, two smaller mineral pools, and saunas. The rustic
complex also has (for a fee) a full service health center and mud baths,
plus a casual dining room and pub. Plain lodgings with a phone and
color TV are available in historic stone buildings and cottages. Toll-
free: (800)458-4393.
   hillside cottage—   2 D or Q bed...$105
   regular room—small, in historic building, 2 D or Q bed...$75
★ **Pala Mesa Resort**   (619)728-5881
13 mi. S (by I-15) at 2001 Old Hwy. 395 - Fallbrook 92028
Resort and conference facilities are blended into a luxuriant site with
an 18-hole championship golf course. Other amenities include a pool
and whirlpool in a garden and four lighted tennis courts, plus a
handsome dining room with a fairway view, a plush lounge with live
entertainment for dancing, and resort shops. Each spacious, well-
furnished room has a phone and color TV. Toll-free: (800)722-4700.
   #448,#458—corner windows & large private
     balcony with fine resort & mountain view,   K bed...$135
   regular room—on fairway,   2 Q or K bed...$110
★ **Temecula Creek Inn**   694-1000
3 mi. S (near I-15) at 44501 Rainbow Canyon Rd. - 92592
Temecula Creek Inn is the area's premier resort. Amenities include a
big landscaped pool and whirlpool; two tennis courts; a scenic (fee) 27-
hole championship golf course; and an upscale restaurant and lounge
(see listing). Each spacious, attractively decorated unit has a large
private deck, a refrigerator/(honor) bar, two phones and remote control
color TV. Toll-free: (800)962-7335.
   #229,#329—big end unit, 2 large patios
     with fine fairway views,   K bed...$150
   "Junior Suite" (several)—as above, good views, K bed...$150
   regular room—   2 Q or K bed...$125

Ventura

Ventura is an inviting blend of coastal grandeur and urbane renewal. The Pacific Ocean is the five-mile-long western boundary. Nearby between the beach and hills, the heart of town covers a gentle bench where Father Junipero Serra founded Mission San Buenaventura in 1782. The existing mission church was completed in 1809. Growth was slow but steady, in spite of periodic disruptions from earthquakes, tidal waves, and pirates. Rapid development began well after World War II following major shoreline and civic improvements.

Today, with a big manmade harbor, miles of broad beaches, and a scenic promenade and pier, the coast is more desirable than ever. Restored vintage buildings and compatible new ones lend newfound vitality to the heart of town. Historic attractions, and increasing numbers of specialty shops, gourmet restaurants, and distinctive lodgings, are within a stroll of both downtown and the beach.

WEATHER PROFILE

V.W.R.*		Jan.	Feb.	Mar.	Apr.	May	June	July	Aug.	Sep.	Oct.	Nov.	Dec.
Great	10					●	●	●	●	●	●		
Fine	9				●							●	
Very Good	8												
Good	7			●									●
Moderate	6	●	●										
	5												
	4												
	3												
Adverse	2												
	1												
	0												

	Jan.	Feb.	Mar.	Apr.	May	June	July	Aug.	Sep.	Oct.	Nov.	Dec.
V.W.R.*	6	6	7	9	10	10	10	10	10	10	9	7
Temperature												
Ave. High	65	66	67	68	70	71	74	74	74	74	72	67
Ave. Low	42	43	44	46	49	51	55	55	54	50	46	44
Precipitation												
Inches Rain	3.2	3.0	2.6	1.0	.2	.1	-	-	.2	.5	1.1	3.0
Inches Snow	-	-	-	-	-	-	-	-	-	-	-	-

*V.W.R. = Vokac Weather Rating: probability of mild (warm & dry) weather on any given day.

Ventura

Population: 92,557   Area Code: 805
Elevation: 50 feet
Location: 74 miles West of Los Angeles
Visitor & Convention Bureau Information Center   648-2075
downtown at 89C S. California St. - 93001   (800)333-2989

ATTRACTIONS

Albinger Archaeological Museum   648-5823
downtown at 113 E. Main St.
Chumash Indian and Spanish artifacts are highlights among displays
from prehistoric times through the cowboy era. All were excavated
from an archeological dig next to the mission. Closed Mon.

Bicycling
Cycles-2-U   985-8557
8 mi. SE at 2101 Mandalay Beach Rd. - Oxnard
The Mandalay Beach Hotel rents bicycles to enjoy miles of separated
bikeways along scenic shorelines from Oxnard to Ventura.
Surrey Cycle Rentals
.4 mi. S (near US 101) at 450 E. Harbor Blvd.
In Ventura, various kinds of bicycles are for rent by the Holiday Inn.

Boat Rentals
Channel Islands Landing   985-6059
9.5 mi. SE at 3821 S. Victoria Av., Channel Islands Harbor - Oxnard
You can rent small sailboats by the hour to explore miles of manmade
waterways in the large scenic harbor any day of the year.

Boat Rides
★ **Island Packers**   642-1393
5 mi. SE at 1867 Spinnaker Dr.
Boats depart from Ventura Harbor at about 9 a.m. (and return around
5 p.m.) for sightseeing and recreational excursions to the Channel
Islands National Park in summer and during the winter whale
migration. Half-day trips, overnight, and ferry service for campers can
be arranged year-round by reservation well in advance.

★ **Channel Islands Harbor**   985-4852
8.5 mi. SE at W end of Channel Islands Blvd. - Oxnard
Well-landscaped homes and business enclaves (many nautically
related) line canals of a manmade harbor that extends two miles
inland. Recreation facilities include pocket parks with beaches, boat
ramps and rentals (see listing), picnic and game areas. Swimmers and
fishermen use both the harbor and the ocean across a narrow
peninsula. **Fisherman's Wharf**, a faux New England seaport village,
has specialty shops and restaurants including a fresh fish market and
cafe. The **Ventura County Maritime Museum** (closed Tues.-Wed.)
with an impressive display of ship models, historic artifacts and
maritime art, opened in 1991 in the complex.

★ **Channel Islands National Park Visitor Center**   658-5730
5 mi. SE at 1901 Spinnaker Dr.
From park headquarters by the entrance to Ventura Harbor, you can
see the islands that comprise this isolated natural preserve and
marine sanctuary looming out of the ocean. The nearest of five major
islands is Anacapa, eleven miles offshore. The center provides an
information desk, well-displayed exhibits, audiovisual program, books
and gifts about the largely uninhabited isles.

Ventura

McGrath State Beach   *654-4744*
4.5 mi. SE at 2211 Harbor Blvd.
Here are nearly two miles of broad sandy beach, sand dunes, two tiny
lakes and a major wildlife area. Lifeguards oversee swimmers and
surfers, and there are restrooms and picnic areas. A campground
without hookups ((800)444-PARK) is behind dunes near the beach.

★ **Mission San Buenaventura**   *643-4318*
downtown at 211 E. Main St.
The last mission founded by Father Serra (1782) was completed in
1809. The massive whitewashed adobe church, with buttressed walls
six feet thick and a picturesque belltower, has been fully restored. A
mission museum exhibits artifacts dating back to the Spanish period.
There is a gift shop. A cloister garden with a fountain enhances the
tranquil enclave that has always been the heart of town.

Olivas Adobe   *644-4346*
4.2 mi. SE via Harbor Blvd. at 4200 Olivas Park Dr.
This two-story hacienda, built between 1837 and 1849, is a classic of
the Monterey style, with a balcony running the length of the upper
level. The restored building has free exhibits of period furnishings and
handicrafts. An adjacent museum displays memorabilia from the days
of the Spanish dons. Landscaped grounds, including a rose and herb
garden, are open daily. The adobe is open on weekends only.

★ **Plaza Park**   *654-7800*
downtown at E. Santa Clara & Chestnut Sts.
A Moreton Bay fig tree planted in 1874 is the centerpiece of Ventura's
oldest and loveliest city park. The magnificent specimen now sprawls
for 140 feet and has a trunk circumference of 22 feet.

★ **Point Mugu State Park**   *(818)706-1310*
23 mi. SE on CA 1
The largest state park on the coast of Southern California extends
along the ocean for four miles and into the Santa Monica Mountains
for seven miles. Features range from a landmark sand dune to
mountains 3,000 feet above sea level. Swimming and body surfing are
popular. Sycamore Cove is the favorite, with a broad soft-sand beach
backed by a grassy, tree-shaded picnic area. Inland, many miles of
hiking trails provide access to highlands now recovering from recent
chaparral fires that swept for miles from the mountains to the sea.
Sycamore Canyon Campground has complete facilities ((800)444-
PARK) in a sheltered location. La Jolla Campground offers primitive
facilities directly on the wide beach.

Port Hueneme Beach Park   *986-6584*
12.5 mi. SE at S end of Ventura Rd. - Port Hueneme
A fishing pier extends from a picturesque palm-shaded park into the
ocean beyond a mile-long broad sand beach. Swimming and
sunbathing are popular. Lifeguards are on duty in summer.

★ **Promenade Park**   *658-4726*
.3 mi. S at S end of California St.
A paved walkway along a splendid south-facing beach is a great place
to check out the scenery and to watch surfers. The Ventura Pier,
California's oldest (1872) and longest wooden pier, was completely
restored in 1993. It now has a snack bar, restrooms, and a large
restaurant and lounge scheduled for completion in 1995.

★ **San Buenaventura City Hall**   *654-7850*
downtown at 50 Poli St. at N. California St.
The old County Courthouse (circa 1912) is now the City Hall. It is an imposing Neo-Classical showplace of Doric columns, marble steps, a polished stone interior, stained glass skylights...and a line-up of padres' heads smiling inscrutably along the facade.

★ **San Buenaventura State Park**   *654-4611*
1.5 mi. SE via Harbor Dr. at 901 S. San Pedro St.
Nearly three miles of the city's coastline has become one of the state's best parks. The broad white sand beach is backed in part by low picturesque dunes extending eastward from Ventura Pier. Swimming and surfing are popular, and there is a paved scenic bikeway. Fishing is enjoyed in the surf and from the long pier and jetties. Lifeguards, restrooms, picnic areas, and snack bars are provided.

★ *Sportfishing*
Sportfishing boats can be chartered daily year-round for deep-sea fishing, and for whale watching in winter. Full or half-day trips aboard modern boats with all necessary equipment can be reserved at these places in Ventura and Oxnard.
   Channel Islands Sportfishing Center   *985-8511*
   10 mi. SE at 4151 S. Victoria Av., Channel Islands Harbor - Oxnard
   Harbor Village Sportfishing   *658-1060*
   4.5 mi. SE at 1449 Spinnaker Dr. - Ventura Harbor
   Ventura Sportfishing Landing   *650-1255*
   3.7 mi. SE at 1500 Anchors Way Dr. - Ventura Harbor
Ventura County Beach Parks   *654-3951*
   2 to 12 mi. NW on US 101
Emma Wood, Faria, and Hobson County Parks offer complete camping facilities near the ocean. All are, unfortunately, also close to the freeway and railroad. Swimming, surfing, surf fishing, and tidepool exploring can be enjoyed from the small rocky beaches.

★ **Ventura County Museum of History & Art**   *653-0323*
   downtown at 100 E. Main St.
On beautifully landscaped grounds near the mission is a handsome Early-California-style complex with several rooms and a courtyard filled with artistic displays of the area's heritage in collections of Chumash Indian, Spanish, and pioneer artifacts. Permanent exhibits include the George Stuart collection of historical figures; diorama paintings, and photographs; and courtyard displays of oil industry and agricultural equipment. There are also changing exhibits, a research library, and a gift shop. Closed Mon.

★ **Ventura Harbor**   *642-8538*
   3.7 mi. SE via Harbor Blvd. on Anchors Way Dr.
About 1,500 boats can be accommodated in a mile-long manmade harbor with launch ramps, guest slips, sportfishing and sightseeing boats. Swimming and shore fishing are other attractions along with specialty shops, view restaurants, and a hotel.

Winery
   Leeward   *656-5054*
   7 mi. SE at 2784 Johnson Dr.
Deep in the Ventura industrial district is a small winery that does nice work with several varieties of premium grapes from Central and Northern California. Tasting, tours, and sales 10-4 daily.

RESTAURANTS

★ **Allison's Country Cafe**   *644-9072*
2.5 mi. E at 3429 Telegraph Rd.
B-L.   *Moderate*
Allison's American breakfast classics are uniformly fresh, well prepared, and creative. (Try the whole wheat and honey hotcakes and the pineapple salsa on the ham and cheddar omelet.) The friendly cafe's comfortable booths with fresh flowers are part of the draw.

Andria's   *654-0546*
4.5 mi. SE at 1449 Spinnaker Dr.
L-D.   *Low*
In one of the most popular seafood eateries in town, fresh fish in various batter fries and stir fries are served in a cafeteria-plain dining area, on umbrella-shaded patios by the marina, or to go. This is the best among several waterfront eateries in Ventura Harbor Village, a faux fishing village complex across some dunes from the ocean.

★ **The Breakfast House**   *648-1130*
1.5 mi. E at 2055 E. Main St.
B-L.   *Moderate*
Delicious all-American omelets, homemade biscuits and gravy, and other classics are served in a cheerful little wood-trimmed coffee shop festooned with live greenery. There may be a wait for a table or the counter, but cognoscenti know that the food is well worth it.

★ **Busy Bee Cafe**   *643-4864*
downtown at 478 E. Main St.
B-L-D.   *Moderate*
Sure! They have cherry cokes, thick malts, and cold meat loaf in this sendup of a 1950s diner. But, with homemade cinnamon rolls, pies, and biscuits and gravy, it's no trendy rehash. Nostalgic chrome jukeboxes back each of the slick-plastic padded booths.

★ **Cafe Zack**   *643-9445*
.8 mi. E at 1095 E. Thompson Blvd.
L-D. Only brunch on Sun. Closed Mon.   *Moderate*
Cafe Zack features some of the finest desserts in California. Decadent delights on display vary, but might include humongous apple dumplings, luscious peanut pie, English trifle, and large light lovely lemon cheesecake. Contemporary California cuisine is also served in the convivial little cottage restaurant, and on a garden-view porch.

★ **California Grill**   *987-1922*
15 mi. SE at 67 E. Daily Dr. - Camarillo
L-D. No L Sat. Closed Sun.   *Moderate*
New California cuisine is represented by tasty creations like warm duck and papaya salad, designer pizzas, and dynamite desserts like grasshopper cheesecake. The airy split-level dining room and lounge are distinguished by candles and fresh flowers on glass-topped tables, monumental live greenery, a grand piano bar, and an exhibition grill.

Chart House   *643-3725*
.9 mi. SE at 567 Sanjon Rd.
D only.   *Expensive*
The chain's local architectural triumph is a low flying-wedge-shaded structure in a lush garden on a hill near the coast. Contemporary American fare is served in a handsome room with ocean views.

Cucina D'Italia   *648-1422*
1 mi. E at 1497 E. Thompson Blvd.
D only. Closed Sun.-Tues.   *Low*
Here is real old-fashioned value for the money. Hearty portions of homestyle Southern Italian dishes are served in a little dining room that's as unpretentious and friendly as an Italian family kitchen.

El Tecolote   *482-4318*
16 mi. SE (near US 101) at 333 Lewis Rd. - Camarillo
L-D. Sun. brunch.   *Low*
California-style Mexican dishes have been featured here since 1952. The big restaurant/cantina includes three comfortable dining rooms enlivened by a notable collection of owls in art objects.

★ **Mrs. Olson's Coffee Hut**   *985-9151*
9 mi. SE at 117 Los Altos St., Channel Islands Harbor - Oxnard
B-L. Closed Mon.   *Moderate*
Mrs. Olson's offers the best beach area breakfast in contemporary California dishes like Joe's special, wheat germ walnut pancakes, and omelets complemented by notable homestyle cottage fries, biscuits and gravy. The food is the thing in this tucked-away cafe with a counter and a cozy homespun dining room.

★ **Old Vienna**   *654-1214*
2.8 mi. E at 3845 Telegraph Rd.
L-D. No L Sat. Sun. brunch. Closed Mon.   *Moderate*
Cured pork shank or (in season) venison four different ways are notable specialties among a wide range of authentically prepared Middle European dishes. Full linen softens the alpine chalet-themed decor in two dining rooms.

★ **Rosarito Beach**   *653-7343*
downtown at 692 E. Main St.
D only. Closed Mon.   *Moderate*
Rosarita Beach is the source for some of the liveliest and most revolutionary Mexican-style cuisine in California. Pork adobado (marinated pork loin), mesquite-grilled tri-tip steak or crab-stuffed chile rellano suggest the masterful chef's versatility. Everything is memorable, including fluffy homemade tortillas and two kinds of salsa that arrive soon after you're seated. Exotic greenery and flowers in cozy dining areas and on a shaded porch contribute to the easy enjoyment of this culinary superstar, now in an enlarged location at the other end of downtown from the original site.

★ **Sal's Mexican Inn**   *483-9015*
11 mi. SE at 1450 S. Oxnard Blvd. - Oxnard
L-D.   *Low*
Oxnard's original culinary landmark has featured authentic Mexican favorites since 1947. A wide assortment of flavorful dishes is consistently well prepared. Three big colorful dining rooms in the sprawling roadside restaurant/cantina are still deservedly popular.

★ **Tipps Thai Cuisine**   *643-3040*
downtown at 512 E. Main St.
L-D. No L Sat. Closed Sun.   *Moderate*
Chicken, pork or beef with a special chile/mint sauce, and hot pot soups typify a well-rounded selection of authentic Thai cuisine prepared with no M.S.G. and an emphasis on fresh ingredients. Fresh flowers and greenery enhance the unpretentious dining room.

The Whale's Tale   *985-2511*
9.5 mi. SE at 3950 Blue Fin Cir., Channel Islands Harbor - Oxnard
L-D. Sat. & Sun. brunch.   *Expensive*
A chalkboard adjacent to a display of fresh fish lists possibilities
cooked all ways and served in a vast contemporary dining room and
entertainment lounge with a panoramic harbor view.

LODGING

A full range of accommodations is available, including three lodgings
by the beach. Summer is prime time. Some places reduce their rates
15% and more on weekdays during other seasons.

★ **Bella Maggiore Inn**   *523-8479*
downtown at 67 S. California St. - 93001
Only a stroll from the beach in the heart of town is an engaging
Mediterranean-style bed-and-breakfast inn with a fountain court and
cafe featuring international fare. The same architect designed both the
Chinese Theatre in Hollywood and this hotel during the 1920s. Full
breakfast and afternoon appetizers and drinks are complimentary.
Each of twenty-eight well-furnished rooms has a private bath, phone,
and remote control color TV. Toll-free: (800)523-8479.
   #37—gas fireplace, big in-bath whirlpool, bay window, K bed...$150
   regular room—compact,   D bed...$75

★ **Casa Sirena Marina Resort**   *985-6311*
9 mi. SE at 3605 Peninsula Rd. - Oxnard 93035
The only lodging on Channel Islands Harbor is a 275-room resort with
a big landscaped pool, two whirlpools, putting green, lighted tennis
court, exercise room, saunas, bicycle rentals, and gift shop, plus
waterfront restaurant and entertainment lounge. Each well-furnished
room has a private patio or balcony, refrigerator, phone, and color TV
with movies. Toll-free: (800)228-6026.
   #602 & even #s thru #636—request gas fireplace,
      private balcony with grand harbor view,   2 D or K bed...$100
   regular room—garden view,   2 D or K bed...$85

★ **Colony Harbortown Marina Resort**   *658-1212*
3.4 mi. SE at 1050 Schooner Dr. - 93001
The only lodging on Ventura Marina was completely remodeled during
1993. The 154-unit resort hotel has a large pool in a tropical garden,
a bubble-dome whirlpool, three lighted tennis courts, a harbor-view
restaurant, plush nightclub/piano bar, and a gift shop. Each well-
furnished room has a private balcony, phone, and remote control color
TV with movies. Toll-free: (800)777-1700.
   "Marina Suites" (many)—request 3rd floor,
      spacious, refr./wet bar, intimate marina views from K bed...$99
   regular room—garden view,   2 D or K bed...$89

The Country Inn at Ventura   *653-1434*
downtown (by US 101) at 298 Chestnut St. - 93001
The ocean is nearby beyond a freeway and railroad tracks by this
contemporary all-suites motel with a small outdoor pool and whirlpool.
Breakfast and cocktails are complimentary. Each well-furnished suite
has a microwave and refrigerator, two phones and remote control color
TV with VCR. Toll-free: (800)44-RELAX.
   fireplace suite (several)—gas fireplace,   K bed...$99
   regular room—   2 Q or K bed...$89

★ **Doubletree Hotel - Ventura**   *643-6000*
1.5 mi. SE (near US 101) at 2055 E. Harbor Blvd. - 93001
Ventura's most avant-garde lodging is a 285-room hotel a block from the beach. Amenities of the post-modern four-story complex include an opulent atrium adjoining a tropical garden court with waterfalls by a large freeform pool and whirlpool. There are also saunas, an exercise room, a handsome dining room and lounge, and a gift shop. Each beautifully decorated room has a phone and remote control color TV with free and pay movies. Toll-free: (800)222-TREE.

> #4027,#4023,#4019—small private balcony
>   with ocean view beyond state park,   K bed...$129
>   regular room—   2 D or K bed...$109

Good Nite Inn   *388-5644*
15 mi. SE (by US 101) at 1100 Ventura Blvd. - Camarillo 93010
This newer **bargain** motel has a small pool and whirlpool. Each compact, comfortable room has a phone and color TV with movies.
> regular room—   Q bed...$36

★ **Holiday Inn Beach Resort**   *648-7731*
.4 mi. S (near US 101) at 450 E. Harbor Blvd. - 93001
Ventura's premier beachfront lodging was upgraded for the 1990s. Amenities of the twelve-story 260-room hotel include a large well-landscaped pool and whirlpool by the beach, saunas, exercise room, game room, bicycle and water sports rentals; restaurant, coffee shop, entertainment lounge; and a gift shop. Each attractively refurbished room has a small private balcony with an ocean/city view, a phone and color TV with pay and free movies. Toll-free: (800)842-0800.

> #901,#903,#801,#803—superb
>   coastal panoramas from   Q bed...$90
> #1101,#1001,#1103,#1003—as above,   2 D beds...$90
>   regular room—   2 D or Q bed...$90

Inn on the Beach   *652-2000*
2.1 mi. SE at 1175 S. Seaward Av. - 93001
One of only three beachfront lodgings between Santa Barbara and Malibu opened in the summer of 1988. Continental breakfast is complimentary. Each of the twenty-four well-furnished units in the Cape-Cod-style three-story motel face the ocean and have either a private patio or balcony by the sand, phone, and remote control color TV with movies.

> #308,#301—top floor, private balcony & corner
>   windows with beachfront panorama,   2 Q beds...$130
>   regular room—private patio,   2 Q or K bed...$80

★ **La Mer European Bed and Breakfast**   *643-3600*
downtown at 411 Poli St. - 93001
By the historic courthouse on a hill overlooking the city and the sea, an 1890 landmark has been artfully converted into a romantic bed-and-breakfast inn. An authentic Bavarian breakfast and afternoon wine and appetizers are complimentary. Each of five guest rooms has a private bath and is beautifully furnished with antiques themed to a different Old World country.

> "Madam Pompadour"—spacious, bay window
>   with fine city/ocean view, private entrance
>   & balcony, French wood-burning stove,   Q bed...$155
> "Queen Anne"—bay window view of city/ocean,   Q bed...$125
>   regular room—private entrance,   D or Q bed...$105

★ **Mandalay Beach Resort - Crown Sterling Suites**   *984-2500*
8 mi. SE at 2101 Mandalay Beach Rd - Oxnard 93035
One of the finest lodgings on the California coast is a contemporary
all-suites hotel by a broad sandy palm-studded beach. Amenities of the
handsome 250-suite Spanish-Colonial-style complex include an extra-
large freeform pool and a unique whirlpool in a tropically landscaped
courtyard enhanced by grottoes, waterfalls and gardens. There are
also two lighted tennis courts, bicycle and water sports rentals, ping
pong and billiards, and a resort shop. Full breakfast is complimentary.
Luxuriant greenery accents a capacious gourmet dining room, and
there is a plush piano bar and entertainment lunge. Each luxurious
two- or three-room suite has two marble-lined bathrooms, a wet
bar/refrig- erator/ microwave oven, sliding glass doors to a private
patio or balcony, two phones, and two remote control color TVs with
movies. Toll-free: (800)433-4600.

#301,#201,#101—2 BR, huge, in-bath whirlpool, fireplace
in LR, private balcony, superb oceanfront view,   2 K beds...$400
#102 & even #s to #116—floor-to-ceiling window &
private patio with great beach & ocean view,   K bed...$219
regular room—garden view,   2 Q or K bed...$179

Motel 6
1.6 mi. SE (near US 101) at 2145 E. Harbor Blvd. - 93001   643-5100
7 mi. SE (near US 101) at 3075 Johnson Dr. - 93003   650-0080
14 mi. SE (by US 101) at 1641 E. Daily Dr. - Camarillo 93010 388-3467
The chain now has three local **bargain** motels near the freeway. Each
has an outdoor pool. Johnson Drive also has a whirlpool. Each small,
plain room has a phone and color TV with movies.
regular room—   D or Q bed...$37

Radisson Suite Hotel at River Ridge   *988-0130*
8 mi. SE at 2101 W. Vineyard Av. - Oxnard 93030
Tucked away by a stark 18-hole golf course is a 250-unit all-suites
hotel opened in 1987. Amenities include two outdoor pools, three
whirlpools, gym, five lighted tennis courts, plus a restaurant/lounge.
Breakfast and afternoon cocktail are complimentary. Each well-
furnished suite has a kitchen, patio or balcony, phone, and color TV
with remote control and pay and free movies. Toll-free: (800)333-3333.
fireplace loft suite—studio with fireplace,
request golf course view for privacy,   2 Q beds...$119
regular room—studio without fireplace,   K bed...$99

Ramada Clocktower Inn   *652-0141*
downtown at 181 E. Santa Clara St. - 93001
This modern motor inn was built around a converted Spanish-style
landmark firehouse. Light breakfast and afternoon wine and cheese
are free. Each room has attractive Southwestern decor, a phone, and
remote control color TV with free movies. Toll-free: (800)727-1027.
fireplace room (several)—large pvt. balcony
or patio, gas fireplace,   Q bed...$95
regular room—   Q bed...$85

Shores Motel   *643-9600*
2 mi. SE at 1059 S. Seaward Av. - 93001
A superb beach is only a block from this small modern motel. Each
nicely furnished room has a phone and color TV.
regular room—(refr. & extra Q for another $10),   Q bed...$45

Index

About the Author

David Vokac was born in Chicago and grew up on a ranch near Cody, Wyoming. During summers while an undergraduate, he served as the first airborne fire-spotter for the Shoshone National Forest next to Yellowstone National Park. Later, he taught courses in land economics while completing a Master's degree in geography at the University of Arizona. In Denver, Colorado, Vokac was in charge of economic base analysis for the city's first community renewal program, and later became Chief of Neighborhood Planning. He moved to Southern California in 1974 to prepare San Diego County's first local parks plan, and stayed to act as Park Development Director.

Mr. Vokac is now a full-time travel writer living in Southern California. He is the author of six guidebooks, including *Destinations of the Southwest* and the acclaimed *Great Towns of The West* series. During the past year, he logged more than twenty thousand miles while field checking previously included locales and features (like the Morey Mansion in the picture above) and adding hundreds of notable new ones. When not researching, writing, speaking, or consulting, he can be found traveling for the sheer joy of it somewhere in the West.

Western Guidebooks for the 1990s

The "Destinations" series of travel guidebooks offers complete, honest information about top vacation areas in the West. All notable attractions, restaurants, lodgings and more are described and rated for each region's most exciting locales.

Every feature was personally inspected by the author, and no payments were accepted.

For nine years, David Vokac's guides have delighted travelers nationwide and earned critical acclaim.

"The beauty of the guide lies not only in the detailed information about lodgings, restaurants, etc., but also in the tips about nearby, unusual places or attractions generally known only to locals."
Books of the Southwest

"Vacation planners will appreciate the wealth of revealing insights provided in a concise, well-organized format."
Booklist

"Vokac wrote his book for travelers and vacation planners, but even the armchair travelers will be intrigued."
Las Vegas Review-Journal

"Until now none of the big publishers has paid much attention to the cities outside the mainstream, many of which are worthwhile destinations. This guidebook does a fine job of covering towns that make travel off the interstate so fascinating."
Seattle Post-Intelligencer

"This is an excellent guide . . . one that you can use again and again."
The Province, Vancouver, B.C.

DESTINATIONS OF SOUTHERN CALIFORNIA 320 pages $9.95
DESTINATIONS OF THE SOUTHWEST   320 pages $8.95
Ask for these guides by David Vokac at your favorite bookstore. Or, order direct from West Press. California residents, add sales tax. West Press will pay postage and handling.

Coming soon: Vokac's Views

West Press will be publishing the inaugural issue of the author's travel newsletter—Vokac's Views. Each issue will feature timely information about new and unusual attractions, restaurants, and lodgings in top destination areas throughout America. For a free introductory copy, send your name and address to West Press.

WEST PRESS
P.O. Box 99717
San Diego, CA 92169